DEATH WITHOUT END

DEATH WITHOUT END

Korea and the
Thanatographics of War

THEODORE HUGHES

Columbia University Press

New York

Columbia University Press wishes to express its appreciation for assistance given by the Wm. Theodore de Bary Fund in the publication of this book.

Columbia University Press
Publishers Since 1893
New York   Chichester, West Sussex
cup.columbia.edu

Copyright © 2026 Columbia University Press
All rights reserved

Cataloging-in-Publication Data is available from the Library of Congress.

ISBN 9780231186063 (hardback)
ISBN 9780231186070 (trade paperback)
ISBN 9780231546485 (ebook)
ISBN 9780231565936 (pdf)

LCCN 2025032629

Cover design: Chang Jae Lee
Cover image: Sea Hyun Lee, *Between Red, 108*, oil on linen, 200cm x 200cm, 2010.
© Sea Hyun Lee.

GPSR Authorized Representative: Easy Access System Europe,
Mustamäe tee 50, 10621 Tallinn, Estonia, gpsr.requests@easproject.com

CONTENTS

Note on Romanization and Names   vii

Introduction: The Thanatographic Imagination   1

PART I   13

1. Jeju Islands   15

PART II   41

2. Seoul Requiem   43
3. Horizons of Happiness   62
4. Motion in Stillness   78

PART III   97

5. Ocean's Edge   99

6. Jet Sublime 113

7. Death in *LIFE* 129

8. The Breaking Point 155

PART IV 179

9. Habitations 181

10. Crossings 197

11. Yet to Die, Yet to Live 211

PART V 231

12. Division as Method 233

Epilogue: Death Without End 250

....

Acknowledgments 255

Notes 259

Selected Bibliography 285

Index 295

NOTE ON ROMANIZATION AND NAMES

This book uses the McCune-Reischauer system for romanization of the Korean language, except for Korean authors who publish in English under a preferred spelling and the names of historical figures and places. Korean names are given in the word order used in Korea, surname coming first. In lieu of the terms "South Korea" and "North Korea," I use the formal names of the two Korean states extant on the peninsula, Republic of Korea (ROK) and Democratic People's Republic of Korea (DPRK). I also use the term Chosŏn for Korea when called for by primary sources.

INTRODUCTION

The Thanatographic Imagination

eath Without End takes the relation between limit and limitlessness as its point of departure. What does it mean to reach an end, to die in a war, the Korean War, that was never declared and continues to this day? In what ways do imaginings of death in the Democratic People's Republic of Korea (DPRK), the United States (US), and the Republic of Korea (ROK)—the three states that would maintain standing armies on the Korean peninsula beyond the 1950s and into the present—organize post-1945 articulations of multiple, clashing worlds? How do stories of Korean War–related dying and death define something that has come to be called a "cold war"?

Verbal, visual, and sonic descriptions in the DPRK and the ROK (two new states located on the periphery of the socialist and capitalist worlds) summon all manner of death and the continuing effects of these deaths on the living, the survivors. The cross from life to death is formative, proffering numerous inflections (in the United States, this included figurings of menticide or brain death). Some deaths were to be remembered, sanctified, others censored, forgotten, unspoken, or rumored. Stories of death (including multiple deaths and mass death) assume the capacity to speak for the silent and the absent, to place the dead in history. Absences, departures, and disappearances could give cause to mourn, eulogize, or simply remain in the realm of the unknown, in the speculative. The thanatography (story of a death) does not strictly oppose a biography (story of a life). Sometimes the cross from life to death turns back on itself in considerations of life in death and death in life.[1] Death and dying bear inextricable relation not only to that which was but that which could have been, will be, or can be. The thanatographic imagination lifts the dead to other places and times, giving life to ways of seeing, feeling, believing, and thinking considered critical to a proper belonging in the post-1945 world.

Working across a variety of genres and media (plays, short stories, novellas, teleplays, TV shows, films, art, songs, nonfiction, intellectual journals, magazines, comic books) in the DPRK, US, and ROK, *Death Without End* approaches the thanatographic imagination neither as unitary nor as confined to something called the "area" or region. This book moves across disciplines to address multiple ways in which the DPRK and the ROK stand at a border that divides (Korea into two) and unites (as the westernmost boundary of the US-led transpacific order). *Death Without End* puts Korean studies (here, both DPRK and ROK cultural production) in conversation with American Studies but not with the aim of providing a comprehensive view of a place and time central to the post-1945 history of decolonization in East Asia. Nor do I endeavor to put all of the pieces of a puzzle together; this book does not, for example, address the role of the People's Republic of China (PRC) in the Korean War. Traversing wartime and postarmistice Korea, *Death Without End* presents fragments that themselves approach the limits of representation, the moments, always multilayered, when dying anticipates death. These are the moments when words, images, and sounds become retrospectives on that which is or will be absent, no longer there. Stretching from the late 1940s through the mid-1960s, these thanatographic fragments underscore the ways in which the idea of limited war (itself thanatographic in its abiding concern with deaths, present and future) and armistice as a mode of governance provide the linchpin for a transpacific expansiveness.

LIMITED-WAR THINKING

In November 1945, East Asianist Eleanor H. Lattimore asked, "Pacific Ocean or American Lake?"[2] Her question was pressing. The matter had not been settled. How best to move forward from the 1945 US military victory in the Asia Pacific? As Lattimore noted, some were already calling plans for US annexation of islands in the Pacific "security imperialism."[3] Plans were one thing; putting them into practice was another. The political scientist Robert Jervis notes that US foreign policy in the late 1940s had yet to achieve cohesiveness, even after the formulation of the Truman Doctrine in 1947. Submitted to President Harry Truman in April 1950, NSC 68 called for dramatic increases in the defense budget and the militarization of the free world, but all of this stood little chance of implementation.[4] However:

By 1951 all the elements we have come to associate with the cold war were present or in train—high defense budgets, a militarized NATO, the perception of a Sino-Soviet bloc, the belief that the world was tightly interconnected and that any Communist victory anywhere would threaten vital American interests. These were changes that drastically altered world politics. It is clear that Korea triggered them.[5]

None of this was a given, if we adhere to Jervis's postulation that "It is easy to imagine a world possessing all the important elements that were present in our pre-1950 world but in which the Korean war did not occur. The later history of this world would sharply diverge from that of ours."[6] Jervis is right that by 1951 a significant alteration had taken place. Central to this shift was a growing recognition that war would not lead to unification of the Korean peninsula. Victory was to be had but not for one side over the other. It was a post-1945 articulation of the notion of limited war that emerged victorious. This victory was put into writing in the July 1953 Armistice Agreement, a consensus that the war would end and not end at the same time. Military, economic, social, and political mobilizations in the Asia Pacific (and the world) would rest upon this codification of an end that was not an end.

In his influential *Limited War: The Challenge to American Strategy* (1957), Robert Osgood underscores the importance of the Korean War as template for the future. He would reiterate in 1979 that "the Korean war served as the great catalyst of limited-war thinking."[7] Osgood affirms that "the cold war was—and continues to be—a period of continual limited warfare."[8] "Cold" names a duration without end; limited wars stretch into limitlessness. At the same time, Osgood now considers the possibility that "a local war that is limited from the standpoint of external participants might be total from the standpoint of the local belligerents, as in the Korean and Vietnam wars."[9] The latter standpoint, though, is lesser. The locals may suffer more casualties and destruction but do not see the bigger picture. For Osgood, the reality is that war remains limited (not all capacities for violence are brought to bear) even if it is experienced as total by the local belligerents (and even if they are victorious).

The Korean War was definitive for the new era of weapons of mass destruction, proof that notions of escalation and limits would be the order of the day. Joseph Darda writes:

> the Korean War launched the Cold War as much as the Cold War framed it. The American planners of the forgotten war constructed the enduring, if

conflicting, idea that the government would, from then on, wage continuous nonwar (defense; the containment of North Korea and China) constituted of a series of discrete, winnable emergencies (small wars; the "liberation" of South Korea).[10]

For Darda, "the Korean War introduced the idea that transformed war into the defense of humanity from illiberal beliefs and behaviors."[11] This defense of humanity from itself would become central to the first-world management of decolonization.

A consideration of what actually happened in the Asia Pacific (security imperialism) and what might have happened (something else) locates the Korean War as tipping point while subsuming it to what Heonik Kwon calls "the business of states and their alliances, largely unconnected to the routines of the civic order."[12] For Kwon, this view elides the reality of places where "people had to live the cold war as part of their everyday lives and in their most immediate intimate domains."[13] Paik Nak-chung considers this lived reality the effect of a "division system" and its accompanying disciplinary mechanisms (such as the Republic of Korea's National Security Law, which Paik calls a "covert constitution").[14] For Paik, "the opposition between the vested interests in both North and South and the majority of the North and South Korean populace who suffer from this system constitutes a more fundamental social structure than the antagonism *across* the Military Demarcation Line."[15] At the same time, one of the "compensating virtues" of the division system is that it "has at least prevented the resumption of war even though it has encouraged continuous tension since 1953 and attendant undemocratic tendencies on both sides."[16] What happened is preferable to what might have happened: "This is a better outcome at least than another internecine (probably nuclear) war that could bring a virtual end to the Korean nation."[17] Paik invokes the organizing principle of limited war, the specter of mass destruction or what we might call the mindfulness of virtual death, here a death that has not taken place but is always in the offing.

What Osgood calls "limited-war thinking" was indeed made manifest in Korea by way of wartime improvisations that would concretize the US standoff with the PRC and the Soviet Union, the formation of a militarized transpacific, and, more broadly, the management of a decolonizing world (which includes the division system on the Korean peninsula).[18] The 1953 armistice serves as a constitution for limited war in its ultimate form, a continuous abeyance—the best recourse in an imperfect world to prevent a greater loss of life (ultimately through nuclear destruction). The armistice frames how everyday life will proceed on the

Korean peninsula, how security imperialism appears as compensatory but unavoidable, virtuous in prevention of potential death.

The armistice governs decolonization via its self-definition as "purely military in character" and provisional, aimed at "stopping the Korean conflict, with its great toll of bloodshed and suffering on both sides . . . until a final peaceful settlement is achieved."[19] Such an arrangement does not acknowledge war (only "conflict") as it inaugurates a militarized regime of mutual self-restraint. The document announces an ameliorative but warlike condition, the transformation of wartime improvisations into something that will become military in character but much more: permanent mobilization, the governance of life as a state of readiness. Less an agreement settling past accounts than a prescription for how to proceed, the armistice would, in fact, offer itself as template of global import.

Limited-war thinking involves self-mourning, an expression of grief for its own necessity, the burden borne in the management of actual and potential death. Such a cumbersome idea was better served by a popular term available for understanding on the level of bodily experience in the world, something sensory, uncomfortable but ultimately livable. This term is "cold war." The management of decolonization (revolutionary, nationalist, or a combination of both) would reside within this thermostatic designation. To follow wartime and postarmistice cultural production in the DPRK, the US, and the ROK is to understand quickly that the notion of a cold war masks incommensurability. The experience of the Korean War differed markedly for the commanders who signed the 1953 military armistice (including the PRC representative), for the militaries that fought on the peninsula, and for the civilian populations from which those militaries were drawn. This war was a catalyst not only for an altered geopolitics but for varying, interrelated forms of social organization that would have profound effects for decades across these three sites (even if the effects of the war were not experienced in an explicit, immediate way by the vast majority of the US population). The armistice remains, as of this writing, as does the global deployment of limited-war thinking.

How do wartime and postarmistice stories of death give life to ideas about revolutionary belongings, gendered selfhoods, anticommunist cosmopolitanisms? At what points do DPRK and ROK works intersect as they offer their own universalisms, visions of limitlessness and potentiality articulated in relation to the bifurcations and borders imposed and hardened by war and extended under armistice? How might the assumption of Korea as template for limited war assume totalizing and lasting cultural forms within the transpacific hegemon (US) itself?

To crisscross DPRK, US, and ROK thanatographic borders is to move beyond the thermometric, to a war that was something other than cold, hot, or a tepid mixture of both.[20] The 1953 agreement to cease hostilities was not a stop but the inauguration of the warlike, the extension and expansion of war into a state of emergency, into semi-sovereignties, competing developmentalisms, mobilizations. Wartime and postarmistice stories of dying and death in the DPRK, US, and ROK extend the idea of the limit itself, which becomes multiple, contested, a place or line, a point of contact, a site in which limitlessness and expansiveness can become blurry, fleeting but also visible, legible. In and around the demise and breakdown of bodies and minds emerges a range of possibilities and empowerments brought to bear in a war that was not a war and had no end. This was a war limitless not only in this never-end but in the attempts to prescribe the course of history itself, to manage everything that would follow.

THE BOOK IN FIVE PARTS

The end of Japanese colonial rule in Korea in 1945 was followed by Soviet (north) and US (south) military occupations from 1945–1948. US-Soviet debates about trusteeship in Korea led nowhere, and the United States would turn to the newly-formed United Nations as vehicle to sanction a general election. This solution was rejected by the Soviet Union, and a UN-sponsored election was held only in the US-occupied zone in May 1948.[21] The ROK was established in the south on August 15, 1948, the DPRK in the north on September 9, 1948. These are the two political entities extant on the Korean peninsula today, with the United States retaining wartime operational control of the ROK military (the latter maintains operational control of its military under armistice) as of this writing.

The United States Military Government in Korea (USAMGIK) was marked by protests and uprisings, the bloodiest among them being the 4/3 Jeju Uprising (4/3 referring to April 3, 1948). USAMGIK was quick to deploy Korean constabulary and paramilitary units to quell the uprising. In the end, the aim was to "permanently pacify the situation" and this involved the transformation of Jeju into "a miniature police state."[22] Part I of this book turns to DPRK, US, and ROK fragments from the late 1940s through 1960 that address the 4/3 Jeju Uprising: Ham Sedŏk's play *Mountain People* (*San saramdŭl*, 1949–1950); postarmistice nonfiction by General William Dean (1954); the Hollywood biopic *Battle Hymn* (1957); Hŏ Yunsŏk's short story "Haenyŏ" (Sea Woman, 1950); and O Yŏngsu's "Afterword" (Huildam, 1960). Invocations of world-historical truths map the island's topography, as do ideas of the exotic, the primordial, the sacrificial, the religious, and the secular. Their juxtaposition mixes extreme violence and death with grand, emancipatory imaginings—revolutionary, counterrevolutionary, sexual, psychological, and redemptive. Visions of postcolonial transformation turn upon much more than the geopolitical. Appeals to the sensory realm, to the intimacy of witnessing, accompany the performance of indigeneity as at once local and universal. Jeju Island becomes a site where the post-1945 exercise of power through proxy and legitimation of mass death appears within the overlap among the visible and the invisible, the knowable and the unknowable, the living and the dead.

Islands, mountains, city, village, skies, ocean, region, continent, world, mind, heart, body. The geographical, geopolitical, psychological, emotional, and sensory intertwine in a post-1945 transformation of the entire Korean peninsula into a site of global border-making. The northern half would manage shifting degrees of affiliation with the Soviet Union, China, and the socialist world, while the southern half was to become an island-like formation at water's edge of an economic, political, and military network under construction in the early 1950s, the US transpacific. Early in the war it was not clear whether the limit line would form at the southernmost shore of the peninsula, at the Yalu, or hold roughly along the thirty-eighth parallel, the line the United States first proposed to divide Korea in 1945. By late 1951, it seemed clear that Korea would be divided roughly along this original limit line. But this did not mean other options, which appeared altogether possible during the first six months of the war, were forgotten or unimaginable.

What does it mean to have fought and died in the southern portion of the Korean peninsula only to recognize that the war would not result in revolutionary unification? How to translate loss of the southern region (and particularly Seoul) into DPRK victory in what would be called the Fatherland Liberation War (*Choguk haebang chŏnjaeng*)? Part II begins with what by all accounts was a failed wartime serial (Han Hyo's *Seoul People*; *Sŏul saramdŭl*, 1951) detailing the September 1950 Battle for Seoul (and subsequent withdrawal to the north) and continues with a canonical novel (Hwang Kŏn's *Happiness*; *Haengbok*, 1953) offering a meditation on the possibility of experiencing joy at the moment of death in combat. Part II shows how acts of revolutionary mourning in the DPRK commemorate loss as a form of progress. Central to this dialectic is women's wartime and postarmistice revolutionary praxis, the relation between martyrdom and notions of monumentality, and a sustained intertextual negotiation with Soviet cultural production. The last involves the critical migration of feelings (that which was felt somewhere else, in some other time) into the unfolding of DPRK history. Part II closes with the writer Im Sundŭk's address to these pillars of historymaking via a question posed in various ways in her work from the late 1940s through the mid-1950s: How to approach the relation among women, war-related death, and the constitution of the "people" (*inmin*) as revolutionary subjects?

The Korean War accelerated the post-1945 US securing of a militarized transpacific and the reimagining of Japan as island safe haven off the Asian mainland. The war also led to lasting forms of militarization and mobilization in the continental United States (CONUS) itself. The Korean War was not forgotten but layered into the fabric of the cold war, structured as it was by the what-might-happen (potential death). Part III opens with companion Hollywood films (*One Minute to Zero*, 1952; *Sabre Jet*, 1953) that fold the what-might-happen into an exemplary state of readiness, that of the virtual widow, the military wife/lover who produces a mobilized domesticity predicated upon the mourning of death-as-possibility (the mourning of a death that might take place). To enter into this realm is to become a member of a community of those prepared to live, die, and mourn in limited wars that will never end, wars that are secular but also religious and even sublime, wars that assume human imperfection and the need for continuing struggle against the darkness without and within.

If the premise of limited war rests upon the management of death, theories of the limit and escalation that populate post-1945 international relations (IR) academic discourse in the United States are themselves part and parcel of a thanatographic imagination. What does it mean to die a reluctant but dutiful death in a war seemingly of little everyday concern to the contemporary CONUS population? James Michener's intertwining of skepticism and voluntarism in his graphic novella *The Bridges at Toko-Ri* (1953, illustrations by Noel Sickles) writes a story of doubt that lends depth, multidimensionality to the corpse. Such a death is exemplary not only of the liberal democratic subject but of the quiet, grim military capacity poised in the transpacific. The burden will be on those who are willing.

Part III traces two inflections of this warrior-self: the pilot and the prisoner. The pilot takes flight in James Salter's novel *The Hunters* (1956), prototype for a masculinity that seeks an empire of the self, a fighter whose prime mission is to push mind and body to the limit, to a heightened aesthetic and sensory experience that approaches the point of death. The prisoner becomes a sign of human frailty, less in susceptibility to brainwashing than in the demonstration of a universal breaking point. A lasting field of empowerment would form around this productive acknowledgment of fragility in two US Steel Hour teleplays (David Davidson's 1953 "P.O.W." and Rod Serling's 1955 "The Rack"), as well as Karl Malden's 1957 *Time Limit* (filmic adaptation of a Broadway play).

How to see the dead body? Harvey Kurtzman, who served as *MAD* magazine's first editor (1952–1956), turns to the visual regime of horror to present a becoming-corpse in *Two-Fisted Tales* (1950–1955) and *Frontline Combat* (1951–1954) that rework *LIFE*'s placement of dead US bodies within a redemptive narrative of sacrifice. At stake in the visual conversation between Kurtzman's Korean War comics and the multimodal display of the war dead in Henry Luce's *LIFE* (which commissioned Michener's *Toko-Ri*) is precisely the appropriation of the corpse. Part III shows how this visual regime helps to frame the multiperspectival, parodic knowingness of *MAD* (self-advertised as "humor in a jugular vein") and its decades-long exhortation to oppose brain death.

Part IV begins with the story of a border, Kang Yongjun's 1960 "Barbed Wire" (Ch'ŏljomang), a thanatography that traces the separation of the protagonist's mind from his body. His crossing from life to death on the barbed wire encircling the United Nations Command (UNC) POW camp on Kŏje Island signals not a disappearance but the appearance of a consciousness that haunts early 1960s reflections on the short history of the ROK and the 6/25 War.[23] This history is of a particular border consciousness, the consideration of the relation between the carceral and the emancipatory. This liminal demise haunts the present, conjures the necessity of another frame beyond what would become life-under-armistice. Part IV etches the search for this elsewhere in the wartime literary scene, with emphasis on the work of Pak Yŏngjun, a central figure in the Embedded Writers Corps. Pak's move from fratricide to sacrifice and finally to suicide in three successive thanatographies—"Dark Night" (Amya, 1952); "Partisan" (Ppalch'isan, 1952); and "In the Sea off Yongch'o Island" (Yongch'odo kŭnhae, 1953)—elaborates a turn to love, sexuality, and interiority as site of transideological authenticity. Such a self finds little sense of home within the bifurcated geospace of the Korean peninsula and its associated forms of governance. Inflections of this dislocation in place would follow in later works addressing national division and the possibility of reunification.

In the mid-1950s, early reflections on division and war often involve a recognition of what will become familiar and what will become unfamiliar, what becomes familiar and unfamiliar at the same time. This play comes to the fore in two early postarmistice testimonials of life (as POW, as educator) in the DPRK—Sŏnu Hwi's *Return* (*Kwihwan*, 1954) and Im Ogin's *Crossing South: Before and After* (*Wŏllam chŏnhu*, 1956). These are stories of departure, destination, and division. They are also stories of return (they narrate arrival in the ROK). Their transit south performs a border-making, a production of meaning that arises from another crossing—to the past, to what is now the place left behind. The name of that place becomes "up north" (*ibuk*). They look back to write histories from the perspective of the war to come and the war that has transformed into armistice. These testimonials speak of redemption within the ruins of postcolonial history, blurring the lines among the confessional, the autobiographical, and the thanatographical. They witness death, destruction from the POV of a threshold, entrance into a struggle to arrange the relation of the before to the after.

Part IV concludes with the filmic battles of the 1960s, a decade that saw the reorganizing of the film industry and the hashing out of the parameters within which to screen the 6/25 War. More than any other director, Yi Manhŭi stood at the center of this warscape, his state-supported, blockbuster war film *The Marines Who Never Returned* (*Toraoji annŭn haebyŏng*, 1963) followed by his arrest for violation of the Anticommunist Law in 1965 (on the grounds of an overly sympathetic portrayal of North Koreans). While Yi subsequently directed several films framing the war in the melodramatic terms of familial betrayal, he would turn to metacommentary with *Homeward* (*Kwiro*, 1967), a film that ends with the protagonist's suicide. A virtual widow mourns the present (wounded in the war, her husband is paralyzed from the waist down) as she wanders the mid-1960s developmentalist city, a site for a film industry mobilized to equate anticommunism with the promise of an ethical life.

Armistice does not produce forgettings but ways of living in the interim, the apparent limitlessness of a pause becoming a place of residence. How to consider armistice in history when it takes constitutive form, frames how history should appear? Part V returns to fragments (two literary texts and a film) from the DPRK, US, and ROK, this time a cross-border accounting of what has happened and what portends in the 1960s. Retellings of war, aspirations, and reckonings also speak of armistice as a form of governance. Armistice settles into location—in calls to heartfelt, revolutionary life in the DPRK, in the US politics of liberal self-restraint extended to futures of sacrifice in wars at once interminable and limited, in a look back at the ROK's entrance into a transpacific world manifesting itself in the struggle for survival taking place in wartime Busan (where the rear has already become the front).

Willing or not, the dead organize universals. The dead are not given to a preexisting world. Nor do they fit in seamlessly. They are to be found in the borders, histories, desires, wants, sexualities, and affiliations that populate the heterogeneous, uneven thanatographic imagination. This form of residence is that of the afterdead. Here, afterdeath refers not to an end but to an inconclusiveness, a temporality reserved for those whose deaths signal that they were yet to live. The afterdead appear in the time and place of those who find themselves in the interim, on hold. For some, this appearance marks a deferral and thus represents a call for the day to come, a call for decolonization. The thanatographic imagination draws on multiple ways of seeing, feeling, and describing the after of the dead in relation to what came before (allusions to death, narratives of being toward death, possible deaths, living deaths, among others). *Death Without End* shows how dispensation of the afterdead plays a central role in the formation of histories and modalities that emerge from the Korean War (whether or not this is acknowledged). Representations of deaths do what the word implies, makes them present. Images of death and their related inflections (meditations on absence, for example) help to define the parameters of what will be a global state of emergency, a continuing crisis embodied most powerfully in the armistice that did not end the war (the consensus of limits that produces limitlessness).

PART I

The terrain at ocean's edge is uneven, the border around which standing armies would organize was to be determined. Invocations of indigenous and gendered belongings, descriptions of transformation and trauma, appeals to class and nation, stories of sympathy, empathy, soundscapes of destruction, transcriptions, interrogations, disavowals of knowledge, rumors, fleeting references—this and much more gathers in DPRK, US, and ROK cultural mappings of Jeju Island in the late 1940s and early 1950s. In what follows, the juxtaposition of fragments from these sites leads not to totality but suggests a sense of beginning, openings predicated upon the location of colonialism as a past.

Images of dying and death. A topography that will not combine to offer comprehension as it harkens to massacre, to sacrifice, to the offering of one's life for the sake of others (death as gift). Potential death assumes multiple valences: Assertions of living death (living as if dead) accompany confrontations with the inability to know whether someone is dead or alive. Such deaths occupy the space and time of the interrogative. They occur in the form of visitations that question what constitutes a limit to violence and what legitimizes death. Their appearance asks of means and ends, how stories of death can organize rebirths, awakenings to histories of the possible.

CHAPTER 1

JEJU ISLANDS

On January 13, 1951, President Harry Truman sent a top secret telegram to General Douglas MacArthur. The Chinese had entered the Korean War in October 1950, leading to the quick retreat of UN forces from the Yalu. Seoul was lost for the second time in early January 1951. The war was not going well.

Truman outlined ten points encapsulating his views on "continuing the resistance to aggression in Korea."[1] These included, among others, the following: Provide a "rallying point" around which the "spirits and energies of the free world" will counter the Soviet Union; "deflate the dangerously exaggerated political and military prestige of Communist China"; "give direct assistance to the organization of non-communist resistance in Asia"; "carry out our commitments of honor to the South Koreans"; "contribute greatly to the post-treaty security position of Japan in relation to the continent"; "produce a free-world coalition of incalculable value to the national interests of the United States."[2] Having established seriousness of purpose and commitment to the global struggle against communism, Truman indicated that the conflict should not include Japan or Western Europe "in large scale hostilities." MacArthur was not to expect an increase in support:

> We recognize, of course, that continued resistance might not be militarily possible with the limited forces with which you are being called upon to meet large Chinese armies. Further, in the present world situation, your forces must be preserved as an effective instrument for the defense of Japan and elsewhere. However, some of the important purposes mentioned above might be supported, if you should think it practicable, and advisable, by continued resistance from

off-shore islands of Korea, particularly from Cheju-do, if it becomes impracticable to hold an important portion of Korea itself.[3]

This suggestion of an island-based perimeter had been discussed in high-level exchanges in Washington in the days leading up to the Truman telegram of January 13. In a January 12 memorandum to Secretary of State Dean Acheson, Assistant Secretary of State for Far Eastern Affairs Dean Rusk wrote:

> apart from Cheju-do Island [sic], there are many peninsulas along the south coast with narrow approaches to mainland Korea and countless islands around the south and west coast which might be held indefinitely by South Korean and a portion of the present UN forces. This would permit us to establish a vast laboratory for unconventional operations against Asiatic communism, for developing the techniques of organizing Asian manpower, and for developing commando and guerrilla operations against and within Korea itself.[4]

Such a perimeter, Rusk proposed, would enable Truman to make a statement that the United Nations was "not abandoning its resistance against aggression" and thus provide "the greatest possible benefits not only in Korea but in Southeast Asia and other vital areas."[5] Acheson would present Rusk's views in a meeting held on the same day and attended by all the major figures in Truman's cabinet, the Joint Chiefs of Staff, Rusk, and Truman himself. The Memorandum of Conversation indicates that Army Chief of Staff Joseph Collins "thought that Cheju-do Island [sic] would suffice for this purpose."[6] What becomes clear in these exchanges taking place at the highest levels of the US government was an assessment of the pros and cons of a continued forward presence in Korea.[7] And this vision placed Jeju Island at center stage, a forward base from which to wage necessarily irregular, limited war against Asian mainland communism.

General Collins and General Hoyt Vandenberg (US Air Force chief of staff and former CIA director) met with General MacArthur in Tokyo on January 18th with the aim of explaining in person the consensus reached in Washington. While the military situation in Korea appeared less dire than feared earlier in January, a complete withdrawal from the peninsula was still a possibility: "They discussed the evacuation of ROK troops and officials (estimated to number approximately a million, including dependents) and agreed that they should be placed on Cheju-do."[8] Jeju Island is to stand in for the island-like Republic of Korea at transpacific edge and at the center of a creative, scientific effort to overcome failures in China and Korea. How to define best practices for the movement away from direct US participation on the ground to a proxy war in which

Asians fight Asians? Such an exercise of power entails observation of the bodies of others (their lives, their deaths). The line of sight is that of an invisible researcher in a laboratory of grand proportions.

The proposal to make Jeju an island of "continued resistance" was not new, as was well-known in US military circles. Six years earlier, another vision had been proposed, this time by the Japanese imperial army. Following defeat in the Battle of Midway in 1942, Japanese military planners increasingly turned to Jeju as the final line of defense outside the Japan home islands. Jeju Island already possessed considerable military infrastructure, including a major airfield used for bombing runs on Shanghai and Nanking in the late 1930s. A quick buildup brought troop strength on the island to around 75,000 men.[9] While US nuclear strikes on Hiroshima and Nagasaki made Jeju the site of a last stand that was never to be, the militarization of the island warranted a second, little-known ceremony of Japanese surrender to the United States Military Government in Korea (USAMGIK) on September 28, 1945 in Jeju City (the first took place in Seoul on September 9). What is the relation between the last line of resistance scenarios gamed by Japanese and American military planners and the reality that roughly 10 percent of the island's population would die violent deaths over a seven-year period, from 1947–1954?

Colonial period militarization on Jeju was accompanied by the formation of a close connection between the island and the Japanese metropole, particularly Osaka. Many islanders migrated to Japan for work. Liberation in 1945 brought thousands of these laborers back to their homes. The subsequent uprising saw tens of thousands flee back to Japan. This movement of peoples was part and parcel of the post–World War II reworking of empires, the shift from a network of island and mainland possessions/occupations that made up the Japanese empire to what Hal Friedman calls the "imperial solution to its security problem in the Pacific Basin" sought by the United States, namely the transformation of the Pacific into an "American Lake," a "supporting base system for future strategic use."[10] The aim to manage the forward projection of power in East Asia was signaled by the formation of the Far East Command and the United States Pacific Command, both established in January 1947 (the former would be subsumed by the latter in 1957). Jeju Island became the site of last stands that never were and the beginning of a war in Korea that would probe limitations, what amount of force to use, how to use it, where to establish the limit line.

In January 1951, the injunction to hold the line somewhere revolves around the question of limited war. How to rework the contours of the Japanese imperium into a new territorial and oceanic border, the westernmost point of the US transpacific? Jeju was a somewhere that became central to the imagining of the

American Lake, to an anchoring of the imaginative with the practicable. Jeju would be a place from which to continue the struggle, all the while securing what was under construction—a vast oceanic network knit together by sea lanes, air routes, military bases, and semi-sovereignties. The Asia-Pacific War and the Korean War were nearly continuous. The former folded into the latter on Jeju Island.

Between the two last stands that never were was the formation of another resistance on Jeju, this one undertaken by the islanders themselves. The date commonly given for the beginning of the Jeju Island Uprising is April 3, 1948. What is known by islanders as the "incident" is also frequently referred to in the ROK by a shortened numerical form of this date, 4/3. Protests had broken out over a year earlier, on the 1947 commemoration of the March First Movement. Many Jeju islanders objected to what they considered to be the continuation of the coercive Japanese colonial state apparatus in the form of USAMGIK and, more specifically, to USAMGIK's impending implementation of a general election to be held only in the south. It was on April 3, 1948 that organized, armed resistance broke out in earnest.[11] USAMGIK quickly organized a counterinsurgency that included South Korean constabulary, paramilitary, and military forces. General William F. Dean, second in command to General John R. Hodge (US military governor of Korea) took charge, and the US role continued in an advisory and support capacity following the creation of the ROK government on August 15, 1948.[12]

As Su-kyoung Hwang indicates, "At the height of the anti-election campaign in May, Cheju was transformed into a space of death."[13] By the time it was over in 1954, approximately 30,000 Jeju islanders had been killed, a number that roughly matches US combat deaths in the 1950–1953 phase of the Korean War (33,739). The early 1951 location of Jeju as central to a vision of limited, proxy warfare was of a future that had been receiving test results since April 1948.

The story of massacre on Jeju Island is more than one of censorship and repressed memories. To invoke the traumatic and nothing else is to disavow the relation between massacre and contemporaneous invocations of the revolutionary, the salvific, and the utopic. The location of possibility on Jeju Island was shared by US strategists and DPRK revolutionaries. Nor was Jeju Island off-limits to mainland ROK writers in the 1950s. They would offer their own emancipatory visions even as they navigated questions of state violence, indigeneity, and mainlander belonging. Military and geopolitical visions intersect with gendered, religious, spiritual, and mythic understandings of conflict and redemption across a constellation of works, among them the DPRK playwright Ham Sedŏk; nonfiction by William Dean and Dean Hess (both US military officers); a Hollywood film directed by the prolific Douglas Sirk; and the ROK writers Hŏ Yunsŏk and

O Yŏngsu. A crisscross of summonings and imaginings constitute the relations between local and extralocal combatants: Jeju farmers, townspeople, factory workers, *haenyŏ* (sea women; the women divers of Jeju), on the one hand; USAMGIK commanders and advisors, ROK regular army officers, Northwest Youth (an anticommunist paramilitary group made up of young refugee men from the north), on the other hand. These works tell the story of how death organizes a contested history of emancipatory claims. This is also the story of a beginning, the combat phase of the Korean War.[14]

ISLAND OF MASSACRE, ISLAND OF REVOLUTION

USAMGIK leadership flew to Jeju Island on May 5, 1948 to discuss strategy.[15] The matter was urgent. Unrest on Jeju was threatening the election scheduled for May 10 in the southern portion of the peninsula.

The May 9, 1948 editions of the influential northern newspapers *Rodong sinmun* (*Workers' Daily*) and *Minju Chosŏn* (*Democratic Chosŏn*) also called attention to recent events on Jeju Island, noting that Ninth Regiment Commander Kim Ingnyŏl (far right in figure 1.1) had threatened to commence combat operations (*chŏnt'u kaesi*) against impoverished and unarmed Jeju villagers.[16] An article more prominently placed on the previous page of this edition of the *Rodong sinmun* serves as context, its headline an exhortation: "Let's Condemn the Election of a Separate Government in South Chosŏn: the Vicious Attempt of the US Invaders and the Struggle of the South Chosŏn People [*inmin*] to Rescue the Country." Later commemorative articles appearing in the April 3 editions of the *Rodong sinmun* in 1949, 1950, 1951 would follow this lead, referring to Jeju Island as flash point of a broader struggle taking place throughout the south (the 1949 edition includes a map of this general resistance).[17] To be sure, the story is of Jeju but with emphasis on the larger struggle of the Korean *inmin* themselves (in north and south) against US imperialism.

May 9, 1948 was, in fact, a day of commemoration, the third anniversary of the Soviet Union's defeat of Germany. It was this story that dominated the news. *Rodong sinmun* underscored the excitement displayed in the streets of Pyongyang and elaborated on the importance of the Soviet victory over the Nazis. The horizon broadens. The peninsula-wide struggle against the UN plan to hold separate elections in South Chosŏn was a continuation of the Soviet Union's Great Patriotic War, which had led directly to the emancipation of North Chosŏn. This shared revolutionary history was now unfolding in the global struggle against a

FIG. 1.1 USAMGIK leadership arriving at Jeju Airport on May 5, 1948. Major General William Dean, USAMGIK military commander, is seen second from left. Courtesy of National Archives and Records Administration.

different enemy, fascist and capitalist. The Great Patriotic War, defensive in nature, marked by suffering, perseverance, and heroism, would inform portrayals of emancipatory struggle against the US invader throughout the DPRK's 1950–1953 Fatherland Liberation War (*choguk haebang chŏnjaeng*). Such discursive overlap was already taking place in the late 1940s. Simply turn the page of the May 9, 1948 edition of the *Rodong sinmun* to move from commemoration of the Great Patriotic War in Pyongyang to the contemporary "terror" (*t'ero*) mobilized by the United States across South Chosŏn.

How to write revolutionary history? The May 1949 issue of *Munhak yesul* (*Literary Arts*; precursor of the journal *Chosŏn munhak*) underscores the Soviet Union's victory in World War II, declaring in its preface that its "continuing struggle in all directions for peace and freedom . . . has provided a powerful lesson and lofty spirit to writers and artists of our fatherland as well."[18] The task at hand becomes all the more clear:

> This struggle to save the nation and the work being done in the northern sector to build up the fatherland stands in complete opposition to imperialism and fascism. Our people [*inmin*] are constructing our fatherland with our own hands,

and our writers and artists, too, must work actively to incarnate [*hyŏlyukhwa*] this reality in their works. This is a pressing matter, and all should employ the totality of their creative activities in this direction.... Our literature and art must present the way we have lived and the way in which our lives today are improving, changing into a completely new form.[19]

The past victories of the Soviet Union and the "way we have lived" cross into a creative contemporaneity. Two pasts move into a shared present. How to incarnate this contemporaneity, this emphasis on taking the past into account while building the new? The struggle against USAMGIK and its Korean supporters is one for national independence and global revolution at the same time. The "struggle to save the nation" unfolds in the revolutionary changes occurring in the north and in the "resistance . . . taking place across the entire southern region."[20] The incarnation of the *inmin* fuses the local and global.

Enter Ham Sedŏk's *Mountain People* (*San saramdŭl*), serialized in four installments in *Munhak yesul* (December 1949–March 1950). Ham's play has stood the test of time, selected for inclusion in the DPRK's "reunification literature" (*t'ongil munhak*), the corpus of texts detailing the continuing struggle taking place in the southern portion of the Korean peninsula.[21] The publication of *Mountain People* in the journal *T'ongil munhak* in 1999 and its later appearance in the multivolume *Selected Works of Reunification Literature* (*T'ongil munhak chakp'um sŏnjip, 2016*) attest to its canonical status.[22] Consisting of four acts (only act one contains two scenes), *Mountain People* details the armed resistance of the people of Jeju against police and paramilitary controlled by USAMGIK officers and their Korean collaborators. The play presents a linear, dated history of the battle as it moves from the seashore to the mountains, where the fighters, under the leadership of Ko Chegon and Kim Sŏngmin, organize to make their own last stand.

Ham's play opens in early March, 1948 at the home of Chegon's Mother, a *haenyŏ* widow now eking out a living as a farmer in a village not far from the water. Stage directions indicate that the house has its back to the hills and is surrounded by a "primitive" wall of stacked stones particular to Jeju.[23] She is described as "like all the other Jeju women who spent half their time in the sea, half of their time farming—strong like a man, with a powerful voice."[24] A small group of *haenyŏ* come up from the sea and join her. Among them is Ŭlla, with her "jet-black, shiny hair, thick eyelashes, and eyes filled with the fire and passion of women of the south."[25] The women speak in Jeju dialect. Chegon's Mother laments the times, which have worsened from colonial days. Chegon used to work in the island's alcohol factory, and between the two of them, they had eked out a living. But now Chegon has been fired after a strike, and taxes/requisitions mean further impoverishment. He will appear shortly, his "face angular, brave, and rough even as he is good-natured and self-sacrificing."[26]

Mountain People invokes a history of *haenyŏ*, Jeju farmers, workers, all who have suffered exploitation under Japanese colonial rule. USAMGIK officers, former Japanese collaborators, and Northwest Youth who have fled to the south due to land reform—such is the reworked coalition of oppression on Jeju Island in 1948. Chegon sums up the situation: "Those dirty bastards are running around massacring all the islanders, and a young guy like me is supposed to feed the horses and weed the fields?"[27]

The curtain rises for act 1, scene 2. Seashore. But no one appears on the sand or in the water. Stage directions call for the sound of the *haenyŏ* signaling to each other in whistles, *hwek hwek*. The audience is invited to image a highly localized and exotic *haenyŏ* communality and island-belonging that quickly moves elsewhere. *Haenyŏ* of all ages come out of the water and gather on the shore:

HAENYŎ 1: The 38th parallel needs to be done away with as soon as possible.
HAENYŎ 2: If that happened, we'd be the first to go to North Chosŏn, wouldn't we?
   . . . .
YOUNG HAENYŎ: And we'd get to see General Kim.[28]

Island indigeneity is inseparable from the mainland manifestation of a proper postcolonial future, one the *haenyŏ* image for themselves and long to see.

The *haenyŏ* set the stage for a death that secures such an imaging. Enter Yongch'ŏl (older brother of Ŭlla), dragged on stage by police and Northwest Youth. He has been caught operating undercover. A crowd forms and Ŭlla, Chegon's Mother, and Chegon arrive. All join to wrest Yongch'ŏl away from the police, but the latter fight back and pull him away. He is killed, shot by the police captain: "Yongch'ŏl's Mother (face trembling with sorrow and rage but calmly as should the mother of a revolutionary): Our Yongch'ŏl is the son of the Chosŏn *inmin*. There is no need to harbor resentment at his death [*han toelgŏn opsuda*]. He has perished for the sake of the *inmin*."[29] His mother names his bloodline: He is born of the Chosŏn *inmin*. She must also organize an emotional topography around the display on stage of his killing, not one of a localized *han* (ressentiment), but of revolutionary anger and determination. Becoming, the future, is at stake, as is shortly emphasized in a quick conversation between Songbaek and Chegon:

(Songbaek, the woman information officer, silently walks on stage.)
SONGBAEK: Comrade Chegon.
CHEGON: Comrade Songbaek. *(In tears, he embraces her.)*

CHEGON: Comrade, quickly give us an order. How long do we have to be bloodied like this, massacred in this way?
SONGBAEK: Comrade, the higher-ups, too, have come to the unanimous view that the only way to survive in the face of this barbarous massacre is to take up weapons and fight.
CHEGON: And so?
SONGBAEK: Yes, all must go to the mountains and rise up as partisans.[30]

Yongch'ŏl's killing was made visible, but the organization of violence on Jeju Island has yet to manifest itself.

Act 3 moves from the visual and emotive elaboration of the relations among the indigenous, the *inmin*, and partisan fighters (of islanders becoming mountain people), to a display of unbecoming (becoming-proxy). Ham's play now takes its audience to the May 5, 1948 meeting of the USAMGIK principals shown in the photograph above: Lt. Col. Kim Ingnyŏl (in the play, Ch'oe Chinyŏl), commander of the Ninth Regiment (far right); Cho Pyŏngok, commander of the National Police (second from right); Song Hosŏng, commander of the Korean Constabulary (third from right); An Chaehong, chief civilian administrator (third from left); Major General William Dean, USAMGIK military commander (second from left).[31] Focusing on Ttin (the play's transliteration of "Dean"), Cho, An, Song, and Ch'oe, act 3 offers an account of a meeting that, in fact, bears a marked resemblance to reports circulating at the time. Stage directions present a stark contrast from act 2. The audience is taken to the provincial capital, to "the same building used as the seat of government under Japanese colonial rule."[32] On the wall, a "US Army map of the world, a map of Chosŏn below the 38th parallel, a map of Jeju Island, the US flag, a picture of President Truman, and a Coca Cola advertisement."[33] The audience is asked to observe Jeju Island through this collage of US military, political, and economic power.

Ttin stresses the urgency of the situation and turns to his subordinates for input. Cho Pyŏngok expresses no hesitation: "The method is simple. We have to wipe out all the reds, every last one of them."[34] Ch'oe Chinyŏl counters with context: "We all know that this riot [*p'oktong*] is taking place in an effort to block the election and create what they think will be a utopia, their people's republic. But there is a more direct cause. What we're seeing is an explosion of the people's pent-up resentment [*wŏnhan*] against the Jeju police and the Northwest Youth."[35] Ch'oe proceeds to offer an analysis that largely coincides with what the audience has witnessed in acts 1 and 2: The guerillas and the people are united in the struggle; farmers and women offer their support; the *haenyŏ* fish out weapons thrown into the sea, and the workers clean and fix them; women students go truant and leave for the hills to wash clothes and cook meals for the fighters; doctors leave hospitals to volunteer their services in the mountains. The conclusion: "This is not something that can be put down through force of arms."[36] How, then, to bring the rioters into line? Things take a turn for the worse when Ch'oe pulls out his pistol and aims it at Cho's chest: "You bastard, I'm just as much of an anticommunist as you!"[37]

How does Ttin manage a war against the Jeju revolutionaries and his underlings at the same time? His method is simple and direct, boiled down to a matter of interests: "Is the failure of the election an acceptable outcome for you? Followed by a communist takeover in the form of a people's republic? And if that happens, where will you go? Not back to America with us. We can't take you."[38] The course of action is clear: "If you plan on living here for the foreseeable future you'd better form a government fast. Bolster Jeju's defenses, make the island into a base that will hold the line against the Soviet Union. That's what's best for you and for America, too."[39] Ttin articulates the confluence of interests that will mark the origin of the ROK. It's a do or die situation.

But just how committed is the United States? Kim Yŏngbae, Jeju Island police chief, tests the waters: "If this doesn't work, there's going to be only one option left. You'll have to bring in the full force of the US military, planes and tanks, to wipe them out."[40] Cho chimes in, calling for "total massacre" (*much'abyŏl haksal*).[41] Ttin offers full military support, but his vision is escalatory. The plan will first be one of "appeasement and persuasion" (*hwoeyu chŏngch'aek*): "We have to isolate the fighters in the mountains, separate them from the people." He turns to his subordinate P'at'oriji (Partridge) with these orders: "Stop the grain quotas, reduce taxes, provide canned food, sugar, and other supplies, allow the *haenyŏ* to freely sell whatever they gather from the sea. That will get us past the May 10 election. Once that's accomplished it still won't be too late to go ahead and do what Cho suggests, massacre the whole lot."[42] End of argument. In act 3, temporal limits (a procession of stages) are placed on the use of violence to bring the enemy around. At the end point is a revelation of relation between mediator and proxy. The former is to recede, and the latter is to appear at the scene of mass killing.

Act 4 draws the play to its close. Stage directions: "Curtain rises. Sampau, Ŭlla and others stand center stage before a door. The group is no longer dressed in the guerrilla attire of act 2. They now wear uniforms, hats, and carry weapons (seized during the previous battles). They move in a regimented manner, reminiscent of a regular army."[43] Productive and purposeful transformation contrasts with the temporality of escalation. Militarization is joyous, accompanied by the sound of a Jeju folk song. Chegon, disguised as a farmer, walks on stage: "Hearing the sound of the people singing after such a long time warms my heart."[44] His deception aligns with authenticity, willingness to take on risk.

The audience will shortly encounter violence and an attempted massacre but neither will serve as source of trauma. We are back in the mountains. The fighters of Jeju, now an army of *inmin*, stand against the Korean counterrevolutionaries. Much of the cast from the first two acts reappears, along with people from the two villages of Hwabuk and Samyang who have taken refuge in the hills to avoid forced participation in the May 10 election. The stage is set. Chegon warns the assembled group that the struggle will be fierce: "The bastards are putting everything on the line for election.... Cho Pyŏngok, An Chaehong, and Song Hosŏng came down personally from Seoul in order to come up with a cunning plan, so we don't know exactly what to expect."[45] The battle heats up: hand-to-hand combat. The villagers refuse to leave. They join the fray but are quickly overpowered by the sheer numbers of the paramilitary and constabulary. Ch'oe Chinyŏl shoots Chegon and is about to fire again when police Captain O Ransu intervenes, telling him a slower death is in order: "Let's make him an example for the villagers, throw him into that cave and set it on fire."[46] He gives the orders to Lt. Mun, company commander of the constabulary:

CHEGON (TO MUN): If you're of Chosŏn, if you have any conscience [*yangsim*] at all, tear off that dirty helmet and point your gun at those bastards over there, the enemies of the people, the ones who are exploiting and oppressing your parents, your brothers and sisters.[47]

Where do the true feelings of the Jeju farmers and villagers lie? Lt. Mun backs off, and others push Chegon into the cave. Ch'oe and O Ransu then inform the villagers of all the good policies and reforms the US occupation will provide. It is Chegon's Mother who responds:

CHEGON'S MOTHER: *(Coming to the fore and shouting in a voice filled with rage)*
We're not going to fall for your sugar-filled words ever again. You're killing children right here, in front of their mothers. So how many of our children have you killed when we're not around to see it?[48]

O Ransu offers the villagers a stark choice: Return to their villages or die in the cave. Chinok, the *haenyŏ* from act 1, steps up:

CHINOK: No need to ask again. We wouldn't follow you, if you were taking us to heaven. We'd rather follow the mountain people [*san saram*] to hell.
VILLAGERS: *(In unison)* That's right. We'll follow the mountain people.[49]

The villagers are shoved into the cave. Lt. Mun's resistance grows: "It's one thing to root out the mountain fighters, but isn't it cruel to kill the ordinary villagers?" Another member of the constabulary protests: "I'm not a red. But the company commander has it right. I'm against the massacre of the people [*inmin haksal*]."[50] More members of the constabulary stand down, only to be disarmed and pushed into the cave with the others. A bonfire is lit at the entrance. The sound of voices lifted in song grows louder as flames enter the cave. And then a shot is heard. A police academy cadet falls. More shots. And more.

The mountain fighters have come. Sŏngmin grabs a stick of dynamite O has placed at the cave's entrance and throws it to the side. Everyone rushes from the cave. Lt. Mun (coming out of the cave and going straight up to Sŏngmin): "It's today, finally, that we woke up from a long nightmare."[51] Ham's play closes with these stage directions: "In high spirits, the fighters lift their voices together to sing 'Song of the Partisans' as they descend the mountain. The *inmin* send them off with shouts of 'Long Live the Mountain People!'"[52]

Lt. Mun makes only a brief appearance at the close of the play but his transformation stands at its center. His witnessing translates into action. His approach to death results in rebirth, embodiment of survival in the face of a power that has no other recourse than to make people disappear. But we have also just been informed that what the play makes visible is not comprehensive. Chegon's Mother invokes the politics of deception—the sugar-filled words of the plotters—when she wonders what massacres have taken place beyond a line of sight. The audience is left with a vision of killing unseen.

BLOODY CONFUSION

As USAMGIK military commander, General William F. Dean formally oversaw operations on Jeju through the end of his tenure, which coincided with the end of the US occupation in August 1948. Dean was later given overall command of the US land expeditionary force, the 24th Infantry Division, deployed to Korea in the earliest days of the 1950–1953 phase of the war. Dean was separated from his men in late July and eventually taken prisoner. He would be the highest ranking US POW, as well as the most famous, awarded the Medal of Honor while still listed as missing in action in January 1951. He was released as part of Operation Big Switch in September 1953 and subsequently penned a widely-read account of his experiences during the war, *General Dean's Story* (1954), a section of which was first published under the title "My Three Years as a Dead Man" in *The Saturday Evening Post* (this earlier version was translated into Korean in 1956).

It is not the transliterated "Ttin" of Ham Sedŏk's *Mountain People* but "Dean" who appears as the protagonist of *General Dean's Story*. Dean, though, does encounter a version of Ttin in the form of a photograph of himself on Jeju Island in 1948, shown to him prior to one of his interrogations. He was there. Dean takes this moment as point of departure to offer an explanation. He had done all in his power to sort things out on Jeju, but "the isolation of the place made control quite difficult."[53] Moreover, Koreans deployed to the island were tough to manage: "When I was governor I sent both constabulary troops and police detachments there to try to restore order, but for a time it seemed to me that they were fighting each other rather than the bandits in the hills."[54] He indicates that guerillas had constantly hampered the occupation government and that he had done his best to "stop the bloody confusion."[55] When Colonel Rothwell Brown discovered that civilian women had been killed without trial, Dean responded by sending a court-martial officer to Jeju, who proceeded to convict several policemen and sentence them all to lengthy prison terms (twenty-five years).[56] Dean mentions, further, that "trouble continued on the island" following the formation of the ROK government in August 1948 and that a mutiny occurred at Yŏsu, where soldiers were to embark for deployment to Jeju. He then returns to the scene of interrogation:

> Hong and Choi, at Sunan, went over and over these events, trying to prove that I had ordered executions and had been responsible for the entire mess. I got tired of all this conversation and said, "Well, you're wasting your time trying to get me to admit responsibility for things that happened when I was military governor. It's your language, not mine: and you have all the names and the figures. I can't possibly put up a factual defense, having nothing to work with, so go ahead and shoot me. I never sanctioned the killing of any soldier or civilian without trial, but if any were killed without trial, in the final analysis it was my responsibility. Anything that occurred while I was military governor I was responsible for. Why don't you just shoot me? Don't wait and go through the farce of a trial."[57]

The Saturday Evening Post title haunts *General Dean's Story*. Here, he informs his US and (later) ROK readership that he offers his own life as sacrifice to that which takes place in the realm of a language he does not understand, to his formal command over that which he cannot fully control.[58] Dean's reflection on his three years as a dead man positions him as witness to what he didn't or couldn't know. And this lack of knowledge extends to the 1954 present, to the postarmistice narrative position of a survivor extricated from the living dead.

Dean's interrogators proceed to press him about coercive measures brought to bear on the May 1948 election: "But so far as I was concerned that had been the only free, secret-ballot election in Korea in four-thousand years, and I was proud of the way it had been handled."[59] The US occupation, though, did much more than work to hold elections. Monica Kim underscores the ways in which USAMGIK secretly provided funding and support for an array of rightist youth groups, prominent among them the Northwest Youth: "The undeniable continuity of such an infrastructure of labor, surveillance, and militarism has been systematically obscured from historical memory because of the US continuous disavowal of its support of violence in order to maintain the image of a successful 'anti-Communist' project in the East Asian region."[60] As Kim points out, "the violence was not merely an inconvenience, but indeed integral to the US project of occupation and subsequent war."[61] Nowhere was such violence and disavowal more manifest than on Jeju Island. For Dean, those deaths that may have occurred recede to the realm of the unknown and the unsanctioned (only several are named as having taken place, and the perpetrators were prosecuted). Instead, it is Dean's life as a dead man that requires telling, for the historical record. Dean successfully managed the formation of the ROK and subsequently served a three-year purgatory as part of the effort to secure its continued existence.

Asked in an interrogation if he had explained to each of his men why they were fighting, Dean responds in the affirmative. He confesses to his readers, though, that this was a lie. His first-person narrative of a virtual death (a form of autothanatography) means to make up for his wartime mistake: "An army can be a show-window for democracy only if every man in it is convinced that he is fighting for a free world, for the kind of government he wants for himself, and he personally represents the ideals that can make a world free."[62] To authenticate such purposefulness, Dean must make his virtual death visible, exemplary, true. He must summon a ghostliness, the testament of his own living death, lay it to rest, experience rebirth. It is in this way that "My Three Years as a Dead Man" becomes *General Dean's Story*.

PROMISED LAND

The original poster for Douglas Sirk's *Battle Hymn* (1957) emphasizes the authenticity of adaptation: The film will present the story of Colonel Dean Hess "as told in his best-seller." This biopic of Hess, the "flying parson," takes the form of a testimonial, the filmic adaptation of a true story of salvation. When Hess (Rock Hudson) tells his wife Mary (Martha Hyer) that he has volunteered for the recall to Korea, Mary replies, "But it doesn't make sense. It doesn't. Going back to war. That's where your problem began." As Hye Seung Chung demonstrates, the "transference of guilt between the two wars and the ultimate moral victory of the American hero constitute *Battle Hymn*'s thematic backbone."[63] Hess, the preacher turned fighter pilot, seeks redemption in Korea (he accidentally bombed a German orphanage in World War II). He will find it in his organization of "Operation Kiddy Car," the successful evacuation of Korean orphans in Seoul to Jeju Island under dire circumstances—the Chinese and North Korean communist advance southward in late 1950.

We learn in *Battle Hymn* that World War II has not ended. Douglas Sirk's film attests to the ways in which the mid-1950s US accounts of psychological breakdown in Korea often turn upon an attempt to portray the largely unacknowledged trauma suffered by GIs returning from combat in World War II.[64] The censoring of John Huston's 1946 *Let There Be Light*, a documentary that features soldiers receiving treatment for battlefield trauma in a Long Island hospital, serves as one of the best examples of this official silencing. *Battle Hymn* speaks to this trauma in its acknowledgment of the possibility of error, the guilt stemming from this acknowledgment, and the redemption sought from good works.

Battle Hymn tells another story, alluded to in the biblical reference of Huston's documentary, *Let There Be Light*. This is the story of a song, "Battle Hymn," shortened title of the famous Civil War abolitionist ballad "Battle Hymn of the Republic." The exhortation is for sacrifice: "As He died to make men holy/Let us die to make men free!/While God is marching on." The US Civil War, the white Christian abolition/emancipation of Black slaves inhabits the march to truth in Korea, the rescue of Asians from communist slavery.[65] There is no longer a need for a localizing genitive: "Battle Hymn of the Republic" now extends its exhortation to the world in the form of a universalist "Battle Hymn." This song, in fact, would circulate widely in the post-1945 era, played at state funerals, inaugurations, presidential library openings, and Veterans Day celebrations at Disneyland. "Battle Hymn" locates white sacrifice at the center of an emancipatory history, calls for an equation of the holy with the free, makes the spirit manifest in earthly works. In *Battle Hymn*, this history travels to Jeju Island.

It is in the final scene of *Battle Hymn* that Hess, Mary, and Sgt. Herman make it to Jeju for the first time. Theirs is a postarmistice visit to the Orphans' Home of Korea. Children and staff await them at the facility. As the trio looks on a boy breaks ranks and rushed toward Hess, jumping into his arms. "This is Old Chu," he tells Mary. "It's wonderful to see them so healthy," Mary declares. "Darling, you look as happy as the children." Hess pauses and looks at Mary meaningfully, "It's always been the children."

Mary appears with Hess only in the beginning frame of the film and in this closing scene. Hess's return to Jeju with Mary folds the domesticity of West Hampton, Ohio (their hometown in the film), into the orphans' home on Jeju

FIG. 1.2 *Battle Hymn* (1957). Still courtesy of Universal Studios.

Island at the same time as it consolidates a harmonious relationship: Hess has found redemption, and Mary now understands him and why he had to return to combat in Korea. Cut back to the children, who break out in song: "Mine eyes have seen the glory of the coming of the Lord." It is here, in the safe haven of Jeju, Republic of Korea flag flying in front of the orphans' home, that verses of "Battle Hymn" are finally sung in the film. The orphans begin the singing (in English), but their voices fade into a nondiegetic chorus of adult American men, as the camera pans up two tall pine trees and into the sky above, overwritten with a dedication from Dean Hess, "to those we could not save." These words of condolence address the past while animating what is to come. Those who could not be saved (in both secular and religious terms) may be dead, but many are not. They were left behind or perhaps found themselves in a location such as North Korea where they could not or would not see the light. The dedication thus calls for a continuous effort, itself represented by the potential of the saved Korean orphans, of their future development (signaled by the camera's travel to the sky above the pine trees and the transformation of their voices into those of adult US men), of the possibility that in the future they too may grow to save others.[66]

Like many other fighter-bomber films, *Battle Hymn* equates flight with a form of transcendence in the sky, a celebration of movement over and across the borders below, both natural and humanmade. Hess, the parson-pilot, makes this relation more obviously religious than most. Emblazoned on his fighter plane is the motto "By faith, I fly." How is it that God countenances suffering? The sacrifice both of innocents and pilots themselves leads to a greater good. The simultaneous elimination of communism and rescue/salvation of Korean souls is actually an either/or proposition, what Daniel Kim calls a "dark calculus" that "suggests that the alternative to adoption is extermination, that if Korean children are not integrated, literally or symbolically, into the American family, they are at risk of

FIG. 1.3 *Battle Hymn* (1957). Still courtesy of Universal Studios.

becoming enlisted by the enemy."[67] Jeju is not simply an improvised, temporary destination for Korean orphans but sign of secular and religious freedom in Asia.

In his book *Battle Hymn* (1956), Hess indicates a familiarity with Jeju Island that extended well beyond Operation Kiddy Car. It was in conversation with Gen. Kim Chung Yul about a replacement site for an ROK training base in late 1950 that he "first heard about the island of Cheju, which was later to become the 'promised land' for a thousand homeless children. Sixty miles south of the west coast of Korea, it is a volcanic island about twenty miles in diameter.... Considering the possibility that we might have to get out of Korea entirely, it sounded promising."[68] It was, in fact, Donald Nichols—a legendary and unusually powerful figure in charge of US Air Force intelligence in Korea from 1946 through 1956—who introduced Hess to General Kim Chung Yul. Hess, who was serving as Syngman Rhee's private pilot, would call Nichols a "good friend" and an "invaluable source of 'inside dope.' "[69] Hess was privy to the highest level of intelligence gathering and military decision-making in Korea. Nichols played an outsized role in covert activities during this period; he too was close to Syngman Rhee, while reporting directly to General Earle E. Partridge, Fifth Air Force commander.[70] The latter appears at the beginning of *Battle Hymn*, sanctioning the film as "affirmation of the essential goodness of the human spirit."[71] The two promises mentioned by Hess ("promising" site for an air base and "promised land" for orphans) connect land to air, faith to flight, the religious to the secular. The former promise refers to the Jeju Island found in the Washington memoranda of early January 1951 (see above), the possibility of Jeju as forward base for a "vast laboratory" in which to develop "Asian manpower" for the purpose of engaging in unconventional operations against "Asiatic communism." Hess's introduction to Jeju Island by way of General Kim had as its aim this mission.

Hess gives us his first in-flight impression of Jeju Island (without giving a precise date):

> Cheju, as I first saw it, seemed essentially one great volcanic peak rising gently, and then more steeply, 6,000 feet out of the sea. It is a bleak place with few trees and volcanic rock and ash everywhere. In 1948 bandits still lived in caves high on the mountain, from which they would periodically raid the little villages on the coast.... Flying over Cheju the first time, I was sharply reminded by its bleak beauty of Scotland.[72]

Hess indicates some knowledge of conflict on Jeju, in the form of local unruliness. The implication is that the bandits still in the mountains in 1948 are there no longer. Bleak yet beautiful, far away yet familiar, Jeju begins its ascension into an unfolding history of the bigger picture, an island of potential significance at the edge of the network of security arrangements, alliances, economic agreements central to the reworking of "Asia and the Pacific as a geostrategic arena neither wholly external nor recognizably internal to the United States."[73] From the sky comes Hess's plane and the song, "Battle Hymn." Jeju enters the picture through a salvific invocation, one in which the offer to lay down one's life for an emancipatory cause (the holiness of freedom) holds no matter where and when that sacrificial death will occur. The offer comes with no conditions in space or time. It is limitless.

TELLINGS AND RETELLINGS

Bookending the 1950s, a decade of war and postarmistice incorporation of the ROK into a precarious, island-like position at the edge of the US transpacific network of bases, Hŏ Yunsŏk's "Haenyŏ" (February 1950) and O Yŏngsu's "Afterword" (Huildam, June 1960) offer accounts of witnessing layered with rumors, stories within stories, and shifts in narrative person. The first addresses gendered violence, indigeneity, naturescape, and sovereignty on Jeju Island. The second looks back from a historical moment that called for a rethinking of beginnings themselves.

Published prior to the date usually given for the outbreak of the Korean War (June 25, 1950–6/25 commonly used in the ROK to refer to the war itself) and in the same month/year as the third installment of Ham Sedŏk's *Mountain People*, Hŏ Yunsŏk's "Haenyŏ" begins with a war scene. Lt. Col. Kim's White Skull

Regiment (*haegol pudae*) lands on Jeju Island.⁷⁴ They are met with utter devastation: "Everything at the harbor and the surrounding village was burnt to the ground, not a single structure remaining. The earth was scorched, nothing remained except blackened corpses scattered about. No one, absolutely no one, had done anything to take care of the rotting bodies."⁷⁵ We will learn shortly that Jeju has been under naval bombardment (*hamp'o sagyŏk*).⁷⁶ What to make of this spectacle of mass, anonymous death and the inference of US shelling of the island? Hŏ's "Haenyŏ" offers a sustained reflection on this question with its title, which could refer to one or more *haenyŏ*. We will meet two. Much of the text revolves around the first, Puni. Lt. Col. Kim brings her in at gunpoint on the first page. We learn she is involved with a leader of the "bandits" (*pando*), Ko Turyŏng. She quickly claims that her wish is for Ko to follow all of the others and come over to the ROK side (*kwisun*, a term often used to indicate defection). Section one (far and away the longest of the text's six sections) moves quickly to a story within a story. Puni's words are retold in the third person, a transcription of what would have been Puni's first-person recitation to Lt. Col. Kim and an unnamed group. This reworked third-person narration takes the form of a report, the summary of an interrogation.

Does Puni's account amount to her genuine recantation? Will her lover, the influential leader Ko Turyŏng come in from the hills? How much information can the captured Puni provide on the activities of the "bandits"? Puni's lengthy testimony will open up a further line of questions by the time it is complete: How does the island encounter the scorching of its surface? What is the relation between islanders to island and, by extension, humans to nature? Do the answers to these questions reframe what it means to *kwisun*?

Puni's story conjures up exoticized images of *haenyŏ* widely circulating in the ROK. She is assertive, sensual, autochthonous, in tune with nature and the island. Nature, in turn, is in sync with her and other women divers: "the moon rose in the sky, a *haenyŏ* clutching her deep red bosom."⁷⁷ Puni speaks openly of her love for Ko, "her dimpled cheeks bursting forth like camellias in youthful red brilliance."⁷⁸ She stands at the primal center of Jeju, a place where "milky *makkŏlli* becomes less like rice wine than moon halos," and does not hesitate to "give her flesh" to multiple men during an indigenous ritual at the ancient, sacred site dedicated to the origins of the three Jeju clans, the Ko, Yang, and Pu lineages (*samsŏnghyŏl*).⁷⁹

The third-person retelling of Puni's story crosses between the anthropological and the interrogatory, presenting a mode of listening that seeks to elicit an indigenous way of approaching the world while securing facts useful for an on-the-ground report. The aim, in the end, is to gather information, confirm the possibility of genuine *kwisun*. How to parse Puni's story in relation to the authoritative witnessing of death and destruction that opens "Haenyŏ"? How to maintain a truth-claim for the statist-nationalist call to *kwisun* itself?

The story of Puni is of a lifeworld that appears to render affiliation with either side, north or south, secondary to island-belonging. Rumors abound—Ko declares at the *samsŏnghyŏl* ritual that Syngman Rhee has fled to Japan, that the Korean People's Army (KPA) has reached as far south as Yŏsu and will soon arrive on Jeju.[80] The KPA does not appear. But the White Skulls do. The report also indicates that Puni looked up into the mountains that night, and "saw that they were still completely aflame." The island suffers: "Bear Rock was lit up in the flames engulfing the mountains. The naval shelling would not let up. A massive cloud of red dust arose in the sky, and Bear Rock crumbled forward. Watching it fall sent shivers down Puni's spine."[81] She rushes up into the mountains, worried that all will be destroyed, that Ko will have nowhere to live: " 'He should *kwisun*. He should *kwisun* while he still possesses his limbs. And then I can harvest seaweed and abalone!' she told herself."[82] Ko's *kwisun* will serve this purpose—the preservation of island life, of life on the island.

As Puni passes by a waterfall, she hears a deafening explosion. She is pushed against a rock, numbed, devoid even of fear:

> Trees fall, boulders rumble down. A small deer rushes by and suddenly jumps into her arms, legs trembling. Puni falls to the earth, deer in her arms. She was dizzied, unable to see anything. The moon was obscured by the dust and smoke.... Moments later she feels her heart beating, the cold wind brushing her nose. "I'm alive!" she shouts to herself, eyes moistening. She gritted her white teeth and tried to suppress her tears. But she couldn't help herself from crying. She cried like a horse, gazing up at the mountain peaks. As she sobbed, the deer sat beside her, smelling of musk, its furtive eyes seemingly seeking the cratered mountains.[83]

The battle on Jeju is framed not in terms of ideological conflict but environmental warfare, the destruction of the land, mountains, its people, animals, flora, and fauna. Does this lyrical retelling of Puni's experience—of the terror, extreme violence meted out against Jeju Island—take cover within a third-person report submitted under the authority of Lt. Col. Kim? Puni begs Lt. Col. Kim to give her the chance to convince Ko to *kwisun*. Kim and others present hesitate but agree in the end. Promising to return the next day, "She rounds the corner beneath the zelkova trees, disappearing into the fog and mist of the moonlit mountains from whence she had been taken."[84]

Puni's multivoiced testimony—her story overwritten by a male interrogator who possesses a lyrical, literary voice—opens a sensory experience of the island under attack that differs markedly from the remainder of the text. Puni will return only by way of the rumor that she has been killed by Ko. No longer coauthored, the third-person narration of the final five sections (aligned with Lt. Col. Kim's POV) presents a linear sequence of events, the unfolding of plot. The question of *kwisun* shifts, revolving now around three new figures, a Northwest Youth become White Skull sergeant, a child, and another *haenyŏ* who is never named.

Terms absent in section one make their appearance: *chŏkkun* (enemy forces), *ugun* (friendly forces), *minjok* (ethnonation). A more precise Korean rendering of the White Skulls as *paekkol pudae* occurs as well.[85] Angered and upset that Puni doesn't return, the White Skulls plan a mission: "They gathered and pored over a tactical map. Here is a rock formation, and here is a river."[86] Their understanding of the island is militarized, instrumentalist. The lines are drawn.

The White Skulls encounter the enemy and suffer casualties. As the firefight draws down, Sgt. Ch'oe (the Northwest Youth) reports the sound of a crying baby. The discovery sends chills down Lt. Col. Kim's spine: "He found himself unable to sort out what he was feeling. Killing them all, one by one, wouldn't mean victory. Why are we out here fighting on a night like this? What's brought us to this point, where we're out here cold-heartedly looking on as we shed each other's blood? And besides, don't we belong to the same nation and race [*tongjok*]?"[87] Kim and Ch'oe argue about whether to fire toward the noise. Silence ensues. And then "The wind brought the baying of island horses, the chirping of birds, and the cries of the baby, now even louder."[88] An irruption of the language of section one. Ch'oe stands down. The White Skulls return to base, bringing with them a baby "giving off the smell of his mother's milk."[89] Sounds of the island, smells of the indigenous will give way to a narrative of adoption.

Sgt. Ch'oe has his own story. He grew up in Yaksan, Yŏngbyŏn County, North P'yŏngan Province (the location of Kim Sowŏl's 1922 "Azaleas," a famous lyrical, anticolonial poem). He left his wife and child behind when he fled south. Rumor has it that his wife was hanged, and there has been no news of his child. Sgt. Ch'oe proceeds to form a close bond with this baby he wanted to kill. Enter the unnamed *haenyŏ*. She and Sgt. Ch'oe appear one day at the base, rounding the same corner under the zelkova trees where Puni was last seen. The *haenyŏ* (whose husband, she says, was killed by bandits) has agreed to nurse the baby for a month but soon decides to remain permanently, "overcome with joy every time she recognized the face of a relative among the bandits coming in [*kwisun*].[90] The *haenyŏ* does double duty. She replaces both Puni and the baby's biological mother. Gone is the sexuality, the primordial agency of her unassimilable predecessor. Transformation takes place by way of substitution. And, at the same time, Sgt. Ch'oe moderates his own violent masculinity (frequently associated with Northwest Youth) in favor of a return to family and fatherhood.[91]

To which *haenyŏ* does the title refer? Or does it refer both to Puni and her unnamed counterpart? The death of the former is located in rumor. The *kwisun* of the latter is affirmed by direct account. Does the schematic of empathetic White Skulls and the *kwisun* of a *haenyŏ*-become-wet-nurse subsume Puni's story, a tale of the bond of the indigenous to their island, its sexual mores, way of life, and sensoryscape?

The second half of the text (sections 2–6) intertwines accounts based on direct experience with rumors. "Haenyŏ" itself closes with rumors, second-hand stories. A young boy named Pawi, son of an associate of Ko, shows up at the White Skull base. A message subsequently arrives: If Pawi is sent back to the hills, Ko will *kwisun*. Pawi, though, heads out of his own accord. "Haenyŏ" concludes with a story (*iyagi*) relayed by bandits that Pawi was killed by Ko at the *samsŏnghyŏl*, "breathing his last with a with a natural, calm look on his face."[92] Those who do not *kwisun* must either die or be considered dead. The move from a more direct, third-person retelling of Puni's experiences to rumors of islander activities accompanies this mix of imperative and assumption.

As the implied narrator, Lt. Col. Kim's observations are tempered by apparent restraint and empathy. He listens. He works to be fair and confer legitimacy upon the position he represents. He recognizes that violence and coercion have limited effectiveness (his position resembles that of the historical figure mentioned earlier, Col. Kim Ingnyŏl). A genuine *kwisun* requires more. He ends up relaying the story of a *kwisun* that does not take place (Puni) and one that succeeds (the unnamed *haenyŏ*, given little description of any kind). Puni may or may not be dead, but her voice, her relation to Jeju Island, the sensoryscape she conveys of the island's suffering lingers. She is a *haenyŏ* who seems to have no choice but not to *kwisun*. A spontaneous, almost naturalist desire remains. If she is exoticized, her lengthy story (cordoned off from the narrative flow of the sections that follow) becomes that of a presence rumored to be absent.

The salvific trope of adoption, the constitution of a pan-regional nation-family that subsumes those dislocated from the north and Jeju islanders, stands in an uneasy and unresolved relation to the account of death and destruction witnessed at the beginning of the text and evoked in the lyrical retelling of Puni's intermesh with the devastation meted upon the island. She is something more than forgotten or erased. She is, of course, never present, ghostly from the beginning, her own account available only through its habitation of a third-person interrogation report. The narrative layers of "Haenyŏ" question the attempt to produce knowledge about the islanders, about what has happened on Jeju, from whence the destruction originates. "Haenyŏ" places the normative call to *kwisun* in uneasy relation to those who recede, disappear, who do not enter history, who are assumed dead.

A REAL GHOST

While writers such as Kim Sŏkbŏm and Hyŏn Kiyŏng (both with family histories connected to Jeju Island) would address the trauma of mass killings on Jeju Island in the 1970s, the mainland writer O Yŏngsu was the first to frame Jeju explicitly in terms of a repressed history.[93] Appearing ten years after Hŏ Yunsŏk's "Haenyŏ" and seven years after the 1953 armistice, O's "Afterword" presents a story within a story within yet another story. First is the first-person narration of Lieutenant Pak. Other than the month he spent in a hospital to recover from a gunshot wound, his entire time in the 1950–1953 phase of the 6/25 War was spent at the front. He has witnessed grim happenings and recounts one of the worst: "I spotted a group of soldiers surrounded by the enemy, unable to break out. They were slaughtered en masse. . . . I watched from a distance of about a hundred yards or so as arms and legs flew every which way, the chunks of whatever remained thrown up with the surrounding dust into the sky."[94] He has killed countless enemy soldiers. There was little he could do other than think of them as objects, pieces of wood that would roll away:

> What else could I have done? It was a kill-or-be-killed situation. That's how I'd put it to rest when I thought about it. And in fact over time it's fading into a distant memory. But there's something I remember, something that just keeps rising up before me ever more sharply, ever more distinctly when I try to forget about it—an apparition [*hwansang*].
>
> It will probably follow me around like a shadow, tormenting me until the day I die. These were the words of the discharged veteran Lieutenant Pak, and what follows is the story he told.[95]

Thus ends the first section (one page in length), as well as the first-person narration. The abrupt turn to the third-person accompanies the conjuring of something more devastating than anything experienced in three years of combat. What does this say about the death, destruction, and displacement that has come to organize the history of the 6/25 War in the ROK over the course of the 1950s?

Written between the fall of the Syngman Rhee regime in April 1960 and Park Chung Hee's military coup in May 1961, "Afterword" belongs to a period that saw a heightened questioning of the post-1945 history of national division. Why is "Afterword" an afterword? The text quickly moves back in time, to Lt. Pak's deployment on Jeju Island, where he served as driver for the commander of the Second Regiment. "Afterword" posits itself as a particular kind of addendum, a postscript to the 1950s that speaks of what came before the accepted history of the 6/25 War. The combat veteran Lt. Pak will serve as witness. He presents a history that remains alive in his mind. An apparition persists. Lt. Pak can't shake it.

"Afterword" addresses what can be put into words, by whom, and when. Lt. Pak's deployment to Jeju Island took place at an unspecified time in the late 1940s, likely 1949. He takes up quarters in an off-base house. He awakens one night to a noise outside and grabs his sidearm, ready to shoot a possible intruder. He cracks the door open to see a face peering at him in the dark: "He almost let out a scream. It was a specter [*yuryŏng*]. Its disheveled hair—a ghost exactly like the ones in picture books. Chills went down his spine."[96] The apparition speaks. She's the landlord's daughter-in-law, she tells him. But Pak has seen no such person during his time at the house. He tightens his grip on the pistol, shuddering at the possibility that "as in tales of old, she might be the resentful ghost of a daughter-in-law who suffered an undeserved death."[97] It turns out that the woman is indeed the daughter-in-law of Lt. Pak's landlord. "Afterword" now moves to the testimonial of a Jeju specter-like woman, relayed in third-person narration, vouched for by combat veteran Lt. Pak. It will, in fact, unfold as the story of an undeserved death, but not as in tales of old.

Partisans broke into her home in the middle of the night and absconded with supplies. The police arrive but only to arrest her and her husband (an elementary school teacher) on the legal grounds of aiding and abetting the enemy (*puyŏkchoe*). She is put in isolation, told she will be killed if she doesn't talk, beaten severely, and "suffered torture too shameful to put into words."[98] Twenty days of this and she is released, put under surveillance. She is given no information about her husband other than rumors that he might have been taken off the island to a mainland jail. It's not long before she is rearrested on false suspicion of having made illegal contact with partisans. She is tortured again, "to the point where I wanted to die, where I begged them to just kill me."[99] This time she is released after forty-eight hours. In the aftermath of the "uprising" (*pallan*), she is taken away yet again, this time "no interrogation and no torture."[100] She and about twenty others are simply loaded onto the back of a truck and driven in the direction of the airport. The truck comes to a stop and they're told to get out: "She and the others were forced to stand in front of a dark pit. She hears something from behind and loses consciousness."[101] How much time passes, she doesn't know, "but she thought she heard something . . . a noise coming from inside her own ear. . . .

What's this noise? What is it? She could see the faint light of stars overhead. She was dazed but her memory started to come back to her. I'm alive! I didn't die!"[102]

She has been shot in her right arm but manages to crawl out of the pile of corpses filling up the pit. She stumbles home, half conscious, head spinning. Ever since then, for three months, she has been hiding in a small, boxlike storage space used for vegetables: "To the world she is dead. The only one who knows she is alive is her mother-in-law."[103] She's now decided she can no longer endure a life that is no different from death. And so she's come to make her case to Lt. Pak, "who appears to be good-hearted."[104] The woman's story assumes stand-alone precedence in the frame of O's "Afterword." Her vivid, carefully worded account of torture and massacre reads as a deposition.

Lt. Pak relays the woman's account to the regimental commander. The latter holds considerable legal authority over Jeju Island, which is under martial law; he asks the legal affairs officer to contact the police for a status check on the woman. They discover that she has been categorized both as a traitor (*puyŏkcha*) and a pro-bandit collaborator (*pando apchabi*). An argument over jurisdiction ensues between the regimental commander and the police. The fact that the island is under martial law tilts the scales in favor of the former. The woman is issued a *yangminjŭng* (certificate of good standing), which negates her previous categorization. Pak, though, worries: Forced to issue a *yangminjŭng* against their will, the police will surely seek a way to exact revenge. He advises the woman to leave Jeju, but she refuses.

Pak is subsequently transferred off the island but returns as part of the wartime buildup taking place on Jeju following the enemy's advance south in July and August of 1950. His neighbors gather and tell him in tears what has transpired in his absence. The police quickly rounded up the families of all of the supposed traitors and recanted bandits (*kwisun pando*). Violence proceeds by way of guilt by association, a social disciplining Heonik Kwon locates as central to statist repression in the ROK.[105] Here, guilt by association extends to unjust, blanket categorization. The woman was last seen weighed down with a stone around her neck, taken out to sea under police guard. The boat returned in the evening. Only the police were on board: "Lt. Pak felt a shuddering in his temples. His eyes began to lose focus, become bleary. He could, though, vividly see the pale face of the woman peering in at him that night, and then the image of her standing on the boat, back weighed down by the stone, as she receded into the distance, ever further from sight."[106] Here is the apparition that will haunt Lt. Pak, a doubled, overlapping image in his mind: First, his encounter with a woman he thought was a ghost; second, an image drawn from the account of others. This double image is more powerful than the mishmash of dismembered bodies Pak has witnessed directly, time and again during the 1950–1953 war on the mainland. While the woman is of Jeju Island and integrally connected with her community, no move is made here to associate her with *haenyŏ* or autochthonous island-belonging.

"Afterword" is the story of a woman who disappeared and can never be laid to rest. The strength of this apparition, its staying power, presents an irruption that will only grow more visible. Try as he might, Pak *cannot* shake it. "Afterword" speaks after the fact to what came before: the truth of corpse piles, untold numbers of undeserved deaths on Jeju Island. The brief appearance of Pak's first-person narration sanctions the third-person accounts that follow; the third-person narration, in turn, extends Pak's trauma beyond his vision, to the story of the woman, to the historical record itself. Written in the opening provided by the Syngman Rhee regime's demise, "Afterword" serves as addendum that can be included well after the fact. This is an addendum that reframes the history of the Korean War in relation to unjust violence meted out by the state against the ROK population itself.[107] "Afterword" underscores the violence of disappearance and in doing so also becomes a preface, looking back at Jeju Island to write a history of the 6/25 War that did not begin on 6/25.

Jeju Island, then, appears in multiples. Narratives of death, dying, returning from death, and disappearing become claims on the future: The call to understand the revolutionary possibility made manifest in the newly-forming DPRK as latent across the Korean peninsula; the imagining—at once secular and religious—of the necessity of US leadership, mediation, and sacrifice in the formation of a free transpacific; the search in the ROK for elsewheres, beyond ideological bifurcations, between the lines of what is to be said, felt, thought, and what is to enter history. The following four parts of this book take these trajectories as a point of departure to address wartime and postarmistice figurings of death as transformative acts of historymaking. Part II will address the attention paid to loss and sacrifice in the DPRK and the accompanying location of a future in acts of revolutionary mourning.

PART II

Seoul was lost. That much was clear by late 1951. How to approach this wartime recognition, acknowledge limitations, sanction withdrawal? How to address those who died defending Seoul, fought on the hills and at the barricades until they could no more? To mourn such deaths is to feel loss as constitutive of revolutionary praxis. To exit Seoul is to enter a place where revolutionary potential can manifest itself, materialize. Left behind is the southern region and those who remain there, caught in time (living consciously or unconsciously in a state of latency). The narrative arc of postarmistice division as long-term prospect finds footing in the wartime Democratic People's Republic of Korea (DPRK) a year after the commencement of peninsula-wide combat.

A question was asked all along as stories of war turned inward, probed feelings of love, affection for comrades, hatred and anger directed at enemies, comfort found in recognition of world-belonging (national and international solidarities): What is happiness? If the answer involves the idea of a joyful death (as it does), it will also consider a life, and a place, that moves to the frontline of the global revolution, pushing history forward. The name of this place is *Chosŏn minjujuŭi inmin konghwaguk* (Democratic People's Republic of Korea). Within this name resides another question: How exactly to define the *inmin* (people)?

Part II tells a story of revolutionary mourning in the DPRK in the early 1950s. This is a story of women in war, their combat deaths, and their manifestation as martyrs. And it is a story of how their own contemplations of death and the dead feature prominently in the call to the lofty, a form of monumentality that is not static but moving, an unfolding of the victorious *inmin* in everyday life, in history.

CHAPTER 2

SEOUL REQUIEM

"Let's Heighten our Mobilized Stance and Construct the People's Economy!" exhorts the second-page headline of the July 30, 1953 edition of the *Rodong sinmun* (*Workers' Daily*). The announcement of the July 27, 1953 armistice meant that war would be carried on by other means, total mobilization on the economic front. "We must immediately turn the strength we used to crush the enemy to increasing production, rebuilding, and coming together as one to advance our front-line efforts" reads a directive on the second page of the July 31, 1953 edition, attributed to Kim Il Sung himself. While making use of wartime references and terminology, such mobilization was almost always couched in terms of "peaceful construction," a figuring that fit with the larger emphasis on the "victory of the Chosŏn people as a victory for peace and a glorious victory for the democratic camp."[1] Total mobilization on the economic front would frame the discourse of "peaceful reunification" for decades to come in the DPRK.

Central to reconstruction, mobilization, and the legitimacy of the DPRK regime was the rebuilding of urban space, as we see in two earlier *Rodong sinmun* articles published on February 27–28, 1953 calling for the building of "green cities," socialist spaces for the people (*inmin*) that stood sharply opposed to capitalist urban planning made in the interests of the dominant class. While planning for the reconstruction of Pyongyang had begun as early as January 1951, public announcements took center stage in the immediate aftermath of the armistice.[2]

The emphasis on the new, the modern, the heroic combine to place Pyongyang on the urban map of the socialist world, with a view particularly to Moscow, itself envisioned in the 1930s as site for "Architects ... to create an incredible space of grandeur that would inspire citizens, impressing on them the greatness of

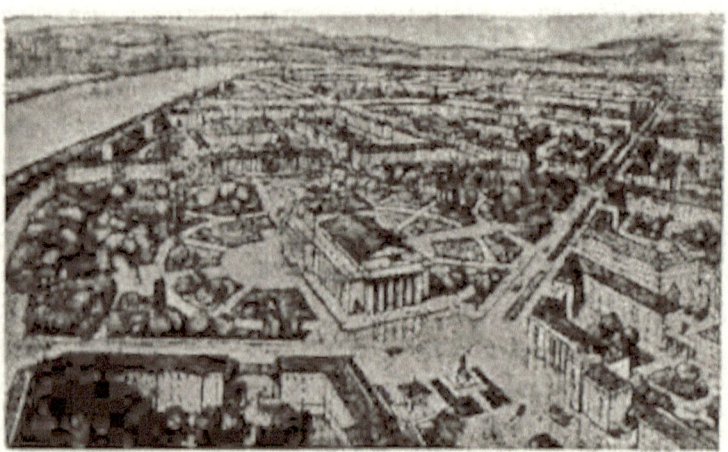

FIG. 2.1.1 AND FIG. 2.1.2 (*Top*) View from above envisioning the initial phase of the rebuilding of the "heroic city" of Pyongyang. (*Bottom*) Rendering of the city that highlights Stalin Avenue. *Rodong sinmun*, July 31, 1953.

their state and inspiring them to become 'grander' human beings."[3] As Tatiana Gabroussenko indicates, "Moscow, as the Soviet capital, was presumed to occupy a special place in Korean hearts."[4]

At the same time, reconstruction of the new capital in the mid-1950s sought to highlight a much longer history. In 1957, celebrations were held to commemorate the 1,530th anniversary of the creation of the Koguryŏ capital in Pyongyang, the founding of the city serving as "a cause for celebration not only in our democratic capital of Pyongyang but for all of the Chosŏn people [*inmin*].⁵ Such a celebration must extend to an awareness of the city's past: "The world knows of the reconstruction of the heroic city of Pyongyang, destroyed by the enemy in the Fatherland War [*choguk chŏnjaeng*] . . . but we should also pay attention to the history and beauty of our Pyongyang."⁶ This is a history that combines aesthetics with a long-standing resistance against invaders, from the Sui dynasty to the United States. Pyongyang embodies the people who created it, defended it, who will rebuild it: "Each and every stone that makes up Pyongyang confers national pride and patriotism."⁷ Pyongyang is also the locus of anticolonial victory and benevolent leadership. As Yun Sep'yŏng writes in 1957, the combined efforts of the "righteous Soviet Army" and the heroic resistance against the Japanese mounted by partisan units under the leadership of General Kim Il Sung allowed Pyongyang to become "the cradle of a democratic Chosŏn following liberation," what was now the "revolutionary, democratic base, the heart for a peaceful reunification."⁸ Pyongyang will renew the beauty and strength of its past within a modernizing and revolutionary future.

Unmentioned in these accounts is the extent to which the early success of the Korean People's Army (KPA) in the summer of 1950 rested largely on the recovery of what at the time was referred to as "our capital," Seoul. The efforts to place Pyongyang on a pinnacle in the mid-1950s by archeologists, historians, poets, composers, theater directors, and journalists (among others) took place in relation to this wartime history, the recognition in late 1951 that the historical capital of Chosŏn would be lost for the foreseeable future. Revolution would take manifest form only in the northern portion of the peninsula. At stake was the extent to which this loss signaled the limitations of the DPRK as historical agent of reunification. Place mattered in the Korean War and would continue to matter in subsequent decades.

In the Republic of Korea (ROK), the story of wartime Seoul was one of loss and recovery, hope and resignation, fear and confusion, destruction and death. Less remembered than stories of suffering and the refugee trail to Busan was the whirl of suspicions and recriminations accompanying those who remained in Seoul under DPRK rule in the summer and early fall of 1950. Who cooperated with the DPRK administration of the city and for what reason? Were those who joined the KPA during this time truly coerced to do so? Who betrayed neighbors? And perhaps their own family members? Such questions would populate stories by writers such as Yŏm Sangsŏp and Kwak Haksong, who would offer their takes on DPRK-administered (*ingongch'iha*) Seoul in the early 1950s, as well as by prominent authors such as Pak Sunnyŏ and Pak Wansŏ who would look back upon this period in later decades. Needless to say, these stories vary, but they do share an observation of the choices, feelings, and life trajectories that played themselves out in the wartime and postwar ROK. This chapter follows yet another tale of Seoul, one that begins with the late June 1950 announcement in the DPRK of the "liberation of our fatherland's capital" (*uri choguk sudo Sŏul haebang*).[9]

The emancipation of Seoul was at once cause for celebration and occasion to recognize the DPRK as the sole legitimate state on the peninsula. Early reports from the liberated capital emphasized the "breaking of shackles," the "enthusiastic welcome" given to the KPA's advance into Seoul, the bravery of Seoul's citizens, "who cast aside the risk of death brought on by the US air raids to come out to the streets and demonstrate their power and will."[10] As the liberated city came under siege in late September, three valences of a last stand came to the fore. First, the emphasis on the "heroic struggle of the Seoul citizenry and the People's Army to defend the capital." The "entire people" (*chŏninmin*) have risen up in defense of Seoul against the US invaders.[11] Second, the importance of Seoul as symbol of the nation: " 'Let's defend Seoul, capital of the fatherland!' has become the rallying cry on the front lines for the troops putting their lives on the line to carry out the sacred mission."[12] Third, as the withdrawal from Seoul is acknowledged as unavoidable, there is a focus on last-stand acts of heroism and bravery. The bitter struggle to defend Seoul at all costs begins with the heroism displayed on Wŏlmi Island against enemy naval bombardment (precursor to the amphibious landing at Incheon) and continues through to mortal combat at the barricades in Seoul.[13] The former last stand, in fact, would serve as the basis for one of the most famous and canonical wartime literary texts, Hwang Kŏn's "Island Ablaze" (1952).

As Sheila Miyoshi Jager points out, it was during the Chinese spring offensive of 1951 that "The war devolved to a battle for Seoul."[14] The fifth and last battle of Seoul took place in April 1951. The failure of the Chinese offensive to retake the city—emancipated by the KPA on June 28, 1950, lost in late September of that year, regained in early January 1951, lost again in March 1951—was widely recognized as the last chance. Seoul would not serve as the capital of the DPRK. Even after the armistice, though, the phrase "going up to Seoul" (*Sŏullo ollaganda* or *sanggyŏnghada*) populates DPRK publications, albeit with decreasing frequency. While the project of territorializing the DPRK as archetype, model of revolution in practice, gained urgency with the recognition that the Fatherland Liberation War would not achieve immediate reunification, bidding farewell to Seoul proved difficult.

Serialized in three parts in late 1951 (August, September, October), Han Hyo's *Seoul People* (*Sŏul saramdŭl*) was accorded prominence of place, the first wartime literary work given a multi-installment run in *Munhak yesul* (*Literary Arts*). Seoul

People mourns the loss of life in the second battle for Seoul, the reluctant evacuation of the capital in late September 1950. Loss, though, leads to the creation of a new notion of Seoul and of people: the *Sŏul saramdŭl*, the Seoul people. Who are they? What do they feel, desire? What history have they shared? What kind of future will they create?

Unlike Ham Sedŏk's *Mountain People* (see chapter 1), *Seoul People* did not enter the canon. Nor did it even appear in book form. Han's text is significant in its disappearance or perhaps because its disappearance seems so understandable in hindsight. This is not a text that thinks of itself as an occasional piece, a detailed account of one battle among others. Han's work fashions itself as monumental, a self-styled epic, a panorama of struggle. Han's epic farewell to Seoul as "our fatherland's capital" attempts to accomplish a task that proves to be insurmountable—to lift Seoul to a realm of revolutionary feeling that travels north.

Pervasive in Han's text is the sense that there will likely never be a return to Seoul *as capital* (the January 4, 1951 retaking of the city, largely by Chinese forces, is for all intents and purposes elided). Seoul travels with the *inmin* who survive the last stand in late September to fight another day. But how will this loss dwell in that which is to come? Seoul is where the *inmin*, including those from Seoul and those from elsewhere, become revolutionary fighters. At the same time, loss of the capital signals what will be the postarmistice future, the increasingly important demarcation between manifest revolution (north) and potential revolution (south). *Seoul People* works through the hardening of this distinction but, as its own title reveals, cannot quite leave the significance of Seoul behind. Seoul is not to move north, even as a noun adjunct (the Seoul of *Seoul People*). Pyongyang was to be the undisputed site of historical resistance. Place will indeed matter. Han's text, though, is more than a colossal failure.

Seoul People sifts through the relations among time, space, the manifest, and the latent in order to define the *inmin* in relation not only to Seoul but to the DPRK's location at the front of a global revolution taking place in the decolonizing world. This move centers upon a lament of the greatest proportions, a eulogy to those who fought to the death to defend Seoul. Han's attempt to imagine a revolutionary spirit and reunificatory desire in relation to a profound sense of loss and acknowledgment of limits placed on what could be done in war would prove suggestive for a mode of revolutionary mourning central to the figuring of the history of the Fatherland Liberation War in the DPRK. This is the story of confrontation with limit as limitation, the wartime moment that proved to be the harbinger of the 1953 armistice. How to figure such a limit as a form of victory in late 1951? *Seoul People* offers a panorama of lives become deaths, a big picture where feeling, seeing, being, and dying comprise the building blocks of a monumental history of the future perfect (what will have been remembered). The exhortation is to a cross-generational act of revolutionary mourning that will always project the past into the future and thus never recede in time.

A LOOK TO THE LOFTY

Active in the mid-1930s literary debates of the Korea Artista Proleta Federatio (KAPF; 1925–1935), Han Hyo (1912–?) quickly assumed a position of prominence in the DPRK literary scene in the late 1940s (a position he retained until his purge in the early 1960s).[15] More critic than writer, *Seoul People* would be Han's first and only novella. While not a mere distillation of Han's literary criticism, *Seoul People* speaks to the contemporary scene in important ways, particularly as a literary exploration of Han's earlier work on "lofty realism" (*kosanghan riallijŭm*), a notion that traveled widely in the DPRK literary, cultural, and political scene from the late 1940s forward. Han's work, O T'aeho points out, had immediate and lasting effect: "The exhortations to *kosanghan riallijŭm* meant that by the end of 1947 it was clear that there would be only one choice left for writers and artists in North Korea."[16] The idea of the lofty would gain considerable traction across the board in the 1950s, appearing directly and via various synonyms denoting height and grandiosity (all requiring no explanation).

Han Hyo's "Incorporating Lofty Realism: General Kim Il Sung's Teachings on the Creation of Literature" appeared in the inaugural issue of *Chosŏn munhak* (*Korean Literature*; September 1947). Here, as elsewhere, Han issues an imperative: "Only works that accurately reflect the reality of the DPRK can be considered truly great, constructive works."[17] The question is how to consolidate the DPRK literary field in relation to its internal and external others, those with "incorrect tendencies": "avoiders of reality," "bourgeois," "formalists," "literary purists." Calling attention to Kim Il Sung's directive to overcome the harmful modalities left behind by Japanese imperialism, Han declares that "Today, what writers in North Chosŏn absolutely need is to arm themselves with an elevated ideology [*nop'ŭn sasang*]."[18] How to reflect reality? Han emphasizes the particulars of everyday life, characters, and events: "When a writer assumes a stance that truly reflects the numerous living phenomena that comprise reality, all comes together in the form of the colossal [*kŏdaehan*] victory of democratic construction."[19] From the beginning, the lofty and its synonyms point to a flexible concept, even as it is closely connected with the "great and profound" teachings of

Kim Il Sung.[20] The lofty assembles particulars into an architecture that moves away from the colonized past and into a bigger and better future.

In a 1952 article, Han Hyo echoes many contemporaries when he states that the Soviet Union's liberation of the DPRK allowed for the emergence of a socialist realism denied to proletarian writers under Japanese colonial rule, setting the stage for "protagonists to emerge from the people [*inmin*] themselves, for the people to become the subject of history."[21] Writers "could now describe the new emotions experienced by the *inmin*, to speak of new human interrelations."[22] Citing Stalin, Han also emphasizes the importance of the distinction to be made between old and new. The location of the new—including "sensibilities" (*kamgak*) and "love" (*sarang*) partakes in the lofty. Offering Han Sŏrya's work as an example, Han emphasizes the "lofty feelings [*kosanghan kamjŏng*] that emerge from a combination of emancipated labor, democratic struggle, and patriotic struggle—all offered up to the fatherland and the people."[23] "Beauty," "romanticism," "creative energy," "new ethics"—Han also views these terms as pointing to the "lofty" that exists within everyday life.[24]

Seoul People compresses five days of battle in late September 1950 into what it self-reflexively calls an epic poem (*sŏsasi*). The task at hand is lofty, monumental, but it will emerge from the ground up, a description of the *inmin*. Han's work combines a record of feelings, love, and affection among comrades with the hatred and desire for revenge that arises from witnessing enemy atrocity. The interlacing of epic form and reportage forges a revolutionary personhood and history from combat, from the multiple registers brought to bear in and around the battlefield. This is a text that seeks to join the fray, to invoke a sensoryscape of war, much of which revolves around bombing, being bombed, and beings who are bombed. I follow selected scenes from the three installments of this novella as it writes details large, this story of death in battle and survival to fight another day. Han's readers learn how Seoul was lost and why the Seoul people, the *Sŏul saramdŭl*, came into being. Most importantly, those who read his work learn how to engage in the act of revolutionary mourning.

Installment one of *Seoul People* is lengthy, comprising over half of the serialized novella. The text opens with the invocation of a name: "Seoul.... We must leave it to the historians to tell us the story of when this city obtained such a name. But what a beautiful and loving name it is."[25] The Chosŏn dynasty aristocrats called the city Hansŏng and the Japanese changed its name to Kyŏngsŏng, but "the people [*inmin*] never stopped calling it Seoul."[26] June 28, 1950 was the moment of liberation of the city from its latest occupiers, the *migungnom* (a common pejorative for Americans) and the traitorous Syngman Rhee regime: "The *inmin* could now fully realize how much they held Seoul in their hearts."[27] Hope and happiness were cut short. The US landing at Incheon and advance on the city was met at every turn by the KPA: "September 21. This was the date on which the solemn epic poem [*sŏsasi*] commenced, written by the warm blood of party members, composed of the fiery patriotism of the brave citizens of Seoul."[28] *Seoul People* is an incarnation, embodiment; the text exists in seamless relation to blood and feeling itself.

We meet six members of the core group of revolutionaries fighting to defend the city in this first section of Han's work: Cultural Affairs Officer Pak Ch'ŏl, Political Affairs Chief Kim Seho, Comrade Kŭmju, Comrade O, Comrade Yun, and Kiok (Yun's younger brother). They serve to highlight a broader network of resistance tightly and efficiently organized by the party. While Kim Seho assumes a central position, weaving his way in and out of the narrative across the three installments, the third-person narration shifts from one comrade's actions and point of view to the next. The text's distribution of heroism intersects with multiple accounts of life histories to form an emotive grid, an assemblage of feelings that creates history. It is in this way, in late September, that "new humans, the new Seoul people, came into being. It was here that the *inmin* were born as heroes of a grand epic poem."[29]

FEELINGS OF DOUBT, DOUBTFUL FEELINGS, AND A LITTLE BELL

Pak is the first to survey the scene. Enemy bombing has left the nighttime city such a fiery, mangled mess that "one wonders if there was any life left at all."[30] Total war. Pak looks inward, weighed down with doubt about his own abilities. His worries are met with more attacks:

> Enemy bombers screech overhead, leaving behind a fearful noise. A flare lights up in the sky and slowly drops over the hills of North Ahyŏn District like a street lantern illuminating a square. The light brings the ruins of the burning city into sharp relief.
>
> But light was shed on something more than just the smoldering city. Workers, members of the youth league, the women's league had come together and were courageously setting up barricades.
>
> As Pak looked upon this scene, it occurred to him that our fatherland's fate would be decided here, in the midst of these burning streets, in this colossal [*kŏinjŏgin*] battle, in the passionate, grand struggle of our people [*uri inmin*].[31]

The enemy's light brings clarity beyond its intention. Those targeted for elimination etch themselves in solidarity. Pak moves from doubt to determination as he discovers the passion and grandness of the *inmin*. The stage is set.

Focus shifts to Kim Seho and narrows to an exploration of intimacy. Born in poverty, Kim left colonial Korea for Japan, studying at night, delivering milk by day. He returns to Seoul (his hometown) after the August 1945 liberation and joins the underground resistance. He is jailed, and his wife is tortured to death. Kim's mother has fled to her eldest son's home in the north, taking Kim's daughter, Okhŭi, with her. Kim visits his old house, now empty, and comes across a small bell Okhŭi would carry with her wherever she went. It is a bell given to Okhŭi by Kim's neighbor, Comrade Kŭmju. As he put the bell in his pocket,

> Comrade Kim was suddenly overcome by a sentiment [*kamsang*] arising from deep within his very bones. It occurred to him that even if he wasn't foolish enough to lose his mind over such sentimentality he still didn't have the courage to simply laugh it off. . . . Comrade Kim resisted the urge to collapse on the floor right then and there. He was disgusted at himself for wallowing in such feelings in the midst of a raging battle.[32]

Comrade Kim's struggle with sentiment speaks to the contemporary literary debates in which Han Hyo played such a central role. Kim runs the danger of falling into the mode of a retrograde "naturalism," closely associated with lyrical emotions, sentiment, and nostalgia, critiqued by Han in the period leading up to the 1954 purge of figures such as Im Hwa and Kim Namch'ŏn.[33] If the task of *Seoul People* is to demonstrate how to write a wartime realist text, this entails the production of an emotive field composed of proper feelings of affection, love combined with anger, rage, and hate—all brought together in a deep sense of care for one's comrades.

What then of the bell? Kŭmju, a factory worker, was more than a neighbor. She assumed the role of surrogate mother for Okhŭi following the death of Kim's wife. Kim will later tell Kŭmju that he found the bell and would like to return it to her: "She was surprised that Comrade Kim would have given a thought to such a thing, or, more than that, that he would have such warm feelings [*ttattŭthan chŏngsŏ*]."[34] Kŭmju accepts the bell "with moistened eyes."[35] *Ttallang ttallang*, the bell has entered the fray. Emotive but not confined simply to an interior "deep within," this feeling will find its expression best in the sound of the bell, beyond words. *Ttallang ttalling*, the bell's ring will follow the text through subsequent installments. The little bell rings with a grand reverberation. It will oppose the roar of US bombers that fill this text (and many other DPRK literary works).

Ttallang ttallang, its chime harkens not to the sentimental past of family and home but to the unfolding of mutuality and affection in a much larger way, in the revolutionary coalition of workers, militia, and party—the network that makes up the warmth of the "Seoul people."

The movement from sentiment to warm affection confers depth and multidimensionality upon the panoply of feelings associated with combat. The enemy's vicious (*yasujŏk*) bombardment of liberated Seoul does not spare the factory (a silk mill) Kŭmju and her fellow workers have made their own over the past several months.[36] A meeting is held there, and Kim Seho's call for payback is seconded by Kŭmju, who finds herself unable to suppress a "burning feeling of revenge [*pult'anŭn poksusim*] welling up in her chest." She leaps to her feet and declares she will join the frontline troops (*tolkyŏktae*).[37] We have seen her moistened eyes. Now we see the constitution of revenge. Anger channels into desire for action.

MASSACRE

Ŏm Hosŏk would offer one of the relatively few early (May 1952) assessments of Han's *Seoul People*. Noting that Han wrote this work, his first novella, based on the accounts of actual combatants, Ŏm calls attention to Han's use of reportage (*rŭp'orŭt'ajwi*) as means to do justice to an enormous historical canvas (*hwap'ok*). Han succeeds, Ŏm tells us, in adding a "deep and profound personality" (*simohan kaesŏng*) to reportage: "And this is precisely what our particular reality [*hyŏnsil ŭi tokjasŏng*] and lofty realism [*kosanghan reallijŭm*] demands."[38] Ŏm emphasizes the importance of a new type of hero, one in possession of a "high spirit" (*nop'ŭn chŏngsin*): "Writers do not merely reproduce reality; they discover new elements appearing in reality. They take those humans who embody [*ch'ehyŏn*] these elements in reality and magnify them, make them higher and bigger, pull them up to the level of typicality [*chŏnhyŏng*]."[39] Such an approach, Ŏm surmises, follows Alexei Fyodorov's *The Underground Committee Carries On*, a famous novel describing partisan resistance against Nazi Germany's occupation of Ukraine.[40] Becoming and magnification bear close relation. One becomes heroic as one grows higher and bigger. If typicality stands at the apex of the lofty, though, it also possesses a horizontal dimension. The lofty crosses borders. In his "Heroes Alive in Reality: On Reading Simonov's *Nights and Days*" (*Munhak yesul*, September 1949), Han Hyo writes that Simonov's Soviet people are doing more than defend their city, Stalingrad: "In their struggle against fascism, we read how they rescued the destiny of humanity and how they propelled history forward."⁴¹ Han emphasizes that Simonov's heroes emerge from below, possess a love of their own fatherland (*chagi choguk*), exist in inextricable relation to "actual experience" (*siljiro ch'ehŏm*).

The antithesis of the lofty takes form in massacre scenes, which bear intertextual relation to Soviet portrayals of the Great Patriotic War. Comrade Pak leads a five-person team to seek out and eliminate comprador ROK elements who have been conducting recon, sending up signal flares to aid enemy targeting. Pak's squad comes across a two-story house, former residence of a Japanese official. A search of the premises reveals a middle-aged woman who speaks in a P'yŏngan Province accent and a group of men hiding in a secret World War II–era antiaircraft bunker. Pak suspects they have come upon a Northwest Youth cell. They also find a youth cowering behind the house next to a pile of signal flares. This teenager, Kiok, tells them that he was captured while searching for his older brother, who turns out to be none other than Comrade Yun (who has sacrificed himself to stop an advancing enemy tank). Third-person narration then shifts to his point of view for a description of a massacre: the slaughter of Kiok's father, mother, sister-in-law, and niece.

This story-within-a-story takes the form of witnessing and testimonial. Yesterday, Kiok was standing on a hill looking down at his village and the surrounding forest covered in smoke. He hears gunshots and screams coming from his home. Kiok rushes down the hill and peers into the yard through a crack in the wall: "The first thing he saw was his mother and father lying outside the door in a pool of blood, and then gun-toting American bastards [*migungnom*], an interpreter, and the smirks on the faces of the landlord and the reactionary Pastor Ch'oe."⁴² Kiok watches a *migungnom* drag his naked sister-in-law and her child out of a room. The group is laughing, jeering. Pastor Ch'oe spots a pot of boiling water in the kitchen:

> "So how do we kill ourselves a little commie bastard?" he asked fawningly, turning his head this way and that. The interpreter translated to English.
> "In the most enjoyable way possible," replied the tall American, shrugging his shoulders and stepping into the kitchen.

The American stuffs the child into the boiling pot. Kiok's sister-in-law leaps toward the kitchen, but she's blocked by another American and thrown to the ground:

> "A nice, fat ass, she's got," Pastor Ch'oe chuckles. He looks like he's enjoying the spectacle and steps toward her. Sister-in-Law suddenly leaps to her feet and slaps him in the face.

"You son-of-a-bitch!"

The sound of her voice is accompanied by a gunshot. Sister-in-Law falls to the ground, gushing blood.[43]

Third-person narration tells us this account is not easy to read or image:

> What Kiok had seen was so appalling, so shocking it would make someone with the coolest head lose their nerve. There is nothing like this even in Dante's *Inferno*. Nor would we find such a scene in tales of the bizarre [*ryŏpki sosŏl*]. Is there something we can compare these cold-hearted beasts to, something that will enable us to speak of them? It was Gorky who once said that fascists weren't beasts but something far worse. Here are demons [*akkwi*], many times more vicious, more evil than wild animals. These gun-toting devils in uniform were the pillars of the German fascist regime, and now they've become the indispensable spearhead for Wall Street's invasion and all of its American thievery. These demons are putting their cruelty on display in our country [*urinara*] for all to see. The reality Kiok witnessed was just one small shard of the evil deeds they were committing here on a daily basis.[44]

This massacre scene draws the first installment of *Seoul People* to a close with its presentation of the enemy not simply as bestial but possessed, inhabited by demons, evil spirits (*akkwi*) that make themselves manifest in acts of violence. These demons appear across space and time (in Nazi Germany, on Wall Street). Han's lofty realism, his historical canvas, lifts the Fatherland Liberation War to a higher, internationalist historical plane.

How to put the atrocities of the *akkwi* into words? Kiok's eye-witness account provides authenticity. But this massacre defies description. Argyrios Pisiotis points out that "Soviet films, posters, and press presented German atrocities as breaking the all-time record of bestiality. *Stalingrad* identifies all Germans with 'Nazi cutthroats,' who commit acts of 'lunacy,' 'monstrosities,' 'unbelievable butchery.'"[45] Seoul may not be Stalingrad, but the battle of humanity against fascism now finds its front in the former. In *Seoul People*, the *akkwi* are mobile and appear in various forms: They inhabit both American bodies and Korean bodies. To observe them is to encounter the unspeakable inverse of revolutionary potential, an evil of epic proportions that accompanies the call to the lofty. Such is the demonic worthy of an epic poem (*sŏsasi*).

Kiok's older brother, Comrade Yun, was difficult to discern in the dust and darkness as he sprinted from his barricade to take out an American tank. But then we hear the sound of a loud explosion: "Comrade O couldn't bring himself to believe that Yun, who'd just been on a recon mission with him, was gone just like that, without a trace."[46] The tank has been obliterated, and Yun along with it. His fellow fighters find themselves calling out his name in unison: "'Comrade Yun Kich'ŏl!' Their voices were choked with tears but were deep and full. The name of Comrade Yun Ki-ch'ŏl echoed powerfully in the gathering darkness, from the ridge of Mt. Kŭmhwa, to Mt. Inwang, to Mt. Pukak, across all of Seoul."[47] Feeling folds into this revolutionary lament for the war dead, for those who have sacrificed. Yun's body is no more but his name remains. The echo extends into mountains that disappear into darkness. The southern portion of the fatherland begins to fade from direct sight, existing now in sound and image. Such a mourning is at once sorrowful and empowering. It will last in DPRK literary texts, in art, in film, in song. It is a collective mourning that comes from the heart and carries itself into the world. It will mobilize manifest revolution in the north and hover over that which can only be imaged from this point forward, the southern *inmin*.

Installment one closes with Kiok learning of this death. Comrade Pak hesitates, pondering how he can possibly relay Comrade Yun's bravery to him. But Kiok seeks no further information: "'I won't cry. I'm not sad. All I have is hate for the enemy [*wŏnssuman miulppunyeyo*].' His voice was shaking tremendously. But each word was filled with an unfathomable strength."[48] Words can only suggest that which cannot be adequately described, measured. The magnification of the small into something larger must be felt. Han's epic poem seeks this height.

PROLETARIAN SUBLIME

"September 25." The first sentence of *Seoul People*'s second installment gives this date and nothing more. Every moment is pressing. Incendiary bombing has grown in intensity, transforming the city into a "sea of flames" (*pulbada*). Enemy ground advance from the south furthers the pressure. But resistance remains strong. More than fifty Northwest Youth members and other enemy agents are brought in as prisoners.[49]

Kŭmju's story takes center stage—a story of sensory and aesthetic becoming grounded in struggle. We are given a quick synopsis of her life history: Her father, a lineman, died on the job, electrocuted in the rain; her mother passes soon after; her sister sold herself as concubine to a childless man but fails to become pregnant and is sent away after seven years; Kŭmju is forced to give up night school and gets a job at the textile factory. She becomes an organizer, devoting herself to "learning the teachings of the party and engaging in the struggle."[50] Attached to a recon unit in the Seodaemun area, she now fights to defend Seoul. Her revolutionary awareness expands.

Taking a position on a hill while out on a mission, Kŭmju is overwhelmed by the wonderful fragrance of the earth (*hŭk*): "Living in servant's quarters, going to night school, moving to the company dorm—this was all she had known. She had lived in an environment distant from the land. So even at this moment of desperation in battle, she found herself completely intoxicated by the smell of the earth wafting through her nostrils."[51] She subsequently observes a KPA squad advancing on a platoon of enemy soldiers about one hundred meters from her position: "Her eyes suddenly grew moist. A squad of just seven soldiers, all low crawling their way toward the enemy. Such bravery, such beauty. It was this sight that brought on her tears. These soldiers, these were the ones always prepared to sacrifice their lives for the sake of the people [*inmin*] and the fatherland [*choguk*]."[52] Kŭmju's life experience heightens her class consciousness and dedication to the struggle. But more is needed. Her recon mission brings the sensory, emotive, and aesthetic together, lifting her into a new dimension. She shortly comes across a US soldier who actually turns out to be Comrade Kim in disguise. As she walks with Kim in a valley, she hears:

> the rhythmic wind flowing through the trees, which makes her forget the tiresome sound of artillery. The smoke and dust of the weapons cannot come here, to this valley.... It occurred to her that if there were to be a moment when sound, light and feelings [*kamjŏng*] combine as one, this would be it. But what struck her eardrums at this moment was not the sound of the wind but surprisingly something else, a voice lifted in song. It was Kim, walking a few feet ahead of her, singing in a quiet but clear voice. The song was "The International."[53]

Kim tells Kŭmju he would sing "The International" in prison. The song gave Kim and his cellmates solace. They would be overcome by a "vast, solemn feeling," knowing that the voices of millions across the world were joining in chorus.[54] They would feel a love for humanity that could not be destroyed by Syngman Rhee, by the Americans, "who had done all they could for five straight years to turn the entire southern region into a vast prison."[55]

The sound of wind blowing through the trees fades into the melody: "His voice was low, but the song shook the entire valley."[56] "The International" traverses the fatherland. This is a voice so powerful it shakes awe-inspiring nature. Kŭmju has entered the proletarian sublime, a sensory and aesthetic apprehension of a place where small is always large, where a squad of seven low-crawling soldiers signals the fatherland, the people, the planet, the cosmos itself. Beauty resides in this intimate and expansive place, as does "sound, light, and feelings."

Seoul People moves from the sublime to elegy as installment two draws to a close. Five days of failure has made the enemy anxious. It was at dawn on September 26 that the enemy brought all of its weaponry to bear upon Seoul: "Those few houses that remained went up in flames. Every last living thing on earth was being blown to pieces, utterly destroyed."[57] Such destruction requires a witness: "the youthful lives sacrificed in defense of their beloved Seoul will remain only in the memory of their comrades. Because language cannot do justice to such a scene."[58] The sensoryscape of the proletarian sublime meets its antithesis, the mindless impetus to make smaller than small, to obliterate. Both require an apprehension that presses against textual description. *Seoul People* asks its readers to approximate the horrible, beautiful experience of this place, to cast words aside and enter the feelings of those who were there and survived, and those fought and died in defense of the capital. We are asked to join a community in revolutionary mourning.

THE DEAD IN THE LIVING

In the final and shortest installment of *Seoul People*, the textile factory workers, heroes of the successful recapture of Mt. An, now join the soldiers in an attack on Mt. Kŭmhwa. Kŭmju is among them. Coming after a massive five-hour bombardment, the attack must have caught the enemy by surprise:

> They must have wondered: "Are they something other than human? How come they don't die? How can they attack in broad daylight like this?" But of course everyone has to die! These bastards [*nom*] were so reliant on their armor, their weaponry they had no conception of the true power and superiority of human beings.... The attack did in fact take place in broad daylight, the worst of conditions. Undeterred, the avengers displayed uncommon courage. Their advance fell beyond the bounds of scientific understanding, a concentrated expression of superhuman strength [*ch'oinganjŏgin him*].[59]

The avengers have become the human raised on high, to the proportions of an epic poem (*sŏsasi*). Losses are heavy but the hill is taken:

Shouts of "Hurrah" [*manse*] rise into the air, overturning all conceptions of space and time. There was no denying that what should be the absolutely solemn, reverberating shout of *manse* was here also filled with a sorrow so overwhelming we could call it tragic. In later days, when people remember the many heroes who sacrificed their youth in this battle, when they stand before their graves and express their sorrow, they should above all reflect on the deep sense of loss voiced by the comrades of those heroes, the grief in that shout of *manse*.[60]

To reflect on such a loss will be to participate in the continuing struggle to emancipate the Korean peninsula. This revolutionary struggle will take place in the everyday of the Democratic People's Republic of Korea, in the labor performed in fields and factories, within the temporal frame of five-year plans. But the future subject of the republic will also exist somewhere else, in the intergenerational remembrance of a place where the heights of the human have confronted the inhuman, where triumph and resilience have met with immeasurable tragedy and loss.

The battle continues. Comrade Kim and Company Commander Min decide to retake the notorious Seodaemun Prison in order to demonstrate the strength and determination of the *inmin*. The attack diverts the enemy, buying valuable time for people to flee the city and escape from impending massacre. Comrade Kim has been directing the fight from a barricade; he approaches the prison after the main gate is taken. A firefight is underway at one of the walls. It is here that Comrade Kim comes across Kŭmju. She lies in a pool of blood. He calls out to her, attempts to prop her up:

> At that moment, the little bell in her pocket chimed, *ttallang*.
> "Comrade Kim."
> Kŭmju opened her eyes. She gazed up at the stars flickering in the night sky.
> "The stars are so clear, Comrade Kim. So beautiful," she whispered softly.
> But then her tone changed and her voice rose with immeasurable dignity, "Long Live the Democratic People's Republic of Korea!"
> These solemn words, those of the woman protagonist of our beautiful epic poem, were her last. She took her final breaths beneath the clear stars and sky of her beloved fatherland.[61]

Kŭmju is a battlefield hero and more. She is a worker, an organizer, a frontline fighter. She is maternal, a stand-in for Kim's wife, caring for Okhŭi. (The text hints that something more might spring up between her and Kim, were circumstances altered.) She apprehends the location of the republic within the cosmos, the proletarian sublime. All of this encapsulated in the intimate but expansive ring of the little bell, *ttallang*. Kim calls out to Kŭmju again and again. There is no response. He turns his eyes to the "beloved capital, more precious than life itself, the capital he had given his all to defend. Seoul was awash in flames, churning in fire like a giant blast furnace."[62]

September 27, 1950. The last day. The hills are lost, all of them. But the fighters continue their defense of the city at the barricades. Here, in this last stand, "it is as if the strength of the dead is transferred to the living soldiers."[63] The epic poem summons the dead to invigorate the living, to move history forward at the moment of withdrawal north. Comrade Kim stands and looks back upon the capital one last time:

> The faces of his comrades appeared before him one by one. Those who had died in this glorious battle, calling out the Party, the Republic, the Leader. Comrade Yun, Comrade O, and Kŭmju. . . .
> He was overcome with a choking sadness. His eyes filled with tears . . .
> His beloved comrades lay in the smoke and flames. Comrades! Sleep well! Your deaths will not have been in vain![64]

Readers of *Seoul People* are witness to two kinds of death: one the result of atrocity/massacre; the other a death in battle. The two combine to produce an ethics of loss. To be sure, loss is conditioned by anger, hate, and revenge—emotions consistently invoked across DPRK media. But these feelings are productive. They do not fester within; they are made visible and circulate. They promote a revolutionary belonging and becoming, a heightened humanity.

To mourn those who died in battle in defense of Seoul is to acknowledge not simply a loss but the historical foreclosure of what presented itself as possibility (decolonization, reunification, revolution). It is to follow the dead in time and in history. It is to become one of the divided (north/south) *inmin*. Such a becoming through mourning moves the past into an ethics of the contemporary moment. At the same time, remembrance calls for a willing obligation to that which is yet to come, which portends. Such is the temporality of the afterdead, the lost ones who are not lost, those whose death stories inhabit this unfolding history of revolution and reunification.

While Han Hyo's *Seoul People* moved quickly to the margins of the DPRK literary scene, its elaboration of the lofty in relation to a wartime recognition that the south was lost for the foreseeable future would appear in numerous iterations for decades to follow. The play between the large and the small would organize postarmistice north/south spatialization, make visible a revolutionary dynamism opposed to a diminished, shackled possibility. In the cartoon above, two images

FIG. 2.2 "The workers' struggle to construct socialism provides the material basis underlying the push for peaceful reunification, independence of the fatherland, and rescue of the South Chosŏn people [*inmin*] groaning under US occupation." *Munhak sinmun*, May 2, 1957.

present division as a form of mirroring, a doubling of what is, in fact, one. The manifest agent of socialist modernization and reunification seeks to break the mirror image and release the potential his ghostly southern counterpart yearns to realize. The worker's facial expression is calm, persevering. He accumulates results, moves toward a breakthrough. He expands space (already wider than the space allotted to his southern counterpart in the cartoon). The smaller right pane of the cartoon is also populated by two miniaturized figures, Syngman Rhee backed by a Douglas MacArthur look-alike. Those who seek to block movement forward in space and time become the smallest of the small, ridiculous figures. The worker chips his way steadily across the illusory divide, bringing light to the darkness.

The cartoon and its captions position viewers/readers as subjects of revolution and reunification, provided with the multiple dimensions of revolution (north/south doubles, manifest and potential *inmin*) and counterrevolution (US/ROK doubles, power behind and puppet in front). To visualize the moment that comes next, where the manifest meets the latent is to take up residence in the realm of the loftier picture, where two images become one.

Chapter 3 shifts from productive failure to canonical success, the work of Hwang Kŏn, a writer who would occupy a position of prominence in the DPRK throughout his life. As was the case with Han Hyo and many other writers, much of Hwang's wartime work centers the revolutionary becomings of women and their eventual martyrdom. Hwang's work continues the pressing task of locating the loss of the southern half of the Korean peninsula in relation to global revolutionary history. Here, too, the question will be of feelings, but now with an eye to their cross-cultural circulation within the socialist world. Can the young people of wartime Chosŏn experience the same emotions as their counterparts in the Soviet Union's Great Patriotic War? Such a question ends up moving in another direction: Can the young people of Chosŏn experience death in the same way as their Soviet literary and filmic forbears? At stake is the negotiation of Soviet forms as feelings, Soviet deaths as transferable icons, and the location of the Fatherland Liberation War in history.

CHAPTER 3

HORIZONS OF HAPPINESS

Preparatory sketches for Chang Myŏngnyong's panoramic painting *Battle in Defense of Seoul* pay attention to individual elements that will make up the bigger picture, ways to signal anger, resilience, and determination via facial expression. The gendered distribution of emotion centers two nurses (one in *hanbok*) who at once align with the fighters in enemy-directed posture (see figure 3.1a) and look to the wounded (see figure 3.1b).

Chang's final version (see figure 3.2) heightens the color contrast between *hanbok* and green combat fatigues, embodied care for the men etched more clearly as the men themselves now engage the enemy in a defense that pushes forward (the angle of the wounded man's body and head altered accordingly). The nurse on the left now joins her comrade (less upright, in a longer dress, sans first aid kit) in a look upon the wounded soldier that adds prominence to her expression of concern.

The gendered, emotive grid assumes form in multidirectional looks, upon the enemy and upon the self, looks ahead and looks back. Feelings arise within this frame—from the activity of its lines, its motion—and take expression in the face.

Chang's 1965 panorama-like painting etches a battle that lends itself to a DPRK-centeredness, a historical moment of possibility that stands on the cusp of withdrawal from the capital (and prior to what would be Chinese leadership in subsequent battles to retake and defend Seoul in early 1951). In Chang's work, the emotions of the Chosŏn *inmin*, women and men, arise from the intensity of revolutionary combat, from hatred of the enemy, care for the self. The painting crystallizes this moment in time, even as it is directed toward a revolutionary future, the portrayal of determined struggle offering the promise of return and reunification.

FIG. 3.1.1 AND FIG. 3.1.2 Two sketches for Chang Myŏngnyong's painting *Battle in Defense of Seoul*. *Chosŏn misul*, June 1965.

FIG. 3.2 Chang's Myŏngnyong's later *Battle in Defense of Seoul*. October 1965 cover of *Chosŏn misul*.

Chang's painting bears relation to another history that does not appear within its frame, the relation between figurings of the Soviet Union's Great Patriotic War and the DPRK's Fatherland Liberation War. Inhabiting the historical connection between the two events is the question of internationalist feelings. How to summon comparable battlefield emotions across time and space, as well as texts and images? The question of internationalism itself is very much a matter of intertextual relations, as is evident in the emphasis in the DPRK on all facets of Soviet cultural production in the late 1940s and early 1950s, prior to the well-documented move away from the post-Stalin Soviet Union that accompanied Kim Il Sung's consolidation of power in the latter half of the decade.

The *Rodong sinmun*'s (*Workers' Daily*) long-running series "In the Glorious Soviet Union" (Widaehan Ssoryŏn esŏ) highlights the wartime location of Soviet culture and progress.[1] Columns such as these provided a present, a meanwhile shared by the DPRK and the Soviet Union, even as the latter appears as exemplar, model for the DPRK future. That "In the Glorious Soviet Union" was eventually paired with a new series entitled "In Our Fatherland" (Uri choguk esŏ) in the early 1950s speaks to this shared but hierarchized temporality. Such a pairing implicitly puts the adjective *widaehan* in play. Is this adjective transferable? Does it provide a telos? What is its relation to the possessive "our"?

A canonical wartime work that has stood the test of time, Hwang Kŏn's aptly-titled novella *Happiness* (*Haengbok*, 1953) is a story about stories, a story about reading, watching, and identifying with the feelings of characters in Soviet texts and films.[2] How to verify that these feelings can be experienced in Chosŏn? *Happiness* frames this question as fundamental to the location of the newly-formed DPRK within the history of internationalist socialism.

It will be up to two nurses, Ryeju and Chŏngim, to move beyond the arc of caregiving and traverse a broader movement of feelings across texts, films, and borders. If this traversal seeks to secure reference and authenticity, it does so in an approach to death as a limit line, a point where the body offers itself to multiple appropriations. The happiness of *Happiness* will lie less in martyrdom or sacrifice than in the transformative pleasure taken in a self-reflexive, cross-cultural mode of reading, viewing, and writing.

A reporter in Manchuria during the late colonial period, Hwang Kŏn (1918–1991) emerged on the literary scene in post-1945 divided Korea. He served as an embedded writer in the Fatherland Liberation War (1950–1953) and would maintain an influential position on the DPRK literary scene for decades to follow, receiving the prestigious Kim Il Sung Prize in 1988. His short story "Island Ablaze" (Pul t'anŭn sŏm, 1952) has done more than stand the test of time. Given the widest possible circulation in the *Rodong sinmun*, adapted for the screen as *Wŏlmi Island* (1982), and repeatedly anthologized, "Island Ablaze" stands at the apex of the DPRK wartime canon. This is the story of a last stand on Wŏlmi Island, Incheon Harbor in mid-September 1950. Platoon leader Ri Taehun leads his unit in a fight to the death against the withering firepower brought to bear by US forces as they press forward to make their amphibious landing. The text centers its POV, though, on Kim Myŏnghŭi, one of three women recently deployed to Ri's unit as a wireless operator.

It turns out that "Island Ablaze" is a story as much about a last report as it is about a last stand. The situation becomes increasingly dire. HQ in Seoul orders Myŏnghŭi and her two fellow wireless operators to withdraw. Myŏnghŭi, however, lobbies hard to remain, and HQ relents. The enemy makes an amphibious landing on the island; the end approaches. Myŏnghŭi places a grenade next to her wireless and telegraphs HQ: "This will be my last report. End of message means grenade has exploded. Make full use of last message."³ She authors the last stand of the platoon and her own approach to death. Stop.

Back at HQ. As the commanding officer stares at the printout of Myŏnghŭi's report, "the image of the operator's corpse covered in a thick bloody mess arose before his eyes."⁴ Words, body, and images fold into each other to produce the truth of "Island Ablaze." Myŏnghŭi's report comes alive in transit, moving from her own last stand, her body at the wireless prepared to die, to the text's relay of the "thick bloody mess" imaged by the CO. Hwang Kŏn reflects on the ways embedded writing should proceed, how death should occur, be imaged, via the transmission of words from the front. Words are to become real via this relay. The stop is actually neither at the wireless, nor in the incarnation of transmitted narrative to image of a messy corpse in Seoul. The stop takes place at relay's end, the movement of image from the page of the *Rodong sinmun* to its readers.

The figure of Myŏnghŭ would become a familiar one, as we see in Han Pyŏng-ik's 1965 painting *The Last Report*. While the wireless operator is not named in Han's painting, the wide circulation of "Island Ablaze" ensures easy recognition of the allusion. She stands astride battlefield and communication network, right leg planted in the former, left leg leaning forward into the latter. She sutures one to the other as she presses ahead while glancing back, witnessing. She will die, but she has become a medium that exceeds her physical body, even

FIG. 3.3 *The Last Report. Chosŏn misul*, November–December 1965.

as the latter incarnates a dying truth, an authenticity into her report, across communication networks and throughout time. Her simultaneous connection to battlefield and touch on the wireless authors this transformation. Han's painting, like Hwang's "Island Ablaze," is less interested in portraying her death than her bodily movement forward, into a space and time where she assumes new form, a larger, more amplified life in signals, transmissions. It is her location as medium itself, her transmission at the approach of obliteration, her travel into a realism that will expand beyond her own death that lights up Wŏlmi Island, the memory of the last stand that took place there.

Hwang's interest in medium as socialist realist message finds further, more sustained treatment in *Happiness*. As does "Island Ablaze," Hwang's novella addresses the moment when the tide of war has turned against the KPA. Ryeju and Chŏngim (elementary school classmates and friends) are living in the southeast portion of the Korean peninsula when war breaks out in June 1950. The text travels to the front, to the Naktong River battlefield in the tumultuous first months of the war. Ryeju will take center stage in *Happiness*. She navigates her feelings toward Kim Chŏngho, a wounded patient under her care at a field hospital, as well as her love for the people/party/nation. She also comes to understand the meaning of hatred (*chŭngo*) for the enemy.

Ryeju's family was poor, but she had managed to secure a teaching position at a village school by the time the war broke out. She remembers how her fellow teachers were filled with anticipation now that the KPA was advancing south. They were already eagerly studying textbooks from North Chosŏn and would talk excitedly about plans for a new school. And then that morning the "roar of planes circling the school" followed by "flashes of napalm from the playing fields."[5] She later recalls spending the night "distraught, blankly watching the flames race through the streets, listening to the voices crying out from near and far, to the moaning, the sobbing."[6] Seared into her memory is this US raid on her hometown that left her entire family dead. She is often unable to sleep, overcome by images of the bombing: "She actually seemed able to see more clearly in the darkness. Before her would be the anguished face of a dead child, lips parched . . . and more faces, everywhere."[7] To enter *Happiness* is to meet Ryeju's trauma, her despondence.

Chŏngim steps in to help Ryeju recover meaning in her life, suggesting that she join her in the field hospital where she works as a nurse. And more: "You need to hate the enemy. Why is it that you don't feel this hatred?"[8] For her part, Ryeju is ready to hate, but "It was just that it all had been so sudden. Her heart [*maŭm*] had been torn to pieces, and everything seemed beyond her control."[9] Unable to place herself or the images that haunt her into narrative form, "She was on the verge of going mad or just wandering the streets until she fell lifeless."[10] Hatred of the enemy, however, will not be enough to extricate Ryeju from the imminent possibility of an abject death.

Ryeju's entrance into revolutionary history will move from passive witnessing to a place where feeling, knowing, and acting intersect. Her initial feelings of affection for Chŏngho are couched in familial terms: "His unadorned language made Ryeju feel that she was listening to the warm words of her blood relations, her parents or an older brother."[11] But this quickly transforms to another layer of intimacy: "Is it the kind of affection [*aejŏng*] that arises between the sexes? If that's the case, am I someone who can love another right now?"[12] Ryeju's discovery of family-like intimacy beyond the family and the emergence of heterosexual love present a new realm that is also a future, a questioning of what may lie ahead. Shortly after, on the fifth anniversary of liberation from Japanese colonial rule, Ryeju formally becomes a party member and finds that "she could not help but feel that within her body a new self was being born."[13] One thing does not stand in for another in allegorical relation. Ryeju's rebirth blends feelings into history, history into feeling.

Upon learning that Chŏngho must be transferred to Seoul for treatment unavailable at the front, Ryeju realizes "how much she relied on him, how much she loved him."[14] Chŏngho—we learn here he was a conscripted laborer in Hokkaido during the Japanese colonial period, joined the army in 1947, and has not seen his hometown in the north since—shortly confesses his love for her: "Comrade, you are so much more than someone who has taken care of my wounded body. You have a place, a hometown [*kohyang*] in my heart like no other."[15] At a loss as to how to respond, Ryeju tells him "Thank you. That you feel this way brings me so much happiness [*haengbok*]. But I worry, Comrade, that it will be unfortunate for you."[16] It is here that the word "happiness" appears for the first time in Hwang's novella.

Ryeju loves Chŏngho but is unable to tell him so. She feels her "affection turn to sorrow," worries she is devoid of cheer (*myŏngnang*), but finally tells Chŏngho that he "will be the first person she looks for after the *migungnom* have been driven out and the war has ended."[17] Happiness, then, is something more than what Ryeju feels in response to Chŏngho's confession. Happiness mediates a crisscross of feelings, experiences, and matters-at-hand that are coeval but not coincident. These feelings include heterosexual love, love for the fatherland, commitment to the party, and hate for the enemy, among others. Happiness is a form of emancipatory recognition, a decolonizing feeling that blends love, hate, and action in the historical moment. But how to define the temporal and spatial horizon of history?

THE HAPPINESS OF REVOLUTIONARY INTERTEXTUALITY

As we see in the commemorative image below, the October Revolution was viewed in the wartime DPRK as a watershed event, changing the course of Russian history while providing precedence, extending itself as exemplary, a beacon of light emanating above and beyond.

To commemorate is to enact this extension, to connect 1917 to the unfurling of history taking place in wartime Chosŏn. 1917 stretches to 1950 Chosŏn, as the headline on page two of this issue of *Democratic Chosŏn* makes clear: "The Great October Revolution is Living and Achieving Victory in the Powerful Struggle of the Upholders of Socialism and Peaceful Democracy on the Front Lines Against Imperialist Invaders and War Instigators."[18] Spatial extension includes a temporal dimension. Mun Sangmin writes in 1957 that "Influenced by the great October Socialist Revolution in Russia, the Chosŏn people's anti-Japanese struggle for national liberation moved to a new stage on the political, economic, and cultural fronts to become an historical event."[19] Here, the anticolonial struggle in Chosŏn (with emphasis on the 1919 March First Movement) enters history itself precisely as an inflection of the October Revolution.

The October Revolution also works its way into the August 15, 1945 liberation from colonial rule. In "The August 15th Liberation and Our Literature" (*Literary Weekly*, August 15, 1957), Sŏ Manil maintains that "The October Revolution was the fount [*saemt'ŏ*] of the August 15th Liberation.... For the people of Chosŏn, the October Revolution and the August 15th Liberation provide guarantee of national independence, the complete reunification of the fatherland, the construction of a happy socialism, all of these things."[20] While yet to fully realize its historical potential ("all of these things" had not come about in the mid-1950s), the August 15th Liberation presents itself as evidence of the movement of global revolution to Chosŏn.

FIG. 3.4 "Celebrating the 33rd Anniversary of the Great Russian Socialist October Revolution!" November 7, 1950. Header for *Minju Chosŏn*.

Sŏ Manil offers a brief literary history that opens a future "firmly grounded in the correct policies of the party while drawing upon the nation's classics [*minjok kojŏn*] and renewing the tradition of the Korean Artists Proletarian Federation."[21] He concludes with both an expression of sorrow that he is not able to include the literature of South Chosŏn in this short outline and a call for "great works that will further the reunification of the fatherland."[22] Sŏ's history pivots on a term much discussed in DPRK literary criticism in the early 1950s, *ppap'osŭ*, or pathos. The transliteration is from the Russian пафос, used to signal the zeal, enthusiasm, and spiritedness which portends revolutionary progress within a current social reality. Sŏ Manil declares that the "spirit of pre-liberation progressive literature was grounded in a *ppap'osŭ* of struggle and resistance aiming to fundamentally change reality; a forward-moving, positive *ppap'osŭ* propelled the revolutionary changes in everyday life depicted in postliberation works." As for the war, "The *ppap'osŭ* of our writers' works is filled to the brim with the conviction of victory and revolutionary optimism."[23] *Ppap'osŭ* as a sustained, emotive principle guiding, running through a literary work is a formal attribute inseparable from content.

Revolutionary historymaking involves the articulation of a *ppap'osŭ* that "moves" on the level of feeling and in terms of travel across space, time, text, and film. It is revolutionary *ppap'osŭ* that links Soviet and Chosŏn histories, Russian literature and DPRK writing. And the distinction between North Chosŏn and South Chosŏn literature lies here as well. The literature of the latter has receded into the distance, sorrowful and ahistorical precisely because it lacks *ppap'osŭ*. But how to ensure that *ppap'osŭ* is truly felt, does not reside in literature as a formulaism? The question is pressing for a site on the socialist periphery that has become the front, locus of direct, violent confrontation with the counterrevolutionary, capitalist superpower.

An uncredited article, "Soviet Literature is the Model for Our Literature" (1957) offers an assessment of Soviet-Chosŏn literary relations relevant to the post-1945 period.[24] Of primary import is the physical presence of translated Soviet literary texts, their increasing availability: "Russian and Soviet literary texts have become close, everyday friends in our spiritual lives."[25] A temporal gap accompanies this intimacy: "Our literature sees its own future in Soviet literature."[26] Does the friendly relation with the available Soviet model guarantee that readers/viewers will actually feel the emotions of the characters they encounter, those with whom they are intimate on a spiritual level that has yet to be realized in Chosŏn? Hwang's *Happiness* addresses the question of intertextual intimacy by locating happiness precisely in the reworking of this temporal gap.

Midway through *Happiness*, Ryeju, Chŏngim, and Chŏngho engage in a lively discussion of the "remarkable personalities" in Alexander Fadeev's *The Young*

Guard (1946, rewritten in 1951).²⁷ Ryeju is currently reading the novel, and Chŏngim has read part one of Fadeev's text (the text mentions that section two has not been translated). All three have seen the 1948 filmic adaptation (dir., Sergei Gerasimov).²⁸ Ryeju and Chŏngim are struck by the ability of the youth in the German-occupied city of Krasnodon (in the Donbass region of Ukraine) to maintain their "cheerfulness" (*myŏngnang*) in the midst of extreme adversity. Chŏngho agrees, adding that "such personalities would not have appeared without the social atmosphere brought about by revolution in the glorious Soviet Union."²⁹ This remark historically situates the emergence of cheer on the Soviet periphery. Can the youth of Chosŏn, too, share this feeling? At stake is the world-historical significance of the October Revolution, its relation to those at the edge of the socialist world who arrive later in time. How, precisely, will cheer travel?

The feelings/thoughts/experiences of these young Koreans do not simply coincide with those of the young Soviets in Fadeev's work, even if we can trace similarities in the narrative trajectories of *Happiness* and *The Young Guard*. Both center on youth—women and men—mounting a resistance against an invading army intent upon destroying communism. Both address two facets central to resistance: The willingness to sacrifice one's life; and the possibility of betrayal, particularly under torture. (These trajectories come together in Oleg's formal declaration of affiliation with the Young Guard.) There are other concrete linkages: Both begin with the roar of enemy bombers; Chŏngho worked in the mines in Hokkaido and Krasnodon is a mining town; portrayal of the Germans resembles that of US soldiers; both works emphasize defense of country and people (*choguk/inmin* in *Happiness*). Such similarities help to invoke an alliance, a shared struggle. But *Happiness* reframes the question of textual precedence (emulation of that which has come before) through its explicit meditation on the act of realist representation itself.

Chŏngim poses what turns out to be the central question *Happiness* asks of *The Young Guard*: "Did those young people feel sorrow or joy [*kippŏssŭlgga*] at the moment of death?"³⁰ Mulling over his experiences in combat as the KPA fought its way south across the 38th parallel, Chŏngho replies that dying with joy in one's heart can indeed take place. He himself felt such an emotion when charging up a hill in the face of withering fire from the enemy, all with no expectation of making it out alive. But Chŏngim remains unconvinced:

> "How could someone who dies knowing they are indeed dying not feel sadness?"
> "It's possible if you think of the fatherland and people with pride in your heart."
> "Really?"³¹

A form of intertextual self-reflexivity, a reflection within *Happiness* on *The Young Guard*, positions Ryeju, Chŏngim, Chŏngho as agents of mediation, critics of their own relation to a Soviet text, questioners of the limits of representation. How can either *Happiness* or *The Young Guard* know what one feels at the moment of death? Doubt closes the temporal gap and locates *The Young Guard* and *Happiness* on the same textual plane. Textual precedence begins to lose significance. The youthful characters of both texts join in common concern that bridges time and space: What will one truly feel at the moment of impending death, a death that is to take place in the name of the people, the fatherland, and the revolution?

TYPICALITY AND INTERNATIONALISM

Discussions of Soviet socialist realism dominated literary journals in the late 1940s and 1950s.[32] Literature from sites along the Soviet periphery also proved of interest in the navigation of a socialist universalism. In a 1949 article, for example, Yun Tuhŏn invokes Julius Fučík's posthumous 1947 *Notes from the Gallows* as an example of Fučík's heroic resistance in the face of impending execution:

> But is this a courage possessed solely by the Czech people? Absolutely not. Given that Marxist-Leninist-Stalinist thought is engaged in a fight with the barbaric enemy everywhere in the world, all humans trained in and armed with this thinking will share these attributes.
>
> We see frequent examples of such courage in the southern region of our land, where our brethren are engaged in a struggle . . . every day, every hour in the Jeju Island resistance, in the Yŏsu, in the factories, in the schools, in the farming villages, in the prisons, in the jails.[33]

To participate in the global struggle is to join in feelings that move across time and national belonging. But this does not entail a jettisoning of the latter, as is evident in a 1949 series of articles assessing "lessons learned from Soviet literature following liberation." Ko Ilhwan, for example, writes that "Without a true love for the fatherland and a defense of the interests of the entire *inmin*, there can be no true literature."[34] He then emphasizes the importance of internationalism:

> Here, our literature should take as its basic line the rejection of a narrow nationalism; instead, we must situate and particularize our literature within the

broader, more equitable concept of patriotism. In order to implement this literature creatively in practice and add weight to it, writers must first and foremost discover and embody the internationalist path. Once imbued with this lofty ideology [*kosanghan sasangsŏng*], their works will be able to educate the *inmin*.[35]

Patriotism leaves restrictive nationalism behind. The former allows for a love of the fatherland open to a higher, global belonging. The Chosŏn *inmin* themselves come into being via this combination of the patriotic and the international.

The assertion of a patriotism that calls for recognition within a broader, internationalist horizon resembles the movement of literary typicality (*chŏnhyŏngsŏng*), much discussed in the late 1940s and early 1950s. Han Hyo writes that "In socialist realist literature, true typicality and concreteness does not mean a onedimensional truth emerging from a slice of reality [*hyŏnsil*]. Instead, it is the freedom of fiction, artistic truth that brings together all that makes up the typical."[36] As is the case with the freedom conferred upon the writer to move beyond the one-dimensional in order to locate the typical, the articulation of patriotism within the more encompassing internationalist path requires creativity, discovery. These gestures turn upon realisms that actualize beyond the actual, the as-is. Han Hyo explains by way of an example, Fadeev's *The Young Guard*:

> Kornely Zilensky demonstrates that Fadeev's ability to bring out the highest level of "concrete and patriotic typicality" of the youthful heroes arises from the writer's ... long experience of observing Soviet youth and combining them in his consciousness to create something different from actual people. Zilensky states ... that "this work is not just a story of the Krasnodon underground youth resistance under German occupation.... The traces of the struggle between fiction and reality are clearly present."[37]

Hwang Kŏn's *Happiness* stages a different scene for the socialist realist Chosŏn writer. The latter must look in several directions, combining an understanding of Soviet cultural production with observations of Chosŏn youth. As is the case for Fadeev, license is given to "create something different from actual people." And in both instances, the story will speak to more than the particular circumstances where resistance takes place. The freedom of fiction conferred on the Chosŏn writer, though, is to approach the wartime heroic on the level of a global typicality, one in which a Soviet text enters the contemporary Chosŏn scene not seamlessly but by way of a critical reading, a self-reflexive inquiry into the relation between fiction and reality. Hwang Kŏn's *Happiness* locates the production of a global horizon of typicality in this line of inquiry, in the doubt that arises not simply about what is felt at the moment of death but about how to approach this moment, one that exemplifies more than any other the "struggle between fiction and reality." The question is of a socialist realist thanatography, how to actualize global revolution in Chosŏn by way of a meditation on dying and death.

HAPPINESS

The war takes a turn for the worse, and Ryeju and Chŏngim finally get their wish: They are sent to the front as combat medics. "This is my battlefield! This is where my everything will be decided!" Ryeju declares.[38] The battle takes place at the Naktong River and via "the struggle within Ryeju herself."[39] While she demonstrates her competence and courage under fire, the wounded to her are little more than "objects, lifeless, machine-like."[40] She cares for them only for a few days before they are transferred to the rear, but soon she begins to see them "as precious lives, comrades-in-arms, each in possession of their own character [*kaesŏng*]."[41] This is the first step in a broader emotional and sensory recognition of the approach to death: "The expression on their faces, the sound of their voices remained in her heart [*kasŭm*], some weaker, some stronger than others. Faces and voices soon blended to form the sense of a broad, large mass, one that awakened in her the intense feeling [*kamjŏng*] that this was the front, this was the place where they needed to throw everything they had against the enemy."[42] Ryeju's consciousness brings forth "something different from actual people." Distinct characters merge, come together. The lifeless come to life in the form of image, sound, and, above all, feeling. It is here that "Ryeju felt for the first time that she had become a Chosŏn person [*Chosŏn saram*]."[43] Particular lives enter Ryeju as images and sounds that connect, overlap in a unity; this series of transformations propels Ryeju into a higher realm of typicality. Becoming-a-Chosŏn-person takes place by way of a feeling-sensory impression of the without as within.

Ryeju is soon shot herself, hit in the arm: "But even though she had been wounded, her heart was still filled with a satisfying joy [*kippŭm*]."[44] The roar of US planes continues, as does the sound of bombs falling from above, hitting the earth, *kwang kwang kwang*. Other sounds, though, fill Ryeju's

> heart with a boundless feeling of gratitude. A mix of voices. They could be the singing of patients loaded onto trucks and headed toward the rear; or the cries of soldiers shouting "*manse*" upon taking a hill from the enemy; or the shouts of

her students running after her during her teaching days; or the voices of Chŏngho and Chŏngim; or her father, mother, or siblings. For Ryeju, the "fatherland" [*choguk*] and "people" [*inmin*] mentioned by others was none other than all of these voices in and of themselves. Taking pride in youth, feeling the joy of battle—these were two different ways of speaking to the same thing. It occurred to her that all of these things came together to mean a new happiness [*haengbok*] bigger and more satisfying than anything she had known before.[45]

A remembrance of sounds from without that have moved within constitute *choguk* and *inmin*. These overlapping sounds embody images, feelings. They become a chorus of material histories, now rising through Ryeju as medium of a song of happiness that will never lose itself amid the clamor of enemy weaponry dropped from on high. The bringing together of all to form the typical does not proceed by way of prescription or formula. It must be felt. It is what happiness means.

And here is where Ryeju suddenly recalls the earlier discussion of Fadeev's *The Young Guard*. She remembers that she and Chŏngim expressed skepticism about the Krasnodon youth, that surely they would have felt sadness when confronted with death. Only Chŏngho had maintained that this would be the case: "But now she could absolutely say that in this fight with the enemy, and for the sake of the fatherland and the people, she was ready to die anytime with a peaceful feeling in her heart."[46] If Ryeju now agrees with Chŏngho, she also enters into a new relationship with the Krasnodon youth of *The Young Guard*, those who gave their lives for the revolution and the liberation of their country. She has become a Chosŏn person within an internationalist emotionscape.

The order to retreat is given. Ryeju and Chŏngim do what they can to help hundreds of wounded make it to the rear. The enemy is upon them, however, and the two take up weapons to ward off the invaders as best they can. Ryeju is hit once again. The wound is severe, and she falls to the ground: "Chŏngim, don't think of me as unhappy.... You don't know how filled with joy I am.... Go now... please go.... Don't stay behind... on my behalf.... If you make it... to the rear... tell our story to our comrades. So that they... can hate the enemy all the more.... Chŏngim."[47] *Happiness* does not mince words about retreat from the Naktong. It comes as a surprise and shock. Loss is tempered with a birth, a becoming-in-the-world. Ryeju put the words and images encountered in the novel and filmic adaptation of *The Young Guard* to the test and became a Chosŏn person by way of the deaths in Krasnodon and those of her comrades. Her own death and the loss of the southern portion of Chosŏn has produced a story of joy, happiness that will rise from where the text stops, in the ellipses that portend Ryeju's death.[48] Ryeju's story is of a journey to impending death, to the limit beyond representation. It is here, at this limit line, that *Happiness* actualizes a global revolutionary front in Chosŏn. Spatial retreat from the south becomes a temporal advance into the world-historical struggle that will continue on the peninsula.

Kim Il Sung's pivot away from the Soviet Union began in the mid-1950s, but the decisive turning point would come a decade later with a broad-based implementation of policies and cultural practices that centered his role in revolutionary history above all else (his name is referenced only once in *Happiness*, and this in relation to Kim Il Sung University). As Andrei Lankov indicates, "It took a large and concerted effort on the part of Pyongyang ideologues in the late and middle 1960s to redefine *chuch'e* as a coherent ideology and the official philosophy of the DPRK."[49] The August 1960 issue of *Chosŏn nyŏsŏng* (*Chosŏn Women*) illustrates the shift taking place in the Chosŏn-Soviet relation, even as it celebrates "everlasting friendship and solidarity between Chosŏn and the Soviet Union, liberator of our nation and provider of crucial aid."[50]

Commemorating the fifteenth anniversary of liberation from Japanese colonial rule, this issue acknowledges the Soviet Union as liberator and aid provider

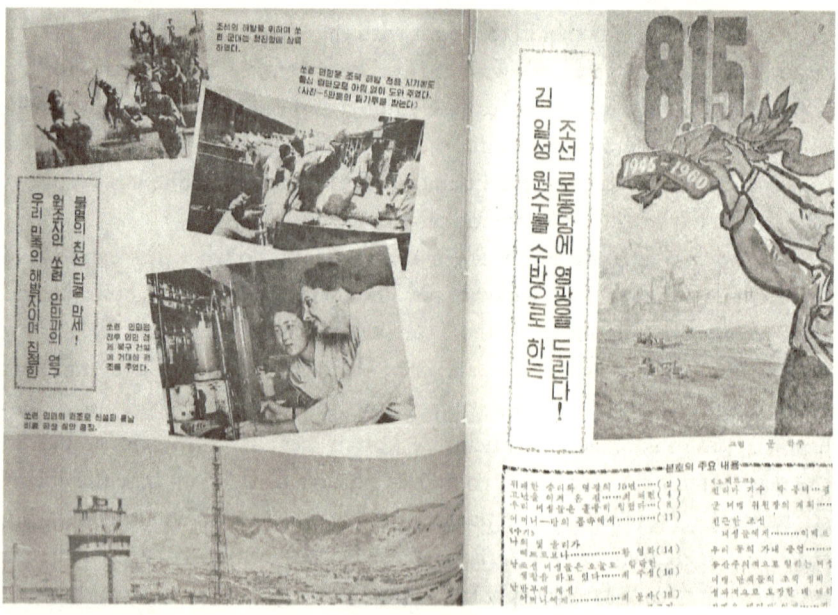

FIG. 3.5 (*Left*) A history of friendship in photographs. Soviet troops land to liberate Chosŏn; wartime Soviet donations of flour; expertise given for postwar development; renovation of the Hungnam Chemical Fertilizer Factory. (*Right*) Illustration caption: "Giving Glory to the Korean Workers Party led by Kim Il Sung." Banner in the upper right hand corner reads "Hurrah for Leader Kim Il Sung!" *Chosŏn nyŏsŏng*, August 1960.

in photographic collage, a series of instances that do not blend seamlessly with the facing page. The artistic and emotive register is reserved for the women sketched on the right. The left photographs a friendship; the right images community and revolutionary possibility under the auspices of the leader and the party. The historical horizon has shifted. This arrangement of photographs, art, and text across two consecutive pages etches an emotive border. Friendship aids, helps, even provides the material means for liberation from colonial rule but does not enter a revolutionary intimacy that looks at once to the leadership of Kim Il Sung and the past and future in Chosŏn.

Women move across the interrelated valences of martyrdom, medium, and mourning to occupy a central position in DPRK portrayals of wartime history. To sacrifice one's life in war is to approach the iconic, to lift a dead body to the life of an image that travels beyond war, circulates into the future. What happens when a woman martyr, the hero to be mourned and celebrated, appears in a hagiography that seeks to redefine revolutionary possibility? How should a bereaved war widow act, think, and feel as active participant in the postarmistice reconstruction of the DPRK? Does a new social order call for a critical reworking of gender relations that moves beyond woman as medium, dying in the name of a story to be told to those who will follow? More than any other writer, Im Sundŭk (1915–?) would proffer alternative forms of revolutionary mourning in her wartime and postarmistice work, drawing on the history of debates on proletarian women stretching back to the colonial period (1910–1945). Chapter 4 unpacks Im's thanatographic imagination as she addresses the relations among feminism, nationalism, and internationalism through 1957, the year of her disappearance from the DPRK literary scene.

CHAPTER 4

MOTION IN STILLNESS

Above a group of strong, confident women workers floats an image of Kim Il Sung. All look forward, in the same direction. The leader is still, photographic, statuesque, and monumental. The women flesh out Kim's bust into body-like form, give him shape in action. The lead-in is to the July 1960 issue of *Chosŏn nyŏsŏng* (*Chosŏn Women*). At once transcendent and corporeal, Kim guides from above and exists within.

Kim Il Sung also takes form as an image within a mass thought bubble. He is consciousness. Thoughts of the leader inhabit the smiling faces of the women. They are strong and happy. Their happiness, as frequently emphasized in *Chosŏn nyŏsŏng*, turns upon their historical emancipation. The article "15 Years of Glory and Great Victory!" declares that it was Kim Il Sung who "in the aftermath of Japanese colonial rule emphasized that construction of an independent, sovereign, democratic country would be impossible without the active and total participation of women. The proclamation of the historic Gender Equality Law soon followed on July 30, 1946."[1] This article concludes its list of the many accomplishments women have made over the past fifteen years with this: "Today women in our country are boundlessly happy. And they will be even happier in the future. This is something that can be achieved only by way of the care and consideration extended to women by Comrade Kim Il Sung and the Party and only within a socialist system."[2] Happiness stems from historical, legal emancipation (Gender Equality Law), inextricable from Kim Il Sung's benevolence and the socialist polity. Kim Il Sung's image is made whole, brought to life in women's movement, their feelings, and their work on behalf of a prosperous socialism. The performative declaration of women's happiness appears in everyday practice. Kim Il Sung appears in the world through this

FIG. 4.1 "To all women! Let's respectfully follow the teachings of the Party and the Leader. Let's continue to press forward, let's continue the revolution!" *Chosŏn nyŏsŏng*, July 1960.

on-the-ground manifestation; women partake in his look from above. The two lines of sight join in a journey to a shared future. Mass happiness involves this form of embodiment, the placing of the still, the statuesque in corporeal, visual, directed motion.

What happens if the lines of sight do not converge, if the still is not vivified, embodied but becomes itself an object of observation, reflection? What if the relation between icon and the practices of everyday life moves beyond the confluence of exhortation and declaration? Can contemplation of a photograph, a statue, or a still (which includes the image of the dead) lead to an open-ended relation between mind and body, a vitalism of consciousness and revolutionary subjectivity that does not require seamless coincidence with the benevolence and vision of leader and party?

This chapter follows the story of post-1945 women's liberation as told by the writer Im Sundŭk (1915–?). It is a story of the monumental, the martyr, the act of mourning. It is also a story that locates emancipatory possibility in the movement between consciousness and becoming in the world. It is a story of possibility, one that requires a redefinition of revolution. Such revolutionary writing can only proceed by unpacking the patriarchal habitations of icon-making, all of which hinge upon the ways in which image is set into everyday motion.

Im Sundŭk's articulations of revolutionary becoming in "Friendship" (Ujŏng, 1948), "Cho Okhŭi" (Cho Okhŭi, 1951), and "Tale of a Bereaved Family" (Ŏnŭ han yugajok ŭi iyagi, 1957) intertwine the gendered with the emancipatory across three key historical moments: The end of Soviet occupation in 1948; wartime Chosŏn; and the immediate postarmistice era. These texts intervene in concerns central to the early formation of DPRK culture and society: DPRK-Soviet Union relations; the circulation of the iconic war hero; and mid-1950s reconstruction. "Friendship" observes the manufacture of a homosocial relationship between the Soviet Union as global revolutionary leader and the decolonizing, peripheral DPRK. "Cho Okhŭi" unmakes the icon it is tasked to create, producing a consciousness and way of seeing that relocates the heroic in active opposition both to US imperialism and DPRK sexism. "Tale of a Bereaved Family" reimagines a widow's mourning for the war dead as the act of transferring strength into a present that dispenses with patrilineal praxis.

Kim Il Sung's increasing consolidation of power in the early and mid-1950s included literary and political purges. Questions as to what socialist realist writing should be and who would write it became ever more uniform, as did representations of women as helpmates, martyrs, and idealized workers. It was in this milieu that Im Sundŭk offered a series of historically situated texts carefully questioning the definition of the term "liberation" (*haebang*). And it was at its close that she disappeared from the literary scene. Im Sundŭk would go silent in 1957, her publications never to enter the DPRK canon.

A MONUMENTAL EMBRACE

Han Hyo's influential "Chosŏn Literature in the Struggle Against Naturalism" appeared in four successive installments in *Chosŏn munhak* (January–April 1953). A dire moment—the purge of major figures such as Im Hwa, Kim Namch'ŏn, and Yi T'aejun was imminent. In the final installment, Han begins his assessment of post-1945 literary history with a standard statement of gratitude: "The liberation of Chosŏn by the grand Soviet army ushered in a new and profound stage in the history of the construction of Chosŏn national literature."[3] After underscoring the emphasis that Lenin, Kim Il Sung, and Stalin placed on party-mindedness, Han declares that "Our true national culture reflects the new spiritual and ethical dimensions of all our people [*uri inmindŭl*] living under the system of people's democracy. The contents of our national culture are reflected in the daily life of our people, those living in our republic."[4] Han proceeds to laud "proletarian internationalism" while condemning a number of ROK writers for their naturalist tendencies, noting that their predilection toward eroticism, grief, anguish, and powerlessness has found its way into the DPRK. He includes Im Sundŭk's "Friendship" in this category:

> In "Friendship," the writer Im Sundŭk presents us with . . . an immature, powerless person, a deformed, cartoonish character whom she contrasts with a Soviet officer. . . . He is an idle fool who can't find his way in a time of liberation, land reform, a time when all manner of democratic reforms are taking place and the creative efforts of workers are bearing fragrant fruit. . . . The unprincipled focus on this strange, perverted [*pyŏnt'aejŏgin*] character necessarily takes a destructive turn. This is a naturalist portrayal that cannot . . . align with the essence of reality.[5]

Han concludes that this "contemptible" character is "suspicious, jealous of the relationship between the Soviet officer and his wife."[6] What to make of the strange perversion that has caused Im Sundŭk's "Friendship" to depart from a proper socialist realism?

Reprinted in the 1955 anthology *Unforgettable People: An Anthology of Chosŏn-Soviet Friendship*, Im's "Friendship" takes the form of a farewell. The third-person narration is closely aligned with Hwasuk (the text will move to first-person narration only at its close). On the eve of the Soviet army's departure from Chosŏn in October 1948, she looks back on her relationship with her husband, Seik, and their friendship with the Soviet naval officer Sserŭba. Much of "Friendship" revolves around Seik's problematic personality—his anger, ill temper, obstinacy, and coldness toward her and others. Hwasuk's marriage is extremely unhappy. Their quarrels "shrivel her with sadness, like a piece of leather soaked in water."[7] The cause, it turns out, is colonialism. Seik has suffered immense psychological pain and can't break out of it, no matter how hard Hwasuk tries to help. For Hwasuk, this is a matter of "self-emancipation." Given that Chosŏn is liberated, Seik must understand that he can follow suit. She considers her accidental meeting with Sserŭba as promising; the openhearted, optimistic Sserŭba can serve as a model of socialist being-in-the-world. "Friendship" gives no hint of Seik's jealousy or suspicion of the Hwasuk-Sserŭba relationship. Indeed, Seik grows quite close to Sserŭba, who turns out to be a mentor worthy of appearance in a Soviet socialist realist text.

Im Sundŭk's perversity lies in her reworking of a genre widely circulating in the late 1940s and early 1950s, the DPRK-Soviet friendship story. Much of the story follows expectations. Hwasuk meets Sserŭba on a truck transporting Soviet soldiers. Hwasuk is a bit nervous at first, but Sserŭba is kind to her baby, Sŭngnyong, and they strike up a conversation in Japanese. As they move along the coast of the East Sea "a conviviality and warmth emerged on the truck, like that of an intimate, happy family out on a pleasurable vacation."[8] Sserŭba later invites Hwasuk and Seik over to his place and tells them of his lover Nyura, killed in battle against the German fascists: "He seemed to fly freely through joy and sadness, like a seabird over the ocean. For Hwasuk, it was as if he had come from another world, but on second thought maybe it was she who had entered into a different world."[9] A heightening of her sensibility occurs in tandem with Seik's first step toward remaking himself. Hwasuk takes action, promoting the Seik-Sserŭba friendship while stepping herself into a new sensoryscape and broader revolutionary history. She apprehends this world much more quickly than her husband, who can be provided with a model but in the end must pull himself out of his "self-hatred," away from what both Hwasuk and Sserŭba joke is his "hypochondria."[10]

Sserŭba is benevolent, teacherly, offering a series of diagnoses: "A lingering despondency, the hope that others will bring salvation, the graveyard of ignorance. These things should not be permitted to take up space in today's Chosŏn for a single second."[11] Hwasuk responds that "suffering for so long under such oppression has rendered many people unable to burn with the proper indignation, has castrated them. So embarrassing." Hwasuk's remark, the narrator tells us, was directed less at Sserŭba than a "letting off of steam, a release of the melancholy she had been holding in for so long."[12] Sserŭba's reply:

> You blame yourself too much, Madam. Why engage in such self-accusation? . . . Only someone with a strong will can stand at the gates of victory. All of the liberated Chosŏn people are fully qualified to become the leaders of their own destiny. Why should I be emphasizing these things when you already know it? No need to trust whatever strength might be in my words. What I will always remember with fondness is the fact that we sat down together and had this conversation, that we became so close, that we shared this friendship.[13]

Im Sundŭk writes a DPRK-Soviet friendship story that is perverse because it is not fraternal. Sserŭba has little to teach Hwasuk, but his encouragement and support are necessary for Seik's rehabilitation (he will later become a diplomat).

"Friendship" concludes with a sudden move to the first-person, provided in the form of an entry in Hwasuk's diary dated October XX 1948:

> To give back to the officer who went so far as to wish our children happiness far into the future, I want to write a story that will commemorate [*kinyŏmk'oja*] something I remember so well, such an honor. For my son Sŭngnyong and for his future wife, for all of those who will follow in future generations, I wish to write in praise of a Soviet officer, in the remembrance of this name, Mihail Ppabŭrowich'i Sserŭba.[14]

Hwasuk's remembrance takes the form of direct authorship at text's close. It is she who writes of her friendship with Sserŭba, who chooses what to remember, how to record the significance of the Soviet occupation.

When Seik finally comes around and declares himself "free of pain," the third-person narration had described the two (Seik and Sserŭba) "embracing in the white winter snow like some kind of commemorative statue [*kinyŏm chogaksang*]."[15] At the close of the text, two modes of memorializing appear before its readership. The first is public, homosocial, two men hugging, embodiments of the DPRK-Soviet Union fraternal alliance and comradeship, a beautiful scene in the white winter snow. The second is the diary entry indicating Hwasuk's authoring of the story "Friendship," her recollection of her relationship with Sserŭba, her desire to push her husband and Chosŏn forward in a revolutionary history enabled by such mutuality. This second memorializing reminds us of something else. It is Hwasuk herself who has authored the third-person description of the manly embrace, the image of the statue; it is she who places the ossified moment of homosocial bonding in the snow for her readers to view.

Hwasuk's text bestows upon future generations something more than the memory of the Soviet officer, Sserŭba. The closing first-person diary entry projects itself into the future as an authorship to be remembered. Hwasuk asks her readers to look at the diary entry, consider who authors it but does not appear in stone, the perversity of revolutionary possibilities lost should such an elision harden into public memory. Hwasuk's act of writing and remembering described a heterosocial relationship and set what it considered a decolonizing, emancipatory history in motion for the future. The fraternal embrace is monumental, a statue frozen in time, still. It appears as an object of observation in the snow. But it does not travel.

BECOMING ICON

The 1952 Fatherland Liberation War Art Exhibition featured prominently in the Pyongyang press. Among critical appraisals was that of the well-known artist and critic Kil Chinsŏp, who offered his view of the "Heroes of the Republic" section:

> First of all, I must point out the consistent lack of typicality [*chŏnhyŏngsŏng*] in all of these works. A hero is neither a mythic protagonist nor one who performs superhuman acts. As one of the *inmin* [people], the hero inheres ideological and spiritual qualities that enable a concrete manifestation of firm resolve and action in a given environment or situation. The struggle for justice, the patriotic fervor that accompanies it, rises up from the *inmin* and reaches a height that empowers heroic action.[16]

The particular acts of the hero take the form of a constellation of strength, feeling, and truth drawn from the potential of the *inmin* themselves. Kil Chinsŏp's invocation of the socialist realist notion of typicality—a favorite topic in the late 1940s and early 1950s DPRK—prefaces his critique of individual artworks, Mun Haksu's famous painting of Cho Okhŭi serving as first example. The choice is understandable. A partisan killed during the US/UN occupation of the DPRK following the loss of Seoul in late September 1950, Cho Okhŭi was officially designated a "Hero of the People's Democratic Republic of Korea" in 1951, the first woman to receive this honor. She has since been immortalized in nonfiction, fiction, art, film, and a school has been named in her honor (Cho Okhŭi Teacher's College).[17]

For Kil Chinsŏp, situation and feelings exist in a mutually constitutive relation, the extremity of the former allowing the latter to rise to the level of the typical:

> In terms of composition and its evocation of feelings Mun Haksu's "Cho Okhŭi, Hero" is a good painting. But the portrayal of Cho Okhŭi's derision for the enemy is lacking. The bastards would have been perplexed by her ideological steadfastness, how cool and calm she was as she was taken to her place of execution. And, in response, their animal-like brutality would have completely revealed itself. But the painting gives us the impression they are going about their business unperturbed. Nor do we see any vestiges, any details of the cruel torture inflicted upon Cho Okhŭi, just a loosely tied rope. An emphasis on the negative would have animated Cho Okhŭi's unruffled demeanor.[18]

FIG. 4.2.1 AND FIG. 4.2.2 (*Top*) Mun Haksu, *Cho Okhŭi, Hero* (1952). (*Bottom*) *The Young Guard* (1948). Courtesy of International Historic Films.

Mun Haksu's painting routinizes violence and hinders a proper response, a heightened expression of the *inmin*'s resolve. If contrast between *inmin* and enemy is lacking, the painting does not depict that which its title promises, Cho Okhŭi as hero. Nor then does the painting provide the expression, material (marks of violence), and emotions (derision) that constitute the Fatherland Liberation War itself.[19]

Mun Haksu's painting, in fact, locates typicality elsewhere. His work clearly alludes to the well-known closing sequence of Sergei Gerasimov's 1948 *The Young Guard*, a film based on the actual underground resistance mounted against Nazi occupation by the Komsomol organization in Krasnodon (see chapter 3). Mun, in fact, replicates the mise-en-scène in which a series of Young Guard members (including Oleg Koshevoy, posthumously given the title of Hero of the Soviet Union), are brought forward at the moment of their execution. Mun's painting seeks what we might call an intervisual typicality, a heightening of the experience of the Chosŏn *inmin* via participation in a broader Soviet canvas. Cho Okhŭi shares with the bound Young Guard members a determined look askance, to the left and beyond the frame of the particular situation, to a place within the history of revolutionary struggle. The Fatherland Liberation War folds into the Great Patriotic War. The typicality of the hero lies in this overlap, in this visual entering of the *inmin* into an "environment or situation" that is itself a coalescence of places and times moving together into a shared mise-en-scène, a collective future.

Mun Haksu was not the first to image a heroic Cho Okhŭi. Im Sundŭk's short story "Cho Okhŭi" appeared in *Munhak yesul* (*Literary Arts*) in June 1951, the issue preceding the first installment of Han Hyo's *Seoul People* (see chapter 3). Here, too, the question at hand would involve the definition of *inmin*. For what and whom does Cho Okhŭi die? Can we consider an action heroic if it does not include gender equality in revolutionary practice? Will the heroic subsume such questions in the name of the *inmin* and the typical or serve as vehicle to address them?

If Mun Haksu seeks a horizon for the typical that Kil Chinsŏp fails to recognize, neither considers the possibility of presenting the image of Cho Okhŭi in relation to proletarian women's struggle for equality.[20] Im Sundŭk's "Cho Okhŭi" offers another take on typicality, an attempt to move beyond the call to make the markings of martyrdom or internationalist solidarity visible. How to tell the story of a hero consistently referred to as the first "woman hero" (*nyŏsŏng yŏng'ung*)? "Cho Okhŭi" becomes a story about icon-making itself, and this will involve a reflection on the relations among heroism, Kim Il Sung, and death.

The portrayal of Kim Il Sung was not a given, as a number of articles in the late 1940s and 1950s make clear. Ŏm Hosŏk begins his "The Portrayal of General Kim in Chosŏn Literature" (May 1950) by citing a 1938 remark on Lenin made by the British proletarian writer Harold Heslop: "Lenin's form can be described in the widest range of artistic modalities. This is because Lenin embodied the October Revolution, the wellspring from which all future possibilities trace their origin. The truth of these words pertains to portrayals of our General Kim Il Sung as well."[21] Ŏm then provides empirical evidence for this applicability of truth: "When the vicious exploitation of the lawless Japanese Empire subjected the Chosŏn people to suffering and despair . . . the people, both within and without Chosŏn, rose up in a patriotic resistance . . . and it was General Kim Il Sung who directly embodied and led this struggle, this revolutionary tradition, this fight for national liberation."[22] If Lenin embodies the past (the October Revolution) that secures the entirety of the future, the portrayal of Kim Il Sung operates in parallel truth. Kim Il Sung serves as the fount of future possibilities based on his embodiment of anti-Japanese revolutionary struggle. And more, Kim Il Sung was the leader of a revolutionary struggle for national liberation that also furthered the international revolutionary cause:

> The revolutionary activities of the Chosŏn Liberation Front simultaneously took the form of an anti-Japanese patriotic struggle to liberate the fatherland and a means to ward off the attacks of the Japanese imperialists on the Soviet Union and China. We see, then, that . . . these struggles took place in an organic relation with internationalist, anti-fascist movements. The particular dignity of General Kim Il Sung, his elevated standing, stems from this internationalism.[23]

It is the general who designates "Heroes of the Republic," approximations enabled by his embodiment of fatherland, his participation in the global revolution.

Im Sundŭk's "Cho Okhŭi," the first literary text to describe this eponymous hero whose fame has survived to the present day, frames her life and death in close relation to the general. Okhŭi lays everything on the line and dies fearlessly. We learn that she is from a poor farming family, a widow whose husband died in the mines during Okhŭi's pregnancy. As the text begins, Okhŭi has already left her child with her mother and joined a group of partisans operating in the hills around Mount Chinam in South Hwanghae Province. She has not, however, left without regret. We find her looking through a box of photographs and other keepsakes and feeling "an almost unendurable affection for her own flesh and blood, the kind of pain she would feel when about to breastfeed."[24] But then she comes across a photograph of the general: "The tears she had been holding inside finally burst forth. Okhŭi gazed upon the general for some time, sobbing quietly, the realization of why she had become a partisan striking her forcefully. 'As one of the *inmin*, how could I too not follow your model, you who sacrificed your youth fighting for the freedom and independence of Chosŏn?' "[25] The heroic model of the general trumps Okhŭi's feelings of motherhood, legitimizes her departure from mothering itself. As Okhŭi addresses the general she makes a claim. She too is one of the *inmin*, the people. But how to define *inmin*? This question leads to the text's central inquiry: How is Cho Okhŭi, as a woman, to follow the general's model? The answer to this question will rest upon yet another definition, that of the heroic.

"Cho Okhŭi" occurs in third-person narration aligned with Okhŭi's POV on her life and death. Her bravery in combat, love of fatherland and revolution, sense of sacrifice, and martyrdom at the hands of an implacable enemy (the United States and its allies) serve as guideposts for her elevation to hero. The kind of cruelty and animallike brutality Kil Chinsŏp will later call for in his critique of Mun Haksu's depiction of Cho Okhŭi are not lacking. Im's work, though, addresses the issue of typicality in a way that does not enter Kil Chinsŏp's prescription for wartime art. Okhŭi finds herself in a situation that is not generalizable to all *inmin*. She faces another enemy, the sexism of her fellow partisans. How can she serve as emblematic of the potential of the *inmin* in the face of an antagonist who is not radically other?

The model of the general calls for approximation, but we learn quickly that Okhŭi's response to this summoning has met barriers. Okhŭi has performed a variety of duties, even been on recon missions, "but her desire was to participate in actual combat at least once. It seemed doubtful, though, that HQ would approve such a request."[26] After all, Okhŭi had just barely been able to join the partisans. The enemy was pushing north into the Ongjin Peninsula in October 1950, and comrades in the local party leadership had urged her to flee: "Comrade, you have a woman's body. And a child. We ask you, please, retreat to the rear, to a safe place."[27] The date February 13, 1947 flashes before Okhŭi's eyes—the date she had become a party member: "How her heart had fluttered that day, how she had resolved to live unashamed, as a Chosŏn person."[28] She makes an impassioned speech, asks her comrades to consider how she has contributed to the struggle, how she cannot bear to depart from their midst in such a desperate situation. All are moved, and the "local party leader comes over to give her his assent with a hearty shake of the hand."[29] Okhŭi has invoked the general as model. She is a party member and Chosŏn person. Will the party match its own assertion of gender equality in practice? Will the party accept her willingness to die in combat as a Chosŏn person?

Political Affairs Officer Kim Sungyong informs Okhŭi that there is no need for her to do combat duty. Okhŭi unhesitatingly disagrees, which leads to his angry retort that it would be best if she spent her time darning socks: "This is what we need right now from you, not your presence on a recon mission or up at the front line."[30] An argument ensues, and Kim turns to affirmative labels: Okhŭi is a "highly valued woman leader," which means "it is her duty to keep herself safe for the sake of the entire partisan unit." Her gendered role as one of the *inmin* is clear: "If you don't accept this reality, you'll have shown that you're mired in narcissism, nothing but a poisonous element."³¹ Kim then invokes familial intimacy. Okhŭi should also do the cooking, since she is "the mother, the older sister for our unit."³² Will Okhŭi accept a role as woman helpmate? The partisan commander assures Okhŭi that HQ has authorized the proper duties for her: " 'Please don't push too hard. It's equal rights between men and women, isn't it? That's what's on your mind, right?' He asked in a tone that was slightly cutting."³³ Okhŭi's response: "Comrade Commander, please don't mock me in that way. Is there anything men can do that I can't?"³⁴

The commander comes around eventually and indicates his complete confidence that Okhŭi can handle a combat situation. Okhŭi's struggle has been successful. She is grateful for the acknowledgment and "burns with excitement . . . as she imagines herself side by side with him on the front line."³⁵ Her path to heroism can now proceed.

Okhŭi will enter one of many massacre scenes we find in wartime DPRK literature. She has already heard of the atrocities committed by the *migungnom* (American bastards) in the village below. She can't bear the images that appear in her mind: "young, healthy children stuffed into ammo storage sheds and set on fire, young women in torn skirts, writhing, putting up as much resistance as they can, their husbands and brothers away at the front."³⁶ She will shortly move from secondhand stories to direct witnessing not of massacre but the fantasy frame within which massacre takes place.

Okhŭi's unit makes its advance through a forest and comes across a group of *migungnom* engaging in a barbaric night feast on tender, young beef. These " 'civilized' American cannibals" seek the "thrills and orgasms" of the night, all part of their "travel in the mysterious orient."³⁷ As they slobber down the meat, "tastier than a Chicago beefsteak," one of the "beasts" (*chŭmsaeng*) declares that "war is actually something quite pleasurable." To which another replies: "Yeah, but this meat here isn't enough to satisfy me. What I need is a juicier piece of flesh! Hahaha."³⁸ The partisans attack. Okhŭi ends up skewering the *migungnom* who made the beefsteak remark with her bayonet, twisting him into the fire. Orientalist fantasy meets the proletarian-national real. If the first stage of Okhŭi's hagiography-as-thanatography—the story of an icon in the making that is at once a being-toward-death—involves doubts, arguments among comrades that take place on the level of the everyday, she now stands in a place where the human has become animal. It is here, where the enemy's fantasy frame transmogrifies to implacable cannibalistic evil, that Okhŭi crosses a threshold into the iconic.

Okhŭi will now face the enemy's massive weaponry, the destruction it delivers from the heavens. This is a violence so terrible it seems unreal. Enemy jets circle above, while ferocious attack dogs ("shepherds," in transliterated English) are let loose on the ground. The enemy is at once animallike and altogether nonhuman, no different than the technology/weaponry it brings to bear on Chosŏn. Twin-engine planes throw loads of napalm onto the hills, turning them into a "sea of fire."[39] But even as the enemy surrounds the partisans with such destructive capability at its disposal, Okhŭi "knows absolutely what her own power can do.... And she knows she must multiply this power of hers a hundred times over."[40] The fight with the enemy has "transformed Okhŭi into a 'ball of fire, filled with patriotism.' "[41] Napalm meets the flames of heroic passion and purpose.

Okhŭi cuts down the enemy soldiers, who "tremble before her in fear, like leaves in the frost."[42] She kills over thirty enemy soldiers, trampling over their corpses, pushing forward. Finally, she is brought down, taking shrapnel from a 60 mm gun fired wildly by an enemy soldier running away in retreat. She is captured and her martyrdom begins: Harrowing days and nights in an underground room "filled with groans and corpses." She is interrogated, tortured sadistically. As Okhŭi's flesh burns, a British soldier (*yŏnggungnom*) screams excitedly that they will soon reach a "climax" (in transliterated English). Okhŭi is left crushed on the floor. But she does not capitulate. She thinks of the fields and streams of Hwanghae Province and the fatherland: "How can I regret shedding my blood and giving my life for the sake of this land?"[43]

On the day of Okhŭi's execution, "Thoughts swirled about in her mind."[44] She recalls her childhood, her mother, the sweat enveloping her body when she gave birth, her feeling like a bird alone in a forest after her husband's death, the joy of the August 15, 1945 liberation from Japanese colonial rule, becoming a party member, being deeply moved by the portrait of a young Stalin she had come across on the day she graduated from the party academy:

> All of these things, the ups and downs—weren't they the symphony that had made up her life?
> Okhŭi quietly closed her eyes.
> So many images of people she longed to see appeared before her. The cold wall of her prison cell, smeared with blood and flesh, was now a fresh and clean screen for her memory [*kiŏk ŭi sŭkŭrin*].[45]

Okhŭi transforms her impending death into a shared experience of her life, a biopic drawn from her own memory, screened on the cell wall. Here is what will be the synopsis of the story, "Cho Okhŭi." Her declaration of sacrificial death extends itself to the future, serves as caption for the images she names and those she doesn't, the presences and absences projected on the wall for an implied audience. "Cho Okhŭi" is a prescient text, reflecting on that which is to be circulated, sensationalized in public memory and that which actually took place but is to be lowlighted, eventually edited out of the picture. The former speaks to the movement from childhood to adulthood in tandem with an emancipatory history, a decolonization mediated by identification with the party and proletarian internationalism. The latter asks what will be left out.

"Cho Okhŭi" is an inflection of the proletarian true story (*silgi* or *sirhwa*), a socialist realist genre in the DPRK. This thanatography-as-hagiography shows at its close (the moment of impending death) how icon-making rests upon a curated narrative of the typical. Beyond the summary that is to serve as symphony is the past itself, as it has just been told to us in "Cho Okhŭi." This history tells us of the otherwise, of the manifestation of the heroic in the atypical, in the mundanity of everyday sexism. From the beginning, Okhŭi's story is framed in twofold terms: She must battle both the various attempts to feminize her within the ranks of the *inmin* and the enemy's animallike violence without. The desire to protect Chosŏn women by relegating them to gendered wartime roles and the enemy's lascivious urge to violate Chosŏn women occupy a sexist continuum. Okhŭi's heroism stands against the sustained reproduction of gendered roles within the *inmin*, while serving as commentary on the requisite and the sanctioned, the fable-like heroism and goblin-like evil that marks Okhŭi's apotheosis. The latter heroism, it turns out, obscures the former, precisely in the name of that which makes up the typical, the realm of heroic sacrifice.

The general returns as the text ends. Okhŭi recalls seeing his face prior to the war, in the square in May: "And below him, all the flags swaying in the wind. Ah, the joy the *inmin* felt in their hearts."[46] The invocation is of a crowd scene, a demonstration of mass happiness. The general's face expresses an emancipatory promise that resides in the movement of the *inmin* into the realm of the typical. "Cho Okhŭi" concludes with a death that remembers this joy as a moment in time.

MOURNING AS PRAXIS OF THE PRESENT

In "Portrayal of the Working Class and Several Problems of Aesthetics," Ŏm Hosŏk follows Vladimir Ermilov when he declares that "To emphasize the beauty of everyday life is to locate the new that resides within life while looking ahead to the elimination of the old."⁴⁷ Ermilov himself draws on Nikolai Chernyshevsky, declaring that "Chernyshevsky's famous thesis, 'beauty is life,' can now be recodified for us as a postulate meaning that beauty is our socialist reality, our victorious movement toward communism."⁴⁸ Ŏm cites *The Tale of Ch'unhyang* as historical example of "the beauty residing in the lofty [*kosanghan*] features of the people engaged in a struggle to transform the ideal into reality . . . and hatred [*chŭngo*] of the ugly and base."⁴⁹ Ch'unhyang, the tale's heroine, is to perform as the sign of the people's struggle, a medium conferring beauty upon the lofty realization of the ideal. The location of beauty in everyday life aestheticizes a temporal, perceptual, and emotional order; the new/future folds into a contemporary moment that includes the old/past. It is the process itself of rejecting this last as ugly, an object of hatred that constitutes the beautiful and propels history forward.

Such oppositions—new/beautiful vs. old/ugly—would prove important in the postarmistice DPRK, where the task at hand was to build a new socialism from the ashes of wartime destruction. Im Sundŭk's "Tale of a Bereaved Family" (1957) addresses this aesthetic frame, as well as the push for socialist transformation of the economy that would move into high gear with the implementation of the first five-year plan (1957–1961) and the subsequent formation of the Ch'ŏllima Movement.⁵⁰ How to transform the ugly into the beautiful in everyday practice? Im's work locates this movement in the proper mourning of the war dead. Such remembrance will entail a reworking of the role dead men are to play in the present. To enact this transformation is to partake in the beautiful, the creation of the new from the old that inhabits the postarmistice everyday in the form of the official category "bereaved family."

Chŏngdŏk, protagonist of "Bereaved," struggles following the death of her husband (massacred during the US occupation of her village) and brother-in-law (killed at the front). Her sister-in-law, Okkŭm, has run off with another man, leaving Chŏngdŏk to look after her father-in-law, two of his children, her brother-in-law's child, and her own child. At the same time, she is the leader of a section in the village workers collective, the only woman to hold such a position.

A package addressed to the principal of the village school arrives on International Women's Day (March 8th). The package, which includes no return address, contains a letter asking that the gifts—school-related items—be given to the three children in Chŏngdŏk's care who attend the school. The young school principal jumps at the opportunity to make a statement about this act of kindness at a school meeting:

It appears that this package is the expression of respect from the *inmin* for the model [*mobŏm*] bereaved family of Comrade Yu Chŏngdŏk. I believe that Comrade Yu Chŏngdŏk will continue to foster a family that will serve as a model for children's education and that she herself will become a model for others as our village of Munulli pushes to increase agricultural production.⁵¹

Chŏngdŏk, though, is familiar with Okkŭm's writing and knows it was she who sent the package. But she self-censors, keeps her knowledge to herself. Critiques of formulaism and bureaucratic inefficiency have always been given leeway in the DPRK, provided they serve as correctible deviations hindering the proper path to socialist modernization. Here, though, it is the invocation of the terms *inmin*, *mobŏm*, and *yugajok* that give pause.⁵² A knowledgeable silence travels among these words, spoken on International Women's Day.

By the time the package arrives, "Bereaved" has already shown ample interest in contradiction, unsure desires (including, quite possibly, sexual desires) that do not conform to those of a widow, head of a model bereaved family. We are privy to Chŏngdŏk's thoughts of isolation, "I'll get by under my own power. I can't trust that someone will appear, that something will drop down for me from the heavens!"⁵³ We have also seen Chŏngdŏk's skills in action as leader of a newly-formed collective comprised of other bereaved families and impoverished farmers whose lands had been decimated by the war. She is, moreover, fully aware of the mores of mourning. She knows well that thinking of the children in the family she now heads as burdensome goes against the "way of the heavens" (*ch'ŏndo*).⁵⁴ She respects what was asked of her in war: "Could her husband and brothers-in-law have left their hometown and confidently faced the enemy's guns without placing their trust in this one woman, Yu Chŏngdŏk, to care for their parents, to raise their children? How could they have remained brave to the bitter end, warding off the enemy's hilltop charges?"⁵⁵ The local people's committee offers Chŏngdŏk special privileges, educational opportunities, to make things easier for her family, but she refuses:

> Chŏngdŏk found herself shaking her head. And then her face reddened with anger.
> "What are you saying?. . . . Why should I be treated as a guest in this village? Really?"
> She clasped her chest, hands trembling.
> Others may think as they will, she had served as secretary of the people's committee, she belonged to a bereaved family, a family that had suffered massacre. And wasn't she also a woman party member, a person who knew party

principles, who understood that her mission was to devote herself courageously to the country's destiny?[56]

Chŏngdŏk's rejection of sympathy and assistance appears to push her elevation to model widow of postarmistice mobilization forward. But something else happens that crosses a line: "No one ordered Chŏngdŏk to say such words. They fell from her lips of their own accord. In her voice, Chŏngdŏk felt something other than herself, a strength coming from others. It was none other than the strength of her father-in-law, her husband who had died all too young, her brothers-in-law who had left her. She felt it rising within her body, coursing through her veins."[57] Chŏngdŏk mourns these dead men as living within her body and spirit. The war dead do not simply give strength to a revolutionary present. She feels the dead within her, on her own accord. They come alive in her voice sans the mediation of state-sponsored memorialization. "Bereaved" tells the story of rejection of the easy invocation of the "model" in favor of a vitalist mourning that converts patrilineal loss into the creation of the new. Chŏngdŏk pays respect to the deaths of the men in her family by altering the lines of transmission, no longer from father to son. She feels and figures their sacrifice as giving life to her embodied, revolutionary leadership in the everyday. Such is the proper form of mourning, away from the ugliness of formulaism and the invocation of static, generic categories (devoid of life, deathlike).

As "Bereaved" comes to a close, Chŏngdŏk literally experiences an awakening to the present. She has trouble sleeping: "Over the past thirty years of her life there had never been a time like this, when she couldn't sleep because of the expansive sense of power she was feeling, because of her excitement."[58] We learn that under her leadership, the cooperative workers' "hearts are now completely filled with the vision of the schools and factories that will appear in in five years' time in the very spot where their grain is now stored."[59] Chŏngdŏk stands in the midst of this new history: "Hers was a mind that might not have been able to sleep, but she could watch the pinkish light of the morning emerge in the east, as if ushering in a new spirit [*sae chŏngsin*]."[60] Her awakening accords with the beauty of the new day.

Munhak sinmun (*Literary Weekly*) devotes considerable space in its September 19, 1957 issue to Kim Chaeha's "Upon Reading 'Tale of a Bereaved Family.'"[61] While largely positive, Kim's review implicitly rewrites "Bereaved." Kim lauds the author's "lofty humanism" (*kosanghan indojuŭi*), approves of its emotive force (*ppap'osŭ*), and calls attention to Chŏngdŏk's "awareness of the warm and comforting breast of the people's government."[62] Implicit prescription, though, moves to directive where the act of mourning is concerned: "The image of her husband should have touched Chŏngdŏk more deeply . . . a clearer image of the husband would have sharpened the story. . . . And we hope that in the future the author will widen her canvas while maintaining the positive aspects of women's lives we find in this work."[63] Chŏngdŏk is to mourn her husband properly. This directive would shortly take collective form. The Critics Committee's roundup of recently published works in the December 5, 1957 issue of *Munhak sinmun* puts it this way: "In 'Tale of a Bereaved Family,' the wise father-in-law is portrayed more vividly than the protagonist Chŏngdŏk. At the same time, how can it be that a portrayal of the person closest to her, her husband, does not appear?"[64] Here, the portrayal of Chŏngdŏk's thoughts, desires, sensory, and historical transformation is to blur in relation to the memories of her supportive father-in-law and the injunction to commemorate her husband appropriately. The relocation of the strength of the familial war dead into the body, words, and new consciousness of a woman leader has no place in the aesthetic economy of the beautiful and the ugly, new and old. This line of transmission stands outside of revolutionary historymaking.[65] No record of Im Sundŭk's work appears after "Bereaved."

Chŏngdŏk reworks mourning and Im Sundŭk disappears into silence within what we might call a warscape, a crisscrossing of war-related representations central to the wartime and postarmistice imagining of gender relations, the social order, and history itself. Such a warscape does not rest within the combat zone (the area in which combat deaths, both military and civilian, occur). The topography of the warscape includes not only deaths in the combat zone but also references, allusions to war and the war-related dead, to multiple forms and varying degrees of death. The combat zone is cacophonous but riddled with silence, the production of inert bodies that no longer speak but offer themselves visually to description, analysis, and memorying. To think of the combat zone as proliferative, assuming multiple inflections in a broader array of representations (a warscape) is to open the possibility of a border crossing that moves beyond the comparable and into the realm of the incommensurable. The war dead travel—in unequal numbers.

Part III turns to the idea of limited war and associated modes of mourning, sacrifice, aesthetics, and gendered belonging that settle upon a border at ocean's edge, the far shore of the American Lake. The address will be to the play of limits and limitlessness that comprise something called the "free world."

PART III

There was only one catch and that was Catch-22, which specified that a concern for one's safety in the face of dangers that were real and immediate was the process of a rational mind. Orr was crazy and could be grounded. All he had to do was ask; and as soon as he did, he would no longer be crazy and would have to fly more missions. Orr would be crazy to fly more missions and sane if he didn't, but if he was sane he had to fly them. If he flew them he was crazy and didn't have to; but if he didn't want to he was sane and had to.[1]

The catch binds. There really is no way out. Anchoring Joseph Heller's *Catch-22* to a single, bounded-off referent might provide a degree of solace. To do so would be to elide the fact that Heller spent nearly all of the 1950s writing his famous work, a portion of which was first published as "Catch-18" (*New World Writing*, April 1955).

In a 1975 *Playboy* interview, Heller makes it clear that nearly all of his characters in *Catch-22* (1961) are "products of an imagination that drew on American life in the postwar period. The Cold War, really. I deliberately seeded the book with anachronisms like loyalty oaths, helicopters, IBM machines and agricultural subsidies to create the feeling of American society from the McCarthy period on."[2] His interlocutor, though, appears not to register this remark, asking a moment later if Heller had returned from World War II with *Catch-22* "rattling around in his head." Heller: "As I've said, *Catch-22* wasn't really about World War Two. It was about American society during the Cold War, during the Korean War, and about the possibility of Vietnam."[3]

Catch-22 is not "about" World War II but the period in which it was written. Heller spent the 1950s writing a book that described how war filtered into the social fabric, how military bureaucracy and routinization wove their way into "American society." *Catch-22* is about bombing runs from the fictional island of Pianosa, paper trails that create their own realities, R&R sites that exist as a world unto themselves. *Catch-22* is not about war as event but as mode, duration. *Catch-22* is about the Korean War because the latter was not a war. And there will be no need to declare future wars since they are wars that are not wars.

The catch organizes around a fear of potential death, as does the idea of limited war. It would be crazy to call a war limited that gives rise to innumerable deaths and disappearances and sane if you didn't. But if you were sane you could still be mobilized to fight it. Round and round, endlessly—and the result is limitlessness. Part III of this book does not seek to remember what was forgotten but to follow the story of the Korean War morphing into multilayered, permanent mobilization in the 1950s. Left behind will be the first-world, managerial figuring of war as cold, hot, or hot-within-the-overarching-cold (the idea of the hot spot). This is the story of a war that was not a war and ended without an end (the logic of armistice as it informs continuous militarization). Is armistice itself the catch? This story will move from the gendered mourning of potential death central to the creation of a transpacific border, across narratives of reluctance, skepticism, antiwar humanism, and into the limitlessness of the skies and the mind. The story's end will be a departure that is an arrival, at the universal breaking point (the place where concern for one's own safety overrides all), where the inevitable desire to quit morphs into a flexible and modulating discourse of mobilization-as-empowerment. Here is where the catch will cross into the twilight zone.

CHAPTER 5

OCEAN'S EDGE

The October 1953 cover of the *Bulletin of the Atomic Scientists* updates the Doomsday Clock, moving it to two minutes to midnight. This revision (the first since 1949) responds to the US test of a thermonuclear device on Eniwetok Atoll in the Pacific Marshall Islands in November 1952 and a subsequent Soviet test in Kazakhstan in August 1953. The *Bulletin*'s editor, biophysicist Eugene Rabinowitch, informs his readers that "Only a few more swings of the pendulum, and, from Moscow to Chicago, atomic explosions will strike midnight for Western Civilization."[4] Rabinowitch calls for a tripartite policy to address the precarious situation. First, educate the public on the destructive capacities of atomic and thermonuclear weapons. Better that fear is "rational, deep, and permanent, not uninformed and volatile."[5] Second, "make aggression clearly unprofitable."[6] This entails a twofold policy of capacity for retaliation and defensive measures to reduce the impact of an attack. Finally, and Rabinowitch considers this the most important point, foster a global network of alliances, "a functional and organizational unity, binding all its nation members by the bonds of the mutual economic advantage of a large free-trade area, and commanding a constantly growing legal and spiritual allegiance of their peoples."[7] Recent history makes this need clear: "The experience of the two world wars, as well as of the Korean war, indicates that the greatest danger of war lies not in a sudden frontal attack on the main antagonist, but in a miscalculated attack on a minor member of the opposing coalition, based on a mistaken hope for impunity."[8] If the Doomsday Clock folds temporality into space envisioned as at once expanding, legal, and spiritual, the emotional frame requires a psychology, a mental preparedness. The call is to a state of readiness predicated upon the production and management of fear.

The San Francisco and ANZUS treaties, both ratified during the Korean War in 1951, were central to the organization of a military network of bases and alliances meant to secure the Asia Pacific as "American Lake." This network stretched from the west coast of the continental United States (CONUS) through Guam, Hawai'i, the Philippines, Taiwan, Japan, and Korea, to New Zealand and Australia. The 1953 armistice ending the combat phase of the Korean War would result in permanent US bases on the Asian mainland, at network's edge. Far East Command (established in 1947) became Pacific Command in 1957. Multiple points of conflict or potential conflict—in particular Korea but also the Taiwan Strait Crises—would inform the changing distribution of assets in the Pacific, itself one command among others spread across the globe and CONUS.

Much of this did little to capture US public attention in the 1950s, let alone give the films *One Minute to Zero* (dir. Tay Garnet) and its companion piece, *Sabre Jet* (dir. Louis King), box office success. Both *One Minute to Zero* and *Sabre Jet*—the first released in 1952 during the Korean War, the second in September 1953, immediately following the armistice—dwell on the presentation of a Japan that is not only domesticated but central to the US war effort in Korea, a model host nation for the forward projection of US power across the Asia Pacific

The prominent *New York Times* film critic Bosley Crowther concludes his sardonic list of the standard fare offered in *One Minute to Zero* with this: "And there are even the wives of pilots who stand at the air base awaiting their return from battle missions. (What the ladies are doing in Korea is never explained.) Plainly, 'One Minute to Zero' is a ripely synthetic affair, arranged to arouse emotions with the most easy and obvious clichés.... Here is another war picture that smells of grease paint and studios."[9] The explanation Crowther seeks will not arrive: He cannot see the transpacific border-making *One Minute to Zero* is at considerable pains to present. The "ladies" reside at Itazuke Air Base in Japan. Nor do they await the return of their husbands. They stand in bodily and emotional readiness, poised to the possibility of no return. Embodying a recognition of potential loss, they make virtual death visible on screen. And it is virtual death that structures ideas of escalation, retaliation, and mutually assured destruction. The path to a gendered recognition of duty is opened to women in *One Minute to Zero*, as it will also be in *Sabre Jet*. These women will need to grow into this exemplary work, serve as models for others, including those who are stateside. They will exemplify something that moves, mobilizes beyond words—to a point where the secular meets the religious. Their story, then, is of another temporality, of proleptic mourning, mourning ahead of time. And this temporality, too, is of limited war, itself anticipatory of its own, continuous (limitless) necessity.

THE CLOCK IS TICKING

The film Crowther finds lacking in verisimilitude aims to show how limited war will proceed in the post-1945 era. Funded by aviation industrialist and RKO studio head Howard Hughes, *One Minute to Zero* screens an intricate, intertwined set of emotional and organizational relationships. We view horizontal lines of flight, vertical drops (bombs and supplies) to combat units in Korea, all taking place via a closely coordinated communication network that includes pilots, HQ, and tactical radio operators calling in strikes on the ground. This arrangement is personified by the story of two colonels, Steve Janowski (Robert Mitchum) and John Parker (William Talman), the former a US Army infantry officer on the ground in Korea, the latter a US Air Force pilot providing air support. Their fraternal relationship signals what should be proper interoperability (interservice cooperation) within the newly formed Department of Defense and United States Air Force (both created by the 1947 National Security Act). Indeed, *One Minute To Zero* was produced at the behest of the DoD, with the request that ground-air cooperation take center stage.[10] Such a request reflects the importance of the Korean War as testing ground for interoperability. As Richard Hallion notes, "Although the USAF performance in Korea has been largely seen through the simplistic prism of Sabre versus MiG, and B-29 operations against the North, in fact counter-air sorties accounted for only 14 percent of all air force combat sorties."[11] *One Minute To Zero* addresses a central modality of the Korean War, given that "80 percent of all combat sorties furnished direct or indirect combat support to Korea's ground warriors: as live fire, ISR (intelligence, surveillance and reconnaissance) or matériel."[12]

One Minute to Zero also tackles the conflict between UN-centered idealism (diplomacy/humanitarian aid) and a realist stance that brings US military power/practicality to bear. This conflict is played out via the romantic relationship of Linda Day (Ann Blyth), a US-UN worker who speaks French, and Steve. Widow of a decorated World War II pilot, Linda seeks meaning in UN ideals; Steve is a retread infantry officer in full possession of an offhand, confident manner typical of Mitchum's characters. Both find themselves in Seoul on the eve of war, with Linda declaring that the UN mandate establishing the ROK will prevent an invasion from the North. Steve disagrees. He is all for allies, including UN allies, but only the ones that understand realpolitik, when and where force must be used (the featured UN combat allies in *One Minute to Zero* will be a British infantry battalion and a Royal Australian Air Force unit). Steve will be proven correct.

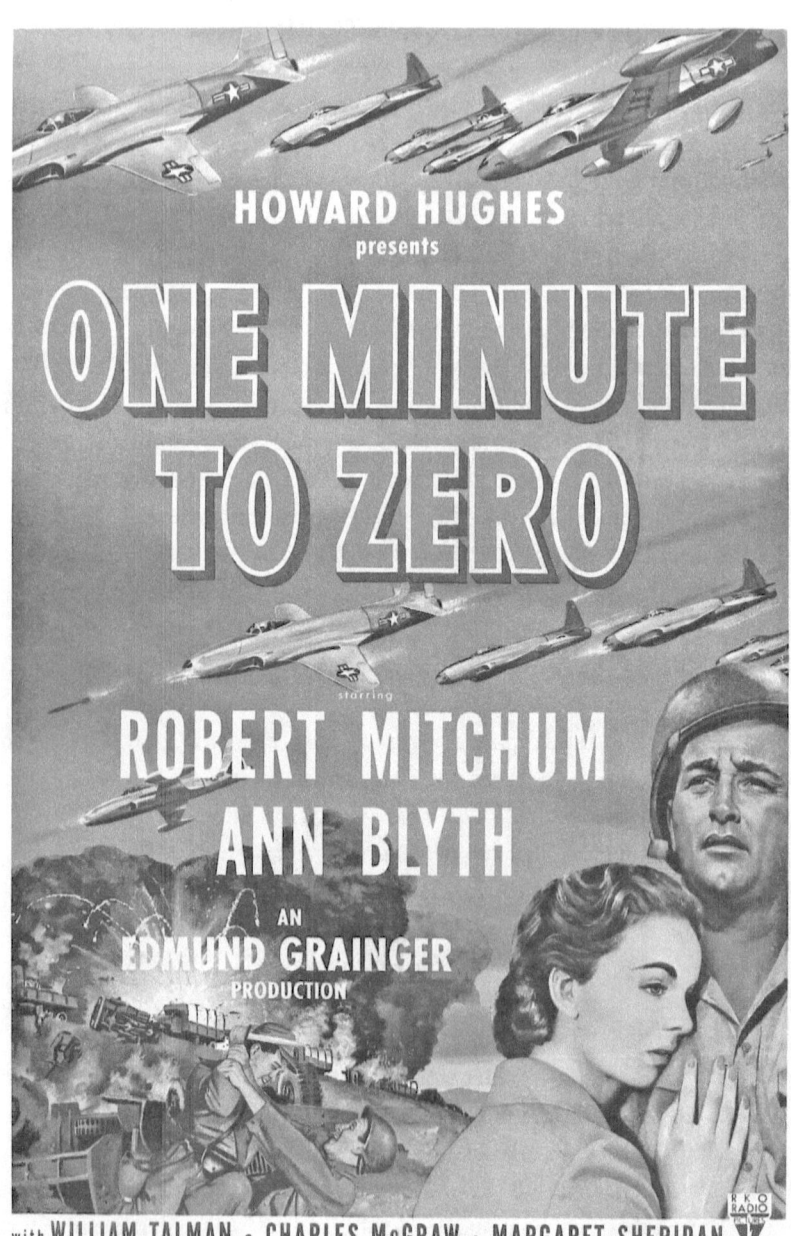

FIG. 5.1 *One Minute to Zero* (poster). Everett Collection, Alamy.

As Seoul comes under aerial bombardment, Steve hoists a reluctant Linda over his shoulder to get her on a plane out of Korea and to Itazuke. A diegetic map establishes their arrival, followed by a dissolve into USAF Command and Control. Bombing runs originate from Itazuke. John lives here, as does his wife (and the women Crowther mistakenly sees in Korea).

Clear-cut military victory is not at stake in this 1952 wartime film. Steve declares early on that "We're not going to win this war, but we're not going to lose it." The formation of the transpacific military network takes place within this temporality of what-will-happen and what-won't. Standoff will be the order of the day, and the 1950 designation of the United States as executive agent of the United Nations Command (UNC) will cement both its continued forward projection on the southern half of the Korean peninsula and the linked presence of US bases in Japan. During the Korean War, UNC General Headquarters was located in Tokyo, providing command and control for the UN Korean War effort.[13] *One Minute to Zero*, in fact, presents base life at Itazuke as model for postwar US forces in Korea and elsewhere in the world.

Steve and Linda meet up shortly at Itazuke. Both have had enough of war. Linda finds no solace in her dead husband's Medal of Honor and the presidential handshake that came with it. Steve is grim but steady. He doesn't like what he has to do, but he'll do it. Their love is sparked over dinner at Linda's place. Linda puts on a record, and Steve, much to Linda's surprise, begins to sing in Japanese.[14] There is much more to him than Linda anticipated. But the film is about Linda, what she witnesses, how she changes. She will gain an awareness of the ethics of escalation, how and why death is unavoidable, what it means to see and mourn the casualties of limited war properly. She will become emotive center of a mobilization, bearer of faith in the need to hold the transpacific line.

One Minute to Zero organizes war in Korea across national borders (with an emphasis on Itazuke's location in the network of interoperability) and in relation to global impact. Such a spatial dimension maps the chronology that names the film. Sixty seconds left. Time, here, is more pressing than has ever been announced on the cover of the *Bulletin of the Atomic Scientists* (the closest as of this writing came in 2025, with adjustment made to eighty-nine seconds to midnight). The interoperable network is under extreme pressure to stop the clock. How to manage precarity of the highest order, the potential destruction of the planet brought on by miscalculation? Recourse is made to a temporality of escalation that allows for varying degrees of death and destruction.

Limited war proceeds in relation to a temporal limit or border, the approach of escalatory time to the atomic moment, the place where the countdown leads to apocalypse. Enter the ethico-religiosity of realpolitik, legitimate killing to avoid a greater miscalculation. Such is the temporal register of *One Minute to Zero* and of limited war. To divide time up into escalatory stages allows for it to run out—within limits. It will be up to US Army-Air Force interoperability to manage the temporality of limited war by placing it on full display. This display will take the form of massacre.

ON THE GROUND IN THE AIR

Back to the battlefield in Korea. Linda has been assigned there to provide medical help to refugees; Steve is in charge of a beleaguered infantry battalion making a stand near the Naktong River. He works to halt a refugee column proceeding south, coordinating with Col. Parker upstairs on air recon to assess its numbers. A checkpoint vets the column for infiltrators (we are shown a gun in a baby cradle and a male guerilla dressed as a woman). It is here that an elder asks in Korean (no subtitles): "What right do you have to come to our country and give orders?" Steve cuts the elder off: "No more refugees past this point!" We are shown two men hiding weapons as this interaction continues. The elder doesn't back down, declaring in unsubtitled Korean that many in the column are sick. "What's the argument?" Steve asks Major Ralston, who replies, "He claims they have the right to go to the aid station down the road." Steve: "He's gettin' aid, from Moscow." Cut to a long shot of the refugee column stretching into the distance, followed by a worm's-eye view of Parker's plane, then to Steve in his command post. He radios Parker for the aerial view, which the camera provides:

STEVE: How do they look?
PARKER: Same. They're still coming.
STEVE: How many are there, Johnny?
PARKER: Too many.

The sequence mobilizes the optics of ground-air interoperability to provide witness of communist infiltration and trickery. Here, as Daniel Kim demonstrates, the question rests on how to distinguish "those subjects who should be annihilated and those who should be brought into the fold and made the proper objects of our sentimental and humanitarian care, nestled within the folds of humanitarian Orientalism."[15] If we are shown clear cases of those Koreans who are communist and to be eliminated, we are also shown an indistinguishable mass (in the long shot; in the aerial view provided from Parker's plane). The question of qualitative distinction becomes quantitative: There are simply "too many." The multiangled presentation provides an object, legitimizes and racializes a potential target.

Linda arrives in a jeep to add in-person witness to what will be a massacre scene.[16] The escalatory countdown begins. Steve orders a series of ever lower, long-range warning shots, but the column does not halt. Finally, he gives the order to fire "for effect." Linda has seen it all and accosts Steve: "Steve, you killed them, those helpless people! You killed them! I saw you, I saw." A slap in the face from Steve interrupts her. Managing Korea and putting Linda in her place coincide; Steve is engaged in a battle on two fronts, a dual deterrence.

Parker and Linda subsequently run into each other in Taegu. He tells Linda she was wrong and takes her to see the bodies of US soldiers, hands tied in wire behind their backs, massacred by the guerillas hiding out in the refugee columns. Long shot of rows of corpses moves to medium shot (flies on the bound hands); to close-up (restraints in focus); and then medium frontal shot of Linda and Parker. Their eyes travel from mass death to individual corpse. They witness the murdered. Parker holds Linda, right hand on her UN armband. This is what takes place "every night," Parker declares. Linda is overwhelmed: "You just don't believe it until you see it." Illicit killing contrasts with the ethics of escalation, Steve's attempt to hold off on the refugee column until he had no choice. Parker's expression reflects this grim realism, projected onto a UN idealism that must be firmly held in check. His hold is a proper and paternal one, contrasting with the illicit restraints the film's audience is compelled to see up close. Linda's transformation is so immediate and profound she cannot speak further. We see it on her face, as does Parker. "I'll tell him," he says, simply.

Linda bears witness to what readers of *LIFE* magazine had already encountered on July 24, 1950: The first fully visible photograph of a US corpse in Korea, hands bound behind his back, caption reading "trussed up and murdered." The sequence, in fact, bears considerable resemblance to descriptions of incidents in two articles written by the war correspondent John Osborne in *TIME* and *LIFE* (both published on the same day, August 21, 1950).[17] Inscribed on the bodies of US corpses is murderous intent on the one hand and willingness to sacrifice on the other. The moment is epiphanic. Linda will no longer entertain an antiwar stance (she can also now mourn her husband's World War II death as something other than senseless). She recognizes the ethics of escalation, the terrible but unavoidable necessity of killing Korean civilians. She has, moreover, arrived at something more than an understanding of war as secular necessity. Hers is a religious journey.

LIGHT AND DARKNESS

Linda will offer a prayer in voice-over at the film's close, an almost verbatim repeat of a prayer she whispered amid the ruins of a church after witnessing the bound US bodies. She shifts the earlier third-person singular (Steve) to third-person plural as Steve's convoy moves through a village into the hills, bombers flying overhead in formation: "O Please dear God, watch over them, protect and guide them, lead them to victory, spare them to no unlasting peace, and in thy infinite mercy, dear God, bring them safely back to us." Cut back to a close-up of Linda's face, tears streaming down her cheeks. The film ends. A prayer for victory is tempered by what Linda has witnessed and what Steve tells us: This is a war that won't be won and won't be lost. And in its very inconclusiveness it is a religious experience, acknowledgment of human limitations.

One Minute to Zero, then, belongs to a world mapped most famously in the 1940s and 1950s by the theologian and political theorist Reinhold Niebuhr. In *The Children of Light and the Children of Darkness: A Vindication of Democracy and a Critique of its Traditional Defence* (1944), Niebuhr offers a Christian view of international relations that posits the idealist assumption of good (the children of light) as setting in motion a false opposition with those deemed to be the children of darkness. Light intertwines with darkness. The children of light must acknowledge the fact that "man is at variance with himself."[18] It is this reality that makes "the simple distinctions between good and evil, between selfishness and altruism, with which liberal idealism has tried to estimate moral and political facts, invalid."[19] *One Minute to Zero* presents not a quandary but a recognition that the temporality of escalation requires the residue of sin, a necessary but reluctant killing that marks human imperfectability.

Linda's twice-spoken prayer contrasts markedly with the Korean elder's words spoken at the checkpoint. These words, as noted above, are not subtitled. Nor are they given in the shooting script, which designates him only as "belligerent male."[20] He is spoken for by Ralston, his questioning of the US presence in Korea translated to moviegoers as the assertion of his people's right to proceed to an aid station. The elder's Korean-language protestation remains in the film's soundscape. But it did not travel into the global aspirations of *One Minute to Zero*'s ethico-religious frame.

LIMITED WAR CALLING

Four F-86 jets cross sky and screen: "This picture is dedicated to the Air Force wives who shared their men with a world made desperate by the most brutal aggressor in history." In case the audience is unsure, Louis King's *Sabre Jet* (1953) emphatically shows the jets' destination, superimposing "ITAZUKE AIR FORCE BASE/Somewhere in Japan" over planes already parked next to the airstrip. As in *One Minute to Zero*, the wives of the jet pilots gather at the gate—a Japanese arch—outside the runway. We will shortly learn that one pilot does not return.

Unlike *One Minute to Zero*, the US Air Force logo precedes the opening sequence, and full DoD and Air Force cooperation appears in the credits (credit is also given to North American Aviation, manufacturer of the F-86). *Sabre Jet*, like *One Minute*, was panned on its release and didn't do well at the box office. *The Hollywood Reporter* considered the film a "weak air story" with a "domestic problem angle," a combination that means it "hasn't much in the way of a story."[21]

FIG. 5.2 *Sabre Jet* (poster). Everett Collection, Alamy.

Contrary to advertisement, the film is not really about "Uncle Sam's 'flying bullets.'" At film's center are what appear in the publicity poster's lower right-hand corner margin, the "Air Force wives" of the dedication. The problem is indeed domestic but with multiple angles at play. The film follows a domestication that takes place both on the geopolitical and the home front. A condensed domesticity where these two registers become inseparable forms within an exclusive community of sharing, a world beyond the profit motive. To share a man will be to awaken to this calling. This is not a world for everyone, but it is for everyone's sake (even the unwilling).

Jane Carter (Coleen Gray) appears unannounced in the office of the Itazuke base commander, General Hale (Richard Arlen). She has come to Japan to write a story about pilots' wives. She also informs Hale that she is married to Col. Gil Manton (Robert Stack), which is news to him. Jane and Gil have been separated for two years, and it appears the latter has kept his troubled marriage under wraps. Jane is a successful reporter. She wears a war correspondent's uniform, complete with tie—and she does not use Gil's last name. All of this will change, including her sartorial choice.

General Hale takes Jane to the gate outside the debriefing room to observe the wives and reunite with Gil. "I've seen this a hundred times before. Westport, New Rochelle, Great Neck. Wives waiting at little stations to pick up their husbands," declares Jane, watching the wives and pilots embrace at the gate. Jane's comment is not far off. Itazuke had undergone a major transformation prior to her arrival, the result of a massive, multiyear construction project that refashioned the former Mushiroda Airfield of the Japanese Army Air Corps into a major US Air Force hub. As Daniel Immerwahr points out, US military procurement orders ($800 million in 1952) had already helped make Japan "a special place within the sprawling U.S. complex," what he calls "baselandia."[22] With its newly built base housing (swimming pool completed in 1950) and commissary, Itazuke offered a microcosm of amenities available to suburban families in CONUS.

Jane's first words to Gil, at the gate: "I had to come here, an important assignment." Gil: "I might have known that." Gil will shortly remind Jane that she stood him up on their second wedding anniversary, choosing instead to interview a woman whose husband was facing execution:

> JANE: That was a terrific story. Great woman's angle. I remember now.
> GIL: Some angle, tearing a woman's heart out.
> JANE: Oh, Gil. That's my job.
> GIL: A job's alright. It's the way you take it, as if you were insulated against all emotion yourself. You never feel anything unless it happens to somebody else.

Jane's journey begins. She is to learn to feel, and this will enable her to understand the difference between a job and a calling. Writing up notes for a story on the women waiting at Itazuke's gate, Jane comes across a letter addressed to Major and Mrs. Ernest Goldman, the previous residents of Gil's base apartment. Gil shares a bit about the couple, that Loretta, Ernest's wife, was disowned by her family for marrying Ernie, who is Jewish. Overcome with emotion, his voice breaks off at the sound of "Taps" (bugle call for "lights out" played every evening on loudspeakers at US bases around the world and at military funerals). Gil resumes, abruptly: "And if you use one word of that in your story, I'll wring your neck." He looks like he means it.

Baselandia is site of something more than war materiel and comfortable quarters. The call of the dead will sound at regular intervals, a reminder of communion with those no longer present. "Taps" creates space, extends to everyone on base as it mourns Major Goldman's death, the absence of the couple. "Taps" has no lyrics, no words, no story. "Taps" calls, inhabits (here, the Goldmans' former address). Major Goldman's absence is not a past or present but that which portends. Jane has not, in fact, seen all of this a hundred times before. The women waiting at the gate differ from those at the little stations in the New York suburbs.

What is Jane supposed to put in her story? The answer is simple: She shouldn't write one. *Sabre Jet* doesn't have much of a story because it wants to show/say something that resists narration. This something is a feeling. *Sabre Jet*'s poster is less deceiving than meets the eye. Something is to be said but not spoken in the image of those looks up into the sky from the lower right-hand corner, almost out of the picture. Marge (General Hale's wife) assists Jane when she tells her that fewer words will be required here:

JANE: Won't the general ever tell you what he did today?
MARGE: Maybe, when it's no longer important. It's a funny thing. An ordinary man comes home at night and beefs about his hard day at the office.... But when Bob comes home, I'll ask him how it was, and he'll say, "A little rugged." And that's all.
JANE: Well, doesn't that make you feel rather feudal?

Jane knows how to spot a story that will sell. But she is lost in the headlines. She will be offered a different world, a meaningful domesticity that combines suburban comforts with attentiveness, purpose.

Jane is interviewing Marge when Gil arrives to inform the latter that General Hale has been shot down. Marge takes it stoically. She sits back down and tells Jane a bit more about Bob:

MARGE: And then he turned down $10,000 a year from North American [makers of the F-86 Sabre].
JANE: Why'd he do it?
MARGE: Because he had to. Because he was Bob Hale. And the Air Force was his life.

Jane turns to leave, and Marge tells her that she's forgotten her notebook. "I don't want it," Jane declares. One feels the call. Or one doesn't. There is no story to be sold. Jane understands. She tries to talk to Gil, but he brushes her off, congratulates her on getting the "scoop" about Marge's reaction that General Hale has been shot down. He'll order a subordinate to process the paperwork for her return to CONUS.

Cut to a flight line of F-86 Sabre jets firing up and preparing for takeoff, Gil making final checks on his plane (marked by its "Watz Matta You" logo) and then to Jane, bags in hand. Jane and Gil are going their separate ways. Next is a sequence alternating cuts of planes taking off and anxious women in their Itazuke bedrooms. Stock footage combines with medium shots and close-ups of the women set in noir-like lighting, with an added element of horror, fear of the unknown

FIG. 5.3 Jane and Gil at Itazuke (*Sabre Jet*). Still courtesy of Everett Collection, Alamy.

FIG. 5.4 Itazuke Flightline (*Sabre Jet*). Still courtesy of Alamy.

intruding into familial space (the baseside bedroom mise-en-scène could be stateside). Military realism lifts all of this into a grim celebration of masculinist, technological prowess (the mass of jet fighters heading to Korea) and feminized fear of disintegration (potential destruction of the pilot-body). Here, too, is an enactment of proleptic mourning as Lee Crane (Lucille Knoch) shifts her body from semi-upright anxiety to an approximation of the iconic Angel of Grief, one hand extended, the other covering her ear. Women attend to the emotive circulation of war machines from base to sky, above and beyond. The horrific fear of what-might-happen makes death proximal, brings it home in virtuality, casts worry as a form of readiness. This sequence requires no words and has none, only a soundscape of thundering jet engines interspersed with nondiegetic music (ominous, dramatic).

Jane will shortly declare to Susan (Kathleen Crowley) that she has no intention of leaving: "Something happened to me. And now all I want is to stay here with Gil." Her transformation is complete when she appears at the Itazuke gate at the close of the film, now dressed like the other women, waiting for a pilot-husband who may not return from his mission over Korea. Baseside is not stateside, even if it might look it sometimes.

In both *One Minute to Zero* and *Sabre Jet*, the Korean war is brought home at the same time as Japan (the former aggressor) is made home. In *Sabre Jet,* Fuji, the Hale family's cook, provides comic relief with his happily broken English. He is chuckled at, caricatured by the children but all in pleasant, good fun. The bitter Japanese foe has become a harmless and helpful domestic. His earlier World War II self appears in the face of an Asian MIG pilot, the only figure in *Sabre Jet* shown dying in gore (blood gushing out of his mouth when he is hit). Fuji's appearance is brief but telling, his racialization overlapping with Jane's awakening at Itazuke, an intersectional, dual domestication that is to attend to the formation of the militarized transpacific.

Chapter 6 addresses two trajectories central to the prosecution of wars without end. First is the limited-war sublime, an aesthetic, masculine experience of pushing individual limits to their greatest height. This is the story of the pilot-in-the-cockpit, the warrior hero whose sensory experience of flight (and risk) moves beyond the mundane. Second is the managing of a reluctance and doubt bordering on skepticism and antiwar critique. Emerging from this constellation will be a flexible form of knowingness, a self-awareness that would blend well with a pliable free-world ethics of empathy and compassion.

CHAPTER 6

JET SUBLIME

The Korean War was a first for jets, as it was for the US Air Force (established as a separate branch of the US Armed Forces in 1947).[1] The face-off between two sweptwing jet aircraft, the MIG-15 and the F-86, was featured regularly in the US press, a fact not lost on Hollywood filmmakers. US jets—the North American F-86, the Lockheed P-80 Shooting Star, the Grumman F9F Panther—would fill the big screens of US drive-in theaters throughout the 1950s. The 1950s jet pilot provided a template for the imaging of white masculinity within a frame of limited war that extends well beyond the fall of the Soviet Union and into the present. The Academy Award-winning special effects highlighting Lt. Brubaker's mission in *The Bridges at Toko-Ri* (1954 adaptation of James Michener's 1953 novella) would find its way into George Lucas's first *Star Wars* film. The blockbuster *Top Gun* (1986) and its even more successful sequel *Top Gun: Maverick* (2022) rehearse the sensory experience of flight and homosocial rivalry West Point alumnus and Korean War veteran James Salter found in MIG Alley and the officer's club in his 1956 novel *The Hunters* (filmic adaptation starring Robert Mitchum and Robert Wagner appearing in theaters in 1958).[2] The pilot, solitary, alone in the cockpit, moving through the skies faster than sound, competing with fellow pilots, engages with an enemy pilot similarly equipped or with a ground target. Aerial cinematography would eventually produce an experience of jet flight so intense the enemy no longer needed to be named, as is the case in both *Top Gun* films.

The Hunters set the stage for a literary and screenwriting career that was less than prolific but would close with accolades of Salter's prominence as an artist, a writer's writer active as mentor at Paul Engle's Iowa Writers' Workshop.[3] Michener's *The Bridges at Toko-Ri* was a bestseller eclipsed by its filmic adaptation. Neither work remains widely read but iterations of both would indeed travel well. How to imagine masculine selves in a limited war that no one cared about "except in a few houses whose men were overseas," as Michener's narrator has it in *Bridges*? Strength, flexibility, and efficiency is to be found in the space opened up by this lack of interest. The Korean War enters US history less as singular event than as unmarked occasion for the emergence of a new modality, a type of functional differentiation that departs from the mobilization of total war. Both Salter and Michener anticipate the increasing split between the everyday life of a civilian population and the emotive register of what will eventually become a postconscription professional military (after the American War in Vietnam).

How to figure combat death in such a milieu? Such is the high concept shared by *Hunters* and *Bridges*. These works diverge in the former's aspiration to highbrow literariness and the latter's appeal to a middlebrow documentary-like realism at once explanatory and hortatory. And this leads to two intersecting modalities with a long shelf life in the post-1945 US imagining of something called a cold war, one an ethos, the other an ethics. The first appears in the form of a rarefied experience, a cosmopolitanism available to the military elite (*Hunters*). This is the aesthetics of man in machine, jet as vehicle to push body and mind to the limit. The second (*Bridges*) elevates the unwilling, transforms bitterness and skepticism into reluctance. This is what Michener calls the "voluntary man." Joining him will be a similarly reluctant but powerful array of military assets that do not simply target but look after the stateside majority, those who remain unattentive and/or unwilling. The disparate approaches of Salter and Michener combine to form a central strand of US limited-war culture, a gendered and racialized inflection of the liberal meaning of defense as mode of consciousness, self-awareness, and sensory understanding of the world.

WARRIORS OF THE CRYSTAL EMPIRE

Korean War jet aces were lauded as heroes, most famous among them triple ace John McConnell, featured in the 1955 biopic *The McConnell Story* (starring Alan Ladd) and familiar to generations of young readers in the 1960s and 1970s by way of Charles Coombs's *Sabre Jet Ace*, included in the widely taught elementary school reading primer *American Adventure Series*, edited by the well-known psychologist and educational theorist Emmett Betts (other titles in the 1961 series included *Daniel Boone*, *Davy Crockett*, and *John Paul Jones*). The jet and its pilot would constitute much of the remembrance of the Korean War for a generation of Americans, MIG Alley figuring prominently in the stories of heroes such as John Glenn, featured in "Making of a Brave Man," a 1962 *LIFE* special pictorial on the astronaut and former Sabre jet pilot.⁴

MIG Alley achieved wartime fame in tandem with a growing awareness that clear-cut victory was likely unavailable in Korea. Postarmistice, action on the ground would recede further in favor of the human/technological prowess proven in the skies above. In the 1950s, the pilot-hunter embodies US limited-war masculinity because he is at the controls in the military theater of operation and in the movie theater (where the vast majority of spectators come closest to combat jet flight). He shifts the playing field from ground to sky and eventually even higher, to space.

As Heonik Kwon points out, "there has never been a conflict called *the* cold war. The bipolarized human community of the twentieth century experienced political bifurcation in radically different ways across societies—ways that cannot be forced into a single conceptual whole."⁵ Kwon's contestation of uniformity seeks to shift "the exemplary central positioning of the cold war as imaginary or metaphoric war to a comparative positioning that privileges neither this peculiar history of war without warfare nor the peripheral 'unbridled reality' of state terror and civil war, on the other."⁶ Such an imaginary did not exist a priori. It took effort to imagine a war as cold. The hot spot, central to the idea of an encompassing cold war, could be thought of as a proxy conflict, a killing field that required no formal declaration or commemoration. But it was also an opportunity to demonstrate new techniques and technologies, to put them to the test. The figure of the pilot was best suited for the human component of this effort. His task was to transform the limited into a broader domain, the experience of the possible itself.

In *The Hunters*, Cleve is an experienced, well-respected fighter pilot, just old enough to have missed out on World War II. Upon arrival at Kimpo Air Base, "For a few unreal minutes, a feeling that he had been in Korea much longer than two or three hours was generated in him. He remembered so many other headquarters, all alike."⁷ Routinization meets the frustration of stalemate. Abbot tells him right off the bat that "it's just no good. I mean what are we fighting for anyway? There's nothing for us to win. It's no good, Cleve, you'll see."⁸ Ausman will follow up, telling Cleve he wants just one thing out of Korea: "My ass." Cleve is struck by this remark: "For one of those naked moments, they looked at each other. It had been a genuine confidence." Cleve quickly recognizes where he is and what he is doing: "He had come to meet his enemy, without reservation. . . . He had come not merely to survive. He suddenly felt the uplift of being that much above those who . . . lived on a subordinate plane of endeavor."⁹ At first glance, the hot spot offers no narrative; it is plotless, no good. The best recourse for most is never to be there or to exit, alive. But place doesn't matter (the base is always the same, anyway). The question is of what Cleve calls "motive," and this will reside in an elevation of body and spirit.

The rules of the game are simple: Secure kills not simply to defeat an enemy but to become an ace. The struggle thus entails two competitors: those in other Sabres and those in MIGs. The former take precedence, and Cleve's nemesis is Pell, the cocky, young upstart, the natural who scores repeated kills: "Of all the absolutes, Pell was the archetype, confronting him with the unreality and diabolical force of a medieval play, the deathlike, grinning angel risen to claim the very souls of simple men. When he dwelt upon that, Cleve felt the cool touch of fear. There was no way out. He knew that if Pell were to win, he himself could not survive."[10] It is not an enemy MIG pilot who threatens Cleve's life. His battle is with Pell, but not really in Korea or its skies. Cleve joins Pell on a higher plane, an epic that stretches back through the literary canon. West Point alumnus and former Korean War jet pilot, Salter would conclude his 1997 preface to *The Hunters* thusly: "It was said of Lord Byron that he was more proud of his Norman ancestors who had accompanied William the Conqueror in the invasion of England than of having written famed works. . . . Looking back, I feel a pride akin to that in having flown and fought along the Yalu."[11] *The Hunters* presents a sensory, sensual, and intensely personal experience. That the pilot is alone, pitted against an archetypal rival, lifts him (and the literary text that describes him) to communion with the epic.

The advantage of being in a jet fighter is that the sensory and the psychological combine to produce an experiential dimension that both literally and figuratively rises above and beyond, jet flight approaching the sound barrier. As the jet takes off, so does everyday bickering transform into something higher. After an ugly exchange with Pell over MIG kills, Cleve straps himself into the cockpit of his plane: "Now in motion, he felt somewhat better. . . . He was aware of an elusive, mystic sensation supporting the physical as they went up."[12] Cleve lifts warrior pasts into the present, opening up a new vista of self-experience:

> You slipped into the hollow cockpit and strapped and plugged yourself into the machine. The canopy ground shut and sealed you off. Your oxygen, your very breath, you carried with you into the chilled vacuum, in a steel bottle. . . . They flew with you in heraldic patterns and fought alongside you, sometimes skillfully, always at least two ships together, but they were really of no help. You were alone. At the end, there was no one you could touch.[13]

Such an aesthetic sensibility extends to experience on the ground below, but not that to be had in Korea.

On R&R in Japan, Cleve visits Miyata, the brother of a friend Cleve's father had known in Washington. He spends a pleasurable afternoon in Miyata's art studio, where he meets his daughter Eico. He is attracted to her, sees her in the nudes hanging on Miyata's walls, and will spend a spend a day with her, one of intellectual but sexually suggestive communion. Cleve and Miyata have a wide-ranging conversation:

> They spoke briefly of Korea and then of the past war with the United States. Miyata had been in Japan for the entire duration of that and must have been deeply affected, but when he talked about it, there was no bitterness. Wars were not of his doing. He considered them almost poetically, as if they were seasons, the cruel winters of men, even though almost all of the work he had done in the 1930s and early 1940s had been lost when his home was burned in the great fire raid of 1944.[14]

Miyata, in fact, "seemed superior to the confusion of life, as if he had been commissioned to spend his own in creative judgment of the world about him."[15] The US firebombing of Tokyo (1945, not 1944) is a creative force: "It was finally like being born again." Their conversation continues: "They talked of Japan, of France where he had lived and studied for six years, of Tahiti, and the former Japanese-mandated islands in the Pacific."[16] Cleve's exchanges with Miyata and Eico open up an intimate and artistic world imbued with the sensual, a sense of expansiveness, discovery. This is a world of potential, of a possible future—and Cleve dreams momentarily of living in Japan forever. The contrast with Cleve's pilot cohort in Korea jars, composed as it is of shallow naturals like Pell and retread pilots going through the motions in a war that is no good, aiming for nothing but a return home.

Back in Korea, Cleve goes up never to come down: "Free of the gravitational forces of reality, he sat in the sunshine and looked out over a crystal empire.... It was almost sleep-inducing. He knew a transcendence as timeless as a dream of deepest waters. If death were ever to touch him here, it would be with a gesture of equality, with fingertips only."[17] A war correspondent interviews Pell about his seventh kill, secured during the action that eliminates Cleve. The correspondent has been watching Pell's offhand manner with suspicion but writes what is wanted: "The article was carried in a national magazine. It was a great success. There was a photograph of Pell in the cockpit, stark and memorable. A whole country found its heroism in his face."[18] Pell is profane, as is the middlebrow US readership. They allegorize, find triumph in identification from afar with a facial surface. *The Hunters* is a thanatography, telling the story of death in a place where war and art combine to produce a higher level of sensibility, in the crystal empire. Salter's work offers itself, its literary style, its aesthetics, to the defense of this empire, opposed to the mundane and the mass.

Little room for Cleve in the national magazines. He is meant to reside in a spare, minimalist prose that invokes transcendence. Cleve experiences the nobility of sport in its most rarefied sense, an intense homosocial competition that exists for its own sake (Salter would find the filmic adaptation financially lucrative but agonizing; he would also later pen the screenplay for the 1969 film *Downhill Racer*, which moves much of *The Hunters* to sport itself). There is no question of conscription here, of a call for mobilization. This is the humanist-masculinist, romantic world of the pilot-in-the cockpit, a disciplined but emancipatory aesthetic in which the enemy loses significance and the fetishization of technology-as-weaponry recedes. There is an end to Cleve's war in and over Korea, but that is reserved for his approach to the gentle touch of death in the sky. Lost in the middlebrow heroes of the national magazines is the self of the crystal empire, that place where minimalism beautifully crosses the threshold to an ungraspable silence, beyond description. Salter presents his readers with what may be one of the finest examples of the limited-war sublime.

THE VOLUNTARY MEN

In *The Vital Center: The Politics of Freedom* (1948), Arthur M. Schlesinger Jr. writes that "History has thrust a world destiny on the United States. No nation, perhaps, has become a more reluctant great power. Not conquest but homesickness moved the men of Bradley and Stilwell; Frankfurt or Tokyo were but way-stations on the way back to Gopher Prairie."[19] The gesture is allegorical (what we might call an individual allegory): The nation is a homesick man. To live in a condition of nonreturn is to do what one doesn't want to do in a place one does not want to be. But history has destined the formation of a world order that will disallow a return home. American exceptionalism achieves ethical agency in reluctance. There will be no choice but to replace way stations with permanent bases.

Early in Michener's *The Bridges at Toko-Ri*, the World War II retread Lt. Harry Brubaker ditches his plane into the sea off Korea's coast. He complains bitterly to Admiral Tarrant following his rescue by helicopter:

"Watching people go on as if there were no war. We gave up our home, my job, the kids. Nobody else in Denver gave up anything."

This made the admiral angry. "Rubbish," he growled. "Burdens always fall on a few.... Nobody ever knows why he gets the dirty job. But any society is held together by the efforts ... yes, and the sacrifices of only a few."[20]

Tarrant's response frames the definition of what he will later call "voluntary men." These are men who "don't veer away. They hammer on in, even when the burden of war has fallen unfairly on them."[21] They do not seek war but will carry out the mission. In this, they embody the post-1945 role Michener allots to the United States in his epigraph to *Bridges*: "In Korea our nation has undergone a new and sometimes bewildering experience. It has been our first taste of exercising the responsibility thrust upon us by our unsought leadership of the free world."[22] Most will never need to leave home; others will get the dirty job. Reluctance travels along a spectrum, from the apathetic to the not-knowing-why-but-doing-it-anyway.

Bridges is at pains to highlight the distinction between the inattentive and the inexplicably hesitant-but-responsible. Nancy, who has come to Japan to see Harry, whispers to him in bed, "What eats my heart away is that back home there is no war."[23] And as Harry later lies in a ditch in Korea facing certain death, "in New York thousands of Americans were crowding into the nightclubs where the food was good and the wine expensive, but hardly anywhere in the city except in a few houses whose men were overseas was there even an echo of Korea."[24] Michener indicates that he himself was hesitant to write *Bridges* "because I feared that Americans might not be interested in Korea." Only when pressed by editors at *LIFE* did he overcome his reluctance, "for I believe that in the years to come our nation will face problems similar to those we met for the first time in Korea."[25] The nation struggles to understand a war that is not a war. The problem of disinterest extends to the way in which a story can be told: "In this special war there were special rules to keep the people back in America from becoming worried."[26] *Bridges* is prescient in its telling of a story of war that does not present itself as an event (Hollywood would drop the Korean War after the early 1960s). What is required is not exactly a mass mobilization of care but the explanation that care must be entrusted to a few.

Nor is *Bridges* about the target it names in its title. Michener will aim for more. *Bridges* is a story about a special war and the bewildering future that faces unsought US leadership. This is a future of war that locates meaning in the results it will achieve and the untranslatable mode in which it will be fought. It will be both transformative (historical) and sublime (beyond history). The future will be of reluctance, duty, and disinterest. Such a constellation speaks to the power of the appellation "cold war" itself—as less standoff with an implacable adversary than address at once to a universalist horizon of worry and a stateside forgetfulness of the present.

CINEMATIC READERS

Bridges was only the second novella *LIFE* published in a single installment (the first was Ernest Hemingway's *Old Man and the Sea*). Both novella and Mark Robson's filmic adaptation were the products of close cooperation with DoD. Michener was an embedded reporter in US Navy Task Force 77 in 1951 and modeled the characters in *Bridges* after real-life figures. The film benefited from a large budget and received extensive US Navy support on location in the Yellow Sea (nineteen ships participating), at Yokosuka Navy Base, and in California. Navy brass were provided with pre-shoot scripts. Little expense was spared for the film's aerial photography (Paul Mantz) and special effects (John P. Fulton, who would later part the Red Sea in *Ten Commandments*). Released by Paramount in 1954, *The Bridges at Toko-Ri* brought in the most star power (William Holden as Harry; Grace Kelly as Nancy, his wife; Mickey Rooney as Mike Forney, helicopter rescue pilot) of any Korean War film in Hollywood history.

Credit for the visual layout of the 1954 film should also go to Noel Sickles's illustrations in the *LIFE* version of *Bridges*. Sickles was an innovator who brought cinematic techniques to cartoon art during his tenure as illustrator for the aviation adventure series *Scorchy Smith* in the 1930s; Robson's film follows the *LIFE* illustrations in storyboard fashion. Brought to publication by *LIFE* and blending almost perfectly with the magazine's visual format, Michener's work is multimodal, almost graphic novel-like in form, beginning with a full-page illustration and concluding with an illustration larger than the body of text that precedes it (all subsequent illustrations fill a half page or more). From the beginning, the reader is asked to experience the cockpit, to fly in precarious synchronicity with Harry, to suture with a jet-mounted camera. The textual body of Michener's work becomes an extended explanatory caption situating a cinematic POV, often of the pilot, the one who targets.

Michener's text follows (caption-like) an illustration of Harry's F2H Banshee (replaced by the sleeker Grumman F9F Panther in the film) strafing enemy soldiers on the ground. We are told of Harry's hesitation. He moves to dive, but

FIG. 6.1 *The Bridges at Toko-Ri* opens with a full-page illustration. Noel Sickles Collection, Billy Ireland Cartoon Library and Museum.

then sees that the communists had fallen "to their knees in the middle of the road, clasped their arms about their heads, and made no effort to escape inevitable death. The tactic so astonished Brubaker that he gasped, 'They're sitting ducks!'"[27] He pulls up but then hears over the radio that this is nothing but a "standard trick. Trying to throw you off balance." And then, as Harry returns, we're told: "Not a communist moved. Not one hit the ditch. They huddled

FIG. 6.2 Brubaker strafes the communists. Noel Sickles Collection, Billy Ireland Cartoon Library and Museum.

and waited. 'Here it comes,' Brubaker whispered grimly, and his finger pressed the trigger."[28]

Sickles's illustration appears as a film still, a reverse shot. The reader-viewer is asked to visualize the unseen but verbally described reluctance of the pilot that frames this image. To visualize reluctance is to engage in filmic adaptation as one reads. It is to image the shots that surround the illustration-as-film-still, what comes before and what comes after. The multimodal format of *Bridges* sutures in this way, asks for reading to take place from a camera-like POV, a cinematic reading that puts words into a motion picture. To cocreate this visual world is to see in a certain way, to assume trickery rather than the possibility of surrender (the "communists" hold their hands over the heads). It is to follow what Harry enacts. He puts into words what he sees, is told how to see it, and acts. It is also to draw a broader visual field from the illustrations themselves, here from the communist mass, almost completely faceless, men hardly separate from the ground upon which they kneel. They appear as an anti-aesthetic, embodiment of inscrutability long associated with Asia and Asians, including, of course, wartime Japanese.

Bridges offers another presentation of Asian bodies, this time in Japan. Nancy has "violated the rules" to come to Japan with the couple's two children, to bring the home front to her husband. Nancy and Harry stay at the Fuji-san Hotel in Hakone:

> In the old days this had been Japan's leading hotel but for the first six years after the war it served Americans only. Now, in the transition period between occupation and sovereignty, it had become a symbol of the strange and satisfying relationship between Japan and America: the choice rooms were still reserved for Americans but Japanese were welcome to use the hotel as before.[29]

The newfound Japan-US amity is performed in the famous bathhouse scene, which, as *LIFE* noted in a later issue, was altered in the film. As Nancy and Harry bathe with their children, a Japanese family enters. Harry and Nancy are "numb with astonishment. But. . . . the quiet beauty of the surroundings and the charm of the Japanese family were too persuasive to resist."[30] The Japanese parents and teenaged children (younger in the film) politely enter the bath. The children of both families quickly bond, and, in the film, the Japanese mother declares to everyone, "Happy family." In *LIFE*, the narrator indicates that "The two families intermingled and the soft waters of the bath united them."[31] Sickles provides a reverse shot, leaving the cinematic readership to image a longer sequence drawn from the verbal description (*LIFE* would highlight this moment in *Bridges* in its February 7, 1955 issue, contrasting the original illustration to filmic adaptation). Sickles's illustration stands at the center of *Bridges*, the visual demonstration of a successful US occupation. As the families come together (no barriers in the bath in *LIFE*, unlike the film), Harry recalls that he "had hated the Japanese and had fought valiantly against them." Such feelings have now, in the sulfur bath, been put in the past perfect tense. A Japanese family joins a white US family in a rehabilitated history. As the former imperial power becomes a model host nation, the occupier transitions to a special guest whose permanent stay is welcomed (the Brubaker girls' shout of "Ohayo goziamasu!" puts the Japanese family at enough ease to enter the pool). Nancy travels to Japan to sanction this embodied, affective historymaking (she will disappear shortly after the sulfur bath).

The free world history of the transpacific will move forward with this visual presentation of genuine amity. Something else, though, happens in Korea and off its coast. It will be described as the indescribable, and its power will be at once reluctant and awesome. It will not be of the event; nor will it lend itself to historical narrative. Much will depend upon on the dispensation of Harry's corpse.

FIG. 6.3 In the Bathhouse. Noel Sickles Collection, Billy Ireland Cartoon Library and Museum.

BODY IN SHIP

Harry is downed. He has been able to make a crash landing after coming under enemy fire while engaging with a secondary target (the mission to destroy the bridges was successful). Low on fuel, other pilots in his squadron have no choice but to leave the area:

> From his filthy ditch, Harry, watched the mysterious and lovely jets stream out to sea. They were supreme in the sky, these rare, beautiful things, slim-lined, nose gently dipping, silver canopy shining in the sun. Once he had been part of those jets and now, huddling to earth, he was thankful that he had known the sweeping flight, the penetration of upper space, the roaring dive with Gs making his face heavy like a lion's, and final exultant soaring back to unlimited reaches of the sky.[32]

Harry imagines the masculinist beauty of jet weapons in flight, but this vision does not offer an end unto itself. *Bridges* has moved to reality on the ground.

Overwhelmed by the stench, Harry leaps out of the ditch and espies four figures standing near some trees:

> They were the family from the nearest farm, a mother, father and two children, dressed in discarded uniforms and brandishing rakes. He stopped to see if they intended attacking him, but they remained still and he saw them not as Koreans but as the Japanese family that had intruded upon his sulphur bath that morning in the Fuji-san and as an unbearable longing for his own wife and children possessed him and it was then—there in bright sunlight in the rice field—that he knew he would not see his family again.[33]

The visual field of *Bridges* includes Korea only as target. Cast where he does not belong, the targeted place, Harry envisions himself elsewhere, in the skies and in Japan, in a transformative history that signals an end to World War II and the beginning of lasting, transpacific friendship. Harry images two experiences of beauty (in-flight and in-bath) as he dies, shot in the head: "In that millionth of a second, while ten slim Banshees roared in from the sea to resume command of the sky, Harry Brubaker understood in some fragmentary way the purpose of his being in Korea. But the brief knowledge served no purpose, for the next instant he plunged faced down into the ditch."[34] He dies a voluntary man, doing his duty without fully knowing why. Time compresses to an instant. His life ends as his afterdeath begins. What are we to make of this corpse, the body that speaks of some sort of knowledge to be gained from a miserable death?

Robson's filmic adaptation offers a remarkable handling of Harry's corpse. He's not left behind. Stephen Prince underscores the way the film dwells upon Harry's death, which "activates an extended interlude of emotional bracketing, marked by a dissolve of extraordinary length—more than 14 seconds—that holds the overlapping compositions of his body in the ditch (the outgoing shot) and the aircraft carrier (the incoming shot)."[35]

As it approaches the *Savo*, the camera wavers slightly as if aircraft-mounted. As Prince notes, following this dissolve into the *Savo*, the final eleven seconds of the scene linger above the carrier before taking us inside its command tower.[36] Robson breaks with the documentary-like realism of the film's aerial sequences to approach what the novella suggested took place in an unspeakable millionth of a second. It will take a little over fourteen seconds in the film to move Harry's death to an afterdeath, to show (not tell) that he belongs to the military sublime.

While the *LIFE* version of Michener's novella was comprised of untitled subsections, the book would be divided into three parts titled "Sea," "Land," and "Sky." The terms correspond with the three phases of military operations

FIG. 6.4.1 AND FIG. 6.4.2 (*Top*) Brubaker lying dead in a ditch in Korea. (*Bottom*) Camera lifts Harry's body from Korea. *The Bridges at Toko-Ri* © Paramount Pictures. All Rights Reserved. Used with permission.

associated with the largest branches of the US military (Navy, Army, Air Force). The "Land" section of the novella takes place entirely in Japan, mostly in Yokosuka. Harry's bombing run, his forced landing, his death on the ground occur in the "Sky" section. Korea does not really exist as terrestrial location in *Bridges*. It is not only Harry's corpse that dissolves into the *Savo* but the surrounding scenery, mostly the ditch in which he died. The camera folds his body into a superimposition of land, sea, and sky, the three phases that appear as section titles in the 1954 Random House version of *Bridges*. The military sublime has arrived at transpacific edge.

"Where did we get such men?" Tarrant asks upon learning of Brubaker's death. And then he repeats the question. His encomium is spare, grim. Where did we get these men? He doesn't have an answer because there isn't one. Nor should there be. These men come from a somewhere that is inexplicable, beyond apprehension. They die in like fashion. They die warlike, in a war that is not a war, that claims to be antiwar. The question is declarative, a pithy eulogy. No response required. Such reflection on their provenance accompanies the awesome display of reluctance, the task force poised in vigilance, readiness, deterrence. The task force that takes care of the world and its own.

Both novella and film give their final words to the carrier loudspeaker: "Launch jets." Interrogative-as-declarative turns to the imperative, amplified by machine. In the novella, "Tarrant watched them go, two by two from the lashing catapult, planes of immortal beauty whipping into the air with flame and fury upon them."[37] *Bridges* names a target but tells the story of a corpse and its dissolve into something else. The reluctant retread has been returned to the task force. The dissolve necromorphizes, absents the corpse to animate the beauty of inexorable resolve. The force brought to bear at transpacific edge proceeds in unfettered communion with its own grim necessity, an inexplicable ethics of reluctance-as-duty. The beauty of the jets, then, does not lie solely in the wrathfulness of their flame and fury, but in a strength of unknown provenance, in the meting out of a destruction that will take place only with hesitation. Here, the military sublime—and the weapon fetish that accompanies it—rests upon the blend of afterdeath with machine.

Bridges provides a vision where reluctance will give way to a purer form of deterrence: "Long ago Tarrant had begun to argue that some new weapon—rockets perhaps or pilotless planes of vast speed—would inevitably constitute the task force of the future."[38] His dream is of "some new agency that could move about the earth with security and apply pressure wherever the enemy chose to assault us."[39] The technomorphic will replace the necromorphic, the jet pilot to be named only as nonpresence (the "unmanned" of the UAV, widely deployed in current limited warfare). Tarrant's look from the command tower (filmic adaptation closely follows Sickles's illustration) calls for the necessity of the voluntary man until he is no longer needed. Korea and the Korean War already exist in this big picture—out there, without fixed coordinates, template for the whenever and wherever. This is why the action on the ground in Korea can occur below the subheading not of "Land" but "Sky."

Limited war is global in its aspirations and timeless in its assumptions. The vision becomes grand, moves about the earth fluidly. From the desire to make small, to limit, emerges the large, a vastness that circles the earth and extends competitiveness in the skies to space, to a freedom from gravity itself. An aesthetics of human endeavor and homosocial competition that cares little for stalemates and those below joins with the ethics of reluctant killing to form a layered, contemplative point from which to make observations. These trajectories join in their observation of self, their turn inward to approach that which will constitute a limit. They are knowing in their experience of something that defies verbal description (*Bridges* ends with an oversized illustration, not words).

To imagine a war as wrapped in a seemingly perpetual coldness that envelopes the mass killing taking place in "hot spots" is to face the difficulty of representing war as event. Nor does the call to fight in a war that will not be declared a war and does not proffer a promise of total victory or triumphal return lend itself to an easily translatable premise, a high concept. The Korean War became the occasion for perusal of multilayered masculinities, among them the warrior pushing the limits of mind, body, and technology and the reluctant, voluntary retread. The reflections of these men can assume as much or more importance than the task at hand for which they are asked to die.

Chapter 7 turns to a sustained, wartime contemplation of self, death, and image. What happens when you are watched over by your own impending death or find out you are already dead, as if in a horror film? The answer (and its implications) lies in Harvey Kurtzman's comics and their observations of what was taking place in *LIFE* magazine and by easy extension across the United States, *LIFE*'s famously oversized covers figuring prominently on coffee tables in millions of American living rooms.

CHAPTER 7

DEATH IN *LIFE*

One of the first things Henry Luce did when he purchased *Life* in 1936 was change its title to all-capitals: *LIFE*. The new title spoke to something big, something that would catch the eye. *LIFE* would be the first magazine comprised of photo-essays meant both to document and instruct. *LIFE* was an unqualified success, by some accounts reaching the largest pass-along circulation of any US magazine in the early 1950s. As Erika Doss notes, the US Post Office asked Congress in 1956 for rate increases, complaining that it "was overwhelmed by *Life*'s sheer weekly bulk."[1] Much of *LIFE*'s popularity stemmed from its presentation of the big picture from the small, a magnification that connected everyday life to the big issues of the day. Short interviews and editorials addressing international affairs dovetail with photo-essays depicting a myriad of global and domestic events; everyday curiosities and happenings in small towns mesh with those taking place in faraway places all over the world.

LIFE's visual layouts (including its glossy advertisements) would teach its audience how to see, experience, feel, and desire. The photo-essay, though, is much more than a vehicle to editorialize ideas in realist garb. *LIFE* demonstrates how theories of international relations, discussions of war and policy are themselves enmeshed in visual regimes, invocations of images, highlightings and lowlightings. Central to the display of war is a thanatographics, a visual-verbal layout of death.

Another word for this thanatographics is deathscape—a horizon of death that turns upon the relation among image (including photograph, illustration) and text/words (including captions, dialogue). Such a deathscape presents a story, makes death popular, involves a mass circulation of death images. How to attach a stable meaning to death, blend feeling with certitude? If *LIFE*'s photo-essays provided one answer, the EC comic books *Two-Fisted Tales* (1950–1955) and *Frontline*

Combat (1951–1954) offered their own take on the Korean War, often in the form of a sudden, almost parodic recognition of how realisms work, how a visual regime organizes the relation between life and death. To enter into such an optics is to gain a particular kind of awareness, what we might call a draw-out from the hook, an exfiltration of the viewer/reader from the experience of *LIFE*'s layouts.

Edited by Harvey Kurtzman, *Two-Fisted Tales* and *Frontline Combat* incorporate the horror genre, extending its visual play between what is seen and isn't to a reflection on how to see what others make visible and obscure, how they present what needs to be seen and doesn't, and, importantly, what is noticed and overlooked. What I call Kurtzman's "thanato-comics" (he called them his "war books") offer a pedagogy, an abiding concern with the transformation of the live body into the dead one, including one's own (a corpse-like view). These thanato-comics dwell upon the ways which ideas of self-preservation and the fear of bodily disintegration involve a politics of seeing death. To approach the intertextual and intervisual relation between *LIFE* and *Two-Fisted Tales/Frontline Combat* is to view the uneven terrain of a wartime thanatographics, its realisms, its ideological/policy contestations, its competing assertions of knowingness, its appeals to the salvific, to the masculine, its devolution into the routine, its claim to the corpse, its call for a liveliness of mind.

Kurtzman put mass-market generic forms, sensationalist hooks into play with the didactic conventions of the preachies (a contemporary term used for socially engaged comics), even as EC—under the direction of its publisher, William Gaines—was morphing from Educational Comics to Entertaining Comics, its horror comics series (*Tales from the Crypt, The Vault of Horror, The Haunt of Fear*) providing the publisher's main revenue stream. Importantly, Qiana Whitted has shown how "Reframing 'entertainment' as an assault on mainstream norms was key to the transformation of the company that Gaines inherited from his father in 1947."[2] The popularity of EC's horror comics also garnered attention from social critics such as the psychiatrist Fredric Wertham, whose *Seduction of the Innocent* (1954) played a major role in a congressional inquiry and the creation of the self-censoring body known as the Comics Code Authority (CCA) in the same year. Amy Nyberg underscores how Gaines and Wertham "personified the struggle over comics in postwar America."[3] By 1956, EC would have only one remaining title, *MAD*, which began as an EC comic and morphed into a magazine, thus avoiding CCA censorship. Harvey Kurtzman served as the executive editor of *MAD* for its first four years (1952–1956), framing what would prove to be a satirical mainstay for decades.

Kurtzman was known as a generous but demanding editor. He wrote almost all of the material for *Two-Fisted Tales* and *Frontline Combat* and insisted that collaborating artists not depart from the layout he created for each comic.[4]

He had a distinct vision for *Two-Fisted Tales* and *Frontline Combat*, both of which contained Korean War content in every issue, along with comics on other wars (including the Civil and Revolutionary Wars, World War I, and World War II, as well as the Spanish Conquest and various battles involving the Roman and British Empires). He sums up his concerns in a later interview:

> I was absolutely appalled by the lies in the war books that publishers were putting out. What they did when they produced a war book is they focused on what they thought the reader would like to read, which was, "Americans are good guys and anybody against us is the bad guys. We're human. They're not. And God is always on our side." This trash had nothing to do with the reality of life.[5]

As M. Thomas Inge notes, Kurtzman "set out to deglamorize combat by showing it to be grim, debasing, and dehumanizing."[6] Kurtzman's unpacking of the contemporary visual presentation of the Korean War, in fact, centered on the display of killing and the resultant corpse, how it would appear, what would be said about it, and how a combatant became one. His concern was with the contemporary deathscape, and his target extended well beyond other war comic books to the most widely circulated verbal-visual presentation of war and death available to the American public, the photo-essays in *LIFE* magazine.

CONTAINMENT AND ITS DISCONTENTS

"Retreat, hell! We're not retreating, we're just advancing in a different direction!" Marine General Oliver P. Smith's famous declaration in early December 1950 would contribute to the title for Joseph Lewis's 1952 *Retreat, Hell!* (filmed at Camp Pendleton, CA with substantial support from the US Marine Corps), a film that follows the 1st Marine Division's pullback from the Yalu in late 1950 and eventual evacuation at the port city of Hungnam. The January 8, 1951 issue of *LIFE* offers its take on this key moment in the history of the Korean War in photo-essay format. Here, what happened at Hungnam is "One for the Book: An Invasion in Reverse," end point for the retreat from the Yalu *LIFE* had been covering over the previous month.

Images of orderly GI withdrawal intersperse with situating shots of the harbor and its demolition, crowd scenes of Koreans waiting to be taken on board waiting ships. A close-up and medium shot of a young girl follows a photo of puppies remaining behind, both now homeless. The photo-essay concludes with a medium-long shot of the last amtracs headed out to the transports, from the

ONLY PUPPIES WERE LEFT BEHIND ON THE DOCK

WE WALK, NOT RUN, TO EXIT

X CORPS EVACUATES HUNGNAM TO FIGHT AGAIN IN THE SOUTH

PHOTOGRAPHED FOR LIFE BY DAVID D. DUNCAN

For 12 frigid days and nights last month the 105,000 men of the X Corps sludged through the streets of Hungnam, across bomb-scarred docks and into barges and transports that took them out into the Japan Sea. With almost no casualties and little trouble they all got out—the 3rd and 7th Army Divisions, two ROK divisions, and the 1st Marine Division which had made the memorable trek from the Changjin Reservoir (LIFE, Dec. 25). With them they took 350,000 tons of supplies, 17,500 vehicles and 91,000 Korean civilians fleeing from dreaded Communist reprisals.

The orderly evacuation at the end of what might otherwise have been a disastrous retreat was an admirable organizational feat. As the Navy put it, "It was walk, not run, to the nearest exit." The Chinese, with their supply lines overextended, were incapable of sustained attacks. The U.N. forces, with complete command of the sea and air, set up an undisputed curtain of gunfire and bombing through which the Reds could launch only sporadic assaults that were easily beaten off by the rear guard. LIFE Photographer Duncan reported that "within that wall of fire, life was probably safer for a man in uniform than almost any other spot on earth. On one typical cold day more soldiers died from the effects of radiator antifreeze whisky than from enemy bullets, and at that the loss of life was but eight."

The X Corps was not heading for home, or for Japan or for much rest. It was on its way to join General Ridgway's Eighth Army, which was bracing itself near the 38th Parallel for a Chinese offensive that was expected momentarily.

WADING INTO THE SEA at Hungnam on the day before Christmas, some of the last troops of the rear guard walk unhurriedly toward a landing craft that will carry them to the transports out in the bay.

CONTINUED ON NEXT PAGE 15

FIG. 7.1.1 AND FIG. 7.1.2 AND FIG. 7.1.3 AND FIG. 7.1.4 AND FIG. 7.1.5 *LIFE* photo essay of the Hungnam evacuation. Text in *LIFE* layout appears with permission of Meredith Operations Corporation; David Douglas Duncan photographs for *LIFE* courtesy of Harry Ransom Center, the University of Texas at Austin.

Evacuation CONTINUED

ARMY'S GUNS, 155-mm howitzers, fire barrages in support of attacked outpost defenses thousands of yards toward hills in front of them. Navy Corsair (left) is returning to carrier after bombing mission.

COMMUNIST DEAD were among 81 killed near perimeter by shells fired from guns in picture above. They are being examined, the morning after their attack, by scouts of 65th Puerto Rican Regiment.

ON THE BEACH engineer and transport units of the Army's 7th Division load supplies and vehicles through gaping bow doors and into the roomy holds of the Navy's LSTs, which are ocean-going vessels.

FIG. 7.1.1 AND FIG. 7.1.2 AND FIG. 7.1.3 AND FIG. 7.1.4 AND FIG. 7.1.5 *(continued)*.

FIG. 7.1.1 AND FIG. 7.1.2 AND FIG. 7.1.3 AND FIG. 7.1.4 AND FIG. 7.1.5 (*continued*).

perspective of a deserted shore. We are told and shown what happens next: "Then the Chinese began to creep over the hills. Minutes later demolition men throw the switch, and in one massive explosion Hungnam's waterfront was blown sky high. The campaign in North Korea was over."[7] Stills and captions of the photo-essay combine to form newsreel-type documentation and narration.

DEATH IN *LIFE*

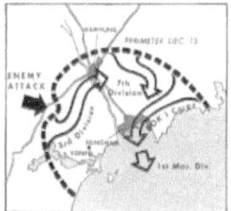

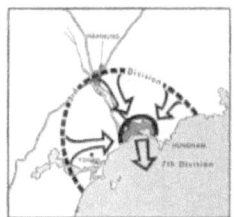

Evacuation CONTINUED

A CHILD CRIES (*above*) when she is told that her home must be destroyed to prepare defenses. She refuses to look (*below*) as bulldozers go to work.

FIRST PERIMETER HELD ENEMY FAR FROM PORT

FINAL PERIMETER BARELY ENCIRCLED HUNGNAM

ONE FOR THE BOOK: AN INVASION IN REVERSE

The orders from Tokyo to General Almond's X Corps to evacuate northeastern Korea came through Hungnam on Dec. 9. U.S. commanders had to improvise an operation—a historic "redeployment by sea," i.e., an amphibious invasion in reverse. Their first step was to establish a perimeter about 12 miles deep to protect their evacuation port (map above, *left*). This perimeter was manned by the 3rd and 7th U.S. Army Divisions and the two smaller divisions of the Republic of Korea I Corps. Inside Hungnam defenses were constructed in case the Chinese broke through the outer lines.

Even as the initial perimeter was formed, 109 transports began the enormous task of evacuation. First to go by Dec. 15 was the hard-hit 1st Marine Division followed by ROK I Corps by the 17th. As the number of men left on the cold, bleak hills decreased, more and more firepower was brought to bear by Navy cruisers and destroyers arriving offshore. From seven carriers Navy and Marine planes averaged about 500 sorties a day. Night was the critical time, but with the beachhead brilliantly lit by Navy star shells, Chinese attacks were spotted and then smashed by Army and Navy guns, which fired more than 10,000 shells a night.

By Dec. 21 the 7th Division had loaded and sailed, and only the 3rd remained on the perimeter. They pulled back to a tight line in the outskirts of Hungnam (map above, *right*) for the final phase, with the additional support of the nine 16-inch guns of the newly arrived battleship *Missouri*. By noon of the 24th only 3,000 men were still ashore. Demolition charges had been set so that nothing usable would be left. At 2:36 p.m. the last 200 men marched down to the docks. Calmly sergeants called the roll. When all were "present or accounted for," the last man left Hungnam. Then the Chinese began to creep over the hills. Minutes later demolition men threw the switch, and in one massive explosion Hungnam's waterfront was blown sky high. The campaign in North Korea was over.

CENTER OF HUNGNAM, AS LAST SOLDIERS PREPARED TO LEAVE, WAS MOSTLY GUTTED FACTORIES. TWISTED GIRDERS AND SMOKELESS CHIMNEYS. THE MAIN

FIG. 7.1.1 AND FIG. 7.1.2 AND FIG. 7.1.3 AND FIG. 7.1.4 AND FIG. 7.1.5 (*continued*).

LIFE's photo-essay follows a four-page "Great Debate" over the policy of containment and an accompanying editorial that calls for "clear talk." Several options present themselves: Do we consider "the conflict with our recognized enemy negotiable, as we have . . . during the recent period of 'containment?'" Or do we conclude that "the enemy's capacity to do us harm and to assault the whole

FIG. 7.1.1 AND FIG. 7.1.2 AND FIG. 7.1.3 AND FIG. 7.1.4 AND FIG. 7.1.5 (*continued*).

non-Communist world must be destroyed?" But then a shift in frame: "There IS a shooting war in Asia. Only one question has meaning for us in Asia now. The question is whether, and when, we fully acknowledge the existence of this war, and set out to defeat the enemy, which is Communist China with the Soviet Union just behind it."[8] *LIFE* then presents photographic evidence of the "IS" (Hungnam) as well as what might be done about it.

The multiplicity of perspectives comprising the photo-essay provide realist effect, a truth that is documented, graspable, shown from every possible angle (from the horizontal to the aerial). Military might (land, air, sea interoperability) and the ability to destroy invests in a powerful but sorrowful withdrawal. The Chinese creep is left to the imagination, visual hint of this alien presence provided by the display of "communist dead," the corpses examined both by troops of the 65th Puerto Rican Regiment and *LIFE*'s audience itself. The muscularity of invasion exists but has been placed in reverse; the newsreel-like photo-essay presents a temporal order that is askew.

The non-Communist world understands the importance of the small. The little girl serves as an emotive focal point, as do the puppies (captions explain that the former's house was necessarily destroyed; the latter are all that remain on the docks after the evacuation). The question of recognition lies in the ability to imagine the vast proportions of the advancing enemy, to witness the military might of the United States, to feel the big picture in terms of the everyday.

The Chinese entrance into the war, the withdrawal from the Yalu, the Hungnam evacuation—these events set in motion the scurry to consider a practicable limit line, possibly on Jeju Island (see chapter 1). To call retreat advance in another direction was, in fact, less nonsense than prescience. Hungnam was a world-historical event, a withdrawal that was an advance into the future. Hungnam was a crossroads, where calls for a broader conflict, for total war would begin to understand their inefficacy. To think of retreat as advance was to begin to overlay grand narratives of victory into the spatiotemporal order of limited war and containment. Such a shift calls for never-ending sacrifice. But, of course, in early January 1951 the matter was not quite settled.

Henry Luce was born in China (the son of missionaries), had penned "The American Century" (*LIFE*, February 1941), and was a major force in the China Lobby. *LIFE*'s view of the Hungnam withdrawal and the do-or-die challenge it appeared to present was subject to critique by those who questioned the idea of a blanket communism. In late January 1951, for example, the historian and China expert C. P. FitzGerald opined that in "American opinion . . . a dispute with China is merely a disguised quarrel with Russia, and there can be no solution short of the overthrow of Communist regimes in both countries."[9] FitzGerald found this view less than nuanced but difficult to counter domestically, given that the Department of State struggles to advance a "realistic" policy, assailed at every turn by the "China Lobby" and its accusations that state is "a nest of Red spies or crypto-communists."[10] FitzGerald offers a set of historical reasons that delink the Chinese revolution from the Soviet Union, as well as to argue that "The Asians, broadly indifferent to the issue of Communism versus Democracy, an issue that is unreal to the mass of the people, see the Chinese movement as an anti-colonial revolt."[11] For FitzGerald, the best outcome would be a "peaceful partition" of the world predicated upon "public agreement regarding where the frontier will be drawn."[12] Such pragmatic assessments of the success of the Chinese Revolution and its anticolonial appeal undergird the view that use of massive military power, even if only conventional, will not achieve desired results.

Even those who were more stridently anticommunist in tone called for more practical means to address the threat. W. Macmahon Ball maintained in 1951 that "it is hard, even with the most skilful use of propaganda techniques, to persuade people that their village has been 'liberated' if it has become a tangle of rubble and corpses. This is not to argue that the military weapon is always useless against communist revolt. . . . If a communist revolt is localised, a radical military operation may remove it before it has proliferated too far."[13] Both FitzGerald and Ball link the use of military force and its limitations to practicable outcomes, and these must take into account the best means of persuasion and the supposed views of Asians themselves. Ball, in fact, considers responsibilization the best approach: "If East Asia is to be saved from coming under the influence or control of the Soviet Union, it will be not by Westerners but by East Asians."[14]

How to see? Americans see communists; Asians see anticolonials. Military intervention should be surgical, no display of rubble and corpses. In the end, it would be best if intervention were not seen at all—East Asians should do it themselves. Ball summons the common medical trope, advocating for surgical strikes against a "communist virus" only when absolutely necessary. The attack against an unseen enemy seeks itself to remain unseen to the greatest extent possible, and in the end westerners themselves should disappear. *LIFE* sought consensus in the "Great Debate" with its first subtitle: "Above All Arguments There Is Agreement on One Thing—The Enemy." But the enemy was a crypto, hidden somewhere or in someone else, difficult to see. As Ball indicates, the emancipatory, the idea of a free world, would do best to render itself visible in ways other than the production of corpses.

In its January 8, 1951 photo-essay of Hungnam, *LIFE* editorializes via the captioned display of enemy bodies. Examination of the "communist dead" provides evidence to *LIFE*'s audience of a proliferation too advanced to localize. The frame of the argument between limited and total war revolves around this dispensation. The communist-as-corpse signals a hopelessly infected entity, beyond surgical cure. Observation of the dead frames the destruction of the port and a massive evacuation. *LIFE*'s task is to put the dead communist body into play in the "Great Debate," a photographic image that organizes the inexorable creep of the enemy. In doing so, *LIFE* layers the thanatographic—the writing and imaging of death and the dead—into the contentious discourse of containment.

SEEING FOR THOSE WHO CANNOT

More than a year passed before Harvey Kurtzman would retrace the road leading to Hungnam, his cover for the March–April 1952 special issue of *Two-Fisted Tales* asking readers to think about General Smith's famous quote with its use of bold lettering in the dialogue bubble: "We didn't retreat. We just **advanced** in **another direction**."[15] This cover, though, presents a soldier whose posture and facial expression coincide less with advance or retreat than with a stop, as the soldier's attempts to help a wounded man do not coincide with his own assertion. The journey thus begins with a disjunct, a visual questioning of movement in any direction. The image irrupts motion; the effect is of a freeze-frame, a photographic still. The approach, here, is beyond direction or purpose but to death itself.

Kurtzman's cover for the special issue remixes several of the looks appearing in *LIFE*'s Christmas Day 1950 edition. What do the eyes say, beyond the surface, or do they dwell on the surface without comprehending a more in-depth or higher meaning? The spread subtitled "Eyes" is one part of *LIFE*'s multisection layout entitled "There was a Christmas in Korea," which in its opening paragraph tells

FIG. 7.2.1 AND FIG. 7.2.2 (*Left*) Photograph for inset cover of *LIFE* (December 25, 1950). (*Right*) Feature photograph for the "Eyes" subsection of "There Was a Christmas in Korea." Photographs by David Douglas Duncan. Courtesy of Harry Ransom Center, the University of Texas at Austin.

FIG. 7.3 David Douglas Duncan photograph for "There Was a Christmas in Korea." Courtesy of Harry Ransom Center, the University of Texas at Austin.

of a journey through the "valley of the shadow of death," moves through images of retreating marines looking down at their dead, and concludes with the story of a wounded marine's evac to Japan.

LIFE tells us in captions that "The eyes of men who have looked at undiluted hell are not pleasant to meet soon after." But "There is no fear in their eyes and no great hatred. They were simply fighting their way out and hoping to stay alive." Marines "look but do not stop as they pass the bodies of men killed in the last Chinese ambush." These men cannot, in the moment, see the bigger picture of which they are a part. *LIFE*'s readers, though, have already been told in the layout's opening paragraph where to place these men and the fear they do not feel. It is in the journey through "the valley of the shadow of death."[16] This war is to be mapped biblically. *LIFE*'s readership must enter the picture by becoming the eyes for those who cannot see.

Following the layout is *LIFE*'s editorial, "The Blessing of God," subtitled "In Each Troubled Heart, and In The Rightness of Our Cause, We Shall Find His Sustaining Presence and His Guiding Hand." The editorial presents a variety of options: "Drop the bomb; get out of Asia and stand in Europe; stand in both; play for time and build our strength for war." But "none is the way of the Prince of Peace." We must remember that "at home and on the battlefield God does walk with us now. With all of us, that is, who will heed His presence and take His hand through the journey through whatever valleys may lie ahead." The retreat-as-advance from the Yalu takes the form of exodus. American corpses, vacant eyes—these are to be seen as markers of earthly suffering at the hands of "an enemy who requires no choice and has only the course of enslavement."[17]

WHAT HAPPENED AT HUNGNAM AND WHO SAW IT

Inside the special issue of *Two-Fisted Tales* awaits a "war map of Korea" a topographical guide to the four comics that will "document" (the term used on the cover to describe the special issue) the retreat from the Yalu. "The Trap!" offers this introductory framing: "A year ago! Just one year ago! How many of you remember what happened at the Changjin Reservoir? Stick with us! We'll tell you! Read our words carefully if you want to know what happened!"[18] The comics take us from the pullout of the 1st Marine Division ("The Trap") through the battle at "Hagaru-Ri" and the combined marine and army action near Sudong in "Link-up!" and finally to "Hungnam!" The story of what happened will unfold as a reworking of *LIFE*'s January 8, 1951 photo-essay. The ask is not only to read carefully but to look carefully.

How to see differently? We find the beginnings of an answer in "Link-Up!" The splash page presents suffering, pain, looks of fear and mourning as the Chinese soldiers gaze upon their own dead. Their advance is not an unseen creep but "through murderous air attacks and a curtain of artillery fire!" The triptych that follows secures a Chinese POV. Move to a later GI observation of the Chinese dead as "Lying there like stacks of cordwood."[19] The layout's message is clear: View both sides because you've just been given one.[20] The title "Link-Up!" is declarative (noun) on one level, imperative (verb) on another. We've indeed been asked to read carefully. The killing of the Chinese is murderous, and these deaths, too, are to be mourned. To link up with this POV is to see this. What the title says must be understood on the level of a visual grammar, which is where the final installment of the special issue, "Hungnam!" (script by Harvey Kurtzman, art by Wally Wood), will take us.

Panel sequences in "Hungnam!" offer a play of angles/durations/perspectives. A turn to filmic form brings dimension, depth, lighting, and mise-en-scène to the mix of images that interact with speech bubbles and caption boxes. "Hungnam!" begins with an aerial establishing shot, what the prefatory note calls the "grand evacuation." This framing image is a composite of two *LIFE* photographs included in its January 8, 1951 layout, with an addition. A C-46 medium transport aircraft and its shadow below interrupts the omniscience of *LIFE*'s presentation. The image provides observation of the aerial viewpoint itself, the perspective of the observer (the observation aircraft). "Hungnam!" will repeat verbatim *LIFE*'s closing line at the end of its own final caption: "The campaign in North Korea was over!"[21] This repetition documents not what has happened but the intertextual relation between the two Hungnams, a doubling that parodies *LIFE*'s production, how it makes up its photo-essays.

Qiana Whitted points out that "As a story-telling maneuver in EC scripts, the snap-ending would become inextricably tied to notions of poetic justice that marked the horror and crime comics in particular."[22] As he frequently noted in interviews, Kurtzman's aim was to make a sensationalist play in the field of vision itself. He found the stuff of pulp conducive to a moment of visual shock, what he called the "twisteroo" or at times the "switcheroo" and did not hesitate to make use of it in his war comic books, often in ways that called for a re-viewing or rereading of the entire work to look for anticipatory but overlooked clues. The twisteroo, in fact, progresses across panels, not always as a sudden switch at a comic's close. "Hungnam!" will center on a twisteroo taken from an emotive detail on the first page of *LIFE*'s layout, the photo of the puppies.

An image of tanks (long shot of barely discernible faces of soldiers above the turrets) and jets overhead, a "bedlam of lumbering war machines and war material," follows the establishing shot. Turn the page to four panels in long shot, medium-shot, medium close-up and full body shot: US and British whites, ROKs, a Black soldier, a Puerto Rican regiment, presented visually in a receding horizon perspective similar to *LIFE*'s photo of members of the 65th Puerto Rican Regiment examining communist dead at the perimeter. The visual trajectory is clear—we have moved from sky to machine, from aerial shot to long shot to medium and close-up shots of an international and interracial coalition. As Christine Hong points out, "the blurring of the color line would prove central to the hegemonic operations of U.S. militarism in Cold War Asia and the Pacific."[23] The assumption is that this coalition will take center stage. These are "United Nations troops, all slogging into the escape port of Hungnam, and . . . as soldiers know . . . wherever soldiers go marching . . ."

The final ellipsis takes viewers across the gutter and to the next panel, which finishes the sentence: "some Pooch seems to tag along!" The visual trick leads the eye back to the previous panel to find the pooch, diminutive at lower left. Pooch now centers the panel on the right, where we're told it's "just a pooch!" The comic's move from sky to ground has established expectation of a POV drawn from the men above, but Pooch only grows larger over the next three panels. And in the midst of this magnification (lower right-hand panel) we are told that Pooch "doesn't know a Korean from an American. . . . Doesn't know a single thing about politics!"[24] This visual experience defines the twisteroo/switcheroo. What happened will take place through Pooch's eyes.

Pooch does not respond to what *LIFE* asks of its audience, to set postracial solidarity in opposition to communism on the battlefield. Overcome by the sounds of war, the shaking of the earth as UN forces explode a gasoline terminal, Pooch joins a crowd of Koreans pressing toward the dock. The crowd is nearly identical in composition to the *LIFE* photograph of refugees at the pier, sans the ship in the background. Removed from its location in the *LIFE* layout, though, the crowd's motivation becomes unclear. They may not be fleeing because they want to (as described in *LIFE*) but because they have no other choice but to join Pooch in a desire to avoid danger and destruction: "Thousands of people running in each and every direction!" Surrounded by panels of Pooch, the crowd loses alignment, narrative place: "Poor innocent pooch! He looks for a kind glance, a sympathetic face . . . but nobody even notices him." In fact, Pooch is hurt when "someone steps on his paw!"[25]

LIFE concludes its layout with a three-photo narrative of departure (photo of the last boat leaving; demolition as viewed from the harbor; Hungnam prior to demolition as seen from hills behind the port). "Hungnam!" presents explosion from within, interspersing phrases borrowed from *LIFE* with exclamatory comic onomatopoeia. An immersion of sound and heat disallows an easy visual distancing; perspective loses itself within the exploding fragments, blasts, and flames. Blown up is an optics of any sort of advance.

The destruction sequence begins with what appears to be a deserted Hungnam from the harbor, shadows stretching across the water suggesting proximity. The peaceful waterfront city is, we are told, wired for explosion. The moment is of intertextual, dramatic irony. The composition of the horizontal panorama replicates *LIFE*'s photograph of what will happen, an exploding Hungnam. But something unseen draws viewers even closer. It is a sound, magnified, ascending: "arf, arf, arf, arf" (each arf increasing in size). Does this visual magnification ask us to consider the possibility of other such calls deafened in the explosion, amid its rubble? Demo does not equate with rescue.

The closing triptych of "Hungnam!" leaves us with a corpse, a star, and a map. This last is of the invasion-in-reverse, from the Changjin Reservoir (Kurtzman uses the Korean pronunciation) to Hungnam. Preceding it is a star shell lighting up the night momentarily, POV from the dock, cross in the rubble on the lower left. And first, Pooch's corpse on the dock, below a caption: "The birthday of the Prince of Peace! And yet, on earth, men were still killing their fellow men!"[26] The visual interruption is of a particular optics of salvation, the assertion of redemption to be had in present and future rescue missions. Demo does not sublimate to succor. Nor should emotive magnification of the small—puppies left on the docks, a little girl—appear merely descriptive, as truth. The caption rests uneasily above Pooch's corpse, a fitting epitaph. Pooch was killed. We heard it happen. We saw it. We are left to consider Pooch's afterdeath. Will Pooch's death be without end, travel in commemoration of a retreat that was an advance in another direction? Does Pooch stand in for civilian casualties, sign of collateral damage? How and why should we care about Pooch?

Pooch's death stands at the center of the end (Hungnam), as a lead to nowhere, to directionless. Pooch does not serve, as *LIFE*'s puppies do, as realist detail shoring up a tragic but magnificent evacuation. We won't be able to step in and see a bigger picture that Pooch does not understand. The star shell illuminates not to rescue but to observe and potentially destroy. Salvation does not arise from suffering here, where a map reminds us that a document can have multiple meanings. Pooch did not sacrifice for others on this day, the birthday of the Prince of Peace. Pooch's ask, in the end, is to consider how a visual layout creates an emotive "us" withdrawing to fight another day and an approaching, creeping "them," how a visual layout emplots our corpses and theirs. Pooch's death is just Pooch's death. Pooch's corpse becomes a meta-twisteroo, its appearance in and of itself questioning how it is that we ascribe narrative meaning to the afterdead.

A DANGEROUS CORPSE

Unlike World War II, it did not take long for *LIFE* to include photographs of the American dead in Korea. The appearance of these corpses follows an earlier decision to present images of World War II dead. James Kimble has shown how the circulation of the first photograph of US dead in World War II—George Strock's photo of three dead marines at Buna Beach in the September 20, 1943, issue of *LIFE*—did not mark a sudden shift in censorship policy but took place in close relation to the earlier release of graphic art depicting dead and dying soldiers as part of the Office of Civilian Defense's "Every Civilian a Fighter" movement. This home front campaign created "a tacit narrative, one that arguably worked to transform the visual interpretation of dead GI imagery away from the profane and into the realm of the sacred."[27] The shift extends sanctioned display of the dead (criminals, the underclass, victims of lynching, the enemy) to bodies associated with the sacrifice of Christ. At stake, as Kimble indicates, is how "to open the Pandora's box filled with spectral soldiers in the unwelcoming visual culture of the moment without activating widespread antiwar sentiment."[28] If the artwork made a "chilling accusation, one that sure made readers feel guilty and worthless," its aim was "not to condemn but motivate." The idea was to channel the feeling that one was not making much of a sacrifice into a redemptive desire to support the war effort at home.[29]

LIFE presented its first Korean War photograph of a GI corpse in its July 17, 1950 issue, a blanket-covered body accompanied by a subtitle making it clear that

FIG. 7.4 Carl Mydans's photograph for *LIFE*'s July 17, 1950 layout. Courtesy of Carl Mydans/the *LIFE* Picture Collection/Shutterstock.

this war "exacts a payment." The alliterative title of this issue's layout—"War by Jet and by GI"—celebrates the masculinist techno-weaponry available on this issue's cover, which presents the easy and routine confidence of an F-80 pilot having a cup of coffee back in Japan (we're told his wife and three children are with him there), now tempered by the price paid on the ground. The corpse provides visual evidence that "What had to happen was happening." The layout's display of the latest military technology—a jet fires five-inch rockets that "scream toward their target far below"—combines with a horizontal shot of the inert casualty: "War is not war until the first miserable, immortal doughfoot has had his guts blown out and his parents have got the word."[30] It is not the body but the body-to-be-mourned that declares war (mourning families will be pictured in another section of this issue). This management of the corpse represents its sacralization, as well as a call to mobilize. This corpse calls for a remembrance of the World War II way of seeing. But the body has not been fully revealed. The blanketed corpse was preparation for a fuller statement that would take place in next week's *LIFE*.

LIFE's July 24, 1950 issue would display a bound corpse, evidence of the enemy's criminality (see chapter 5). The corpse reveals a mode of enemy profanity associated with a war that was never a war, the downgrade voiced by President Truman in the June 29, 1950 press conference in which a reporter suggested "police action" as a term to aptly describe the conflict—to which Truman agreed, labeling the adversary a "bunch of bandits." What meaning attaches to death in a police action, at the hands of a lawless adversary? The article accompanying the image offers a quote from Lt. Edward James: "Why don't they send over something we can really fight a war with?" Why not make this war a real war? Profanity of the lawless enemy intersects with that of domestic lawmakers, those who support budget cuts downsizing the US military. It will now cost the nation $10 billion extra "to fight back to the 38th parallel. Until then we will go on being kicked around."[31] The corpse can call for a heightened use of military capability to destroy the enemy. To die with one's hands bound is also to die under restraints issued from the home front.

Such a multilayered profanity would endure beyond the Korean War. This corpse is a victim of those who refuse proper support or simply don't care. At the same time, a sense of sacrifice accrues to those who have suffered and those who have died not knowing how to see the purpose of their own death. The corpse can also provide evidence of senseless battlefield violence, death in a time and place that doesn't seem to enter history properly, as event. Here, one answer lies in the rejection of warfighting itself. The war that was not a war, the police action in Korea, gives rise to a dangerous corpse, a body that blends pro-war and antiwar positions into deaths that struggle to find meaning and perhaps are best forgotten.

THE CRYING FACE: A STORY OF TWO PAULS

The FBI opened an investigation on *Two-Fisted Tales* and *Frontline Combat* in 1952, an internal memo stating that "a review of the contents of these comic books reveals that some of the material is detrimental to the morale of combat soldiers and emphasizes the horrors, hardships and futility of war.... G-2 considers these publications subversive because they tend to discredit the army and undermine troop morale by presenting a picture of the inevitability of personal disaster in combat."[32] While the investigation found no "specific intent" to engage in seditious activity, Harvey Kurtzman would maintain an ongoing relationship with DoD throughout the run of *Two-Fisted Tales* and *Frontline Combat*.[33] The FBI noted correctly that Kurtzman was interested in the horrors of war. But this interest was not confined to the level of content.

Kurtzman was an active contributor to EC's *Tales from the Crypt* and *The Haunt of Fear*, both of which rehearse a visual frame central to horror: The play of the seen and the unseen that surrounds the watched watcher. Al Feldstein's cover for the November–December 1950 issue of *The Haunt of Fear*, for example, presents a man-in-the-middle casting his lantern on what he cannot see, the imminent possibility of death at the hands of a mummy who looms menacingly behind him. His look is fearful but unknowing—a look in the wrong direction. The empty coffin is not for the mummy but for the man; he unwittingly looks into his own future. Kurtzman would carry this visual scheme to his war comic books, to *MAD* (the subtitle on *MAD*'s lefthand cover margin was "Humor in a Jugular Vein"), as well as to his later presentation of soft porn in the long-running series *Little Annie Fanny* (*Playboy*), the eponymous character unaware of how she is watched within the diegesis and without.

Kurtzman's 1951 cover for the March–April issue of *Two-Fisted Tales* follows the horror template.[34] A GI addresses his buddy, Joe, as he looks upon a column of civilians in the distance. He has "heard that a lot of the enemy are infiltrating with these refugees!"[35] But he sees neither the figure looming large behind him nor the similarly outsized section of a corpse (Joe) in the foreground. The enemy is a monstrous combination of the hypervisible and unseen. He is also a slasher. The GI cannot see what we do, what the immediate future portends: He is on the cusp of getting his throat slit. The GI is about to become Joe. But the twisteroo was there from the beginning, in the careful visual alignment of the GI and the murderous slasher (their location, direction within the image, their bodily pose, left hand on their weapons). The tripartite perspectival composition of the image—background, middle ground, foreground—magnifies the GI in relation to the column in equal proportion to the magnification of the supposed infiltrator (in relation to the GI). They both stalk; they both appear to loom; and they both may be of the same size (as the size of Joe's corpse in the foreground indicates). If the GI does not see what is behind him, neither does the refugee column in the distance appear aware of the GI's presence.

We know the GI faces a dilemma as he asks, "How can we tell?" But the bubble also informs us that discernment begins only with what the GI has heard. The cover offers a visual play, a set of layered perspectives that seemingly asks for a way to distinguish between refugees and infiltrators while confirming the latter's presence in the form of the unseen slasher. But its tripartite structure presents something else, an ask to think about where the GI stands within a deathscape, in relation to seeing, killing, and the corpse (the one in the picture and the one he doesn't see, his own becoming-corpse). The twisteroo lies in the transformation of the sensationalist presentation of a lawless slasher (who is everywhere, unseen behind and hidden in the column) into the fear that the GI might not know how to see his own monstrosity (in relation to the column).

Such a turn to the self, a self-reflection, was central to Kurtzman's address of killing, othering, mourning, and the display of the corpse in one of his most famous *Frontline Combat* comics, "Big 'If!' " (March 1952). In an interview conducted long after the EC era, Kurtzman mentions in passing—and much to the surprise of his interlocutor—that he found inspiration for his depiction of

FIG. 7.5 David Douglas Duncan photograph for *LIFE* (October 9, 1950). Courtesy of Harry Ransom Center, the University of Texas at Austin.

the crying face in "Big 'If!' " in a photograph he came across in *LIFE*: "I built the character around that one picture. That was so impressive to me. The crying face was the strong point, the visual strong point of the whole story."[36] Bill Schelly considers the reference inaccurate, noting that Kurtzman's renderings (they are multiple) much more closely resemble shots of the crying face included in *LIFE* photographer David Douglas Duncan's popular book *This is War!* (1951, Bantam reprint in 1967).[37] This two-photo close-up of the crying face would circulate widely, part and parcel of the visual presentation of emotions experienced in Korean combat. As Junghyun Hwang points out, in *This is War!* "Duncan intends to represent a patriotic sentiment by capturing American (white) male bodies in a heroic light. His Marines are portrayed as heroes of a developmental drama, fighting their way from initiation to maturity."[38] Angle differs slightly, facial expression alters across the paired photos. They are stills that enter a filmstrip-like movement, a multidimensional, humanist take on what this is, war. Duncan's title makes a realist claim with its copula, the assertion of coincidence between photographs and referent.

It is quite possible that Kurtzman drew from all three photos (the one in *LIFE*, the two in *This is War!*) for "Big 'If!' " (the latter reworking the "is" into a visual presentation of supposition and chance). Kurtzman also replicated and repurposed another image from *LIFE* (the "Devil Posts" included in a July 10, 1950 *LIFE* layout of Korean everyday curiosities), while working off the storyline of the October 9, 1950 *LIFE* sequence covering the US advance on Seoul. The *LIFE* crying face appears in a medium shot located in a narrative and visual context, its caption explaining that Corporal Paul Ebensteiner's tears fall "not in pain but in sorrow." He "is crying, not because he is wounded, which he is, but because he thinks it is his fault that another Marine was killed, which it is not" (Duncan's narrative block preceding the photo sequence in *This is War!* recapitulates the *LIFE* caption).[39] Both *LIFE* and *This is War!* tell us that facial expression combines attribution of self-blame with mourning. Tragedy lies in dramatic irony, the certitude *LIFE* provides to its viewers/readers that this death is not Paul's fault (it is impossible to spot every North Korean mine), even if he may think this is the case. The move to doubled close-ups in *This is War!* highlights this abiding recrimination that wells from within and across frames, an expression of care for others above and beyond self.

Kurtzman will turn the crying face in another direction, toward a different doubling of Private Paul Maynard, one that involves his own death. This version of Paul will eventually break into tears as he declares "If!! . . . If!! Not much of a word! A little word! But lots of meaning!" Paul's reflection is on the past, how what happened twenty-seven minutes ago might not have happened, only if . . .

Paul enters the "if" of horror. He positions himself as home front spectator of a war movie (or perhaps reader/viewer of a war comic book) when he spots a P-51 overhead, exclaims that "Someone's gonna get it!" and decides it's time to "have chow and watch the show!"[40] We'll find out that he's the one who's gonna get it. He's stalked by the "if," by chance itself. That's a big "if." It's only on the final page that we're shown his crying face in a triptych that signals a double twisteroo— diegetic in reference to "Big 'If!,'" nondiegetic in reference to *LIFE/This is War!*. The body blown up in the previous, captionless panel is Paul. Paul was stalked by chance. We now know that all along the Paul who appears in the "Big 'If!'" is undead.

If there is a diegetic watcher, it has been the Devil Posts. From the beginning, the posts look down at Paul "as if to mock his thoughts ... as if they know he's thinking of the big. ... Big 'If!'"[41] *LIFE*'s presentation of the posts as orientalist curiosity retains an air of inscrutability but not as object. The "if" is so big it's given a narrative in reverse, a version of the auto-thanatography, the story one tells of one's own death. Here, the vantage point is from the living (Paul), the dead (his corpse), and the inanimate (the posts). The final twisteroo is that we're asked to read/view backward, consider what we didn't know and now understand. We're asked to animate the corpse, think about Paul's undead reflections. But what if we're in Paul's position, thinking we're watching a show? Paul wanted to step into the nondiegetic world. "Big 'If!'" pulls its readers/viewers into the diegetic frame. What if no certitude or meaning can be attached to your death at all other than it can happen anytime (you are stalked by chance itself)? What if, and this is a big if, you too are undead without knowing it? "Big 'If!'" is a horror story of chance that animates the corpse by placing it somewhere else than in the sacred, profane, or sacrificial.

TO SEE THE LIGHT

As is clear from multiple interviews and acknowledgments within the pages of the thanato-comics themselves, Harvey Kurtzman was in regular contact with government officials. He would publish materials related to recruitment/mobilization initiatives and dedicated special issues to service branches. He was given access to military personnel returned from Korea for interviews, and at least on one occasion was put in contact with the ROK consul general in New York City in order to consult on content.[42] He and his collaborating writers and artists created their comics in NYC, but this was a scene with its own set of pressures and very much on a continuum with what we would call embedded, on-the-ground wartime work. To be sure, *Two-Fisted Tales* and *Frontline Combat* often appear supportive of the war effort, celebratory of its weaponry, laudatory of the men who perform their military duties with resolve. Such portrayals, though, did not simply rest in uneasy juxtaposition to a critical thanatographics. Kurtzman's work makes use of these very moments to underscore the draw, the hook of war, the power of its optics. To display the visual regime that sanctions war-making (what we might call embedded cultural production) is to place it under observation. The presentation is not of the horrors of war but of the workings of the horror genre as means to watch the watcher.

The *Frontline Combat* special "Air Force Issue" (May 1953) includes an editorial note: "To get the stories in this issue, we spoke to several Air Force pilots who all saw action in Korea . . . saw action flying bombers, jet fighters, and helicopters!" Authenticity established, the editors tell their readers that "preparing this issue has convinced us of one thing! And that is that our Air Force is doing a fine job all over the world!"[43] The editors likely haven't visited US Air Force installations around the world but appear to have been persuaded. How will this manifest itself in the visual layouts? The note is caption-like—and in the fashion of *MAD*, says one thing that promises to show another (the latter making the one thing appear preposterous).

The special "Air Force Issue," includes a number of titles that use aircraft designations: "F-86 Sabre Jet!"; "H-5!"; "F-94!"; "B-26 Invader!" Weapon fetishism— the animation of the aircraft, their aesthetics-in-motion, their position as protagonist, the social relations among them—is on display. But the central concern will be with an in-flight optics that manages a view of the killed in a war that had become, by mid-1953, definitively limited (while establishing a modality that appeared replicable). "B-26 Invader!" best shows how the twisteroo involves a horror-inflected meditation on visibility/invisibility that extends to the routinization of destruction.

"B-26 Invader!" explores the beauty of bombing runs, the aesthetics of a relation between making-absent and absence itself. The presentation is of participation, a call to enter the cockpit: "Now we are going to fly with the bombers!" We'll be deeply embedded, not only with personnel but with weaponry itself. And we're asked up front to make this a visual experience: A jeep's headlights "illuminate the Korean night," providing impetus for this claim: "Lights! . . . This story can be **told** in lights!"[44] Indeed, this will be a story of lights, lights in the dark—an invitation to the immersive experience of combat film as shown in a theater. We are part of "Operation Strangle" and something more. Lights of a convoy are spotted, and "A thrill runs through the four-man crew as they get ready for business!" Bombing commences, and the convoy's lights quickly go out. The B-26 now proceeds on a "rekky" (recon) route and engages in a strafing run, "firing on any peep of light that shows . . . tearing a swath of light, like a string of huge firecrackers, through the night."[45]

As the B-26 heads back to base, the mood changes quickly: "Routine! The crew is sleepy and impassive!" But we now enter a "bomb's eye view." We've already seen the "long graceful arcs" of the bombs, flares compared to a "brilliant necklace." Now we experience ammunition trucks lighting up, "brilliant orange flashes! . . . Soon they blend in a flaming smear that slowly dies away like a log in the fireplace . . . red embers vanishing one by one!"[46] An aesthetics of light and dark, a lighting up of the dark to the point of destruction, a view of disappearance, and a return to darkness.

We've been told earlier how to distinguish between the two Koreas. As the B-26 heads to its target area, the look below reveals that "Lights twinkle in South Korea! City lights! Road and railroad lights!" North Korea is lit up by fireballs from cannon, searchlights ("probing patches of white"), "tracer bullets, like glowing orange beads arching, away through the blackness!" When the lights go out, "North Korea spreads pitch back below! For North Korea, unlike South Korea, is hiding!"[47]

The final three panels of "B-26 Invader!" offer a conversation:

> "Well, fellas! How'd she go?"
> "Aww, usual routine rekky route!"
> "Did you hit any good targets—get anything big?"
> "Naw, nothin' big. Not while **we** were there."[48]

Crisp, laconic, masculinist. But not a bomb's-eye view. "Operation Strangle" pushes the horror genre to a visual border, where death by strangulation will take place in the aestheticized play of light and dark. The operation is to touch without touching, to squeeze the neck without making physical contact. The operation is routine and gorgeous. Coloration, at once somnolent and explosive, intermixes with the "monotony" of a soundscape in which "Pratt and Whitney engines drone on and on, hypnotically." This is a thanatography of absence: no corpse, no strangler. The unseen does not stalk, loom from behind. Instead, the unseen is the target itself, the enemy bodies assumed both to be present and to disappear in colorful flashes, ensuing embers. The blanket strafing is of any "peep of light."

The bomber lands and the engines are cut off, the B-26 now "A lifeless machine sitting in the gloom!" What begins as celebration of the "B-26 Invader!" ends with the closest we get to the description of a corpse. The "sleepy crew" heads off in a jeep, "anxious to get to bed!" "B-26 Invader!" presents more than what the crew sees. We were there, embedded—in the cockpit, sutured to a bomb's-eye view that closed in a burst that did not reveal what was struck. An optics of magnificent destruction—at once fantastical and real—turns upon inference. What has happened?

A soporific masculinity replaces the celebratory aesthetics and heightened sensory realm of the jet pilot (see chapter 6). Body and mind have not been pushed to the limit. The visual presentation is of a dreamy, movie-like experience, moments of excitement tempered by drowsiness, even a sense of hypnosis. We've been put to sleep by Pratt & Whitney engines. It's just been the usual rekky route. Has this route actually taken us to a place where we've become machinelike? And the horror of it all is that we see neither this possibility nor the dying and mass death obscured by the awesome beauty of the light show below?

If the horror genre stages bodily disintegration, a becoming-corpse, it does so within a field of vision. Fear is made manifest. How to see fear? In the 1950s, the question of fear would turn inward, to a fear not only of the unseen but of the self that does not know how to see. This is the unaware self, open to a range of manipulations. In this horror scene, the fear is of brain death.

Harvey Kurtzman's May 1954 *MAD* reprints *LIFE*'s May 18, 1953 cover alongside a replication of its own cover as part of an "advertisement" for *MAD*: "Beware of Imitations!" declares the header, and below, in smaller print, a question: "Which one is the dirty imitation?"[49] *MAD*'s choice of this May 18, 1953 cover is not spurious.

The upper right-hand corner of *LIFE*'s cover heralds the second installment of former US Eighth Army Commander James A. Van Fleet's two-part article on the Korean War. Van Fleet forcefully makes the case against the "policy of limited war" that held back advance in Korea in late May of 1951 following the pushback against the final major Chinese offensive. The latter's weakness, Van Fleet argues in the first installment, makes victory in Korea possible and necessary if communist aggression, particularly in Southeast Asia is to be checked: "Korea is for us the right war in the right place at the right time and . . . with the right allies."[50] How to see the photograph of Sallilee Conlon on *LIFE*'s cover in relation to the lower-left caption "Harvest of Arts in the Midwest—Coed Opera Student from Indiana" and the upper-right title "General Van Fleet Tells How We Can Win in Korea?" *MAD* replaces the first with an alligator-like image captioned "Beautiful Girl of the Month," the second with "Humor in a Jugular Vein." Consume the visual/verbal montage that accompanies the one-word declaration *LIFE* at your own peril. Your brain will explode (as happens in the three-panel cartoon below the two covers).

Hillary Chute notes that Kurtzman "went from meticulous representation of then-contemporary historical wars to establishing *MAD*'s satirical send-ups."[51] Kurtzman, though, edited *MAD* during the Korean War while also serving as editor of *Two-Fisted Tales* and *Frontline Combat*. The antiheroism of *Two-Fisted Tales* and *Frontline Combat* takes a satirical turn in *MAD*, but all three publications share a pedagogy, a desire to etch how visual regimes offer an authenticity of feeling, belonging, purpose—an affective and sensory recognition that what is should be.

It is no accident that Kurtzman would follow his satirizing of the "glamorous war comics" in "G.I. Shmoe!" (*MAD* #10, April 1954; art by Wally Wood) with a self-reflexive take on comic-making in "Sound Effects!" (*MAD* #20, February 1955). "Hero Worship Dept" and "War Comics Dept," we're told, are two of the entities that have brought us *MAD*'s "Superduperman!" and "G.I. Shmoe!" The offer remains the same—look askance at the ways in which a visual field produces a sensory experience of self and mission in the world.

Dan Byrne-Smith writes of *MAD*'s impact that "Parody could allow for taking pleasure in one's cultural surroundings while simultaneously demonstrating that one is not taken in by it."[52] A flexible skepticism was both pleasurable and permissive, allowing for the possibility of a productive rebelliousness. Above all, a tempered anger and playful insanity (alluded to in *MAD*'s title) was an exhortation to the liveliness of the mind. *MAD* was not a war comic book, but it was thanatographic, fearful of a brain death that would result from not knowing how to see. In the end, such a thanatographics questions the image itself—as is evident in the May 1955 cover's injunction "THINK" centered on a completely blank background.

Chapter 8 will follow the questioning of conformism and fallibility, associated in varying degrees with menticide in the 1950s. The threat faced by the mind took its most sensational form in the wartime appearance of a neologism, brainwashing. But this would only be part of the story. To be sure, iterations of a mind-manipulative enemy (both within and without) would remain popular, but so would another frame. The quick call for a calibration of weakness in the ranks (and society at large) led to the consolidation of something universally present but impossible to locate, the breaking point. Around this acknowledgment would emerge a pragmatic self ready to acknowledge the challenge presented by a necessary, constitutive fragility. From the sense of crisis occasioned by the police action in Korea came the imperative to self-mobilize, to push it to the limit.

CHAPTER 8

THE BREAKING POINT

"NSC 68: United States Objectives and Programs for National Security" locates geopolitical crisis in totalitarian idolatry: "Where the despot holds absolute power—the absolute power of the absolutely powerful will—all other wills must be subjugated in an act of willing submission, a degradation willed by the individual upon himself under the compulsion of a perverted faith."[1] The individual wills their own enslavement because "The system becomes God, and submission to the will of God becomes submission to the will of the system."[2] Totalitarian power works to break the individual from within: "It is not enough to yield outwardly to the system—even Gandhian nonviolence is not acceptable—for the spirit of resistance and the devotion to a higher authority might then remain, and the individual would not be wholly submissive."[3] Making its way to President Harry Truman on April 7, 1950 (signed by him in September 1950, following the outbreak of the Korean War), NSC 68 tells us that if absolute power proceeds by willing degradation, the crisis turns upon frailty, the moment when a spirit of resistance flails before a false God.

Nor is the crisis limited to what NSC 68 calls the communist "slave state." In his commencement address at Notre Dame in May 1953, George Kennan extends arguments made famous in his 1946 "long telegram" from Moscow to the contemporary US cultural scene. As would many others in the 1950s, Kennan decries conformism: "What is it that causes us to huddle together, herdlike, in tastes and enthusiasms that represent only the common denominator of public acquiescence rather than show ourselves receptive to the tremendous flights of creative imagination of which the individual mind has shown itself capable?"[4] The battle is over unthinking but willing submission to the absolutism of public acquiescence itself, wherever it might be. The huddle assumes a rigidity, a fearful self-righteousness.

For this reason, it is imperative "to remember that the ultimate judgments of good and evil are not ours to make: that the wrath of man against his fellow man must always be tempered by his weakness and fallibility and by the example of forgiveness and redemption which is the essence of his Christian heritage."[5] The complexity, depth, and humanity of the free world self finds strength in "the flowering of the human spirit" that can only proceed by acknowledgment of vulnerability. Such an understanding counters "the forces of intolerance in our society," those that assert the authority to render judgments in absolutist terms.[6]

"Brainwashing," a neologism that first circulated during the Korean War, quickly became the popular name for manipulation of the mind, a bending of the will to a radically conformist ideology, an absolutism of the highest order. The brainwashed POW figured prominently in attempts to define what had happened in Korea, as well as in subsequent portrayals of a ubiquitous but unseen communist threat. The brainwashed are devoid of will and therefore unfree. They are zombielike. The brainwashed are the living dead. The term is alluring, and its shelf life has been long.

While brainwashing would achieve wide cultural currency, a more pragmatic universalism also came into play, one that dispensed with the sensationalist focus on mind control and coercive techniques of the communist enemy. Around the figure of the brainwashed arose a sustained reflection on frailty, a call for an understanding and assessment of a distribution of behaviors under stress. Already available in contemporary critiques of absolutism and conformism, the emphasis on fallibility as a marker of human depth and complexity would find inflection in the idea of the "breaking point" (a notion discussed in World War II military psychiatry). While brainwashing would retain a certain efficacy/visibility, recognition of the breaking point would play a large role in what we might call a flexible mobilization, one that turned to modes of self-empowerment to bolster US free-world humanism.

At what point would someone break (which they inevitably would), and how best to make use of that knowledge? The breaking point would differ according to the individual, while remaining common to all. The break occupied a place on a variable grid and a moment in time; it was a where and when that made imperfectability palpable, visible. The distinction between the communist and free worlds would lie in the latter's acknowledgment of human frailty and its accompanying regime of self-becoming and self-discovery, the pushing and testing of one's inevitable limits.

Here, the story begins with Samuel Fuller's wartime *The Steel Helmet* (1951) and its fold of the World War II battlefield into a site of unsure coordinates, Korea. Fuller's gritty combat film is a slow, careful revelation of the battlefield as "mindfield," the psychobiography of a broken retread. From trauma comes acknowledgment of weakness. Two US Steel Hour teleplays and the filmic adaptation of a Broadway play—David Davidson's "P.O.W." (1953); Rod Serling's "The Rack" (1955); and Karl Malden's *Time Limit* (1957)—continue the exploration of the battle-mind. The question of trauma moves to the brainwash. How to address disorientation, loss of control, collaboration under pressure? The answer will lie in realisms, truths offered by confession and therapeutic understanding. A tell-it-like-it-is portrayal of human inadequacy and self-interested behavior puts the idea of the brainwash itself on trial and determines its lack of credibility. The turn is pragmatic and hard-boiled at the same time, an opening to a calibrated form of heroism and masculinity underwritten in ethico-legal terms.

The story closes with the distillation of the breaking point in Rod Serling's pilot episode for *The Twilight Zone*, "Where is Everybody?" (1959). Here, the Korean War occupies a place in the shadows, assuming form in mediated reference, a kind of framing allusion. *The Twilight Zone* begins its run and ends the 1950s with an ask to its television audience: Observe the breaking point, see it now as part of a testing regime, a place that combines the management of body and mind with the promotion of limitless human endeavor in the cosmos.

THIS IS WAR

The Steel Helmet was shot over a two-week period on a very low budget (under $200,000) in Los Angeles's Griffith Park six months after the Korean War began.[7] A decorated World War II veteran (16th Infantry Regiment, 1st Infantry Division), Fuller was known for his work on the edges of the Hollywood studio system and for a gritty realism ready to tackle controversial material. Indeed, *The Steel Helmet* addresses anti-Black racism and is the first US film to raise the issue of Japanese internment during World War II. The film also screens the murder of a North Korean POW, which led to considerable outcry in the media, as well as to extensive internal discussion of Fuller and his work by the FBI, the MPAA, and DoD. After much back and forth, DoD did provide limited stock footage for Fuller's use in the film but only on the condition that no acknowledgment be made of its provenance.[8] Despite all of this, *The Steel Helmet* was something of a surprise box office success.

The Steel Helmet tells the story of a multiracial infantry squad (formed of stragglers who secure a forward observation post in a Buddhist temple and engage in a firefight with North Korean forces). A steel helmet appears throughout the opening credits, followed by a slow reveal of eyes peering left and right under the helmet. The soldier (Sgt. Zack; Gene Evans) cautiously moves his head upward. As his body emerges from a ditch, the audience is presented with a further revelation: He's bound. He'll low-crawl forward through a field of corpses, all with their hands tied. Accompanying this familiar image of bound US corpses (see chapters 5 and 7) is the appearance of a young Korean boy (Short Round; William Chun). He wields a knife and appears about to use it—but this will be to untie Zack rather than kill him, evidence that he is not murderous but friendly.

Daniel Kim points out that "What we see in *The Steel Helmet* is not just the emergence of the anti-Communism that provided the primary rationale for US entry into the Korean War but also a collision between residual and emergent vocabularies of race."[9] Zack will shortly use the term "gook" to refer to all Koreans, only to be corrected by Short Round, who declares that he is not a "gook" but "South Korean."[10] The distinction between helpmate and enemy lies beyond the surface, racial marking. Zack, though, is not really interested in racial or ideological polarities. His comment on the dead takes the form of an imperative: "See if there's any ammo on those guys." He'll then direct Short Round to get a helmet and take PeeWee Johnson's boots. *The Steel Helmet* locates the bound corpse within a thanatographics of survival. The corpse-field is littered with what might be of use, nothing more, nothing less.

If this take on the dead appears as the film's first sequence, lost in the mix is the first reveal, the slow appearance of Zack's face under his helmet. Sgt. Zack later shoots a North Korean POW (Harold Fong) when the latter mockingly reads a note written by Short Round prior to the latter's death. Lt. Driscoll (Steve Brodie) is furious: "Soldier, you're no soldier. You're just a big dumb stupid fatheaded sergeant. And if it takes me twenty years, I'll see that you're shot for killing a prisoner of war, understand?" Zack doesn't, and the film soon provides evidence why. As the firefight at the temple reaches its most intense moment, the retread Zack breaks.

Medium shot of Zack covered in haze, firing at the attacking enemy, opening and closing his eyes. Close-up as Zack pauses, looks up, no longer targeting the enemy. Return to medium shot in which Zack drops his weapon. Cut to Zack inside the temple:

LT. DRISCOLL: Hey soldier!
SGT. ZACK: Did you hear?
LT. DRISCOLL: [No response]
SGT. ZACK: Did you hear the Colonel?

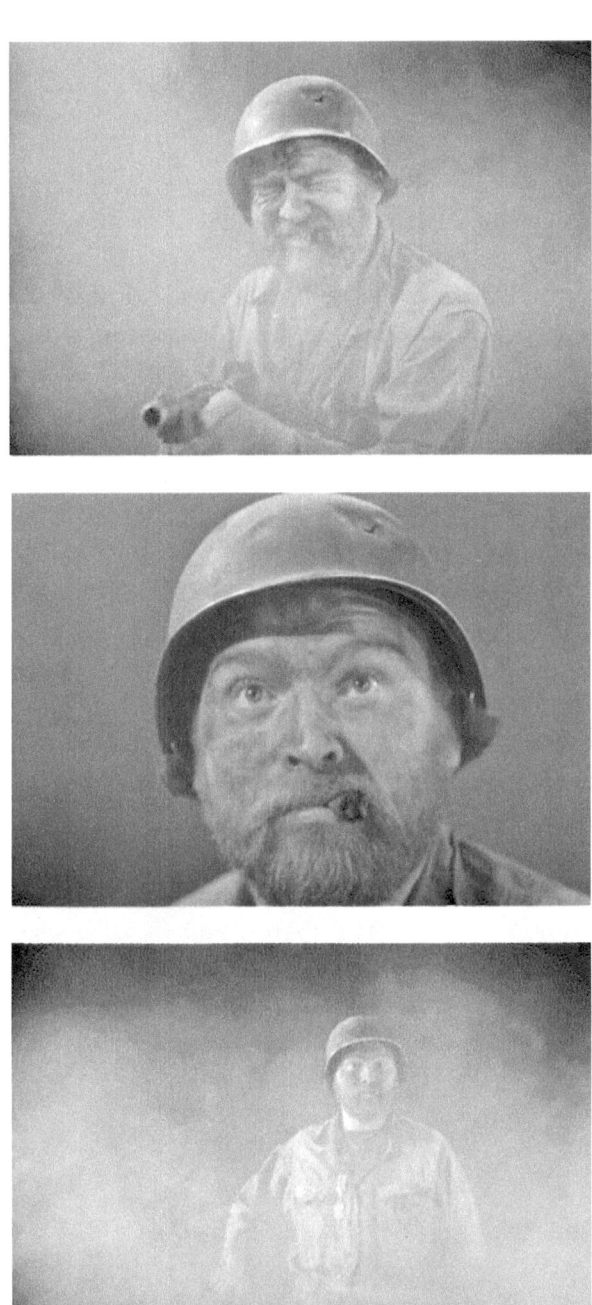

FIG. 8.1.1 AND FIG. 8.1.2 AND FIG. 8.1.3 Documenting the breaking point (*The Steel Helmet*). Stills courtesy of the Criterion Collection and Janus Films.

LT. DRISCOLL: Yeah, I heard what he said.

SGT. ZACK: What are we waiting for? Get off the beach. Get those Krauts. Get off the beach. Gotta get off the beach.

Dialogue explains not only this sequence but also *The Steel Helmet*'s opening slow reveal. The hard-boiled truth lies in something obscured by the stories that make the headlines (or, here, the film's credits). This is a film about what's under the steel helmet, inside the head. It's about Zack's brain, what's left of it. Sgt. Zack's a doggie, gruff, tough. But the film will show that he is zombielike, doesn't have control over his mind or his bodily actions. The first US commercial film to engage the Korean War screens combat trauma.[11] The retread Sgt. Zack never left the beach at Normandy and was from the beginning located beyond the accountability of an ethico-legal register.

What remains of the squad wards off the attack, and a fresh unit headed by an unnamed Lt. arrives at the temple: *Lt.*: "What's your outfit, soldier?" Silence as the camera pans from left to right, giving individual, still-like shots first to Sgt. Zack, then Cpl. Thompson (James Edwards), and finally to Sgt. Tanaka (Richard Loo), with Pvt. Baldy (Richard Monahan) slightly in the background to his left. *Zack*: "U.S. infantry."

Sgt. Thompson and Sgt. Tanaka have already acknowledged and addressed the North Korean POW's critique of segregation and the internment of Japanese Americans during World War II. Neither break in this film (and Tanaka is also a World War II veteran, 442nd Infantry Regiment). If the pan seeks to level racial hierarchies in the name of the US infantry, only one facial expression (white) presents a legibility of depth, presents itself as revelatory (based on what the film has shown its viewers). Zack's damaged brain—the call to see what is not readily apparent on the surface—marks his location as primus inter pares. It is Zack who bears the burden of retread breakdown, who shows that place doesn't matter—nor do causes.

THE OLD RETREAD

Drawing on his field experiences in the Korean War, the psychiatrist Albert J. Glass concludes that breakdown occurs when the "realistic dread of death or mutilation" heightens to an "influx of fear stimuli that cannot be either contained or discharged."[12] When these stimuli reach a certain point, "all intra-psychic sustaining powers are overcome and breakdown is inevitable."[13] While Glass finds

FIG. 8.2.1 AND FIG. 8.2.2 AND FIG. 8.2.3 *The Steel Helmet* (1951). Courtesy of the Criterion Collection and Janus Films.

it impossible to predict who will break, he turns to earlier World War II cases to argue that "Intense combat conditions with heavy losses in killed and wounded cannot be tolerated for more than brief periods of time by most persons."[14] The question becomes how to engage in preventative practices that will provide productivist ends. Early detection by psychiatrists embedded at the front (Glass finds that this has led to success in Korea), implementation of rotations, and the fostering of emotional investment in the unit serve to transform the "inward direction of fear" into a "release of energy that can be utilized for aggressive behavior" against "external objects."[15]

Glass's work follows Raymond Sobel's 1947 article "The 'Old Sergeant' Syndrome," which addresses the "chronic and progressive breakdown of the normal defenses against anxiety over long periods of combat."[16] Sobel concludes that "The question that these men presented was not, Why did they break? but rather, why did they continue to endure?"[17] He closes his argument with reference to Sergeant Porter in Lewis Milestone's *A Walk in the Sun* (1946) as an "illustrative" example.[18] Milestone's film was an adaptation of Harry Brown's 1944 novel (condensed version reprinted in the magazine *Liberty* in the same year), written while Brown was on active duty working for *Yank*, a weekly distributed to US military personnel throughout the world. Both film and literary text sympathetically detail the psychological breakdown of Sgt. Eddie Porter, who finds himself unable to proceed as his platoon heads inland after an amphibious landing at Salerno, Italy: "It was hard to say just what was the matter with Sergeant Porter. Perhaps he had just had too much war. Men vary in the amount of war they can take. Some are good only for one action, others can stand it for years."[19] *A Walk in the Sun* locates heroism in the very acknowledgment of Porter's breakdown, care and understanding becoming part and parcel of unit cohesion, purposefulness.

An unknown in Hollywood in 1946, Fuller had offered a scathing critique of *A Walk in the Sun* in a letter to Milestone (who kept it in his personal papers): "Blowing a whistle, waving an arm like Frank Merriwell and leading a parade of riflemen in an attack like Superman is one for serials—but I believe that people would like, if they like the idea of a war yarn at all, a story that is on the level."[20] Fuller considered *A Walk in the Sun* recuperative, displaying trauma only to conjure up well-known fantasy heroes from the serials (Merriwell) and comics. To tell it like it is means to "be real with no message."[21]

The Steel Helmet was Fuller's on-the-level answer to *A Walk in the Sun*. It is a film about a steel helmet, a film about World War II, the Korean War, future wars (*Steel Helmet* closes with the declaration that "There is no end to this story").[22] Linearity would give way to repetition. War would be a bodily, sensory experience, with profound effects upon the brain. *The Steel Helmet* is the story of what

Fuller—who soldiered in the Big Red One's amphibious landings in World War II, including Normandy—calls the "American doggie." This doggie, like Porter and the "Old Sergeant" can break. But from the beginning his only purpose is to make it out alive from the killing fields. He murders. And no care is given for his trauma. Bound corpses will not organize meaning; nor will invocations of law carry weight. The message that there is no message does not depart significantly from contemporary military psychiatry, sans the clinical consideration of measures to keep the doggie effective in the field.

BRAINWASH

The brainwash joins with military psychiatry in its exploration of the break and more generally of the mind. The scene of combat, though, gives way to a terrain more global in scope—the battle for minds themselves. This is a life and death struggle, a drama of mind-murder. This break marks a disorientation, a liminal state in which a mind-corpse now inhabits a live body. The journalist and former World War II OSS agent Edward Hunter is widely credited with introducing "brainwashing" into the English language in a September 1950 article in the *Miami News*.[23] His later *Brain-Washing in Red China: The Calculated Destruction of Men's Minds* (1951) and *Brainwashing: The Story of Men Who Defied It* (1956) outline a "conversion" process that, in the end, manufactures the "trance state" found in the "'new Soviet man' with the instinctive obedience of the termite instead of a free will which is subject to reasoning faculties and is therefore never 'reliable.'"[24] Elsewhere, the new Soviet man is described as a "robot creature," the kind of figure who appears in Richard Condon's *The Manchurian Candidate* (1959) and its 1962 filmic adaptation (remake in 2004).[25]

The Soviet appropriation of Ivan Pavlov's work has moved to China, where "The Chinese as a race are now undergoing mind treatment inside a Great Pavlovian Wall."[26] Similarly, the POW camps of the Korean War "were simply large clinical laboratories in which the prisoners were dealt with as patients and as mental cases."[27] Drawing on a conversation with a neuropsychiatrist named Dr. Leon Freedom, Hunter confirms that "The Reds were using the highly specialized knowledge of medical science to take balanced minds and make them unbalanced.... This was the exact opposite of the efforts of medical science in the Free World, which were directed toward discovering the source of a patient's mental disorder."[28] The brainwash perverts the clinical setting, the rehabilitative trajectory. For Hunter, resistance will be faith-based, and the Black experience is exemplary: "What soon became evident to me was that the U.S. had a great deal to learn from its Negro [sic] citizens faced by adversity in the p.o.w. camps."[29] Corporal Robert Stell, a Black POW, informs him that "Religion for a Negro [sic] is something he can live.... That was the personal man-to-man religion—each man and his God—that we took to the p.o.w. camps. How could the Reds take that away from us? They were helpless against it."[30] Salvation is to be found in the imperfect but emancipatory history of the United States. Stell tells Hunter that "It isn't that I appreciate hardships or like to suffer.... We wouldn't like to have to call on God as much as we do. But we've learned how to do it from having to, and it sure stood by us in Korea."[31] It is this imperfectability and the accompanying desire for progress, both religious and secular, that anchors the free world.

The brainwash, then, is at once therapy in reverse and antihistorical: "The aim is to create a mechanism in flesh and blood, with new beliefs and new thought processes inserted into a captive body. What that amounts to is the search for a slave race."[32] If brainwashing empties out the soul, it does so in its elimination of the inner conflict that propels an emancipatory history, premised as it is upon an embodied experience of suffering and faith across racial lines (and therefore universal).

A CODE FOR ALL

In 1954, the Eisenhower administration tasked a Defense Advisory Committee with a one-year study on the ethical and legal questions involving POW conduct, enmeshed as it had become with talk in mainstream media of capitulation, collaboration, and the brainwash. The committee's July 1955 report led to the creation of the Code of Conduct for Members of the United States Armed Forces. The code was implemented in August 1955 via Executive Order 10631 (amended in March 1988 in order to excise masculine nouns) and remains a staple of basic training across the services as of this writing. The committee's report sought to set the record straight: "Public opinion tends to settle for generalities because they are convenient. The 'single slot' is easy to handle. The some-equals-all deduction, quickly arrived at, does not entail bothersome thinking. But these handy and quick devices serve to distort factuality. Misconceptions result."[33] Central among these misconceptions was the idea that most, if not all, of the US POWs were subjected to brainwashing:

> The Committee made a thorough investigation of the "brainwashing" question. In some cases this time consuming and coercive technique was used to obtain

confessions. In these cases American prisoners of war were subjected to mental and physical torture, psychiatric pressures or "Pavlov Dogs" treatment.

Most of the prisoners, however, were not subjected to brainwashing, but were given a high-powered indoctrination for propaganda purposes.[34]

The brainwashing of POWs was less dangerous than uninformed public opinion, which lazily makes the "some-equals-all deduction." While the Committee called for a continuing set of training protocols for service members, it emphasized that "skill must be reinforced by will—by moral character and by basic beliefs instilled in home and classroom long before a lad enters the Military Service."[35] The locus of the war resides not in the training of bodies, but in the workings of the mind: "As a serviceman thinketh so is he."[36]

The nuclear threat means that "Today there are no distant front lines, remote no man's lands, far-off rear areas. . . . Under such circumstances, the new code of conduct for the American serviceman might well serve the American citizen."[37] The fix identifies two targets, domestic (the distortion of public opinion) and foreign (propaganda). The public's ready assumption of a generalizing brainwashing is itself a form of flattening, conformist weakness. The Defense Advisory Committee dismisses the brainwash as exception to the rule. That the majority who broke were not brainwashed shifts the blame to a common weakness rather than the invidious techniques of mind control.

Article V of the code indicates that POWs are required to give name, rank, service number, and date of birth. But service members also memorize the next sentence in basic training: "I will evade answering further questions to the best of my ability." The code sanctions the variability of the limit. Borrowing from military psychiatry, techniques of self-strengthening surround an acknowledgment of inevitable frailty. Only here emotional investment in the unit expands to a military-civilian nexus, to childhood, the home, the classroom. The question of the breaking point is not merely a military matter. Civilian minds must possess the wherewithal to push it to the limit.

2130 HRS. (9:30 P.M.)

A live dramatic anthology series broadcast biweekly from New York City, the enormously popular United States Steel Hour transitioned from radio to television on October 27, 1953 with an inaugural episode advertised that same day in the *New York Times* as "a brilliant study of one 'brainwashed' G.I. and the tortuous road back to life."³⁸ "P.O.W." would premiere in living rooms across the United States while the postarmistice exchange of prisoners, Operation Big Switch (August–December 1953), was still taking place. Viewers were asked to tune into ABC at "2130 hrs." (civilian translation provided in the *New York Times* ad as 9:30 p.m.).

If World War II combat trauma was to be addressed sparingly (*Let There Be Light*, John Huston's 1946 documentary on returnee trauma and rehabilitation in a Long Island hospital was censored through the early 1980s), Korean War brainwashing was given a national television audience. Like Huston's documentary, "P.O.W." (script by David Davidson) screens individual and group therapy sessions in a military hospital where a cohort of former POWs (prisoners of Camp 9) receive physical and psychological checkups following their return stateside. The two voice-over narrators of the episode are a medical doctor, Captain Willis (Donald McHenry), and a neuropsychologist, Major Mead (Gary Merrill), who plays an important role in the teleplay. Voice-over framing takes the form of medical reports on the patients' condition. The rehabilitative process will aid the returnees while providing a documentary-like examination of what happened at Camp 9. It turns out that "brainwashing" is given scare quotes not simply because the term is a neologism.

The teleplay begins with what amounts to testimonials from a number of former POWs who aver that Lucky (Richard Kiley), the central character, was a well-liked leader, the kind of guy who kept everyone together. He had a reputation for standing up to the Chinese. "There was a brain they couldn't wash," Marty declares. Danny tells a nurse that he contemplated suicide, "But then … Lucky stood up to those Commie slopes [*sic*] and turned their own brains inside out."

Lucky breaks down when he visits home, hearing voices while alone, awake in his room: "Be honest, that's all we ask of you. Truth, tell the truth! Liar! Liar! Liar, tell the truth!" It will be up to the neuropsychologist Mead to figure Lucky out, as well as to understand why "Iron Man" Bonsell (Brian Keith) is plagued by a perforated ulcer in his colon. Epitome of gruff, laconic white masculinity, it was Iron Man who led an escape attempt foiled by the Chinese. We are shown Iron Man's subsequent torture by Chinese guards: He coughs up his rank, serial number, and nothing else. Lucky will confess that he talked after being thrown in the hole: "I don't know what I said, I just told them everything." Mead will proceed to boil it down for the benefit not only of Lucky but for the US Steel Hour's audience:

> *Mead:* I'll tell you the way it is. We've been lucky, we Americans. Stuff like that never happened to us. Secret police, labor camps, torture, confessions. Europe

and Asia, they've known about it a long time. But between us, Lucky, in that kind of communist degradation, we've had a couple of oceans. Also a Bill of Rights. But in Korea, in Korea some of us found out, the awful secret. That Americans too have a breaking point.

This point is brought home when we learn that Lucky never broke—he was duped into thinking so. The real culprit is Iron Man: "The pain inside me here was like a rat, chewing me apart, day after day. I had to stop it. I had to. I went over to 'em. I, I crawled. I talked." We will need a different definition of manhood. Mead explains: "The most any of us can do is to be the best man that's in him. And, after that, to try to live with himself. These are the kinds of experiences that captured American GIs underwent as a result of their treatment in the communist prison camps." Truth resides in the unseen, not the surface. Otherness lies within—this is the constitutive otherness of the limit, of the breaking point.

LIMITED SELVES

Even as Hunter's brainwash located malicious intent in a communist other, his work intersects with the broader critique of the delusory and the trancelike associated with domestic mass culture. A number of mid-1950s bestsellers sought to unpack zombielike consumption and organizational behavior, among them Sloan Wilson's *The Man in the Gray Flannel Suit* (1955; filmic adaptation in 1956), Robert Lindner's essay collection *Must You Conform?* (1956), and Vance Packard's *The Hidden Persuaders* (1957). An across-the-board critique of fascism, communism, totalitarianism, unthinking "public opinion," advertising proffers a spectrum of organizational behavior that can kill brains, rape them, wash them, stretch them out on the rack, or simply lull them into submission, make use of all available means to turn them into what the psychoanalyst Robert Lindner (author of *Rebel Without a Cause*) calls a "walking zombie."[39]

Eric Bennett underscores the movement from a critique of the model totalitarian citizen to a generalized push against "technocratic puppeteering":

> From the elements of critique common to such figures as Mailer, Adorno, and Arendt . . . there emerged a common antidote: the indivisible integrity of spirit; the individuality of the victim, his actuality as a person, her fullness of self—for it was precisely this selfhood that the death camps, the advertisers, and the propagandists aimed to destroy. . . . With great deftness, the Cold War establishment

in the United States transformed such analysis into a vindication of the liberal democratic capitalist subject.[40]

The call to acknowledge the breaking point, though, moves away from a given selfhood, a fullness. The antidote would arrive elsewhere, in acknowledgment of a reality Joost Meerloo—who follows both Hunter and Lindner in his concern not only with totalitarian societies but with the troubling tendencies found in the West—locates in the first chapter title of his popular *The Rape of the Mind: The Psychology of Thought Control—Menticide and Brainwashing*: "You Too Would Confess."[41] Meerloo, who avers to have coined the term "menticide" (by drawing on the etymology of "genocide"), describes in sensational detail how "it is now technically possible to bring the human mind into a condition of enslavement and submission" precisely as means to address "our lack of understanding of the limits of heroism. We are just beginning to understand what these limits are, and how they are used, both politically and psychologically, by the totalitarians."[42] Empowerment in the era of limited war will proceed from this recognition.

If the Korean War POW precipitated a codification of conduct that invokes a military-civilian nexus, the ontology of the warrior-self would also prove central to a mobilization, not of the event (an ad hoc mobilization in the name of total war) but for undeclared wars, limited conflicts whose purpose could appear more nebulous and whose outcomes were not always legible. These were imperfect, utilitarian wars that reflected vulnerability in and of itself—they were to be fought in its name. Victory would not be immediate. The brainwash would play in popular culture, but the figure of the Korean War POW also provided a site for the exploration of a warrior who troubled the either-or, who would make ethical compromises for the greater good. This was a figure proper to the articulation of limited war, sanctioned as it was by its perceived reticence, its attempt to temper escalation as a series of steps meant to achieve consensus.

The idea of the breaking point also fit well with definitions of human nature circulating in contemporary international relations (IR) scholarship. For the theologian and IR theorist Reinhold Niebuhr, critique of communism called for a measured understanding of the self, a "sense of contrition about the common human frailties and foibles which lie at the foundation of both the enemy's demonry and our vanities."[43] Those in possession of such an awareness are the "children of light." They are knowing but dismissive of those they counter: "The children of light must be armed with the wisdom of the children of the darkness but remain free of their malice. They must know the power of self-interest in human society without giving it moral justification."[44] Self-righteousness is a form of self-delusion: "This is why a frantic anticommunism can become so similar in its temper of hatefulness to communism itself, the difference in the respective creeds being unable to prevent the similarity of spirit."[45] That is, "the spirit of humanity is not preserved primarily by a correct division of the nature of 'humanitas' but rather by an existential awareness of the limits, as well as the possibilities of human power and goodness."[46] Such a play between limit and possibility requires vigilance, management, and honesty—not radical othering or simple attribution of manipulation.

As the political scientist Hans Morgenthau pointed out in his magisterial *Politics Among Nations: The Struggle for Power and Peace* (1948), "the world, imperfect as it is from the rational point of view, is the result of forces inherent in human nature. To improve the world one must work with those forces, not against them." Given that "moral principles can never be fully realized but must at best be approximated," the aim will be "the realization of the lesser evil rather than of the absolute good."[47] Arthur M. Schlesinger Jr. echoes this position pithily in his widely-read *The Vital Center: The Politics of Freedom* (1948): "The rise of totalitarianism . . . signifies more than an internal crisis for democratic society. It signifies an internal crisis for democratic man. There is a Hitler, a Stalin in every breast."[48] The internal crisis is a continuous war. Failure to understand this struggle arises from a misunderstanding of what Morgenthau calls "human nature as it actually is," as well as "with the historic processes as they actually take place."[49] This invocation of realism and the ascription of a vitality, an energy at the center intersect with the pragmatics—the optimizing management of limits—surrounding the figure of the Korean War POW.

FOR THE GREATER GOOD

On April 22, 1955, the US Steel Hour aired its second and last episode on Korean War POWs, Rod Serling's "The Rack." Serling's teleplay, a legal drama, would be adapted for the big screen in 1956 (the MGM remake stars Paul Newman, with screenplay by Stewart Stern, veteran of the Battle of the Bulge and screenwriter of *Rebel Without a Cause*). "The Rack" was shortly followed by *Time Limit* (1957), a popular legal drama starring Richard Widmark, directed by Karl Malden, and based on a successful 1956 Broadway play. Both "The Rack" and *Time Limit* are at pains to add nuance to the assessment of Korean War POW conduct, dwelling on the ways that the Uniform Code of Military Justice (UCMJ) and associated military investigations seek to present an impartial assessment of possible collaborative acts. At stake is the question of human nature, how to temper an understanding of behavior under duress in relation to the rule of law. An investigation of the truth becomes an exploration of ethics that will frame what it means to mobilize a free-world population via acknowledgment of the limit.

This mid-1950s constellation of teleplay, play, and filmic adaptation moves decisively away from brainwashing to the ethical question of conduct the Defense Advisory Committee considered relevant not only on an interservice level but across the American social fabric. These dramas lift the narrative of POW suffering, victimization, and breaking—central to representations of the Korean War in the 1950s—into an ethico-legal register that, in turn, extends the rehabilitative process to the broader, civilian sphere. How to build an effective military-civilian nexus suitable for what promises to be a continuous global struggle?

In "The Rack," Captain Ed Hall Jr. (Marshall Thompson), "an infantry captain with a star and a cluster," stands accused of collaboration with the enemy in a POW camp. Major Sam Moulton (Wendell Corey) has been assigned to investigate and prosecute. Thirty witnesses are lined up to testify against Hall, and Moulton's boss, Colonel Hansen (Meville Ruick), considers the case "cut and dried." He lacks nuance.

Ed appears for the first time in the teleplay, limping into the living room. He'll start flipping a light switch on and off, a diegetic play of light and dark that will frame the teleplay. His shadow appears only to disappear. He's more in the neither-nor than the either-or. Ed has a silver star, but he also collaborated. He's a shadow, a child of the twilight, Serling's favorite time and place. The teleplay will revolve around his ethico-legal dispensation, Moulton and the defense counsel, Captain Steve Wasnick (Keenan Wynn) hashing out the problem off-the-record. Moulton postulates what will happen if Ed's declared innocent:

> **MOULTON:** In that second you must establish a precedent. If a man must break he must break. That's all there is to it. We're not trying to crucify a man, Steve. We're trying to put a little muscle in every other man who may have to face the same things he did.
> **WASNICK:** We sentence a man as an example. We put a man on a rack for want of an alternative. Well that may be law, but it's a hell of a long way from justice, Major.

Acknowledgment of the universal breaking point made, pragmatics demands an example, a move that mirrors the rack presumed to have existed in the POW camp.[50] Closing arguments will underscore the stakes:

MOULTON: The security of the United States is an unbroken chain that extends from an eight-man patrol in the foremost area of an unpronounceable island to a school in Dubuque Iowa to a flat in Brooklyn. Every front porch. If you find Captain Hall innocent of collaboration, you find 3,000 men who did not break guilty of stupidity. You must find Captain Hall guilty as charged.

WASNICK: To condemn a man for cowardice is altogether right and just. But cowardice does not occur when bravery ends. It is not either-or. For if it were, all men would be heroes or cowards. I humbly submit to the court that there must be an in-between.

The question of the in-between calls for flexible management of the universal breaking point. When Moulton preps Lt. Anderson, a witness for the prosecution, the latter declares that Ed "was a brave man" who saved his life and "is a human being." The breaking point is inevitable but does not define a self in toto. Nor does it represent a dividing line. It refers less to space than to time.

Following his submission of the draft for "The Rack," Serling was called to the Pentagon and spent three weeks on site meeting with officers involved in the prosecution of POW collaborators. He would later indicate that some of his dialogue was taken verbatim from these interviews.[51] "The Rack" navigates the need to mediate exemplarity, to place time (the break) in relation to space (the unbroken chain, the extension of home front to tip of the spear). The debate reflects upon and tempers the rack while allowing punishment to proceed.

Time Limit offers a slow reveal of the need to compromise. Major Harry Cargill (Richard Basehart) is accused of lecturing his men on the merits of communism, espousing the enemy's cause in radio broadcasts, and signing a confession indicating that the United States had engaged in germ warfare. Queried by Colonel William Edwards (Richard Widmark) as to why he broke, his response appears straightforward: "I suppose that some men are weaker than others." He will later compare the "mind of man" to granite, noting that under pressure both turn to liquid. The mind is frangible.

Edwards himself is under pressure from General J. Connors (Carl Reid) to wrap up his investigation and recommend court-martial (this pressure signals the first meaning of "time limit"). The case is pressing for the general, as his son, Captain Joe Connors (Yale Wexler) was killed at Camp Gee Gee. We are shown just one witness deposition, that of Lt. Miller (Rip Torn). It is the oddly repetitive testimony of witnesses that eventually gives Edwards pause. Miller echoes others when he declares that Cpt. Connors and another soldier, Lt. Harvey, died of "acute dysentery." He's got a vacant expression on his face, almost trancelike. Has he been brainwashed, and the others, too? The film provides the verbal/visual cues to put this suspicion into play.

Edwards pushes Cargill hard: "I think you're haunted by the ghosts of dead minds as well as dead bodies. Minds that you helped to kill by your broadcasts. Minds that were pushed over the brink by you. Isn't that right, Major?" Later we will discover that Joe Connors ratted on Harvey, who was involved in an escape plan. The men in Cargill's shack agree to draw lots on who should kill Connors, all vowing never to speak of the incident. Cargill urges them to desist and refuses to participate. Miller draws the unlucky stick and strangles Connors. At this point, the camp commandant, Colonel Kim (Khigh Dhiegh, who would later appear as Dr. Yen Lo in *The Manchurian Candidate*) threatens to kill all sixteen men in the shack if Cargill doesn't cooperate. Cargill chose to save his men.

Later, General Connors enters Edwards's office to find Miller talking about a stool pigeon they'd been forced to kill. He'll interrogate Cargill but the latter clams up. When he calls Cargill a "dirty swine" and a "traitor," Edwards steps in and tells him the truth:

> **CONNORS:** You have no proof.
> **EDWARDS:** I have. Conclusive proof. [A long pause; Edwards places his hand on Connors' shoulder] Every man has his limit, sir. There's no crime in being human.

Cargill to Connors, after the latter declares his own son guilty of cowardice: "You can't ask a man to be a hero forever. There ought to be a time limit." *Time Limit* has dismissed the brainwash. And Cargill's pragmatics do not oppose Joe Connors's cowardice. Presented with no good choice, the latter performed to the best of his abilities. Cargill and Joe are simply case studies of performance under pressure. They have done their best; they both confronted risk and pushed their way to their own limits. The lesson of the POW camps extends beyond military circles; the military-civilian distinction diminishes in this maximalist regime of self-empowerment. The call is to see how far you can take it, to "Be All You Can Be," as a popular 1980s US Army recruiting slogan (revived in 2023) would have it.

Robert Lindner's critique of the "Mass Man" he found in 1950s US society similarly rested upon a form of goal-oriented, personal expansiveness. For Linder, communism functioned as a religion that fulfilled the need for stability and sense of belonging felt especially by the psychologically weak and neurotics.[52] The battle lines are clear: "the forces of conformity have collected against the spirit of man."[53] Against these forces stands the hero of "positive rebellion," a figure who is "restless, seeking, curious, forever unsatisfied, eternally struggling." The positive rebel is "the only animal which persistently wages war against all that limits it."[54] This rebelliousness includes a battle with "the limits of his body: it has led him to extend his senses almost infinitely, so that his fingers now probe space."[55] Nor can the positive rebel rest "content with the limits of his mind." This is a masculinist rebel with a cause, "pledged to progress, defined as those advances against all limitations or barriers to a break-through into the next dimension of evolution, whatever that dimension may be."[56] The foe, then, is as much internal as external, the struggle continuous.

A best-selling author, Lindner has become something of a footnote to the 1950s. His notion of positive rebellion, however, has traveled well, if not as visibly as the sensationalist allure of the brainwash. In the end he distills from pathologies of subservience a call for a "pedagogy of freedom" that "lies within ourselves. . . . With this act, we manifest our own maturity and obtain the *right* to instruct others."[57] The declaration is of free-world governance. This is struggle in its highest form, a battle in which the killing fields are second-order ephemera. The expansion of inner freedom pushes limits outward and upward, to the world, the universe.

EVERYWHERE, NOWHERE

Camera pans across trees to a man in a jumpsuit walking aimlessly down a dirt road. He finds himself in an empty town. He has no memory of who he is or why he is there. His only human interaction will be with an image of himself in a mirror. No one else is in the town, although he comes across traces of life—music from a diner jukebox, a lit cigar in an ashtray. He is utterly alone. The title of *The Twilight Zone*'s 1959 pilot episode is fitting: "Where is Everybody?"

The episode's conclusion nears as the man trips over a bicycle and encounters a large eye, which turns out to be an image adorning an optometrist's window: "Somebody help me. Help me. Help me, help me. Please help me." The "help me's" continue as we cut away from his face, covered with sweat, into a dark room where a group of men are observing him: "Help me, somebody's looking at me, somebody's watching me, somebody help me." The man, Mike Ferris (Earl Holliman), has been confined in an isolation pod in an aircraft hangar, subject of a carefully controlled test—replete with numbers, graphs, scientific observation via electrodes placed on his body—designed to see if he can endure for the length of time it will take an astronaut to reach the moon. Rod Serling inaugurates *The*

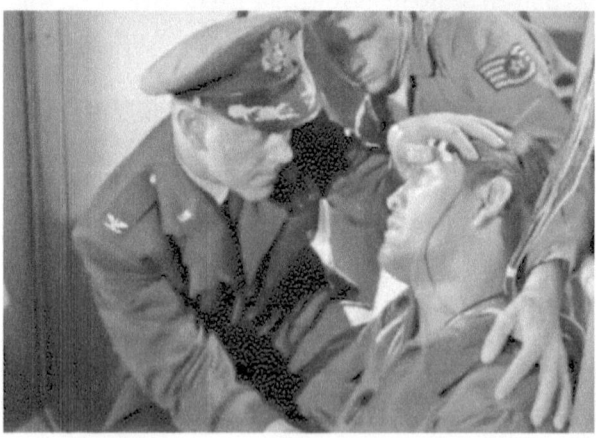

FIG. 8.3.1 AND FIG. 8.3.2 AND FIG. 8.3.3 *The Twilight Zone*: "Where is Everybody?" Stills courtesy of CBS Broadcasting.

Twilight Zone with a screening of therapy in reverse, a mirroring of Edward Hunter's definition of the brainwash. Both aim to employ scientific methods to produce the breakdown.[58]

In what the television audience will later be told is his delusion, Mike, clad in a flight suit, wanders out of the trees into the empty town as if he's been shot down. But he finds himself on the ground in the United States. The audience is watching the condensed trajectory of a downed pilot, returned to the United States from an overseas war (World War II, Korea, or a retread combination of both?) to find himself in the uncanny. Bracket the surprise ending and "Where is Everybody?" becomes the most sustained presentation of a traumatized US service member since Samuel Fuller's *The Steel Helmet*.

While the concluding scene may have appeased potential censorship (which always worried Serling), it cannot erase what now appears as illusion. Mike himself is curious as to what happened: "What was the matter with me? Just off my rocker, huh?" "Just a kind of nightmare, Ferris, that your mind manufactured for you," replies the medical officer. But Serling's pilot episode has spent nearly its entirety presenting Mike's experience as real.

Night falls as Mike first approaches the blinking lights of the Savoy Theater. He pauses in front of a poster for the film *Battle Hymn*, Rock Hudson in a flight suit standing below the wheel well of a jet fighter. He recognizes himself in the poster, as if it were a mirror: "Air force. Air force. Air force, I'm Air force!" He rushes into the empty theater. A massive bomber suddenly appears on the screen,

FIG. 8.4 *The Twilight Zone*: "Where is Everybody?" Still courtesy of CBS Broadcasting.

the roar of its engine accompanied by dramatic music. Mike leaps up the stairs to the projection room: "Hey, who's up there? Who's running the pictures?" No one there, just the bright light of the projector beaming at him, like an interrogation lamp. He rushes back down the stairs and runs directly into the camera, which turns out to be a glass wall. The glass shatters and Mike falls to the ground, picks himself up, and runs wildly away from the theater, as if he is trying to escape. Filmic adaptation of Dean Hess's best-selling autobiography outlining his redemption in Korea (see chapter 1), *Battle Hymn* provides no uplifting, salvific melody. Mike's recognition of himself not as a person but as "Air Force" appears to provide little consolation. *Battle Hymn* sends him crashing into the fourth wall. He breaks as he attempts a breakout.

Mike isn't really moving forward, even as different temporal markers (the measured chiming of church bells, for example) appear. He repeatedly smashes the glass on the clock mounted inside his isolation pod: He's going round and round, as his last name implies. Serling's pilot takes Enrico Fermi's famous musing on the possibility of extraterritorial life ("Where is Everybody?") as a point of departure to place a radical disorientation on display, an apocalypse in and of the mind. Erik Mortenson points out that Serling staged "a realm that was neither the brightly lit epitome of American optimism nor the darker pessimism of earlier film noir. *The Twilight Zone* was instead a space where light and dark struggled for dominance."[59] This struggle to present the neither-nor would be continuous. The *Twilight Zone*'s pilot episode presents a play between the inner workings of the mind (just a kind of nightmare) and the attempt to harness its potential, push limits into an expansiveness best represented by techno-progress in space. "Clock him!" shouts the general. These are the first words we hear from the group of men watching Mike in his pod. If the task of military psychiatry is to assess the breaking point within a productivist, forward-looking temporality, what hovers in the shadows is the relation between illusion and allusion, the elliptical play opened up by the referencing of something without naming it. The move to allusion is to the twilight of history. Where is the Korean War? It is everywhere in "Where is Everybody?" And it is nowhere. It is in a battle hymn, a promise for redemption that appears in sensory overload, the deafening roar of a bomber. It is in the testing regime, the push to the limits, the skies.

Serling's "Where is Everybody?" and Fuller's *The Steel Helmet* serve as bookends for 1950s US visual portrayals of the Korean War in popular culture. The Korean War never really named an event in US history. Instead, the war served as catalyst for a reflection on limits, limitations, and limitlessness in varying realms, from IR theory, to teleplays and films, to psychoanalytical articulations of rebellious instinct and the nature of freedom. The question is not of forgetting or remembering but approaching the post-1945 US reworking of war as modality centering on techniques of the multilayered self (the warrior of the limit), as frame for a lasting military-civilian nexus: 2130 hrs. is 9:30 p.m.

Why was the Korean War not a war? Because it was the scene of a utilitarian relation that blended the secular and the religious, that proffered a temperate salvation, the best that could be done to manage life and death given the fundamental flaws of human nature. The Korean War was not an event but an example, evidence of how conflict would proceed and restraints would manifest themselves, armistice signaling a particular kind of victory, not for one side over the other but for the continuing elaborations of the notion of limited war itself (in theory and in practice).

Part IV moves to the wartime and postarmistice travels of the living dead, those killed or left behind who remain in images and imaginings, those who may or may not be alive, those who live as if dead, those who have yet to die and yet to live. Within these thanatographic realms are summonings, departures, endings, and becomings. The living dead cross borders of presence and absence to contribute to the figuring of what in the Republic of Korea (ROK) is called the 6/25 War.

PART IV

Anticommunism did not arrive in a package on the doorstep. Multilayered forms of wartime and postarmistice anticommunism (*pan'gong*) appear in ROK literary texts, films, and nonfiction. The "anti" (*pan*) was difficult to define or contain, at times serving as point of departure from which to search for an elsewhere, beyond the ROK, the island-like site taking shape at the edge of the would-be American Lake. Calls for a way out, imaginings of spaces and times beyond the confines of the free world inhabit both figurings of the DPRK and mappings of what would be a permanent US military presence (and encounters with US popular cultural forms).

Communism manifests itself as specter when it appears in the form of a powerful, ubiquitous cliché, the *koeroe* (傀儡) or puppet. The givenness of *koeroe*, its status as a cliché to live by (and kill for) renders its immateriality real, present in everyday life. Recourse to this term is so easy it asks for comparison to "brainwashing." But *senoe* (the term used to translate brainwashing) has never approached the lasting currency of *koeroe* in the ROK. Brainwashing in the United States is untethered from its Korean War origins. *Koeroe* still works to figure the DPRK, as well as political parties in the ROK deemed overly appeasing to the DPRK (the term also remains a staple of official DPRK pronouncements regarding the ROK). *Koeroe* names the living dead, their place in a history of division and war.

Crossings to the south, stories of return and departure, of departure as return. Crossings to the past, to life experiences receding into image, available only in the look back. Crossings into the past to write of ruins—liberatory possibilities foreclosed, divisions now hardened by war. Redemptive looks, returns from the dead, rebirths. How to make war appear later, after the fact? Impossible. Part IV accounts for a warlike visual regime in the ROK that requires communism to reveal itself as exuding only the appearance of life (puppetlike, inherently inert). But such a gesture doubles back, serving as acknowledgment of the armistitial present itself... of the unwar, the war that is not a war, the war that remains (without end).

CHAPTER 9

HABITATIONS

Kang Yongjun's "Barbed Wire" (Ch'ŏljomang; 1960) travels back in time to the wartime POW camp on Kŏje Island. Outed as part of a coup attempt against the "red faction," Minsu finds himself in a secret underground cell, a prison within a prison. His interrogator comes at him with a hot iron:

> What happened after that, Minsu couldn't really remember. There was the thought of something horrifying.... His body was being ripped apart, it was, finally, dying. The flesh that had surrounded this thing called "I," the skeletal frame that covered him was torn way, scattered into pieces that floated around him and then disappeared, one after the other. His consciousness [ŭisik] was watching over it all, intently. A dizziness came over him. He completely lost his bearings. And then he was hurtling into the unknown, an empty grayness.[1]

Minsu has entered the neither-nor of the "gray element" (hoesaek punja), the suspicious one who belongs to neither camp. Later, he will come to, crawl past a dozing guard, and make a dash for the barbed wire. He once more feels his flesh torn asunder, this time by wire and bullets. His body falls to the ground. Several figures (guards from the red faction) surround the corpse in the shadows, commenting on the futility of the attempt. "The yankee bastards [yangnom] built a strong fence," says one.[2] The text closes: "Darkness fell. The barbed wire fence stood as before, giving the appearance of a desolate ruin."[3]

The third-person narration (aligned with Minsu) tells the tale of a corpse that lends itself to observation, reflection. It is the story of a separation of consciousness from body. It is also the story of a consciousness of the body, of its shredding, its porosity. Minsu's death in the barbed wire presents a ruinous

FIG. 9.1 Illustration header for the first two pages of "Barbed Wire." *Sasanggye*, July, 1960.

embodiment. What the text calls *ŭisik* is material; consciousness hovers in the darkness, no longer encased by a skeletal frame but by the barbed wire itself. This is a consciousness embedded in a border, in its enforcement, the limits put into play for those who have no choice but to live and die within a well-made perimeter. It is a limit-consciousness.

"Expressionless faces" had marked the majority of the camp as they listened to communist indoctrination:

> These were people who had never even heard of the term "prisoner of war." And they didn't really know what had happened, what a terrible crime they had committed by becoming POWs. They'd just been dragged in, and now they were prisoners. They'd done what they could to survive on the arduous path they'd set out on, only to be collared by foreigners [*igukin*]. They were what you might call refugees [*p'inanmin*].[4]

Passive rejection of communism does not translate to the category of the "anticommunist prisoner" (*pan'gong p'oro*), closely associated with another 1950s designation, "anticommunist youth" (*pan'gong ch'ŏngnyŏn*). Used synonymously in the 1950s to refer to all prisoners allowed to escape from UN camps in 1953, these terms signaled patriotic zeal while retaining an element of mistrust, a mark that the escapee would never fully be released from a certain suspicion.[5]

Kang (himself a former *pan'gong p'oro*) shifts the rejection of communism from "pan" (anti) to the elemental humanity of the *p'inanmin* and the question of incarceration.[6] The barbed wire sets the terms under which antagonisms will emerge, how violence—latent and manifest—will proceed.[7] The perimeter becomes a parameter—to attempt to escape is to risk death. The look back to what is already ruinous, covered in darkness is to a history difficult to discern, a history of refugees become prisoners, of an embodied consciousness—torn, shot through—lingering on the wire, hovering above the corpse from which it has departed but does not leave. This is the story of an afterdeath that extends to the 1960 present, a thanatography that concludes with no conclusion. "Barbed Wire" speaks of an unbecoming, a transformation into that which does not disappear but remains, neither present nor absent. This 1960 return to the Kŏje POW camp proffers a history of habitation, a dwelling not only upon history as ruin but on the uneasy history of the relation among, doubt, suspicion, and the living dead.

Appearing on roadside signs in the 1970s and 1980s was the exhortation "If in doubt, look again; if suspicious, report it" (*ŭisim namyŏn tasi pogo susanghamyŏn sin'gohaja*). Suspicion harnesses doubt, ensures that doubt is the first stage of suspicion rather than doubt of a regime premised upon suspicion. In the 1950s, such a statist disciplining proceeded by way of the appellation *koeroe* (傀儡, or puppet, the first sino-Korean character in the compound connoting the appearance of a person who acts on behalf of another entity, a person who is inhabited by someone else). In both the Republic of Korea (ROK) and the Democratic People's Republic of Korea (DPRK), the term was frequently used to designate the inauthenticity of the other (in the ROK, *koe* is often attached to north to form the noun *pukkoe*). Largely dismissed as cliché or simple translation for the idea of a "puppet regime," *koeroe*, in fact, organizes a habitation of death in life, the naming of either side—communist or reactionary—as appearing alive while in fact dead. In the ROK, this names less a specific nation-state than communism itself. If the *koeroe* embodies a mirroring suspicion, it also harkens to an inauthenticity associated with misguided belief and the accompanying possibility of recantation. The notion of the *koeroe* involves a technique of the self. To purge the *koeroe* within and kill the *koeroe* without is to depart from the status of proxy; it is to approach a salvific return to fullness of presence.

To return to the already-ruins is to inhabit the scene of an anticommunism (*pan'gong*) that did not come ready-made for easy consumption in the 1950s ROK, even as it drew on colonial period antecedents and the contemporary, transnational travel of anticommunist ideas. *Pan'gong* is a misleading rubric, even when seemingly invoked to articulate an oppositional position. Even in wartime the strictly denunciatory was accompanied by the affirmatory, a search for emotive and appealing forms of belonging in the world. If *pan'gong* turned upon a figuring of return (*kwihwan*) as repatriation to the ROK (proper locus of belonging/national sovereignty), this search for an emancipatory self opened the possibility of multiple imaginings, including doubts cast upon statist summonings, mutual accusations of puppetlike living deaths. Kang Yongjun's portrayal of an attempted escape to an elsewhere beyond the perimeter speaks to these earlier articulations of doubt and accompanying killings/deaths.

This chapter follows the wartime literary front, with emphasis on the state-sponsored journal appropriately titled *Chŏnsŏn munhak* (*Frontline Literature*), organ for the Embedded Writers Corps (*chonggun chakkadan*). Three texts by Pak Yŏngjun—"Dark Night" (Amya, 1952); "Partisan" (Ppalch'isan, 1952); and "In the Sea off Yongch'o Island" (Yongch'odo kŭnhae, 1953)—combine in confession and mourning amid the ruins of the present, traveling from the need to kill one's brother, to the offer of one's life as sacrifice, and, finally, to suicide.[8] This is the story of war becoming armistice. It is also the story of a return that never arrives at the destination.

WAR FOR THE WORLD

"6/25" and "intra-ethnonational war" (*tongjok sangjan*;) serve as the most common terms for the "Korean War" in the ROK.[9] The former names the day of the war's outbreak; the latter invokes internecine conflict.[10] The common figuring of the intra-ethnonational war as tragic (*tongjok sangjan ŭi pigŭk*) points to the complex relation between self-harm and the intervention of outside powers (*oese*). The seven issues that comprise the full run of *Chŏnsŏn munhak* address this relation in global terms. On the cusp of armistice, for example, Yi Muyŏng explains that the phrase "holy war to exterminate communism" (*myŏlgong sŏngjŏn*) locates the ethnonation in world history. Wars may bring suffering, but they also offer "grand lessons for the future." To engage in a holy war is to understand the meaning of sacrifice: "Today, our holy war to exterminate communism represents nothing more than the suffering of all humankind. Our nation [*minjok*] stands at the forefront, carrying out a war on behalf of others, obviating what could easily become more tragic, a war involving the entire world, all of humanity killing and crushing each other."[11] Yi is quick to point out that this definition of "holy" requires historical review: "In the past, the Japanese imperialists attached the term 'holy' [*sŏng*] to the Asia Pacific War, but we are not fighting this war, as Japan did, in the interests of one nation [*minjok*]. The truth is that we are carrying out a sacrificial war for the sake of the peace, happiness, and welfare of all humanity."[12] Sacrifice is redemptive, creative of a present and future that renders the Asia Pacific War improper both in its parochial, deceptive imperialism and its forced mobilization. A proper death for others is not tragic but philanthropic. The ROK stands at the front line not as proxy for the great powers but as world-historical subject.

Such an entrance into history requires continuous self-examination. Pak Kijun explores the proper stance for writers in his article "Self-Reflections of Korean

Writers" (Hanguk chakka ŭi pansŏng), which accompanies Pak Yŏngjun's "Dark Night" in the inaugural, framing issue of *Chŏnsŏn munhak*: "We must again ask of writers: Is their subjectivity [*chuch'esŏng*]—that is, their view of life or of the world—oriented in the proper direction?"[13] Such a look inward is to expansiveness, the extension of self and nation to world: "The highest level of national consciousness [*kodo ŭi minjok ŭisik*] and subjective spirit [*chuch'e chŏngsin*] breaks ground for our Korean writers and, at the same time, makes the path clear for humankind itself."[14] The "extermination of communism" (*myŏlgong*) on the level of consciousness and reflection—the inner surveillance of that within the self which disorients—extends outward, to the necessary excision of communism from recalcitrant bodies. Subjectivity (*chuch'e*, a term that would later assume prominence in the DPRK) signals a clarity that is also a meeting point. The name for this place will be "Han'guk" (ROK).

The trope of fratricide that inhabits intra-ethnonational killing turns upon a particular kind of homosocial intimacy, a place where self and other converge and

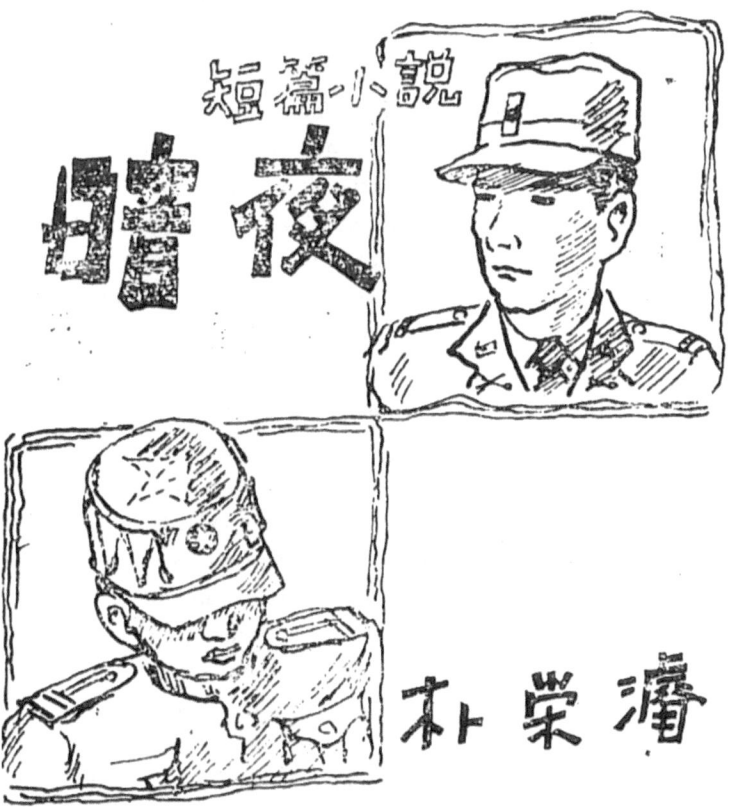

FIG. 9.2 Illustration header for "Dark Night" *Chŏnsŏn munhak*.

diverge, an uncanny mirroring. Such self-reflection manifests itself best in action by way of brother-killing, which is the elimination of the communist in the mirror.

Director of the Embedded Writers Corps, Pak Yŏngjun played a central role in the formation and publication of *Chŏsŏn munhak*.[15] "Dark Night" (Amya, 1952) works through the relation of a literal fratricide and intra-ethnonational war. This killing will not serve as trope for the war but the production of the *koeroe* as itself strangely familiar, a form of homosocial intimacy.

ROK forces are pushing north, in pursuit of the retreating *koeroegun* (傀儡軍; puppet army). The fighting is fierce, and Captain Im is exhausted. Summoned to the rear for a meeting, he encounters a column of KPA POWs. Shockingly, one of them looks like his younger brother. A closer look confirms. Captain Im had written his younger brother off as dead: "And even if he wasn't dead, he figured he would never see him again. So long as communism and democracy traveled along different paths, there wasn't any room for compromise [*t'ahyŏp*]. . . . Wasn't this the sad fate of the nation [*minjok*]?"[16] Younger Brother had remained in Seoul under communist occupation, a choice that rendered his status questionable.[17] He ended up in the *koeroegun*. Was this, too, his choice? He tells Captain Im that he was forcibly conscripted, did everything in his power to escape. But Captain Im hears a different story from his commanding officer (CO). Only one of the POWs had refused to surrender: Younger Brother, subdued only after he's killed an ROK soldier. The CO sums up the situation in short order: "Even in the case of two brothers, if the ideologies are different, there's nothing to be done."[18] But Captain Im needs more. He sifts through his memory and recalls that his brother had opposed his enrollment in the military academy two years earlier: "Perhaps it was from that time that he became a communist?" He confronts Younger Brother, asking directly if he really has gone over to the other side. The latter's reply: "Older Brother, now even you doubt [*ŭisim*] me?"[19] The appeal is to familial trust, brother to brother. But this does nothing to explain Younger Brother's refusal to surrender: " 'So you ended up a red. Family, nation, all forsaken,' Captain Im moaned, tears falling down his cheeks."[20] The moment speaks to an ROK anticommunism where, as Heonik Kwon points out, "the wrongness of an ideology is judged on the basis of what the ideology does to people who make a commitment to it, turning them into a nonperson from the perspective of kinship and morality."[21] Younger Brother indicates what he has become: an object of doubt. He has become that which resembles a person but is now something else. He is a *koeroe*, and his return is from the dead. He is the one who appears familiar but is unfamiliar, residing somewhere between the literal and the figural. He approximates personhood, bearing an uncanny resemblance to the human but stands for something else. To become red is to approach the border between death and life, to remain on earth but only in bodily form, as a duplicitous appearance of that which is no longer present. It is to haunt. His relation to family and nation is not radically other but that which inhabits, that which is to be doubted, the suspicious one.

The CO meets with Captain Im to offer a last word of advice: "Captain Im, there is no question that we are living in troubled times. To the point where trust between father and son, as well as between brothers, has been lost. Isn't this precisely the gift bestowed upon us so cold-heartedly by a communism utterly bereft of humanity? Don't be so sad, put it all behind you. . . . This is your duty, and it's the world's duty."[22] The *koeroe* threatens not kinship in a general sense, but the ethics of patrilineage, the homosocial order. It is not communism itself but the inhabiting of communism within a male, nationalized body that marks the appearance of the *koeroe* in Korea. To see the *koeroe*, to acknowledge its presence is to locate oneself as masculine, national, human, and global. This is not a fratricidal war. It is a war upon the *koeroe*. And it is a war for the world, for one's place in it.

Night begins to fall. Captain Im rounds up his troops and heads out for a deployment. In the twilight, they come across a couple of guards in hot pursuit of two prisoners making a run for it. Captain Im "feels a stinging sensation in his heart. Could one of them be his brother?" He circles to the point they are sprinting toward and takes up a position in a furrow. The answer is yes:

> "Bastard! Why are you running right toward me?" he screamed, but only internally, to himself.
>
> He had no choice but to shoot. Anything else would be a violation of military discipline.
>
> "Bang!"
>
> "Bang!"
>
> Eyes shut, Captain Im fired his pistol. His eyes remained closed as he lay prone on the ground. Fist-sized tears were streaming down his cheeks. In his left hand, a clump of red earth.
>
> Captain Im just lay there for five minutes or so, completely motionless. Then he jumped to his feet and turned to his radioman.
>
> "Let's get going, come on, let's go," he shouted.[23]

The corpse will remain, a recovery of the body in death, now bearing proper relation to the color red (the earth). Captain Im has brought Younger Brother home. To soldier is to pull the trigger with eyes closed, wishing you didn't have to do it but understanding necessity.[24] It is not a question of free will but duty.

The *koeroe* appears as likeness but must be recognized as a habitation that others. The internal scream, the scream unvoiced marks the tragedy of this distinction as an inner struggle. Is Captain Im implicated by his younger brother's fall to communism (guilt by association)? Does the text provide moments where the obscured face in the lower image of the header illustration travels, inhabits the upper image, threatens to dwell within it? The *koeore* disciplines, mobilizes. Younger Brother's face is obscured in the illustration (see figure 9.2). To see him as *koeroe* will require considerable affective labor (which "Dark Night" performs). He is the reflection in the mirror that must be disavowed, recognized as a presence no longer present.

RECANTATION

The battle within shifts to recantation in Pak Yongjun's "The Partisan" (Ppalch'isan), published a month after "Dark Night."[25] This text assumes form as transcript, a spoken confession (signaled by formal-style verb endings used in speech), although there is no interlocutor/interrogator. "Partisan" thus addresses everyone and no one. Kim Hyŏngsik or Ch'uil (his partisan name and preferred moniker) narrates the story of his life up to capture by the *kukkun* (national army; ROKA), the term used throughout for ROK forces, as opposed to *koeroegun* (puppet army), used for the KPA. The partisan looks back upon his life as a communist from an ROK-sanctioned frame: Regardless of Ch'uil's position, the *kukkun* were always *kukkun* (DPRK texts never use this term without scare quotes). Ch'uil's testimonial cannot cross this line, even as it reveals a gradual awakening based on actual experience of life under communism.

Ch'uil's belief in communism stemmed from his view that the exploitation of the many at the hands of the few was unjust. He tells us, though, that he "came to realize the reality of North Korea [*Pukhan*]. I witnessed with my own eyes how high-level party members constituted a privileged class while below them lived an oppressed class far more wretched than the workers in a capitalist society."[26] He receives orders to go south as a partisan, and he's happy to have the chance to prove himself: "In case you haven't heard, soldiers who performed great feats in the war could receive the hero designation, officially conferred in the name of Kim Il Sung."[27]

The Chinese enter the war, and Ch'uil's unit receives additional support. Among the newly arrived partisans is a young woman, Yun Kwihyang, "twenty-one-years-old and beautiful."[28] Could the regional commander be testing him? Ch'uil orders his troops to refrain from any kind of untoward conduct. And more—he takes away as much personal time as he can from his soldiers. More study groups and self-criticism sessions: "Such is the most effective method by which communism turns humans into machines. Permit no freedom for reflection. Teach the same thing again and again, repeat it over and over! Only under these conditions can uniformity of thought be achieved.... But this is precisely what is necessary in order to stick it out under communist rule."[29] Kwihyang eventually criticizes Ch'uil: "Comrade Commander! Isn't it cowardly to try to prove how pure and upright you are by picking on a woman and wearing her down with so much work?"[30] Ch'uil finds himself apologizing, and the two confess their loneliness, grow closer, and soon become secret lovers. Now everything starts to change. He worries that love has caused the two of them to weaken their will to fight, but "When I thought about it, I realized that it wasn't a weakness of the heart. It's that love opened my eyes to my heart, to my humanity. Was I to remain untouched by the sorrow of my compatriots, those whose faces looked like mine, who wore the same clothes, who spoke the same language?"[31] He has stepped into proper selfhood.

Kukkun attacks intensify, and the partisans are now on the run. Kwihyang is shot and killed; Ch'uil is subsequently captured. As he was being taken to an unspecified camp, he never once thought he would remain alive:

> Even now I have no desire to plead for my life.... I'm someone who lost their humanity once and got it back. And this makes my attachment to life so much deeper than for someone who hasn't had this experience. That's what I can say. That's the reality for what it is.... Even if I must be killed, I will harbor no complaint.
> I leave my mediocre life in your hands.[32]

The partisan positions himself beyond suspicion. His is a testimonial that calls for acknowledgment of someone who returned from the living dead. To kill Ch'uil would be to deny his humanity, unmoor the very dividing line Ch'uil has etched with his crossing, the line between *kukkun* and *koeroegun*. Ch'uil's offer of his middling life is in the name of such a reality.

DEAD BEFORE ARRIVAL

Chŏnsŏn munhak is sometimes lost in the mix of the postarmistice emergence of major literary and intellectual journals, among them *Hyŏndae munhak* (*Modern Literature*, 1955) and *Chayu munhak* (*Free Literature*, 1956). But the literary texts, roundtables, and scholarly articles published in *Chŏnsŏn munhak* were not a one-off; they would leave their own mark on the approach writers, filmmakers, and artists would take to the 6/25 war, the issue of national division, questions of ideology (the "isms").

Kim P'albong, for example, offered a series of articles in *Chŏnsŏn munhak* that grapple with the relation between the human spirit and materialism. He minces no words in his 1952 "Soldiers and Religion": "We are now engaged in a third world war here, on this tiny Korean peninsula. One camp defends the spirit—human dignity, freedom of the individual, human equality. The other is made up of a bunch of demons who have nothing but earthly desires, who consider the human spirit as emanating from the material and nothing else."[33] Kim would increasingly question this bifurcation, in line with others who found ways to critique both communism and capitalism.[34] In a 1953 article, Kim makes a familiar call to writers of war literature to address head-on the communist ideology of dialectical materialism, to expose its "mechanistic" approach to reality, its neglect of the working of the human spirit. Here, the critique provides a lever for writers to dispense with despair (wartime suffering and loss) in favor of an active, positive vision: "If hope always accompanies light [*kwangmyŏng*], our literature must be of light."[35] If literature must work to recover the "actuality, the essence of human life," Kim emphasizes that such a call occurs in the aftermath of the 1952 detonation of a hydrogen bomb by the United States (Kim's example of the destructive power available in the world).[36] The implication is clear: A literature of hope and light must seek a way out.

Kim will, in fact, later laud the Korean proletarian literature of the 1920s for its critique of capitalism (he was a prominent figure in proletarian writing circles in this period):

> Compared to naturalism and the literature of decadence, which considered their descriptions of the dark side of society the end-all, the socialist literature of the 1920s ... grounded itself in a materialist view in which the liberation of the proletariat was part of a "necessary historical process." The spirit [*chŏngsin*] of socialist literature, therefore, was more elevated, offering a fresh approach.[37]

Kim proceeds to underscore the historical progression of the "elevated spirit" (*kodo ŭi chŏngsin*):

> The contemporary world, however, is markedly different from the 1920s. To be sure, America's Wall Street, its finance capital, is alive and well.... Even under enormous national debt, though, the US has, since 1950, made massive

expenditures and suffered great loss of life on behalf of Korea [*Han'guk*], for the sake of human dignity and freedom.... We see, then, that the 1920s spirit of socialism is a relic, yesterday's news.... The spirit [*chŏngsin*] we must now develop and foster is a human spirituality [*ingan ŭi yŏngsŏng*]. Such a spirituality (*yŏngsŏng*) is itself the essence of a wisdom that lies in love and sympathy [*chabi*].[38]

Kim will conclude his article with a distinction between the flesh (*yukch'e*) and spirit (*chŏngsin*). To preserve life, we must protect the former: "But it is impossible to save the flesh if we do not save the spirit." This recognition made, a path opens to the creation of a literature of the "elevated spirit" (*kodo ŭi chŏngsin*). What Kim is calling *yŏngsŏng* is itself the unfolding, the historical elevation of *chŏngsin*. Such a move does not simply dismiss socialism but views socialism as a stage through which a higher spirit develops. Kim charts a path in which *yŏngsŏng* mediates socialism and capitalism. The literature of spirituality will serve as a site from which to critique both the socialism of the DPRK (already a relic) and the materialism of a capitalism associated with profit and the flesh. 6/25 is a world-historical event to the extent that sacrifices made on behalf of human dignity offer a concrete manifestation of *yŏngsŏng*. Such an argument helps to frame contemporary critiques of self-interest, opportunism, of the *sosimin* (petty bourgeois), a term frequently invoked in the 1950s and 1960s ROK. Critique of communism includes a critical look within, and not only to purge impure elements lurking in the corners of the mind or between the lines of a literary text.

In his 1952 "Has a Cultural Front Taken Form?," Yi Hŏn'gu calls upon intellectuals to engage precisely in such a self-critique (*chagi pip'an*).[39] Here, Yi quickly distinguishes such self-criticism from its communist counterpart: "Rather than suffocate humans, turn them into machines, render them slaves to the party line, such self-criticism entails an earnest effort to elevate and express the human spirit."[40] Korea now occupies a vanguard position in a newly-forming "international cultural front" which aims not only to defeat communism but to take advantage of a historical turning point hastened by the two world wars, namely the opportunity to overcome "colonial capitalism, nationalist bias, racial discrimination, and religious zealotry ... in order to set in place a truly democratic ideal in which all of humankind can co-exist."[41] Here, as elsewhere, such an exhortation to stand at the forefront of the free world jettisons contemporary communism on the Korean peninsula while legitimizing the ROK as the entity entrusted with the mission of fashioning a truly emancipatory history (not a proxy). To posit such an exemplary role, of course, is to open a gap between what is said and what is done, between the assertion of freedom and an embodied experience of the postarmistice order as potentially something other than decolonizing.

Pak Yŏngjun's "In the Sea off Yongch'o Island" stands, as the title implies, where sea meets land, where one is not quite the other, where one is in the process of becoming the other. Published in *Chŏnsŏn munhak*'s final issue (December 1953, the month in which Operation Big Switch concluded), "In the Sea" begins with a group of POWs loaded into a covered truck, informed by "officers in the puppet army" (*koeroegun changgyo*) that they're headed to Panmunjom. Really? No one knows for sure: "They were so used to all of the lies it wouldn't have come as a surprise if they ended up in Siberia."[42] This story of repatriation will become the story of Yongsu's journey toward death.

Yongsu (ROK officer; hometown, Seoul) and the others arrive at Panmunjom to the sound of a band playing the "Yangsando," a Kyŏnggi Province folk song that signals recovery and rebirth. They cross through "freedom's gate" into the south and are finally able to cast off the "puppet clothing" (*koeroe ŭi ot*) they have been forced to wear: "The music continues, causing streams of tears to cascade down Yongsu's face.... He found himself dancing with joy, the body-warmth of the nation [*minjok*] flowing from the music, embracing him softly."[43] He has been taken "under the wings of the Republic of Korea."[44]

Transport by helicopter to Seoul follows. Espying the ROK flag waving atop a tall pole below, Yongsu spontaneously mutters a line from the national anthem, "Under God's protection, long live our nation." But then he rephrases: "Under God's protection, I made it back alive."[45] Thoughts of self and survival lead him to recall a fellow POW stamped a Christian and thus given less rations. This man owns up that he's spied on fellow prisoners in order to make up for the shortfall. He deserves death, he tells Yongsu. He'll thank God for his illness in his evening prayer and die the next day.

It's at this point that the face of Chŏnggap, a man Yongsu feels he has betrayed, flashes in his mind. Along with five others, Yongsu was coerced into testifying against Chŏnggap, who stood accused of providing water to a fellow POW performing forced labor. And more, Yongsu was asked to sentence Chŏnggap— which he did, thinking that six months in solitary would be the lightest punishment Chŏnggap would receive. But the sentence was immediately reduced to three months by a KPA judge.

"In the Sea," then, will revolve around Yongsu's abiding sense of betrayal and self-doubt, interwoven among three registers: the national, the religious, and the personal. If the stream of images, thoughts, and feelings that arise of their own accord, by association, serve as counterpoint to communist repression, they also question the performance of freedom at Panmunjom. Yongsu's return (*kwihwan*) to Seoul and the ROK, the warm embrace of the nation he felt at Freedom's Gate, will feel less real than what he imagines while awake and what he experiences in his dreams.

Elsewheres follow Yongsu. On his first night in Seoul, he dreams of Hyemin—a local woman he was able to meet while on a POW work detail, tasked with building an air raid shelter. He sees her in front of her house, watching as Yongsu and his fellow POWs are marched off to an unknown destination. A soldier butts her to the ground with his gun as the column rounds the bend: "He awakened from his dream. But it didn't seem like a dream. Hyemin was standing there, beckoning toward him, asking him why he'd left her and gone south."[46] The image torments him, follows him day and night. Return to the ROK becomes something else: Hyemin's return, her insistent crossing south in the form of her appearance in his mind.

Yongsu and fellow former POW Sŏngju are sent to Yongch'o Island (site of a former UN POW camp, now repurposed as a debriefing location).[47] On board a transport ship, Yongsu dreams again of Hyemin. He'd been able to get water at her house a few times, and the two had quickly developed feelings for each other. She once again provides water:

> After he'd had his fill, she drew him close, placing his head in her lap, caressing him. He fell asleep, in his own dream. It wasn't long, though, before Hyemin woke him up, telling him it wouldn't do to just doze off like this. Her voice was filled with tenderness, worry. Softer, more gentle in the dream than it had been in reality. A voice that emitted true affection, so beautiful that he wanted to touch it. Yongsu wished to hear more of the voice, so he kept his eyes shut even though he was awake.
>
> "You should get up," urged the voice, fragrant-like.[48]

The voice crosses from dreamscape to awakescape. Feeling manifests itself within a play of senses (aural, tactile, olfactory). The voice from "up north" (*ibuk*, the term used throughout the text for the DPRK) crosses, returns, lingers within Yongsu—a much more powerful affective embrace than the music of return performed at Panmunjom, the site where *ibuk* becomes just that, up north.

"In the Sea" dwells in the somewhere and the sometime, neither here nor there, then or now. Such is the awakescape, the crisscross of images, memory fragments from dreams to awakened reverie. Sŏngju presses Yongsu to break out of it. Look at the sun rising over the water (harbinger of return), stop mention of dreams: "Why try to make something out of such things?" Yongsu refuses: "No, there are many things that you can see only in dreams."[49] All that happened in the camp flashes before his eyes, all of the dying; the massacre of those who couldn't walk or were declared "reactionaries"; the deaths from disease; the fellow prisoners gone on work detail at the airstrips who never came back, mowed down by US bombers: "There was only death. Not for a single instant had the images of death left Yongsu's mind. Nor had they departed from his body."[50] These images appear after Yongsu's mention of dreams, not within a dream itself. They manifest in the awakescape as an attachment of image to mind and body, an image-embodiment. The awakescape is where death will not detach itself from consciousness. Truths reside in dreams, irruptions that appear beyond the pale of free will. These truths are embodiments of the elsewhere, deaths that are alive as images, habitations that assume primacy over postarmistice summonings.

Yongsu is moving south by ship. But he is struggling to apprehend this southerly journey as return, rebirth, a future of freedom—a marked contrast with Sŏngju's easy accommodation to changing circumstances. "In the Sea" frames the notion of return via this juxtaposition. An ROK soldier (hometown: Busan), Sŏngju is captured by the Chinese. He converts to the communist cause and fights as a "liberation warrior" (*haebang chŏnsa*) in the KPA for two years. He's sent back to a POW camp when prisoner exchange becomes imminent so he can return to the south as a spy, under the cover of returnee. He's made up his mind fairly quickly, though, to leave communism behind: "As far as poor people go, there's probably no difference between communist and capitalist society. But I like the fact that you can live as you want here. All you need to do is take care proper care of your own affairs."[51] Yongsu is relieved that Sŏngju has wiped himself clean (*ch'ŏngsan*) of communism and even envies the ease in which "of his own determination he had completely recovered a lighthearted cheerfulness."[52] But Sŏngju's easy recantations, his linking of freedom to self-interest presents the ROK as haven for a petit-bourgeois or *sosimin* mentality, a representation often associated with contemporary depictions of wartime life in Busan (in the works of Yŏm Sangsŏp and Yi Hoch'ŏl, for example). Pak Yongjun himself had already described Busan as a city rife with war profiteering, its inhabitants engaged in battle for themselves and their own interests in his eponymous "Busan" (1951). Considered by many the founding text of division literature, Ch'oe In-hun's later *The Square* (Kwangjang, 1960) would elaborate this frame via the journey of its protagonist, Yi Myŏngjun, who rejects the ROK as corrupt and undemocratic site of "secret room" (*milsil*) politics and leaves for the DPRK, where he discovers nothing but empty slogans. He will later cast himself into the sea while in transit to a neutral country (having left behind two lovers—Yunae and Ŭnhye—in south and north).[53]

As the ship nears Yongch'o Island, Yongsu begins to feel a sense of freedom: "No one will call him a POW anymore. He can live life to the fullest, in the way he wants."[54] Shouts that Yongch'o has come into view—Yongsu turns to see. But it is Chŏnggap who appears, or so it seems. More jubilation. Sŏngju is filled with excitement: "But Yongsu only stiffened. His gaze shifted away, toward the vastness of the sea. The joyous cries seemed to be cursing him."[55] In the midst of the celebration, he hears Hyemin's voice from the night before, now calling him from the watery expanse. His last words: "Seems like a lot of people are happy." Yongsu leaps over the railing. The shout of "Man Overboard! . . . but Yongsu had slipped into the cresting waves, gone without a trace."[56] The wartime call for writerly self-reflection invokes the politics of suspicion, a command to truth, the production of a record. Pak Yŏngjun's embedded (*chonggun*, literally "follow the military") work travels from the injunction to kill (and a brother-corpse offered as testament of necessary elimination) to the absence of a body altogether (a death that is not only war-related but return-related). The latter, a suicide, presents a reframe, a movement from the suspicious back to the elsewhere of doubt, to Yongsu's disappearance. He will not arrive on Yongch'o Island, last stop for repatriated ROK POWs before release back to home units and into the civilian population.

Ripped apart at the fence in 1960, into the sea in 1953. Kang Yongjun's "Barbed Wire" returns to Kŏje Island to write a history of incarceration in the free world, to summon an embodiment of consciousness that finds no rest, lingering in the 1960 present. "In the Sea off Yongch'o Island" stops short of entrance into the ROK proper. Pak's text brings *Chŏnsŏn munhak* itself to this kind of close, looks back on the discussion of an elevation of spirit that took place on its pages, offers as a farewell a kind of desublimation, an immersion. Yongsu passes into the *kŭnhae*, the near waters, just off the coast. What is there to know of his death? Lost up north is Hyemin, who calls to Yongsu from his dreams and from the waters. He does not join in the happiness of the "returnee soldiers" (*kwihwan changbyŏng*). We know no more of his thoughts. Nor is his corpse available for viewing. "In the Sea off Yongch'o Island" tells us of a man who looks and feels askance, whose mind and body will disappear (offering no clear answers). Left behind is the transport headed into the armistitial order, into the future of a war that will not end. Kang Yongjun tells a story of the limits of representation that is at once a story of non-return. But what is the story of those who do not leap from the ship, who report to their final duty station, Yongch'o Island?

Chapter 10 moves to elaboration of departure as return, a leaving-behind that settles the "up north" in place—on the emotive register, in geopolitical terms, in postcolonial history, within a religious temporality. Sŏnu Hwi's *Return*

(*Kwihwan*, 1954) will take us back to Yongch'o Island, not to the waters off its shores but to the island itself, to the gate that stands between past and future. The offer is of an arrival that welcomes testimonials of the walk through the land of the living dead, of a truth that ushers renewal and rebirth. Im Ogin will perform her own return in *Crossing South: Before and After* (*Wŏllam chŏnhu*, 1956), a memoir of life under Soviet occupation, a return to the pre–6/25 War past that recedes in time as it appears in recollection. At stake in this eyewitness account will be the multilayered meanings of *koeroe* and liberation itself.

CHAPTER 10

CROSSINGS

To "cross to the south" (*wŏllam*; 越南) in the late 1940s or during the 6/25 War (1950–1953) was to become a *sirhyangmin* (those who have lost their hometown; 失鄉民), a term associated with a sense of sadness, nostalgia. Home is lost to the communists of the Soviet Civil Administration (1945–1948) and its successor, the Democratic People's Republic of Korea (DPRK). The loss associated with the *sirhyangmin* would inform the lasting issue of separated families (*isangajok*; 離散家族), their later televised reunions becoming, as Nan Kim points out, "ciphers of unspoken grief, with often little or no articulation for what is being grieved."[1] The object of lamentation is shapeless, has no form. The presentation of a body in the moment of reunion, though, calls attention to a widely circulated history of departure and dispersal (離散). To gather in momentary reunion can neither elide this history of dispersal nor an impending, postreunion return to the status quo ante.

To cross to the south under military occupation or in wartime is to enact this history, to engage in a purposeful act, even if no other choice seemed to present itself. *Wŏllam* invokes both displacement due to forces beyond one's control and an active decision made to move away from those forces. Enter the impropriety of immediate post-1945 history, the crisscross of the commemoration of "liberation" (*haebang*) from Japanese rule with the acknowledgment of military occupations, division of the peninsula, and the seeking of refuge (*p'inan*; 避難).

Postarmistice narratives of crossing south navigate this late 1945 simultaneity (liberation/division) when they figure the emancipatory (the flight from communism) within what now appears to be a much more lasting state of division. The 1945 liberation achieves new meaning in a crossing south that secures Republic of Korea (ROK) legitimacy. Liberation thus repeats itself, the flight from communism assuming signal importance. This chapter follows two early postarmistice crossings, Sŏnu Hwi's *Return* (*Kwihwan*, 1954) and Im Ogin's *Crossing South: Before and After* (*Wŏllam chŏnhu*, 1956). These are stories of division, departure, and destination. They are also stories of return (they narrate arrival in the ROK). Their transit south performs a border-making, a production of meaning that arises from another crossing—to the past, to what is now the place left behind, the north.

Drawing on interviews of more than five hundred former ROK POWs at three processing sites (Munsan, Incheon, Yongch'o Island), Sŏnu Hwi's *Return* traces a passage that involves the talking cure, a confessional that acknowledges the need to return to what has been left behind but remains in the mind. *Return* narrates a panoply of reentries, pullbacks from what amounts to virtual death. Im Ogin's *Crossing South: Before and After* travels in time, returns to everyday life in 1947 North Hamgyŏng Province under Soviet occupation. *Crossing South* is premonitory, an early postarmistice text written with an awareness of what will follow: the 6/25 War. Im's return to the north reconfigures the idea of *haebang* as she centers an emancipatory, free Asia feminism within post-1945 history. And this necessitates yet another return, to the colonial period literary scene and Im's engagement with Yi T'aejun, a writer who has crossed north, lost his direction. Im's resurrection of his aesthetic project will locate the relation between life and death in a sensory understanding of presence in the objects and art of the Chosŏn dynasty past. Taken together, these testimonials speak in different ways of redemption within the ruins of postcolonial history, blurring the lines among the confessional, the autobiographical, and the thanatographical. They witness death, destruction, and physical separation. But they do not lament needlessly as they write histories of what happened as histories of the future.

RETURN FROM THE LIVING DEAD

In the June 1957 issue of the journal *Saegajŏng* (*New Family*; the title *Christian Home* also appears on the cover in nontransliterated English), Nam Haeyŏng follows her brief testimonial of suffering and massacre in Sŏngjin, North Hamgyŏng Province under communist rule in the late 1940s with a description of liberation at the hands of advancing ROK forces in October 1950. But this was momentary, soon followed by retreat. Nam and her family make it to Hamhŭng by small boat arranged through the goodwill of a pastor embedded in a military unit: "The Lord delivered us from impending death."[2] They then travel to Busan by landing ship tank (LST), where they spend Christmas, followed by transfer to a camp on Kŏje Island. Here, some among her group are able to meet with separated family members they did not expect to see again: "Can we call this anything other than a miracle?"[3] To cross is to experience Christian deliverance as postcolonial praxis.

As Henry Em indicates, "the *architecture* of South Korea was designed not just by certain Korean political factions and the United States Army Military Government in Korea (USAMGIK), but also to a surprising degree by missionaries, Korean Christians, and their transnational networks."[4] Nam's story takes place within this architecture, via transit through networks that align Korean Christian networks with US military resources (the LST). Nam's story attests to that which was already present, waiting (safe haven). Her testimonial speaks of an architecture of the arrival, of promise, of faith made manifest in the world.

Sŏnu Hwi's *Return* (*Kwihwan*, 1954) is a founding document, the presentation of a textual congregation, a gathering of testimonials that give due witness.[5] The 6/25 War becomes a past comprised of present attestations to salvific, free-world belonging. These attestations make up the architecture of this text, and they locate the history of the 6/25 War on two temporal levels, anno Domini and *tan'gi* (the calendar calculated by Tangun's founding of Old Chosŏn in 2333 BCE, adopted by the ROK in 1948 and used through 1961). The first two pages of *Return* are blank, with the exception of a small box in the lower right-hand corner of the second page enclosing the following: "These are events which took place in a corner of the world from fall in the year of our Lord Jesus Christ 1950 through the fall of 1953."[6] In the body of the text, *tan'gi* marks secular happenings (for example, date of capture). Reference to the Tangun calendar also appears at text's close, its requisite location in the 1950s (along with anticommunist pronouncements included in all publications in this period). Between these two temporalities—Christian and ethnonationalist—lies the assertion of history from below, a record of those who experienced POW life in the DPRK and are now experiencing the temporal and spatial process of return. Their testimonials inaugurate the postarmistice era, not exactly in July 1953 but in fall 1953, when the last of the prisoner exchanges took place.

Return begins with third-person singular accounts of the moment of capture and vignettes of life and death in various DPRK POW camps, perspective shifting to third-person plural, that of POWs jointly encountering their release, in a section entitled "Freedom's Gate." The next section presents first-person accounts explicitly designated as "memoirs" (*sugi*), each reflecting on lessons learned from life experiences. This section names itself as a place, "Yongch'o Island."

Sŏnu Hwi's task is "to present the facts as they are and leave the freedom of interpretation up to the reader. For this reason, I am nothing more than a chronicler [*kirokcha*]."[7] He was there to listen and transcribe. The selections are "representative of the experience of hundreds, indeed thousands of their fellow soldiers."[8] *Return* (*Kwihwan*, 1954) purports to offer a truth greater than the sum of its parts. Selected interviews and shifts in person congregate in witness of the meaning of the 6/25 War, of the events that took place in a corner of the world.

In their very appearance on the written page, the *sugi* perform an arrival at Yongch'o Island, the true story of survivorship. The island and its repurposed UNC POW camp name a threshold, the last stop on the journey to civilian life in the ROK. The *sugi* sift through a personal history of feelings, thoughts, and sounds that accompany the move from incarceration to emancipation. What happens at Yongch'o is exemplary, as are the testimonials selected for inclusion, the transcripts that gather under the island's name. These are records of war, more real than the wartime literature written during the time period they cover. The truth can now be told, and it manifests itself in arrival, not in suicide off the island's shore (see chapter 9).

The collection point at Yongch'o Island became a border zone, the time spent there ranging from three to eight months.[9] To cross south as repatriated prisoner was to provide a response to the summons of the nation and its future, part and parcel of the broader regime of free world subjectification. To return is to acknowledge the weakness of the body, as we see in "Hallelujah," the chapter that closes Section One of *Return*. Here, accounts of bodily suffering, death in the POW camps serve not only to excoriate the poor treatment of POWs (much of it by the Chinese PLA), but also to demonstrate the ephemerality of the body in the face of the spirit. Return calls for a reinvigoration, a filling in of the body that comes from confession, verification of a coincidence of awareness, feeling, and belief.

The first-person testimonials of "Yongch'o Island" speak directly, voice their sensory experiences, their transformations. "Ch'oe" (we learn his name only from the dialogue of others included in his account) tells of his joining the ROKA while still a high school sophomore, his deployment to the front, his capture by the Chinese, his subsequent descent to the "the lowest of any human, an unfree, shackled person."[10] Above all else, what depressed him was his loss of pride. He'd dreamed of medals but became a POW. How could he return? He was nothing but a "living corpse" (*sansongjang*), a term invoked throughout *Return*.[11] His life as a POW is a sound-hell on earth: "In the camp, other than the crack of leather whips on the flesh, the clickety-clack of PLA boots, and the clank of rice bowls, the only sound I heard was that of sobbing and moaning."[12] Imprisonment is one thing; indoctrination is another. He has further to fall.

Ch'oe is forced to attend study sessions (*haksŭp*): "I didn't pay attention to their nonsense. But the daily repetition of the lines, always with the same melody [*kat'ŭn karakŭro*], naturally did pass through my ears right into my head."[13] The POWs were told that the enemy bastards (*wŏnsu nom*) had drawn the wool over their eyes, made them betray their class position. Only now could they fulfill their duty to the people (*inmin*), wash themselves clear of their crimes.[14] Ch'oe becomes a leader of the study sessions, speaks of the evils of capitalism, lauds the Soviet Red Army's liberation of the *inmin*, praises the great Stalin and Kim Il Sung. By the time armistice arrives, he has become an informer.

Given the choice to stay in the DPRK or go south as a sleeper agent, Ch'oe chooses the latter. The drop-off point for the POW exchange comes into sight, and Ch'oe finds himself spontaneously joining in the hurrahs (*manse*) let out by everyone else. Some begin to sob, but all sounds are lost in the melody of a Korean folk song, the *pangat'aryŏng* (standing in contrast to earlier mention of the "Slavic melodies" played in the DPRK POW camps): "I felt dizzy all of a sudden and grabbed my head. My heart was throbbing, tears were gushing forth."[15] Ch'oe recalls stepping out of an army truck, asking himself "Why does the *pangat'aryŏng* move me so? Why did I cry like that? What happened to all I had learned of revolution?"[16] He's completely confused: "Just that one melody alone was enough to topple what I'd built up for almost two years."[17] Spontaneity speaks of a truth beyond words, in folk melodies that move the heart. But this is not enough. Another return is required, and this can only take place on Yongch'o Island itself.

Ch'oe learns of process and imperfectability from the commanding officer (CO) of the education unit detailed to Yongch'o. While democratic countries possess deficiencies, the "elevated consciousness of the national citizenry [*kungmin*]" will result in the creation of a social order that meets the people's demands: "He told us that Rome wasn't built in a day and that both the means and the ends are important. He also pointed out that human life and personality [*kaesŏng*] were precious, and that it would actually be rather odd if societies or individuals didn't have flaws."[18] Recantation or *chŏnhyang* (轉向; literally, a "change in direction") turns upon the rejection of absolutes, the recognition of imperfectability, an awareness of one's complex, multidimensional personality.

Ch'oe is later confronted by a POW who had been in the same POW camp. This man accuses Ch'oe of being the worst kind of informer and proceeds to beat him severely while others stand by cursing him: "At that time, of course what I hated more than anything was myself."[19] Ch'oe cuts up his stomach with a razor blade the next morning but is saved by another soldier and recovers in the hospital: "I asked myself: Was I embarrassed because of the evil deeds I had done? Or because I had been beaten up? In my case, it was clearly the latter. And this made me more ashamed."[20] His torment intensifies, calmed only by the sounds of a hymn coming from a nearby church tent:

> And then suddenly rising up out of the deep dark earth was the PLA training officer's loud voice, telling me that I had allowed myself to be exploited by the class oppression of the enemy, that I had betrayed the people [*inmin*], that I should cleanse myself of these crimes, that I should engage in relentless struggle. And then the CO, "By appropriate means, consistent with the elevated consciousness of the national citizenry [*kungmin*]," "It would actually be rather odd if there were no flaws," "With a heart full of understanding and humility," "How precious is the life of the individual" ... The hymn ended, followed by the sound of a reed organ. And then just the wind rushing through the pine trees.
>
> I looked within, thought about it. My suffering, even my arrogance—these had been beneficial to me. None of these pages of my life should be thrown away. I can now endure any kind of suffering that comes my way. Filled with deep understanding, and with humility.[21]

The Christian hymn blends first with the battle of voices making up Ch'oe's internal struggle—the change in direction, away from *inmin* toward *kungmin*—and then with the sounds of nature. Ch'oe's awakening rests upon the externalization of the injunction to become *inmin*—now heard but unfelt, spectral. The departure is from the living death of the POW camp to life itself. The return is to an embodied, melodic experience of nation, faith, and self-forgiveness. Folded into this return as rebirth is the attempt to take one's own life, the experience of earthly suffering pushed to its limit.

Return does more than name a passage from north to south, from indoctrination to awakening. *Return* provides another return, to the narrative trajectory of Pak Yŏngjun's immediate postarmistice "In the Sea off Yongch'o Island" (see chapter 9). Ch'oe's sensory, affective experience in the Panmunjom soundscape, his tale of collaboration in the POW camp rework the story of Yongsu's postarmistice transit south as a being-toward-suicide. Ch'oe suffers as much or more than Yongsu, but he will arrive at an experiential threshold that rejects communism (as does the protagonist of Pak Yŏngjun's confessory "Partisan"). He will make it to Yongch'o Island and beyond his own suicide attempt. He incarnates what Yongsu should have become, could have understood (human imperfectability). *Return* draws Yongsu from the sea.

Return reverses communist indoctrination, presenting a cathartic combination of the secular with the religious, the preciousness of the individual with Christian humility and ethnonational belonging. The rescue is of the one who became a living corpse (*sansongjang*), the one inclined to death, who lived in endless repetition, who will even attempt to take his own life. It is in the recovery itself, in the pull of life (*san*) away from corpse (*songjang*) that Ch'oe and others approach the transnational "anti" (*pan*) of anticommunism (*pan'gong*). The therapy offered and experienced at Yongch'o Island has global implications.²² The extraction of life from the automaton confirms that "the corner of the world" mentioned in the box on *Return*'s second page occupies more of a central position than appears at first glance. The box is, in fact, island-like, a focal point within an expansive, blank space. Redemption will dissolve opposition. *Return* is indeed of the world, representative, an offering of life to humanity.

COLONIAL REMAINS

The final serialized installment of *Crossing South: Before and After* includes a brief afterword (omitted from anthologized versions) that outlines the manuscript's history.²³ Im Ogin began the project right after coming south, writing whenever she could find the time. This original text (*wŏn'go*) was lost in the war: "I couldn't, though, give up my lingering desire to write on this subject. So I did what I could to remember what I had put down, mixed it with new feelings and realizations, and the result is the present work [*pon'go*]."²⁴ The 1956 serialized version gathers up the remains, reflects upon them even as it extends immediacy to its witnessing. *Crossing South* will draw on what is no longer there (the past, the original text) from the perspective of a new after, the postarmistice world.

Im Ogin's return takes place via the first-person memoir of a protagonist, Kim Yŏngin (whose life trajectory closely resembles that of Im herself).²⁵ Yŏngin's account of life in North Hamgyŏng Province under Soviet occupation is autoethnographic. She is participant-observer, fleshing out the on-the-ground formation of a satellite state. *Crossing South* fits well with the contemporary call to write of life in the DPRK. The Asia Foundation, for example, sponsored a "Freedom Writers" program that "published eyewitness accounts of experiences in North Korea by North Korean refugee writers."²⁶ *Crossing South* would, in fact, receive the Asia Foundation's 1957 Freedom Literature Prize. Im's work is embedded in a free-world context that asks for nonfiction, personal accounts of a life (under communism) that had to be left behind.

Chang Sejin points out that in the mid-1950s "North Korea was not framed as an independent object of study but only as part of the communist bloc or as a Soviet puppet [*koeroe*]."²⁷ Yŏngin provides testament to the incorporation of the north into the communist bloc, and this includes graphic description of the devastation caused by the 1945 Soviet bombing of Yŏngin's (and Im Ogin's) hometown, Kilchu. She witnesses firsthand dismembered corpses in the streets, demolished buildings, a population in turmoil: "Liberation has been declared, so why the bombing?"[28] As stand-in for Im Ogin, Yŏngin will reflect on the formulaic, the one-dimensional, the spectral; she will witness what it means to become communist, to enter into a puppetlike existence, a virtual death.

Crossing South begins with the Red Army marching into Korea: "Round and round it goes, that's life. And aren't political regimes just empty, dreamlike things? These were the thoughts that came to my mind as I stood by the side of the road watching the seemingly endless procession of Red Army soldiers." It takes days for the Red Army column to pass. And then another army appears, this one comprised of worn-out Japanese soldiers shuffling their way south: "Plodding along in filthy, matted uniforms. Vacant, listless eyes staring out from ashen, pale faces. This was not the march of the living. It was a column of specters [*yuryŏng*]."[29] Round and round it goes: "I thought of the contrast between this wretched column and the same soldiers who just the other day had swaggered past the *Senjin* [a Japanese pejorative for Koreans]."[30] As Yŏngin stands at the crossroads of history, her witnessing takes the form of afterimage. She bitterly recalls a Japanese policeman slapping her on a train as she was returning home with a bag of rice, "the bone-biting anger of powerlessness, of one who has lost her country."[31] The faceless Red Army columns do not replace the ghostly, defeated Japanese soldiers (*p'aejanbyŏng*) but represent them at a different historical moment, when they waxed as colonial oppressor. Round and round it goes. The 1945 Soviet advance into North Hamgyŏng Province is colonial and communist, a lifeless superimposition.

SENSIBILITY AS HISTORY

Yŏngin's nonfiction account of life in the north concerns itself centrally with textual remains, the literary project abandoned by Yi T'aejun, the colonial period modernist who chose to cross north in 1947. Mention of her "Balsam Flower" (Pongsŏnhwa)—a short story actually published by Im Ogin in 1939—helps to underscore Yŏngin's familiarity with Yi T'aejun, who had helped Im publish her early stories (including "Balsam Flower") in the prominent journal *Munjang*. The title of Im's text plays on the title of Yi T'aejun's 1946 short story "Liberation: Before and After" (Haebangjŏnhu). Censored at the time of *Crossing South*'s publication, Yi's "Liberation" includes the subtitle "a writer's memoir" (*han chakka ŭi sugi*) and features his own frequent stand-in, Hyŏn, who comes to reject life under US occupation. *Crossing South* offers a virtual, allusive encounter of Yŏngin and Hyŏn, stand-ins headed in opposite directions. Im's novella is not interested in blanket dismissal (of the kind enforced by the contemporary ROK ban on the entire corpus of any writer who had crossed north) of Yi's work.[32] The task will be to rescue Yi T'aejun both from himself (his decision to cross north) and the ban on his colonial period imaginings, to recover and rework a lost aesthetic sensibility. Yŏngin will redirect selected elements of Yi's literary trajectory to her own memoir and its circulation in the early postarmistice present.

Yŏngin's communist cousin Ŭlmin (who now works closely with the Soviet occupation) brings her to the county office to see a cache of antiques—pottery, writing implements, furniture. These are objects left behind by Nakayama, a wealthy Japanese official and businessperson "a guy whose interest in mining and trade was matched by his mania for collecting."[33] Post-1945, these remains are doubly inflected. Marked by appearance in Japanese collections, they are now *chŏksan* objects ("enemy property"; property left in Korea by the Japanese). While she is filled with a "a feeling of rapture and happiness," Ŭlmin predictably takes the party line: "Yeah, it must be delightful for you to see all these playthings. That's the bourgeois mentality. Messing around with all this luxurious stuff. No use value here, not an ounce of it."[34] How to extract these antiques from an overlay of materialist critique and colonial collection mania?

Yŏngin will reflect on her communion with the collection in a way that strongly recalls Yi T'aejun's own deep engagement with Korean antiques, the creation of what Janet Poole calls "Yi's private Orient: a highly individualized exploration of the self within a geopolitical aesthetic of empire as orient."[35] Yŏngin's encounter with the antiques will also take the form of an experience that is aesthetic, emotive, and embodied. Im Ogin's exploration of Yŏngin's self brings Yi T'aejun's banned project to life both within a geopolitics of Soviet occupation and a postarmistice scene of writing enmeshed in the effects of the 1950–1953 combat phase of the 6/25 war.

In a 1953 article, the influential critic Cho Yŏnhyŏn follows others in his emphasis on the ways contemporary experience lays the groundwork for how writers should approach what amounts to an unfolding history. For Cho, war is one of the "greatest of literary topics." But even an issue of this magnitude fails to achieve importance without "internal motivation." In other words, "What is most important in literature is not the topic but a writer's subjective ability [*chuch'ejŏgin nŭngnyŏk*]."[36] The war is experienced not as something external but as the "self's subjective life, its reality."[37] In fact, the war is a good thing insofar as "our nation" (*uri minjok*) can now count itself as one among others with such "direct experience."³⁸ And how does representation of war work? Cho, who would go on to play a formative role in the mid-1950s literary scene as founding editor of the prominent journal *Hyŏndae munhak*, first distinguishes between *ch'ehŏm* (which he designates active, in-progress experience) and *kyŏnghŏm* (the experience of reflecting upon, remembering *ch'ehŏm*): "Where do we place literature in relation to these two [dimensions]? Literature is less a seamless record of *ch'ehŏm* than a portrayal based on *kyŏnghŏm*. Such is the physiological process [*saengnijŏk kwajŏng*] by which *ch'ehŏm* gives birth to a proper literary work."³⁹ Quietly alluding throughout to what will come after (the 1950–1953 phase of the 6/25 War), *Crossing South* will provide its own version of reflection. The self's subjective life unfolds in the form of a memoir, and here experience involves picking up the pieces of Yi T'aejun's lost project. Yŏngin ends up spending the entire day among the antiques: " 'Why did I have such a loving attachment [*aech'ak*]?' I muttered to myself. I realized that it was this constitution of mine, what I had in my bones [*saengni*; literally, "physiology"], that made it impossible to fit into this North Korean atmosphere."⁴⁰ Nor does Yi T'aejun belong there. His choice, outlined in "Liberation: Before and After," was disastrous; he will be a ghostly presence in such an environment (it is altogether possible that Im Ogin had heard news of his 1954 purge).⁴¹

As Ŭlmin later expands on what he knows of Nakayama's mania, Yŏngin "feels suddenly all enjoyment and interest dissipate . . . the fact that one person would collect all these things was beyond words."⁴² But suddenly she realizes that "these things were something more than items left behind by the Japanese; they seemed to shine, to carry their own inner light."⁴³ She mulls over the profound effect this recognition has upon her, even as she also recalls what she had seen in an adjacent room, the communist interrogation of a prisoner, bound and kneeling on the floor. Her heart grows heavy: "The warm, quiet joy buried in the antiques disappeared somewhere, replaced by an image that wouldn't go away, the innocent young man."⁴⁴ Light and joy emanate from the antiques themselves, provided one knows how to see and feel them. Im Ogin will locate Yŏngin's physio-aesthetics within the in-progress experience of a dividing Korea.

The antiques are alive, they animate. Here, they are accompanied by torture, the embodiment of pain (*Crossing South* includes mention of a similar scene in the colonial period). The image of the bound young man bundles the physio-aesthetic experience of joy emanating from the antiques into a memory of what will be lost. The juxtaposition is premonitory in its gathering of colonial past, communizing present, and wartime future.

KOEROE AT THE CROSSROADS OF LIBERATION

The *koeroe* (傀儡; puppet) is a disembodied form. The *koeroe* moves, is animate, but without experience or understanding of the world. The *koeroe* can torture, kill indiscriminately because it does not really feel or see properly. Although devoid of will and agency, the *koeroe* does not represent a natural condition. The *koeroe* is redeemable (see chapter 9). If the *koeroe* signals a highly visible form of emptiness, it also refers to a play of presence and absence—to that which it is not. In this sense, the *koeroe* actually assumes a sense of radical nonnormativity. That both DPRK and ROK make varying use of the term *koeroe* to refer to each other underscores the *koeroe*'s subordination, its placement as geopolitical proxy, Soviet or US puppet. In many ways the *koeroe* has served both to organize ways of thinking about national division in Korea, as well as approaches to reunification. The notion of *koeroe*, in fact, informs ideas about what constitutes the nation (*minjok*) itself. *Crossing South* enters into this conversation by way of its return to the colonial period debates on women's liberation and their inflection within a dividing Korea.

Yŏngin's emphasis on self-knowledge, women's education, literacy, and community draws heavily on well-known colonial period women educators, journalists, and artists such as Kim Hwallan, Ch'oe Ŭnhŭi, and Na Hyesŏk. Her work in Kilchu provides a blend of the earlier women's enlightenment movement, a cultural nationalist awakening, and Christian faith—all of which had contrasted markedly with proletarian figures such as Hŏ Chŏngsuk, those who sought to articulate a communist feminism that would intertwine women's liberation with class-based emancipation. Post-1945, Hŏ Chŏngsuk would return from exile in China to Seoul. Her stay under US occupation was brief; she would shortly cross north and go on to assume a position of prominence in the DPRK.[45] Yŏngin's memoir takes up both Yi T'aejun's 1947 crossing and these crossings. Where is feminism to be located in a dividing Korea? *Crossing South* offers a reply in its witnessing of the communist women's movement in North Hamgyŏng Province, centered on two differing leaders, Ch'oe Sunhŭi and Kwŏn Tŏkhwa.

Yŏngin's love of Korean expressive forms is evident throughout *Crossing South*: Her ardor for Korean writing, song, and the language itself (all of which have colonial period precedents). At the same time, we learn that Yŏngin's advocacy of women's literacy stems from personal experience: Her great-grandfather would "take her books and throw them over the backyard wall."[46] Yŏngin locates a confluence of historical agency, cultural nationalism, and aesthetic sensibility in her attempt to enlighten and educate women in her hometown. They are to assume historical agency and enter into proper ethnonational belonging.

Here, as happens elsewhere in the 1950s, *Crossing South* summons the figure of the "man-like" communist woman, the woman who has become other than herself, alienated from her femininity. When Ch'oe Sunhŭi appears at a Women's League meeting, she tells her audience that "Now is not the time for cosmetics and silks. Now is the time for payback, the time to build a government for the working class." Yŏngin notes that "As Ch'oe Sunhŭi spoke, her face betrayed not a hint of femininity, softness, or sympathy. She was no different than a machine."[47] Elsewhere, Yŏngin emphasizes Ch'oe Sunhŭi's manlike attributes: She sits "cross-legged like a man"; she "strokes her chin as if she had a beard."[48] Ch'oe Sunhŭi and other Korean communists have also become "unfamiliar, like foreigners [*igukin*]."[49] These communist women appear as a particular nonnormative inflection of the *koeroe*, emptied of a sensory, human self (machinelike), womanhood (manlike), and ethnonational belonging (foreigner-like).

Kwŏn Tŏkhwa differs. Even when she follows so many other communists in speaking of the "evil customs of the feudal system" and sings "The International" at a meeting for Yŏngin's night-study students, Yŏngin views her as "straightforward and reliable, humane."[50] And her singing of "The International" is somehow moving, "similar to the rhythm of a Korean folksong while reminiscent of 'The Red Flag.'"[51] Tŏkhwa has not othered herself. Like Yi T'aejun, she simply has made the wrong choice. Her inclinations, her sensibility provide room for reclamation: "She received the full support of the communists in the area but differed from them in the warm blood that flowed within her as a woman, in her humanity, These were the things that made her a welcome presence to me."[52] It is precisely these qualities that the communists would summarily dismiss as "cheap sentiment."[53] We are told that Tŏkhwa maintains this sensibility while keeping it from view. Best to maintain depth below surface in this kind of atmosphere.

Tŏkhwa confides in Yŏngin, telling her of the freedom she felt after her divorce: "I decided that now I could truly engage in the struggle. I was done being a puppet [*koeroe*]. I would be a true revolutionary, the equal of anyone."[54] Tŏkhwa's declaration makes uncommon and seemingly passing usage of *koeroe*, this term mobilized in both the DPRK and the ROK to delegitimize the other side as inauthentic puppet-proxy. Here, *koeroe* assumes intersectional significance, alluding to a patriarchal order that remains alive and well in a dividing Korea. It is this that brings Tŏkhwa and Yŏngin together in common cause, while parted by the parallel worlds they will have chosen. Yŏngin cannot accept Tŏkhwa's remark that "the ocean will no longer stand in the way of my ability to swim." Her rejoinder is stark: "Swim as you would like. But for me it's the Dead Sea."[55] Tŏkhwa, like Yi T'aejun, will find herself awash in a deathscape. Theirs will be an unbecoming, a dissolution. They will become *koeroe* in spite of themselves, even as both sought liberation in the north.

The relation between experience and abstraction will set the stage for a multilayered definition of liberation: "They were saying we had been liberated [*haebang*], but for me it was just the opposite. As for my environment and my personality [*kaesŏng*], I felt like an insect caught in a spider's web. Backwards, forwards—I couldn't budge. I felt nothing but absolute frustration."[56] *Kaesŏng* connotes an expansiveness of the unique self, its growth and development in the world, its liveliness.[57] Yŏngin cannot move—she has been rendered something other than human and inanimate. As *Crossing South* draws to a close, Yŏngin recalls Ŭlmin's earlier declaration that the 38th parallel won't be done away with in peaceful fashion. It is only the spider's web that will increase its reach.

Aware that she is now under surveillance, Yŏngin hardens her resolve to escape (*t'alch'ul*). She gets as far as the Hant'an River, where others have gathered to make the crossing. Shouts ring out that armed Russians are after them, and everyone jumps in the water. The passage is cold and treacherous, but Yŏngin makes it across:

> So here it was, the southern sky.... This wasn't an idea, something abstract. I was experiencing it myself, in my own body, my physicality [*saengni*]. I was feeling that sense of relief a bird released from its cage surely has as it spreads its wings through the clear blue skies. I exhaled a number of times, deeply. It would be best, I felt, if the air around me would just take me, all of me, and swallow me up.[58]

The communist spider web meets the birdcage of Henrik Ibsen's *A Doll's House*, the latter frequently featured in what Hyaeweol Choi calls the "highly contested" discussions of women's liberation in colonial Korea.[59] At the moment of crossing, Yŏngin's memoir lifts this debate not only to North Hamgyŏng Province under Soviet occupation but to the postarmistice ROK. Crossing south, Yŏngin brings her experience of what will be the DPRK (a deathscape) with her, along with a more careful, aspirational call to remember that *koeroe* can have multiple, unexpected meanings.

Sŏnu Hwi's *Return* and Im Ogin's *Crossing South* testify to the before and after of the 6/25 War. These postarmistice nonfiction accounts locate the global history of the 6/25 War in sensory, experiential becomings that are at once secular and religious. As the broad strokes of the term *wŏllam* (crossing south) imply, regional affiliations would lose a certain degree of primacy. To be sure, the idea of a home or hometown lingers in the emotive *hyang* (place of birth, with a layered connotation of village/countryside) that informs the term *sirhyangmin*. But the geopolitical organization of a south (*nam*) and north (*puk*) would assume center stage, as it does in both *Crossing South* and *Return*. It is this divide, and its vested interests within and beyond the peninsula, that would become paramount.

Is it possible to seek an elsewhere that interrupts residence within armistice? Does such a search threaten to unravel borders? If so, what kind of policing should be brought to bear? Such questions assume an urgency when images appear on screen, catch the attentiveness of those gathered to watch in the darkness of a movie theater. Chapter 11 will follow the story of the 6/25 War on film as it unfolds in the mid-1960s, a moment central to film history (particularly in the attempt to codify and categorize what should appear and what shouldn't). How to approach the *koeroe* as surface on a screen, demonstration of what someone should not have become? How to address the gendered distribution of affective labor and ethical belonging in a war that did not end? Film becomes a form of embodiment that folds wartime into a postarmistice management of life and death, life in death.

CHAPTER 11

YET TO DIE, YET TO LIVE

P ark Chung Hee's assumption of power in a 1961 military coup gave rise to a developmentalist call to condense the time needed for a Rostovian takeoff in the ROK. To push time forward was to pull the future in. Economic modernization became the order of the day. Mobilization for this effort would require clear definition, and this entailed a reckoning with the 6/25 War in popular culture. The stakes were high for what appeared on movie screens.

Accompanying the first (1962–1966) of a series of five-year plans under the Park regime was a succession of Motion Picture Laws (the first enacted in 1962) that worked to tighten pre-, in-process-, and postproduction censorship.[1] The categories of "Best Anticommunist Film" and "Best Anticommunist Screenplay" appeared for the first time in the government-sponsored Grand Bell Awards of 1966. In 1967, the introduction of an import quota regime limited the allotment of distribution rights for foreign films, while mandating a fixed percentage of days per year for domestic film screenings. Production companies that received an Anticommunist Film Award received distribution rights for an additional foreign film. Coincident with the reorganization of the film industry (the number of production companies was quickly reduced from seventy-one to sixteen) was the attempt to codify the portrayal of the 6/25 War. To make a war film in the 1960s was to navigate both a legal apparatus and censorship regime under construction, a play of punishments and rewards (which included funding, production support). Add to this mix the question of the market, the potential for commercial success or failure.[2]

As censorship policy took form in the 1960s, the proper representation of *koeroe* (傀儡; puppet) became a touchstone for war films. How, precisely, to define anticommunism in relation to ethnonation? Such a question harkened back to the earlier, wartime mobilization of the ROK cultural scene (see chapter 9), as did its response. In the 1960s, 6/25 War films tended to revolve around the figure of intra-ethnonational conflict (*tongjok sangjan*), often encapsulated in a scene of village and/or battlefield camaraderie emerging in relation to the location of malice and betrayal in an enemy considered at once the same and radically other. Family-like affective communities (which includes brotherly bonds formed in combat) hinged upon the manifestation of this self-other, the one who appears as a vacated surface (there and not there at the same time), the *koeroe*.

The early developmentalist state sought to organize the film industry by way of an informal embedment that was not simply repressive. Hieyoon Kim points out that "filmmakers could read what they were supposed to do differently from the written or spoken codes and represent their position to censors through communication during the censorship process."[3] Such a process was central to the production and screening of war-related films in the 1960s. To enter into this filmmaking scene, itself a kind of warscape, is to engage in the creative act of genre-making, in conversation with censors, as well as with domestic and international film movements.

Most prominent and prolific among the filmmakers navigating the war film genre was Yi Manhŭi (1931–1975), his blockbuster success (*The Marines Who Never Returned* (*Toraoji annŭn haebyŏng*, 1963), followed by arrest, incarceration, and subsequent rehabilitation. His story is in many ways that of the 1960s scene, a probing of the limits (yet to be clearly established) within which the war film should address family, ethnonation, *koeroe*, and masculinity. How to carry the 6/25 War into the 1960s? This chapter begins with a constellation of Yi's war films that address the anticommunist injunction, exploring a horizon of contemporary expectations. Yi would eventually find a way to screen this process, to offer visual comment on the carryover of wartime into the present in a vehicle that does not appear to be a war film at all and has never been categorized as such, *Homeward* (*Kwiro*, 1967). Yi's turn will be to a virtual widow (her husband, a veteran, is alive but paralyzed) wandering the contemporary cityscape. The film dwells upon a multilayered summons to mourn one who remains, to accede to the demand that commemoration of his wartime past take the form of filmlike, militarist reenactment.

What might it mean, though, to self-mourn one's own position as *mimangin* (widow; literally, the one-yet-to-die)? Would such a turn inward open the possibility of moving to an elsewhere, beyond wartime? *Homeward*'s posing of these questions is at once a return to a figure afforded little place in 1960s representations of the 6/25 War, the 1950s "ap'ŭre kŏl" or "après girl," the "after (war) girl" who threatens the family in different ways, usually through her assertion of subjectivity and desire beyond the expectations of the patriarchal domestic sphere.⁴ This chapter will follow in kind, concluding with Ch'oe Chŏnghŭi's exploration of sexuality, decadence, and death in the illustrations/text that comprise "Maelstrom" (Soyongdori, 1955), a short story about widowhood that is as much or more about images, how they transit from Hollywood film to produce elsewheres within the everyday life of immediate postarmistice Seoul.

CROSSING THE LINE

Filmic adaptation of Sŏnu Hwi's 1963 novella, Yi Manhŭi's *The Legend of Ssarikkol* (*Ssarikkol ŭi sinhwa*, 1967) centers on what amounts to parricide. Trapped behind enemy lines, a squad of ROK soldiers (the *kukkun*, or national army) obtain the approval of village elder Kang (Ch'oe Namhyŏn) to don civilian clothes and disperse into the community (each staying with a different family). They blend harmoniously with the villagers, all interactions taking place under Elder Kang's benevolent watch. DPRK troops arrive in short order, led by a former villager, the ill-natured P'yo Munwŏn (Pak Nosik). P'yo's subsequent tyranny over the village ends only with the return of ROK troops, who join with their civilian-clothed counterparts and the villagers to drive him and the others out. But Elder Kang has perished at the hands of P'yo, cowardly shot by the latter as he steps forward at P'yo's request to negotiate. The patriarch's last act is an attempt to repair the village fabric.

Medium-long shot presents villagers bent over Elder's Kang's body, draped by an overcoat. As ROK troops arrive, the villagers arise. Shown the elder's body, Sgt. Yun (Kang Minho) declares solemnly that "He was just an ordinary person, nothing special. But he is a Korean (*Han'guk saram*)." As successive medium shots of the villagers proceed, voice-over narration irrupts for the first time in the film: "Ssarikkol exists nowhere on Korean land [*Han'guk ttang*].... But this story is not mere legend. This is a story that did take place on Korean land and it is a story of Koreans." A final medium shot of Sgt. Yun cuts to a medium-long shot of the villagers blended with the soldiers. The death of the patriarch has given birth to a civilian-military nexus that constitutes village communality as that which is to be fought for, that which is Han'guk (ROK) itself.

The extradiegetic voice underscores Sgt. Mun's declaration by bringing life to virtuality, the simultaneous absence of a Ssarikkol and its presence everywhere. Elder Kang's ethics, his good faith attempt to talk it over with P'yo was met with betrayal, but his community-minded spirit remains, manifest in those gathered together around his body. Absent is P'yo, the villager who is no longer a villager, the one who revealed himself irrevocably as murderous. His return to the village, his tyranny, his life and death—all of this, too, is not the stuff of legend but part of a story that took place on Korean land. It is the story of the *koeroe*.

The Legend of Ssarikkol was a follow-up to Yi Manhŭi's *Hero Without a Service Number* (*Kunbŏn ŏmnŭn yongsa*, 1966), inaugural winner of the Grand Bell Award for Best Anticommunist Screenplay (Han Ujŏng). *Hero* also screens the story of a *koeroe*, this time one who commits a literal patricide—he kills his own father. The film's turn to the melodrama of a battle of brothers—the older, Yŏngho (Shin Yŏnggyun), is leader of an ROK-affiliated guerilla group operating near his hometown in the DPRK while the younger, Yŏnghun (Shin Sŏngil), is an officer in a DPRK unit—occurs within another story, referenced in the film as "original sin" (*wŏnjoe*). This story, as the priest in the film indicates, is the biblical story of Cain and Abel. Commanded to give a firing squad the order to shoot his father (Ch'oe Namhyŏn, tethered to a cross), Yŏnghun does so—a sacrifice in the name of fidelity to the party.

He will repent, turn spy for his brother's guerilla unit—a performance of *kwisun*, or recantation (more literally, "return"). But he recognizes he can never be forgiven, even as others are willing to do so (including his father). If he enters the realm of nonredemption, his act points to the confluence of Christian belief and familial ethics.[5] The one who violates the religious and ethical order constituting community is the object of commiseration. To become *koeroe* is to transgress. Such a devolution, in turn, situates those who resist communism as subjects (not objects) of forgiveness. Maintaining what Yŏngho calls "hope for humanity," they rise up and resist of their own accord (they do not require service numbers).

FIG. 11.1 Yŏngho faces his father. *Hero Without a Service Number*.

Ssarikkol and *Hero* screen a navigation with the censor.⁶ Both are hortatory in this sense, working to define anticommunist film. And both follow Yi Manhŭi's 1965 arrest and brief incarceration.

It was *Seven Women POWs* (*7in ŭi yŏp'oro*, 1965) that led to Yi Manhŭi's prosecution under the Anticommunist Law (the film would eventually undergo extensive edits and be rereleased under the title of *The Women Soldiers Who Returned* (*Toraon yŏgun*, 1965). While the indictment cited the film on multiple accounts (including fomenting hatred against Americans), the central trespass lay in its portrayal of the *pukkoe/koeroegun* (northern puppets/puppet soldiers). The film derided the motivations of the *kukkun* (ROK troops), treated the *pukkoe* as representatives of a sovereign state, and viewed the "the puppet soldiers [*koeroegun*] as good-natured compatriots [*tongp'o*], brave troops."⁷ That the DPRK soldiers intervene to rescue ROK nurses from predatory Chinese communists casts them as independent actors who do not serve at the behest of the Chinese PLA. Further, that they join with ROK nurses to kill the Chinese communists praises the "strength of their love of nation over communism."⁸

The *koeroegun* have crossed a line. They have "returned" but without any kind of mediation; nor have they repented. Their defection or *kwisun* takes place on their own terms, agentive, as savior-men, in full possession of ethnonational love (*minjok ae*). The state's application of the Anticommunist Law locates parameters for the definition of *pukkoe* in relation to independence of action, ethnonational belonging, and prescriptive gender roles (the last only implicit in official documents). *Ssarikkol* and *Hero* proffer a quick fix, rework the *pukkoe,* produce an ethico-religious register that displays their ghostliness, their terrible, tragic vacating of community. In doing so, the *koeroe* become *koeroe*—denationalized, emptied out, spectral. That *Hero* won the inaugural Grand Bell Award for Best Anticommunist Screenplay is testament to a successful rewrite. Han Ujŏng, the screenwriter, had also penned the screenplay for the censored *Seven Women*.

Patricide/fratricide (and its accompanying family melodrama) did not appear solely of their own accord as primary figure and frame for the 6/25 War in the mid-1960s. The state's intervention (the Anticommunist Law; the succession of film laws promulgated in the 1960s) in the figuring of the *koeroe* would play a role in the location of the family at the heart of the warscape. The betrayal of the *koeroe* and the accompanying production of a subject of forgiveness (often the father and/or mother) only consolidates a gendered familial order. To set the stage as a battle between brothers, then, is to present the patriarchal family as transhistorical, violation of its ethics unnatural, unhuman. And to live within this familial frame is to remain chaste in its broadest sense, morally pure, desire properly directed.

SEOUL, 1967

Yi Manhŭi directed ten films in 1967, his most significant effort, *Homeward* (*Kwiro*), appearing in theaters four months prior to *Ssarikkol*. *Homeward* offers a portrait of the relationship between Yi Chiyŏn (Mun Chŏngsuk) and her husband, Ch'oe Tong'u (Kim Chin'gyu) that centers on the former's virtual widowhood (Tong'u is a Korean War veteran paralyzed from the waist down). Winner of the 1967 Grand Bell Award for Best Film, *Homeward* folds Chiyŏn's sexuality and psychology, her malaise into the cityscape (Mun Chŏngsuk's performance as virtual widow-flaneur earned her the Grand Bell Award for Best Actress). Indeed, *Homeward* places Seoul in visual conversation with Michelangelo Antonioni's early 1960s Rome.[9] As Hong Chinhyŏk points out, "*Homeward* screens long takes in which characters do not speak. This is what makes it a modernist film. In these moments, the film rejects effective narrative progression."[10] The move to the contemporary city, to the long takes, will provide a modernist reflection on the warscape well beyond the referentiality of a combat film. Gone is the wartime setting; present is the architecture of Seoul, the mood of the city. *Homeward* summons the idea of destination only to preclude its possibility. Filmic form will interrupt notions of return associated with family, home, and community. Yi Manhŭi turns to a filmic grammar that addresses the register of the ones who mix life with death, those who trouble narrative representation. Nor will *Homeward*'s virtual widow honor the injunction to live in perpetual memorialization of sacrifice. The film will end with Chiyŏn's suicide.

Homeward, though, will return to the 1950–1953 scene of war but not to present another narrative take on the war itself (as would *Ssarikkol*). The contemporary, modernist frame transforms the anticommunist war film into an object of observation. *Homeward* is meditative, reflecting elliptically on warscape past (the five years of filmmaking that preceded its production) as it considers warscape future (the crystallization of anticommunist film as category disciplining contemporary filmmaking).

Chiyŏn takes the train from Incheon to Seoul regularly, delivering installments of Tong'u's serialized novel to a newspaper office. She wanders the city, heading home to Incheon and up the stairs to the second-floor room in which her husband is confined to bed. Her experience of the city occurs within a back and forth—return is lost to repetition. A key sequence begins with a long shot of Chiyŏn lost among others on a pedestrian bridge, moves to her POV, then to low-angle medium shot, and back to long shot, this time returning her to a crowd scene, barely discernible, one anonymity among others moving in different directions in space. Mood, desire, interiority withdraw into observation followed by collapse into the city. The linearity of a *kwiro* (literally, "return road") gives way to circulation in an everywhere and nowhere.

In Chiyŏn's briefcase is Tong'u's installment, a novel in which she herself is a character placed in a narrative arc that demands her chastity. She moves this injunction—and the narrative form within which it takes place—into circulation as she flaneurs the contemporary city. The novel, as Reporter Kang (Kim Chŏngch'ŏl) comments to a colleague, is "insipid." This appears to be an office consensus. The newspaper's editor asks Chiyŏn what she thinks of the protagonist (namely, herself). Her response: "Isn't it the duty [*immu*] of a writer to plant ideals in a society that has none?" The editor maintains his skepticism: "But can a healthy woman married to a man incapable of sex go on living that way for decades? Are we to view this woman's sacrifice as a truth?" His conclusion: "The author is offering a deified portrayal of the woman. And therein lies the problem." Chiyŏn will address the relation between injunction and truth as she steps into the 6/25 War.

A letter arrives from the survivors of the 17th Regiment on the fourteenth anniversary of the taking of Hill 724. A nondiegetic voice reads the letter, and Tong'u asks for his uniform. He will proceed to act out a combat scene, accompanied by a military march (diegetic, on a record player): "Soldiers arise. Dawn is breaking..." Tong'u now assumes the narration: "A man with no legs was running. I saw a headless man walking. I charged in front of them." Nondiegetic guns blare as he attempts to arise from his wheelchair and falls forward to the ground. "We move forward, we move forward"—the music blares as gunfire continues. Tong'u falls to the ground. Tong'u and Chiyŏn then begin yelling, but their voices are drowned out by the march, the gunfire. As he lies prone, Tong'u points ahead dramatically at an unseen enemy. His hand drops, and Chiyŏn's posture pays homage to the Angel of Grief. She then pulls herself up and turns to him as the two continue to shout wordlessly.

Focus moves from Tong'u's body in foreground to Chiyŏn. She decides to end the scene, pulling needle from record player, which continues to spin for ten seconds. All goes quiet—diegetic and nondiegetic sounds end. "Please," Chiyŏn eventually says. "Don't talk of the war. Be brave. Don't think of yesterday. Think of tomorrow." Tong'u bemoans his inability to perform as a husband for the past fourteen years, but Chiyŏn tells him she lives in accordance with her own choice.

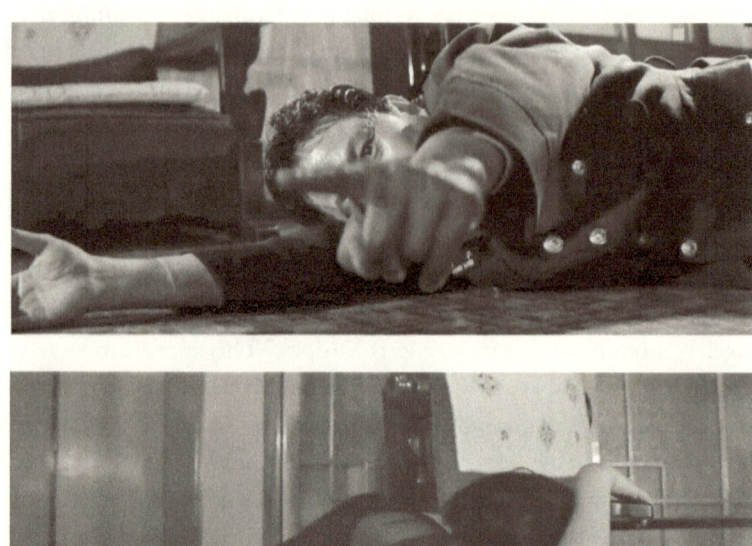

FIG. 11.2.1 AND FIG. 11.2.2 Combat and mourning, Reenacted. *Homeward.*

Fade in to the soundscape that accompanies Chiyŏn's flaneuring in the city, then cut to her walking along the water, and to a train passing by.

The sequence moves from closed, interior space to the city, from reenactment of past to confrontation of this past in the present. Such a staging replicates the temporal structure of the mid-1960s warscape—a screening of wartime meant to construct an affective grid, a contemporary mobilization that will organize everyday life. The Angel of Grief manifests itself in synchronic relation to the perpetual absence that will inhabit the disabled body.[11] Chiyŏn makes a directorial decision to silence the soundscape, end the scene. She pulls away from her position as participant-observer (gazing upon the prone body, calling for a "tomorrow"). She moves to an elsewhere. To cut to the city is to enter a different space, time, and genre. The cut is self-reflexive, a look upon a war film-like moment from the time and place in which it is produced, directed, and screened. Trauma, here, lies in a relation to the present, to the injunction to reenact a melodramatic combat scene, to mobilize as a participant-observer. It is from without that the call to action first proceeds; the call of the disembodied, nondiegetic voice begins the sequence of this film-within-a film. But such an injunction—like that made in

Tong'u's insipid novel—is behind the times, out of joint with Chiyŏn's location in the modernist filmscape that maps Seoul.

The injunction from without aims to become a voice from within—and this requires a visual repeat.[12] Later, Chiyŏn hears a voice as she opens a wedding invitation in her husband's bedroom. The voice is of General Song Ch'anghŭi presiding over her own wedding ceremony. As Chiyŏn looks upward, the camera follows suit with a series of low-angle oblique shots of the ceiling. The voice emanates from on high, Wagner's "Bridal Chorus" playing in the background. Cpt. Ch'oe has suffered a "glorious wound" during the taking of Hill 724: "When it's too cold, we must strive to be sunlight. Let's wholeheartedly create a new life. [music grows louder] I become Cpt. Ch'oe's honorable wife. I absolutely become Cpt. Ch'oe's wife. This is what Yi Chiyŏn said to herself time and again." Military march played on the record player in the earlier combat reenactment fades in as the wedding march fades out; camera angle switches to a high-angle shot of Chiyŏn. The march takes over, repeating the lyrics played earlier: "Write to your loved one, before the dawn breaks. . . . Let's fight and win before the sun goes down. . . . We are sol." It is up to Chiyŏn to complete the exhortation, broken off mid-word. She is to enact the blend of "Bridal Chorus" and military march. Her soldiering is to take on the chastity, a sacrifice of the wife as survivor. She is to become the *mimangin* (widow), "the-one-yet-to-die."

Chiyŏn's body begins to heave, but expressivist inner struggle once again gives way to genre travel. If the injunction to commemorative sacrifice appears in vertical form, the visualizing of a voice from on high, the POV shot of horizontal lines crossing the ceiling pulls the authority of command in other directions. Chiyŏn's look up (low angle) cuts to a look down upon her (high angle) that transfixes, captures her. Chiyŏn's lines of sight mirror her travel up and down the staircase into her husband's room, toward and away from the city. She begins to writhe, accentuated by a low-angle medium shot that places her at the crosshairs of a vertical and horizontal axis, as well as between sonic injunction and a cinematography that pulls in multiple directions. *Homeward* begins to fold sexuality—figured as bodily struggle with repression and natural, human impulse—into a cinematic desire to perform visual experimentation, to engage with bodies meeting, dispersing through the cityscape.

Chiyŏn will have an affair with Reporter Kang. He will call her on the phone near the film's close, exhort her to leave with him, join him for a life as far away as possible, on Jeju Island. Chiyŏn receives the call at home but leaves the phone off the hook, preventing further calls even as she declares "I'll be there in a moment. I don't want to miss the train." We have seen her already putting on makeup, gazing at herself coming in and out of focus in the mirror. She will shortly

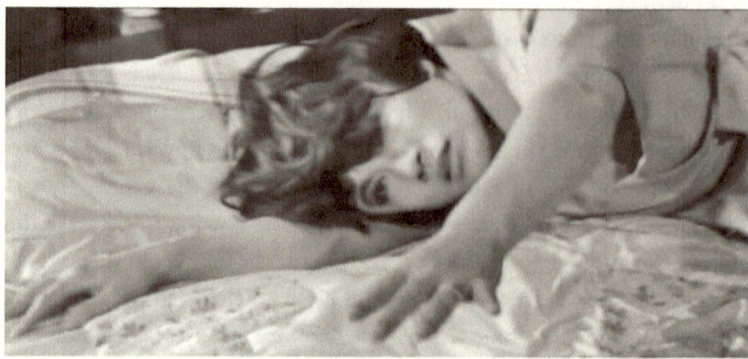

FIG. 11.3 Repetition of reenactment. *Homeward*.

die of an overdose but not before we see a final image of Tong'u lying corpse-like on his bed, followed by Chiyŏn, prone on her own bed, hand reaching out to the phone.

Her pose replicates Tong'u's earlier failed embodiment of the call to charge forward. The terms of mourning shift. Chiyŏn has moved from the *mimangin*, the one-yet-to-die, to one-yet-to-live. Desire interrupted is to be mourned. Chiyŏn has, in fact, left Tong'u (the one-who-did-not-die), who attempts to script her life. She reaches out to another frame, to a place beyond the home, site of filmlike combat reenactments and the production of Tong'u's serialized novel. Chiyŏn dies, a casualty, not of war but of the contemporary summonings that manifest themselves in representations of war (the 1960s warscape).

A cinema of fragmentation and desire imagines something other than the mobilization of a mid-1960s spectatorship of survivors, those who are to approximate a virtual widowhood, to feel the effects of war and loss in relation to the call to charge forward, to mobilize. Such an audience is to sanction itself as chaste. To travel to a modernist experience of the city is to forego an attempt to rework the consolidating anticommunist parameters of the 6/25 War film in the 1960s. The choice becomes to either make one of these films (as Yi Manhŭi would continue to do) or somehow leave the genre altogether. *Homeward* comments visually on the contemporary 6/25 War film by juxtaposing ways of seeing. Yi Manhŭi's film steps outside and observes the 1960s warscape, its reenactments, its attachments, desires, its call to move history into a militarist future by mourning the casualties of war in perpetuity, intimately, as if they were yours.

A PLACE IN THE MIRROR

Homeward inflects a version of the 1950s après girl, the war widow in its display of desire crossing through the relation of the one-yet-to-die and the one-yet-to-live. Chiyŏn approaches the threshold where one passes into the other. She resides in abeyance, in an "after" that moves forward neither in time nor space, demanding only return in the form of endless repetition. Chiyŏn's travel across film genres implicates not only bodily practices of commemoration but the idea of war as bounded-off event, presented in contours available for remembrance. The location of a lifeless body at the end point of a narrative about desire questions the idea of war itself, where it resides, who fights, and for what. Such a questioning inhabits the notion of an après girl. She is not simply rebellious, seeking a westernized individuality, exploring her agency, sexuality. She is the one who resides in an after that does not properly acknowledge what came before. The after (war) girl just comes after—she delinks from war as much as she interrogates normative ideas of domesticity/family. To what extent does this mean that she desires within a play of surfaces?

Serialized from August 30, 1955 to September 13, 1955 in the *Chosŏn ilbo*, Ch'oe Chŏnghŭi's "Maelstrom" (Soyongdori) offers a portrait of Yunsu's Mother, her out of control lifestyle, decline, and eventual death.[13] The story unfolds largely through the eyes of Miyŏng, a distant cousin who lives in Seoul with Yunsu's Mother and her two children, Yunsu and Yunnyŏ. Miyŏng lost her parents in the Korean War, fled to Busan with relatives during the January 4, 1950 retreat from Seoul, and, by way of her relatives' introduction, has come to live with Yunsu's Mother this past winter. Miyŏng will offer a sustained ethical critique of her cousin, who ignores mothering in favor of a dissipated existence, drinking with questionable friends, infatuated with the American fashion she encounters on the streets of Seoul and Hollywood films, above all Elizabeth Taylor's outfits in *A Place in the Sun* (1951, costarring Montgomery Clift; screened in the ROK in 1953). It is only at the close of the text that we find out that Yunsu's Mother is a virtual widow.

"Maelstrom" resembles a "film novel" (*yŏnghwa sosŏl*), a colonial period genre that found its way into 1950s film journals—a film put into words. As was the case with many serialized literary works, illustrations (here, by the renowned New Realist Group painter Baek Young-soo) center installments, drawing the eye to center and then back to a second traversal of the image as reading/viewing takes place down and up from right to left. A cinematic text both in form and content,

FIG. 11.4 Installment Three of "Maelstrom," *Chosŏn ilbo*, September 1, 1955. Page courtesy of Digital Chosun; "Maelstrom" image courtesy of the Baek Young-soo Art and Culture Foundation.

the visual experience of "Maelstrom" is not limited to the borders of the cross-page rectangle that contains each installment.

Below the installments are larger and more detailed advertisements, mostly for Hollywood films. Installment Three, for example, includes ads for *A Streetcar Named Desire* (1951), *Samson and Delilah* (1949), and *The Mississippi Gambler* (1953). Other installments of "Maelstrom" appear above *Tap Roots* (1948), *The Mark of Zorro* (1940), *Mogambo* (1953), *Mighty Joe Young* (1949), *Ulysses* (1954), *The Silver Chalice* (1954), and *Blackbeard the Pirate* (1952). To encounter "Maelstrom" in the pages of the *Chosŏn ilbo* is to enter into a verbal and visual conversation with Hollywood film. "Maelstrom" is at once filmic in form and a meta-look at the circuits of desire put into play by the reappearance of Hollywood film in mid-1950s Seoul (the films that find their way into theaters, that dominate contemporary film journals and magazines, that draw looks on the same page as "Maelstrom" itself).

A filmic text about film, "Maelstrom" places the relation of an observing subject to mimetic desire on display. In her study of the modernizing impulse found throughout 1950s women's magazines, Kang Soyŏn points to two contrasting types of women consistently invoked in relation to the consumption of US cultural forms: The first envious of Hollywood actresses and eager to imitate their external appearance; the second, "sophisticated women of cultivation," engaged in an informed, mature encounter with the influx of US culture.[14] "Maelstrom" presents this dichotomy in the form of the latter (Miyŏng) disapprovingly observing her cousin's embodiment of what she sees on film: "Glued to the mirror late into the night, Yunsu's Mother would assume Elizabeth Taylor's various poses."[15]

Steven Chung indicates that in the 1950s "Filmmaking and its extensive promotional apparatus became the best way to see the latest fashions, and fashion became a crucial means through which to emulate and embody the roles and fantasies films inspired."[16] Yunsu's Mother watches a film with reenactment in mind: "Yunsu's Mother had no thought of appreciating and interpreting [*kamsang*] a film. Her focus was on remembering the fashion of the actresses as they moved on the screen so that she could later copy them, and on the relationships between the men and the women, these kinds of things."[17] Even Miyŏng acknowledges that when posing in the Edith Head knock-off dress she has commissioned for herself, Yunsu's Mother "actually did resemble Elizabeth Taylor."[18] Baek Young-soo's illustration (Installment Nine) presents its own take on Yunsu's Mother looking at herself as she poses as Elizabeth Taylor. Here, the illustration adds to textual description, depicting the mirror as screenlike (clothes, comportment differ from the images Yunsu's Mother sees). Is Yunsu's Mother looking at herself or Elizabeth Taylor in the mirror? Mirror and screen combine, a

FIG. 11.5.1 AND FIG. 11.5.2 *Chosŏn ilbo*, September 3, 1955 (Installment Five); *Chosŏn ilbo*, September 8, 1955 (Installment Nine). Courtesy of the Baek Young-soo Art and Culture Foundation.

conflation of surfaces. Yunsu's Mother sees herself as the Elizabeth Taylor who appears in films, daily newspaper advertisements, and film magazine covers circulating in the ROK.

Miyŏng appeals to the body-as-referent in an effort to reveal the fantasy: "You're not really up to the level of Elizabeth Taylor. Korean women can try to be as stylish, but it's not the same. Western women have been sitting in chairs since they were young, so they've got long legs and their butts stick out."[19] She adds that "Korean women are better suited to long skirts than to western clothes" and, finally, "Hair like Audrey Hepburn, clothes like Elizabeth Taylor, it's ridiculous, isn't it?"[20] Yunsu's Mother dismisses the appeal to reference, shape, and form of the body, as so many words: "There you go, more of your sermonizing [*sŏlgyo*]." Such an exchange rehearses the many colonial period debates on modern girls, fashion, westernization, chastity, and marriage in which Ch'oe Chŏnghŭi herself occasionally took part.[21] "Maelstrom" presents a verbal/visual mise-en-scène that speaks to the reworking of these debates, the appearance of a version of the modern girl—promiscuous, mimetic, obsessed with western fashion as surface—within the postarmistice 1950s ROK.

From the beginning, the contrast between Miyŏng's attempt to reconstitute the family downstairs and the pandemonium, dissolution in her cousin's room above takes the form of a parallel edit. "Maelstrom" begins with this mirroring of the proper and improper. Miyŏng and the siblings, Yunsu and Yunnyŏ, spend a restless night below followed by an interrupted breakfast: "All hell breaks loose upstairs."[22] The three throw down their utensils and rush up to Yunsu's

FIG. 11.6 *Chosŏn ilbo*, September 7, 1955 (Installment Eight). Courtesy of the Baek Young-soo Art and Culture Foundation.

Mother's room. There they will find Yunsu's Mother "ridden like a horse" by Chang Kiho as the two rip and tear at each other. Chang, who is married, has caught Yunsu's Mother cheating on him. Baek Young-soo's illustration captures the irruption of a family-like setting—breakfast downstairs—that Yunsu's Mother has abandoned. Cut to Installment Two and the aftermath of the battle between Chang Kiho and Yunsu's Mother. The latter lies crushed, bruised on the floor, almost lifeless. Chang Kiho's departure was at the hands of Miyŏng, whose "strength filled him with trepidation."[23] Chang Kiho not only quails before Miyŏng's physical presence, he also seeks her "sympathy" (*tongjŏng*), her ethical approval of his excoriation of Yunsu's Mother as "nothing more than a dog" and "worse than a westerner's whore [*yanggalbo*]."[24] Miyŏng dismisses Chang's pleas even as she commences her teacherly project: "It's all your fault," Miyŏng tells her cousin. Their argument will only intensify. Miyŏng will pack her bags to leave but pull back, still hoping to draw her cousin out of "the dirty water that was her life."[25]

Chang's remark indicates the mid-1950s overlay of the colonial period, westernized, modern girl with the mid-1950s condemnation of the *yanggalbo* or *yanggongju* (western princess), those women, especially sex workers, associated with US soldiers stationed in the ROK. Yunsu's Mother, though, reworks this term—her desire is for departure in place, to join Hollywood royalty while residing in Seoul, a desire, in fact, that fills mid-1950s film magazines (*Yŏnghwa segye*, *Ssinema p'uro*, *Kukche yŏnghwa*, among others), their covers populated with white Hollywood actresses, pages filled with layouts of the Hollywood scene, the latest Tinseltown gossip, articles detailing how the stars present sexuality, beauty, and glamour on the screen.

FIG. 11.7.1 AND FIG. 11.7.2 Downstairs. *Chosŏn ilbo*, August 30, 1955 (Installment One); Upstairs. *Chosŏn ilbo*, August 31, 1955 (Installment Two). Courtesy of the Baek Young-soo Art and Culture Foundation.

"Maelstrom" offers its own history of the modern girl, her travel into the 1950s, her location within the play of images, the fantasies that accompany those images. Yunsu's Mother seeks sexual and economic freedom but demonstrates no interest in her two children. If "Maelstrom" searches for reference as counter to fantasy, the reconstitution of the family can only take place in relation to a corpse.

The maid, Kisuk, finds the body at approximately 2:00 p.m. on August 15, 1955, the date marking the tenth commemoration of Korea's 1945 liberation from Japanese colonial rule. Yunsu's Mother had been hiding in a secret attic, an effort to avoid creditors. She has offered her own defense in a final conversation with Miyŏng: "When Yunsu's father was alive I knew how to behave. You think you're the only one who's gentle and modest? . . . My husband left for the war and never came back. What was I to do?"[26] While we know that her husband hid in the attic during the communist occupation of Seoul, no indication is given of which side he ended up fighting for, whether he was forced into service for the PLA, or if he is indeed dead (he could be alive in the north).

Underscoring this ambiguity is the seemingly passing reference to the home as "not only enemy property [*chŏksan*] but also traitorous property [*yŏksan*]."[27] The former refers here to homes formerly owned by Japanese and distributed to Koreans following the end of colonial rule in 1945, a process that began under US military occupation in the late 1940s and continued through the 1950s, often involving varying degrees of influence peddling (the text implies Chang Kiho's involvement in matters pertaining to the property's title, which, in the end, he appears to control). The latter, not a legal designation, refers to properties owned

FIG. 11.8 *Chosŏn ilbo*, September 13, 1955 (Installment 13). Courtesy of the Baek Young-soo Art and Culture Foundation.

by a subset of "remainers" or *challyup'a*, those who remained in Seoul under DPRK occupation and were therefore tinged with varying degrees of suspicion. Some were deemed collaborators (often on the basis of rumor) following the retaking of the city and forced to forfeit title to their now "traitorous property."

"Maelstrom" pauses only at its conclusion to reflect on the casting of aspersions. Yunsu's Mother has, in fact, been leading a precarious life, held within the confines of multiple condemnations. Ch'oe Chŏnghŭi's work can only suggest elliptically that Yunsu's Mother and her husband might be the victims of unfounded rumors that led to the designation of their property as "traitorous." And if her husband had voluntarily gone north, where does that leave her? She would simply be guilty by association.

Gazing upon the corpse, "Miyŏng regretted that she had always hoped she would just drop dead."[28] But the text has already performed her wish. Yunsu's Mother joins her children for the first time in Baek Young-soo's final illustration, but she "cannot hear their crying." Miyŏng's regret, the text's withholding of Yunsu's Mother's backstory, a closing scene of mourning—all combine to ask for a look back on the postarmistice mise-en-scène presented over the previous twelve installments. Could it be that readers/viewers of "Maelstrom" have joined in a way of seeing that arises from their own desires, a sermonizing gaze, a form of chaste viewing that itself hovers on the surface? Should more attention have been paid to the fact that it was the shady Chang Kiho who declared that Yunsu's Mother was "nothing more than a dog"? Depth appears in death. To look upon the corpse is to consider the mix of her fantasies, identifications within a radical precarity. The entirety of "Maelstrom" takes place within a home designated as traitorous, a term that moves beyond suspicion to implicate all of the residents of this space.

Miyŏng momentarily wonders "if Yunsu's Mother died alone in the attic, lonely, shutting off the noise of the celebrations all over Seoul commemorating the tenth anniversary of Liberation."[29] She was, all along, present in relation to her husband's absence and its accompanying uncertainty (whose side, if any, was he on?)—a cast off and a virtual *mimangin*, one-yet-to-die. Now that she has become corpse, "Maelstrom" pauses to reflect on a death that appears to be of little or no note (in history or anywhere else). If Yunsu's Mother did not hear the celebratory shouts of liberation, those in the streets do not see her.

Yunsu's Mother has crawled into the attic, hidden herself. "Maelstrom" tells the story of how she got there with care. She remained in Seoul under DPRK wartime occupation. She saw Elizabeth Taylor in the mirror. She resided in a former Japanese/now traitorous home as one-yet-to-die and one-yet-to-live. She, too, was caught in the maelstrom of a dividing, wartime, postarmistice Korea. Ch'oe Chŏnghŭi's verbal descriptions combine with Baek Young-soo's illustrations to commemorate her place and time, in the end offering her dead body for viewing on this celebratory day, the tenth anniversary of liberation.

The introduction of "Anticommunist Film" as a category in the 1966 Grand Bell Awards serves as more than injunction. The new category provides exemplarity, a pivot around which to circle. That such an exemplarity begins with the premise of family betrayal locates the *koeroe* on the spectrum of those with communist inclinations, *yonggong* (容共). The *koeroe*, the traitorous one, neither mourns properly nor enters the future as one to be properly mourned. The *koeroe* is thus atemporal, located outside of time. That the *koeroe* destroys the family renders it worthy of elimination. That the family in question is patriarchal, heteronormative means the *koeroe* disturbs a set of gendered, hierarchical relations. To invoke the disruptive *koeroe* is to suture anticommunism to this would-be transhistorical familial order. The *koeroe* itself becomes an antiexemplarity, around which the anticommunist state gathers up the family and makes it its own.

The developmentalist call to mobilize in the 1960s includes a return to a wartime-like mode of cultural production, one familiar to writers, artists, and filmmakers who had lived through the 6/25 War (and a slightly older generation who had also experienced the Asia Pacific War). Familial tropes were available, as was the *koeroe*, and articulations of what 6/25 should mean for the ROK's place in the world (see chapter 9). Yi Manhŭi's 6/25 War films would draw from this past as he sought to address emerging anticommunist parameters. He could make films that worked to establish what the 6/25 War film should become.

Following his arrest and incarceration, he could offer a more settled anticommunist familial paradigm, coupled with an oblique observation of the very theater of exemplarity he was presenting in those films.

Homeward quietly invokes a version of the familiar, sensationalist figure from the 1950s, the après girl. She is the virtual widow who must remain chaste, true to the prescriptive manuscript she carries through the city; she is to act, puppet-like, in accord with the serializations that unfold in the newspaper, that circulate to a national audience. She will seek to break the frame, exit the theater. *Homeward* offers another return to the 1950s scene, precisely in its pull of the après girl as widow into the midst of a filmic mobilization, the attempt to codify the 6/25 War film. Yi Manhŭi, combat veteran of the 6/25 War, presents a version of the question asked by Yunsu's Mother: "What was I to do?" The question in *Homeward* is of the mode survivability will take. How to live? How is it that I have yet to live? And this question involves a reckoning with the lifting of the 6/25 War into the present, on the screen, in newspaper serializations, in everyday life . . . in Seoul, 1967.

Part V returns to fragments drawn from the DPRK, US, and ROK. Here, reflection takes the form of a mid-1960s look back upon the July 1953 armistice as future.

PART V

If the sino-Korean *hyujŏn* (休戰) signals respite or abeyance from war, *chŏngjŏn* (停戰) connotes more of a stop. If the former leans toward ceasefire, the latter more closely approximates armistice, in its sense as a staying of arms. While 休戰 would appear in ROK newspapers announcing the July 27, 1953 cessation of hostilities, 停戰 would appear in contemporary DPRK print media, as well as in the official DPRK and PRC versions of the Armistice Agreement itself. Over time, *chŏngjŏn* would join *hyujŏn* in the ROK, both used to refer to the same document (which does not include an ROK signatory).

Placed in productive relation (rather than claim to accuracy), the two terms present an uneven proximity to war, a play, back and forth, between respite and stop. These two terms hover over the force posture, the social, political, economic orderings surrounding the maintenance of a demilitarized zone (DMZ) four kilometers wide, stretching from one coast of Korea to the other.

The space of the respite-stop locates itself in time, to the fighting that came before and the fighting that might break out after. To reside in *hyujŏn/chŏngjŏn* is to live in the present progressive, enveloped by a war-past that demands recognition as a war-future. One name for this time and place is state of emergency—a *status* (standing, permanence) of the *emergens* (the coming forth, rising up). What is constant, immovable is the possible, that which might arise.

Armistice is the institutionalization of rest in restlessness, stability in instability. Armistice is stillness in motion, a stay of arms that mobilizes.

CHAPTER 12

DIVISION AS METHOD

To attach years in parentheses (1950–1953) to something called the Korean War is to locate an event in history. Armistice in Korea, though, was not an event but a method, a way of governance. The armistice did not simply put an end to the bloodshed of the "Korean conflict." The armistice has proven durable as future-oriented arrangement of the temporary, securing an interminable interim and thus becoming a template for what was to come not only after war but after colonialism on the Korean peninsula. The armistice was as much an attempt at time management as it was the implementation of the DMZ, a border that possesses its own temporality. As embodiment of a cease and desist order to those on either side who would attempt to reunify the peninsula by force, the DMZ looked at once to the past and the future, to the settling of the Korean peninsula into the unsettled state of division. This chapter takes as its point of departure the codification of this unsettled state in a document (the armistice) that would have lasting, global effects. The armistice tethered the peninsula implicitly and explicitly to the post-1945 reworking of the world order, which included the continuing projection of US economic, political, and military power across the transpacific, to a forward position within the Korean DMZ itself (south of the Military Demarcation Line).

To reflect on the wartime past is to bring the dead into conversation with survivors, past and present. This chapter turns to mid-1960s stories from the Democratic People's Republic of Korea (DPRK), the United States, and the Republic of Korea (ROK) that retroactively set the stage for postarmistice worlds. Ri Yunyŏng's short story "Dawn Behind Enemy Lines" (Chŏkhu ŭi saebyŏk, 1965), Denis Sanders's film *War Hunt* (1962), and Yi Hoch'ŏl's novel *Petty Bourgeoisie* (*Sosimin*, 1964–1965) organize pasts as leading to the 1960s and beyond. These works intersect as they reflect upon on beginnings, even origins. These are testimonials less of confirmation than exhortation, and in this they dwell on those who did not survive. They search for and attempt to define what we might call a dividing point, a moment in time that allows for dividing (process) to approach division (condition). Here is where division appears as method, in the form of feelings, attitudes, ways of life, and histories of presents poised to become futures.

DEATH WARRANT

Peaceful, productivist columns of tractors and supplies stand ready to move south by train and vehicle convoy, from the Korean peninsula's northernmost border, Sinŭiju, to the southernmost city, Busan. A DPRK woman extends a peaceful embrace to southern women in tatters, wizened faces darkened. She draws them toward her even as they seek her approach. Her compassion splinters the Military Demarcation Line (MDL) separating the Koreas, reducing a corpulent US soldier, his weaponry, and a doglike figure labeled as Chang Myŏn (the ROK prime minister) to miniature, without direct confrontation (as if they've become afterthoughts).

Figure 12.1 presents an asymmetrical, tripartite fragmentation. The capaciousness of a single figure, a totality larger than the others, stands above while reaching below to two smaller women and a third set of hands, disembodied. This rendering of expansiveness makes visible the opposition of happiness to misery, fullness to lack. The splintering of the MDL occurs within an emotive horizon, the desire for the place and time when productivist revolution becomes familial reunification. The temporal register of this image rests upon a visual and emotive movement from the larger to the smaller, to the miniature—to a future perfect in which the shards of armistice that remain visible will have become what they always were, out of place and time. The desire of the despairing and dying will be met. They will have been brought back to life.

For Kim Il Sung, the armistice signaled a return to the status quo antebellum, his prewar attempt to achieve reunification sans war having been interrupted by the southern puppet regime's attack on the north in June 1950.[1] He declared the armistice a "huge victory" in 1953, and it would indeed be celebrated as such in subsequent decades (becoming a national holiday, "Fatherland Liberation War Victory Day," in 1996).[2] In short, "we have now attained the possibility of resolving the issue of our fatherland's reunification peaceably."[3] Kim explains his view of the armistice by outlining two incorrect responses to its implementation.

FIG. 12.1 "To all women! In order to move forward the day when we will live together warmly as one family with our brethren in South Chosŏn, let's produce more, let's build more!" *Chosŏn nyŏsŏng*, December 1960.

The first considers reconstruction impossible because war can break out at any time. The second assumes a carefree, lackadaisical attitude, satisfied that little needs to be done insofar as the armistice has, in fact, brought an end to the war. The task, though, is to "keep firmly in mind that this achievement, the victory of the armistice, came at a heavy cost, the enormous sacrifice brought on by the suffering and destruction of war. What we must now do is engage in a resolute, unbending struggle. For the sake of lasting peace in Chosŏn. For the sake of the peaceful reunification of the fatherland."[4] The armistice strengthens the originary vision of peaceful reunification, of a struggle by means other than war. This struggle must now remain mindful of the price paid in war, the victory achieved in the cessation of hostilities, and of a limit, the disallowance of war as an option to achieve reunification.

As Kim Il Sung made clear in 1956, the policy of peaceful reunification is meant to connect to a broad base in the south who yearn for the same policy but suffer under a fascist dictator, the US puppet Syngman Rhee. It is Rhee's "trampling all over the armistice agreement, his continuing attempts to stir up trouble along the Military Demarcation Line, his request for the long-term basing of US troops, his incessant clamoring for a so-called 'northern conquest' [*pukpŏl*] that will once again give rise to intraethnic strife [*tongjoksangjaeng*]."[5] The construction of a sovereign, socialist state—manifest in the north, suppressed in the south—will enable reunification by peaceful means, allow for proper decolonization of the Korean peninsula.

Kim Il Sung's reference to "northern conquest" targeted "Unification by Northward Advance" (*pukchin t'ongil*), a well-known catchphrase in the 1950s ROK.[6] As is evident in his correspondence with US President Dwight D. Eisenhower in the months leading up to the late July 1953 armistice, Rhee's insistence on northward advance framed his staunch anticommunism, as well as his position that "If . . . the United States should decide to withdraw entirely from Korea, they may do so."[7] Rhee would subsequently expand on the latter point, offering a scenario in which all foreign belligerents ("both the Communist and United Nations forces") simultaneously depart from the peninsula, leaving the ROK "the self-determination to decide the issue ourselves conclusively one way or the other."[8] Eisenhower's response: "The blood of your youth and our youth has been poured out on the altar of common sacrifice. Thereby we have demonstrated not only our dedication to the cause of human freedom and political liberty, but also our dedication to an equally important principle which is that there cannot be independence without interdependence."[9] The assertion is of blood alliance (*hyŏlmaeng*), a term that would find currency in the 1950s and beyond. Here, US blood establishes credibility, an embodiment of purpose and willingness that binds center to periphery in equal measure. Made in the name of ideas (freedom, liberty), this common sacrifice posits itself as universal truth but was in fact the offer of a "securitized humanity, a defensive construction of 'bonds forged in blood' that posited militarized development as a foil to notions of sovereignty or self-determination based on the people."[10] US global management—the arrangements and determinations it makes—will proceed in the form of oversight of this bond, of the exigencies and accommodations accompanying interdependence itself. The armistice stands at the center of this arrangement.

Eisenhower makes it clear that armistice is the only route forward: "We would not be justified in prolonging the war with all the misery that it involves in the hope of achieving, by force, the reunification of Korea."[11] The statement is made in the name of life, and it is clear. The war has reached its limit. Rhee would counter in kind, replying to Eisenhower that "to accept such an armistice is to accept a death warrant."[12] This would be Rhee's final protest in writing prior to the conclusion of the armistice on July 27, 1953 (signed by military representatives of the United Nations Command, Korean People's Army, and Chinese People's Volunteer Army).

The Rhee-Eisenhower exchange represents a significant moment in the wartime history of what Robert Osgood termed "improvised restraints," the "language of actions as well as of words" that "kept the Korean War limited."[13] That Rhee combines a call for Wilsonian self-determination with the proposal that US/UN forces withdraw from the peninsula signals that he was ready to rescind his July 14, 1950 agreement handing over operational control (OPCON) of ROK forces to the United Nations Command (UNC). A US general would assume OPCON of the ROK military in both peacetime and wartime through 1994 and in wartime after that date. Coupled with Rhee's advocacy of Unification by Northward Advance, the lack of an ROK signatory to the armistice did more than harden domestic anticommunism and polarize south-north relations. The subsequent implementation of the US-ROK Mutual Defense Treaty in 1954 meant that the United States would occupy a limiting function on the Korean peninsula, with no time limit.

To figure the armistice as death warrant is to contest the regime of the limit in the name of an authentic anticommunism, the nation (and its sovereignty). Rhee understood, quite correctly, that for the United States the armistice served as a check on anticommunist nationalism as much as the containment of communism (a form of dual deterrence). Eisenhower's power to represent the meaning of life (avoidance of further death) and death (common sacrifice made in war) on behalf of the United States and the ROK assumes a sovereignty over the idea of the limit, with ramifications well beyond intra-peninsula concerns. Kim Il Sung's elevation of the armistice to victory acknowledges that the possibility of reunification by military means is foreclosed. The sacrifice made to repel US-sponsored aggression, though, locates the DPRK at the forefront of the global history of revolutionary struggle, while legitimizing the DPRK's postarmistice position as harbinger of a properly decolonial future for the peninsula.

HOMETOWN OF THE HEART

The June 1965 issue of *Chosŏn munhak* (*Korean Literature*) begins with an introductory call: "Let's Create a Greater, More High-Spirited Epic and Poetic

Canvas of the Fatherland Liberation War!" The summons is to commemorate the war (fifteen years have passed since its outbreak) by making it appear in its totality: "We must remember that only when the focal point of an epic canvas carefully follows a unificatory principle that brings together a broad, organic set of relations does it take multidimensional form."[14] The war is to coalesce in multiplicity, to mobilize: "The primary concern is to create the everlasting typical character of the heroic warrior as people-patriot-fighter. To put this into practice, we must assemble . . . a collective of positive characters who . . . bring the rear into organic relation with the front."[15] The war is to make itself manifest across time and space: "the collective heroism of the army at the front and unyielding everyday vitality of the people in the rear cannot be thought of apart from their socialist fatherland and their future, and their loyalty to their Party and the Leader."[16] The war inclines to its own present and the presents that will follow. The war is unificatory in its continuous contemporaneity, its stretch of wartime across rear and front and into the future. No one is to fall behind this homogeneous wartime—then, now, or later. Multidimensionality requires a combination of depth and intensity: "We must pay deep attention to the historical development of main characters," and this is best done "by presenting a sharply tense, dramatic situation in which a *hero's spiritual experience and unyielding spiritual strength* . . . have the opportunity to come to the fore."[17] The epic canvas seeks to animate, materialize the spiritual, make it visible.

Ri Yunyŏng's "Dawn Behind Enemy Lines" (Chŏkhu ŭi saebyŏk) appears directly after these introductory remarks in the June 1965 issue of *Chosŏn munhak*. "Dawn" is a text about light, what will be brought to light, how one is drawn to light. The call to live in the light will turn upon a slow reveal, a presentation of how to see and feel a story within a story, the story of a mother's dead body, her nurturing strength, her animation of the present.

Pak Kiyŏl is on recon behind enemy lines in Kangwŏn Province. He's under orders to track the movements of a US general, advance scout for a mission to take the general prisoner. Pak is hurt, his arm useless when we meet him at the beginning of the story. He's doing all he can to carry two children (one a baby, another a young boy) with him while making his way back north, evading American checkpoints: "In a couple of days you'll be at Army Political Affairs, and they'll find an orphanage for you. You'll be raised well there. On the day we win this war, I'll come and get you. I'll take you to our home [*uri chip*]."[18] As the three move through a beautiful, moonlit night, traversing the glistening snow—marred only by the sound of enemy gunfire—the boy's eyes shine brightly as he asks Pak, "Is the north far from here?" "It's close," Pak replies, the boy's notebook coming to mind: "Our House" it was titled.[19] "Dawn" will dwell upon this notebook and Pak's flashbacks to the shack in which he found it.

The boy writes his story in the first-person (although Pak senses that the boy's mother provided a guiding hand). The boy's father died in the Mt. Odae guerilla battle; his mother was arrested and brutally tortured. He and his mother till their landlords' fields, barely eking out a miserable living until the People's Liberation Army comes from the north and everything changes. They are given a house, land, the boy is sent for the first time to school: "Our country is a really good country. I want to grow up fast and become an important person in our country."[20] Pak pauses. "Yes, let's go north," he mutters, looking up as "the North Star, always a friend on nighttime missions, seemed to beckon, filling him with emotions deeper than ever."[21]

Pak's wounds steadily weaken him as the three continue their trek northward. He gathers strength when "an unusually beautiful dawn" arrives and finds himself "drawing pictures in his mind, looking at what had happened as if it were right before his eyes."[22] He fights off the enemy, makes his way forward through gunfire, hears what he thinks is someone screaming. It's like a dream. A young boy's voice, the word "Mother."[23] And "Moooththeeer, Moooththeer."[24] Pak espies a shack, rushes inside. He pauses, shocked: "A middle-aged woman lying there, eyes open, a baby, maybe a two-year-old, asleep on her chest, hand tightly clenching one of her mother's breasts, one of the mother's arms wrapped around the baby. A boy of about ten, arm draped around his mother's neck, sobbing."[25] Pak places his hand on her chest: "Still warm. It looked like she'd been dead for only a short while."[26] Pak's imaging of the mother's body circulates, the touch of her warmth travels to readers of "Dawn." She nurtures postmortem.

Pak's mission demands that he return to base as soon as possible. The children are slowing him down. Should he leave them behind? The boy has told him more of the story, what his mother had said: " 'Uhong, take the baby and leave now. Go north. It's the only way you'll survive.' She'd fallen silent, and then continued, 'This mother of yours won't close her eyes until I see you two go north and live well.' Those were her last words."[27] As Pak considers what to do, "It was as if the mother's eyes, paler than ever in the moonlight, held him in her gaze."[28] He's overwhelmed: "His brain went 'thud,' like he'd been hit with a hammer. Ever since the division, he'd heard the expressions 'north,' 'up north,' 'northern sector' countless times. But how was it that these words of the mother, conveyed by the boy, could hit him so hard, touch him to the core, cause such a powerful emotion to erupt?"[29] For the southern brethren (*tong'po*), the north was the base of the Chosŏn democratic revolution. The north was their "hometown of the heart [*maŭm ŭi kohyang*], their mother's bosom, the hand of succor."[30] The moment is epiphanic: "Pak's worried, squinting eyes opened wider and wider and began themselves to glimmer with light."[31] Awakened to the north within, he becomes a light source: "Here, deep in the mountains behind enemy lines, isn't it that I am the 'north'? Why should 'north' be in a faraway place?"[32] The north is a direction, a call, a guidelight beckoning from the skies, a safe haven, the look in a mother's eyes, the look in your own eyes, a feeling, a place deep within.

"Dawn Behind Enemy Lines" returns to the war to commemorate an experiential, transformative moment. To recognize that the only way to survive is to find your way north is to organize a way of seeing, feeling, and belonging in a peninsula divided. This return to the Fatherland Liberation War responds to a contemporary exhortation, as well as to the messiness of the early 1950s literary scene. The revolutionary mourning of Han Hyo's *Seoul People* (see chapter 2) recedes. No need to mourn for what has been left behind and carry it with us. The southern brethren themselves have awakened to the north that lives within their hearts. Happiness resides in this feeling-north. It will arise from experience, self-awakening. No longer is it in need of mediation, a consideration of feeling-transfer by way of a Soviet text or film (see chapter 3). Nor does a postarmistice woman's revolutionary agency emerge from reflection on the meaning of the war dead, of the transfer of their blood into her subjectivity in the present (see chapter 4). The mother's dead body transmits its last warmth to Pak, to the text's readers, to the north within.

Calls to lift the wartime past into mobilization of the present and future would echo in the mid-1960s. In a 1965 article, Pang Hyŏnsŭng declares that "In reflecting the Fatherland Liberation War, writers must locate the kernel [*almaengi*] that is worth imparting to the humans of this generation and later generations; they must elucidate it in an artistic manner that expands their ideological approach and spiritual world [*chŏngsin segye*]."[33] Such an expansiveness resides in the portrayal of "spiritual power" (*chŏngsinjŏgin him*) and "action" (*undong*) that pushes simple, earnest, average workers and their children to the level of "heroes of the age" (*sidae ŭi yŏng'ung*). The "grand human" (*kŏdaehan in'gan*) that appears before their eyes must also be one that is familiar, a "fellow traveler" (*kil tongmu*). Key is the "proper understanding of the unification between the ordinary and the heroic."[34] The latter resides in the former, the "heroic in the ordinary human" ensuring that workers devote themselves "not to a socialist system that benefits a chosen few" but instead, are themselves "hosts of the nation" (*nara ŭi chuin*) engaged in struggle (*t'ujaeng*) for their own "happiness and resplendent future."[35] The kernel expands from the Fatherland Liberation War to a broader, more encompassing struggle, a mobilization of all for all times, for time itself.

LESSONS

The Kennedy administration's Project Beef-Up and the accompanying creation of US Military Assistance Command Vietnam (1962) signaled an increasing US commitment to South Vietnam. By 1965, though, Kennedy and some of his advisors (including Secretary of Defense Robert McNamara) entertained ideas of withdrawal. As Marc J. Selverstone indicates, McNamara in particular was concerned "about making long-term, open-ended commitments to the developing world. For McNamara, the object lesson was South Korea, which the United States had been supporting with substantial amounts of aid since the end of the Korean War."[36] These discussions aside, Selverstone locates Kennedy firmly within "the era's technocratic, problem-solving ethos, which inclined Americans toward managing the global order."[37] For Selverstone, "The linchpin of that new understanding was the slippery yet salient concept of credibility. Although open to interpretation, credibility communicates a nation's willingness to act in defense of its fundamental interests."[38] In the early 1960s, Korea could serve both as object lesson of commitment and evidence of credibility, proof of US willingness to intervene globally.

The Korean War was distilled in other lessons, among them the continuing need to redefine the meaning of war for an American public unschooled in the complexity of global management. Credibility involves not only international but also domestic belief. In *Limited War: The Challenge to American Strategy* (1957), Robert Osgood reflects on what the outcome in Korea means for the future modality of war. Two extreme positions require mediation. On the one hand is "sheer bellicosity," what amounts to a call for "total destruction in the name of universal principles." On the other hand is a "peculiarly irresponsible form of self-righteousness" that advocates for a "general renunciation of force." Osgood argues for a more nuanced ethics: "Intelligent morality is superior to capricious moralism." The former speaks to measured perseverance, the ability to "endure the sacrifices and frustrations of limited war." The latter is unreflective, serving only to gratify "superficially moral instincts." In lieu of "buoyant sentiments and aspirations" Osgood argues for "a kind of practical idealism, even a kind of heroism."[39] How to mobilize a population in the name of a heroism that is less than clear-cut? Osgood worries that the public will struggle to "sacrifice life and happiness without ever exerting the full military strength of which it is capable."[40] Will the nation "permit its sons to die for the sake of holding some secondary position on the rimlands of Asia?"[41] Osgood ponders "disguising new imperatives in terms of traditional principles" but then determines that candor relying on the American "record of pragmatic adaptation" would be the best course.⁴²

Osgood's earlier formulation of "enlightened self-interest" also sought to temper a national egoism with internationalist idealism, a move that proceeds by way of the underlying reality that "national self preservation is predicated upon the fear of death."⁴³ Like sacrifice, fear portends, speaks to a future. That pragmatics would retain heroism—a kind of intelligent and realistic heroism that understands the long game, the big picture—means that death in limited war was never to be in vain, nor will it be shorn from the promise of a victorious outcome.

In *Korea: The Limited War* (1964), a text widely read in international relations and US military circles, David Rees similarly eschews what he calls a "liberal-puritan tradition" that views war as justified only "when fought as a crusade against tyrants in a mood of righteous indignation."⁴⁴ Korea serves as a wake-up call: "Only when the West fully appreciates that power and policy . . . can never be separated and that limited war is the fusion of both, will we ever meet the Communist challenge decisively on the most important battleground—our own minds."⁴⁵ Writing in 1964 (the Gulf of Tonkin Resolution would follow later in this year), Rees calls for the understanding that "Limited war . . . is political war *par excellence*, in that 'purely military' considerations are excluded."⁴⁶ At stake is the credibility of limited war itself, belief in its necessity, the formation of a willingness to support it.

For T. R. Fehrenbach, the question of credibility and commitment of the general population to limited war requires a different form of pragmatics. In his influential *This Kind of War: A Study in Unpreparedness* (1963; Colin Powell blurbs for the 2008 edition) Fehrenbach also presents Korea as a past and a future. As the title implies, a lesson had been learned: "In the Korean War, Americans adopted a course not new to the world but new to them. They accepted limitations on warfare and controlled violence as a means to an end."⁴⁷ Here, credibility reaches its own limit. Belief in a new way of waging war will never extend to a willingness among the general population to die in its name: "None want to serve on the far frontiers, or to maintain lonely, dangerous vigils on the periphery of Asia. There has been every indication that mass call-ups for cold war moves may result in mass disaffection."⁴⁸ Korea offered yet another lesson. The reality is that "Korea, from Task Force Smith at Osan to the last days at Pork Chop, indicates that the policy of containment cannot be implemented without professional legions."⁴⁹ At the same time, the only way to end the regime of limited war will be total annihilation, what Fehrenbach calls "blowing the whistle on the game."⁵⁰ In the future, the " 'modern' infantry may ride sky vehicles into combat, fire and sense its weapons through instrumentation . . . but it must also be . . .

iron-hard, poised for instant obedience, and prepared to die in the mud."[51] The image is of death limited to the willing (see chapter 6).

It would take Vietnam to bring the point home. Richard Nixon would authorize a commission to explore the possibility of an all-volunteer force in 1969 (Project Volar was launched in 1971). Replacing the grand narrative of crusade would be the symbology of "ultimate sacrifice" particular to limited wars (whose causes are not immediately clear and whose ends are murky). This is a sacrifice given as gift not only to those in the domestic population unwilling to die but to humanity itself (in the name of a struggle to contain both its own powers of annihilation and communism). As such, this death assumes a dimension unapproachable by the involuntary death and dying taking place in the limited-war zones themselves, regardless of severity. Bruce Cumings indicates that in the Korean War "as many as three million Koreans died, at least half of them civilians."[52] Limited war appeals to a grim realism, which includes the assumption that those suffering disproportionate casualties and destruction understand this necessity. As Su-kyoung Hwang points out, "The idea of communism as the ultimate evil not only turned the Korean War into a just war, but also made the bombings seem like the lesser evil and the people's fear of the bombings as the lesser fear."[53] Fehrenbach concludes his study of unpreparedness with a call to attentiveness: "It is while men talk blithely of the lessons of history that they ignore them. The lesson of Korea is that it happened."[54] So it goes, as Kurt Vonnegut's *Slaughterhouse-5, or the Children's Crusade: A Duty Dance with Death* (1969) has it. Korea was less important as a past than as interminable lesson for the future.

THERE'LL BE ANOTHER

The 1960s began with the disappearance of the Korean War film from Hollywood. *War Hunt* (1962; dir. Denis Sanders) would be one of the last; this film would also be the first to offer a sustained meditation on the July 27, 1953 armistice. That war might be a hunt poses an ethical and temporal question: When does combat killing become murder?

War Hunt revolves around the conflict between Raymond (also called Endore; John Saxon) and the liberal Loomis (Robert Redford, in his first significant Hollywood role). The film begins with the image of a corpse followed by Loomis's voice-over narration explaining that his journey from the continental United States (CONUS) to the Korean front is to the "tip of the spear." He will shortly meet Raymond, whose sole mission is to creep behind enemy lines, gather

FIG. 12.2 *War Hunt*. Everett Collection, Alamy.

intelligence. He kills silently (with a knife) and perhaps needlessly. Raymond does more. He follows his kills with a death dance around the victims (a ritual overlooked by the commanding officer (CO), who places a premium on Raymond's recon successes). As one *War Hunt* poster exclaims, "In this exploding hell—you couldn't tell where the hero in a man ended . . . and the killer began!!!"

War Hunt is indeed about this hell, where borders blur—which is why Raymond tells his protégé, the young Korean boy Charlie, "No one's ever seen me at night. It's because I'm invisible. The truth can blind." But it's also about border-making. Raymond's disappearance with Charlie immediately after word of the Armistice Agreement leads to considerable consternation (the agreement stipulates a ceasefire within twelve hours). Worried about the possibility of a major international incident, Pratt (the CO) leads several soldiers (including Loomis) into the DMZ under the cover of a grave detail (as allowed in the Armistice Agreement, Article II, Section 13f). They find Raymond on a ridge. "The war's over," Pratt shouts. Raymond replies with a query: "Which war?" Pratt continues: "We've all been confused at times Raymond. But you'll come back with us now. Won't you son? The war is over." Raymond's response: "There'll be another." Raymond's location on the blurry border between sanctioned killing and murder does something more than reflect on criminal psychology (much-discussed in the 1950s). His truth is of the murderous impulse, the human proclivity to violence and destruction that knows no borders, that in the end celebrates homeostasis (something of a death drive, perhaps).[55] Such an impulse can be found anywhere—on a city's streets, on a battlefield (as the *War Hunt* poster has it). The friend/enemy distinction recedes as the battle moves to the question of human nature (death drive trumping ideas of self-preservation). No choice remains but restraint, the establishment of a limit line assuming universalist dimensions as a form of self-deterrence. The film's question, then, is less whether or when Raymond's killings become murder than how to understand his death.

Pratt orders Raymond to drop his knife, declaring emphatically that he is the latter's commanding officer. Raymond's response: "I am commanding. The command is that I am commanding the commandment." The statement is of what Joost Meerloo calls "totalitaria," locus of the absolute (see chapter 8). Pratt will shoot and kill Raymond, even as the idealistic Loomis shouts "No!" The dissenting voice is less imperative than descriptive, "no" signaling "this cannot be." But it must. Armistice in Korea requires accommodation of the play of dark and light, murderousness and idealism that constitutes the human condition. Armistice is a form of governance that seeks equilibrium, a reigning in of the worst of human impulses. It is Raymond who must be hunted down in the DMZ, embodiment of this uneasy but necessary governance. "You alright, soldier?" Pratt asks Loomis. Loomis: "No." "No" because there is no way out, only recourse to a pragmatic commandment: thou shalt kill so as to limit more killing. And "No" because what will matter are the feelings and state of mind of the witness-participant who travels to the tip of the spear.

The journey into the war zone does not locate truths worthy of a crusade. Instead, Loomis, stands in his own universalism, sensitive, witness to a terrible but necessary kill, an American death inaugurating armistice (constitution for limited war). The film ends with Loomis, Pratt, and Raymond's corpse in the DMZ, south of the Military Demarcation Line (MDL). "Mark him!" Pratt declares. They mark a spot, appearing in a location under new administration. In accordance with the Armistice Agreement (Article 1, Section 10), the KPA and CPLA commanders assume administrative authority over the section of the DMZ north of the MDL, the UNC commander (always a US general) given administrative authority over the section of the DMZ south of the MDL. The command is that the UNC is commanding this limit. Raymond's body commemorates this spatial distribution of authority. And his corpse is credible, prophetic, embodiment not of event but of a truth that will manifest itself in the future. There'll be another.

MAELSTROM AS HISTORY

Reflecting on postarmistice life from a 1959 vantage point, Kim Sŏngsik considers mid-1950s ROK society as largely defined by a "depoliticization stemming from a sense that people were powerless to effect any kind of change amidst the infighting and corruption.... Money determined the outcome of all affairs; moneyism [*kŭmgwŏnjuŭi*] took the place of nationalism."[56] Kim extends this view to his own moment at decade's close: "True, Korean society is presently threatened by communism; however, it is equally threatened by commercialism."[57] Such a description was not uncommon (see chapter 9). Indeed, the terms "petty bourgeois mentality" (*sosimin kŭnsŏng*) and "petty bourgeois consciousness" (*sosimin ŭisik*) were frequently invoked to critique the contemporary scene, particularly in the 1960s. But what is a *sosimin* exactly? The prominent intellectual Paik Nakchung provides historical context in a 1969 essay:

> The Korean *sosimin* of the 1930s was a combination of the pre-modern feudal subject [*ponggŏn sinmin*], the Japanese imperial subject [*ilche singminji ŭi sinmin*], and the *sosimin* that appears in early industrial society. Liberation from

Japanese rule, the April Revolution, the industrial development which has taken place following May 16 [Park Chung Hee's 1961 military coup]—all of this has changed many things, but insofar as we have still been unable to establish a modern civil society, we can say that the amorphous character of the 1930s *sosimin* is very much with us today.[58]

For Paik, the "amorphous character" of the *sosimin* makes it a "flexible, encompassing concept, one which emphasizes the general attitude taken towards everyday life, political consciousness, and overall worldview."[59] If the *sosimin* (小市民) is writ large, sign of the continuing colonial modern, this figure/concept turns upon its smallness (小; so), more precisely, the historical production of this smallness as constitutive of the social, political, and economic order.

In his novel *Petty Bourgeoisie* (*Sosimin*, 1964–65), Yi Hoch'ŏl finds these conditions in what he calls the maelstrom (*soyongdori*) of refugee-filled, wartime Busan.[60] Pak, the first-person narrator, explains:

> When a society, every layer that comprises it, is torn asunder, no element of the old order remains unscathed. It's as if everything gets thrown into a swampy mess only to be churned up in a violent maelstrom [*soyongdori*] and spit out the other side, down a muddy rush of waters. Surplus goods from the U.S. continuously poured into the war zone that was Korea. U.S. industry seemed to be getting a second wind from all that was happening. . . . In Busan, the American-made products were by no means distributed evenly—they followed their own logic, zigzagging here and there. A new kind of competition for these goods emerged, and a bloody one at that. And a new class, the nouveau riche, came into being. . . . This was a time of drastic change for Korean society. Those lacking the energy to survive were swept aside like used goods. Only those with strength and vitality were able to stay alive.[61]

Based on a wartime diary Yi Hoch'ŏl kept after crossing south (*wŏllam*) by boat and arriving in the port city of Busan, *Sosimin* details the everyday lives of a noodle shop's owner and workers, linking these characters and their individual histories to the general "depravity" (*t'arak*) of a newly-forming social order.[62] Yi's text dwells upon the ways Busan serves not as destination but entrance into a world more unforgiving than the combat zone. The rear becomes the front, more lasting in its effects. The battle taking place in Busan portends more than an improper future. The wartime birth of the *sosimin* signals an improper survivability. The choice of life is of a certain way of life, an attitude, a bearing toward life. The novel's title, *Sosimin*, declares not an end but a beginning, the appearance of the maelstrom. To be sure, this is a history of survivors, but it is also a history of casualties, those who become thinglike, inanimate (used goods)—those who recede, disappear.

Yi Hochʻŏl's memoir-like novel dwells upon a painful separation, the growing distance between Pak and Chŏng (senior among Pak's refugee cohort, all from the same hometown). The latter's refusal to compromise is portrayed as bringing about his own death—a "half suicide." Pak finds Chŏng's ethical stance admirable but formulaic:

> I couldn't give a clear-cut reason for it, but the truth was that I wanted so badly to let him know that I was on his side. Of course, this had nothing to do with the weightiness of the philosophical system Chŏng had cherished for so long. It was, more or less, sentimental on my part, but even so, I just knew deep down that my feelings were ... more to the point than Chŏng's weighty schematism [*tosik*].[63]

A feverish consideration of his own "conflict with society" ensues, and Pak suddenly thinks of Lenin: "He never once made a middle-of-the-road, moderate judgment regarding anyone. His eyes operated like a microscope. All that entered into his line of sight was amplified to the extreme degree, no matter the particularities of the situation."[64] The mid-1960s implication is clear. Chŏng's schematism, like Lenin's amplification, distances him from himself, from an understanding of the everyday. But if Chŏng is uncompromising, one-dimensional, so is the leveling of the maelstrom, the spit into the muddy waters.

Pak will attempt to understand his own accommodation via a mid-1960s self-reflection: "Standing at the crossroads of the individual and the collective, I had no choice but to choose the path of protecting myself. You might declare this a betrayal of history, but wait a minute, whose history, what type of history do you mean? Sure, I wanted to protect myself, but I was also properly stricken by the pangs of conscience."[65] The memoir of a refugee in everyday Busan. A story of dislocation from the DPRK that becomes something else in the ROK, dislocation in place. A title, *Sosimin*, that, in fact, carries many meanings, that asks for some kind of middle ground (where the small might meet the big), an amorphous term around which critical views might coalesce in their search for a proper history.

A remorseful past of survivorship extends to the mid-1960s (marked by protests against the normalization of diplomatic relations with Japan, the beginnings of Park Chung Hee's developmentalist push, ROK deployments to Vietnam). Punctuating this history of the present is a revenant, the return of the dead Chŏng in the form of his son. His view is clear. Anyone of his father's generation worth their salt were destroyed in the maelstrom: "Those who remain are the disgusting egoists who avoided and ignored things from the very beginning. Those now in their thirties learned a little lesson from watching the older generation perish— that they should not let this happen to themselves. . . . And so they became worldlings, avoiding everything that was of vital importance."[66] Chŏng's son looks forward: "A group or generation comprised of those who were once loyal subjects of the emperor has no business taking the lead."[67] The search is for a history of one's own making that will stem from a "sense of self-reliance" (*chuch'e ŭisik*) and eschew "copying someone else's method."[68] What followed division of the peninsula and war was a general state of despair in which "'freedom of the citizenry' became nothing more than a meaningless placard held up high by fascism."[69] In the end, "What enables such a force to emerge is precisely the passive, uneasy nihilism of the *sosimin*; fascism is the process of transforming this passive nihilism into an active one."[70] The work of the maelstrom continues. Chŏng's son sparks a transformation. Pak no longer reflects but confesses: "During the past fifteen years, I had become something of a bystander, just looking on as events took place around me. I had decided to live day-by-day on my wits alone, avoiding . . . everything that was of crucial importance. It was through Chŏng's son that my filthy cowardice became clear to me."[71] The revenant's call anticipates Paik Nak-chung's remark that the condensation of history found in the *sosimin* "is very much with us today." The call is to become something else; the call is for decolonization.

Like Jeju Island (see chapter 1), the dividing point appears in multiples. Mid-1960s returns to wartime—behind enemy lines in Kangwŏn Province; in the DMZ, south of the MDL; in a rear which stands at the front (Busan, transforming by the day into US transpacific edge)—stand in relation to what will have happened, the implementation of armistice. Reflections on the past as present and future, these fragments speak of life in the present as a form of debt, a look back, in different ways, upon those who did not survive as exhortation to what should happen.

EPILOGUE

Death Without End

The thanatographic is less genre than gesture, a habitation of death stories across media and disciplines. Stories of dying and death from the DPRK, US, ROK do not step neatly into ready-made worlds. This book does not aim to cross borders but to show how the thanatographic addresses border-makings (at times constructed by the act itself of crossing). The Korean War has no strict temporal border, if we consider that no formal declaration was made of its end. Indeed, the relative absence of commemoration of the Korean War in the United States stems in part from the difficulty of placing the Korean War in time, as event.

The Korean War names a duration, a modality, a method, an exemplarity. One of the names given in the 1950s to this constellation of qualities was limited war. Korea was the future, point of reference for a global applicability that has, in fact, found its way into contemporary forms of warfighting and conflict resolution (the war in Ukraine serves as a recent instance).

Thomas Schelling wrote in 1957 that "the problem of limiting warfare involves not a continuous range of possibilities from most favorable to least favorable for either side; it is a lumpy, discrete world that is better able to recognize qualitative than quantitative differences."[1] The description is of a "focal point" (later known as a Schelling point). As Schelling's famous phrase has it, what one party "expects to be expected to expect" will eventually converge "on a single point, at which each expects the other not to expect to be expected to retreat."[2] Schelling provides Korea as a prominent example, given that the "thirty-eighth parallel seems to have been a powerful focus for a stalemate."[3] For Schelling, a latitudinal line existing in the form of a quantitative relation to others (degrees north or south of the equator) became lumpy, qualitative. If a lump becomes a focal point, the latter assumes concrete form, becomes substantial, thinglike in a way that resembles Im Sundŭk's elaboration of icon-making as motion-become-stasis in the DPRK (see chapter 4). Im, too, addresses a temporal world that works to gauge and manage the future. As she demonstrates, this process of signification turns upon an agreement among men (something Schelling does not consider in his conceptualization of the focal point).

It is no accident that Schelling, who would become one of the most influential strategic thinkers in the post-1945 United States, found exemplarity in the 38th parallel early in his career. The 38th parallel has, in fact, become a synecdoche, synonymous with the division of Korea and with risk management itself (even though the armistice agreement drew a different line for the DMZ). We might say that this line is a lumpy, symbolic limit, a place where conventional war and nuclear war assume qualitative difference. Emerging from this difference, or bargain, is the post-1945 applicability of limited war as one mode among others of global governance. The legal implementation of this mode in Korea would be armistice.

In a 1956 article, Colonel Howard S. Levie (chief of JAG's new International Affairs Division at the time), underscores the rise of the armistice in the post–World War II world (only two in the interwar years but ten general armistice agreements over the previous decade, 1945–1956).[4] Levie concludes that "The elaborate armistice agreements of recent years have, in effect, rendered the preliminaries of peace obsolete. It is not inconceivable that the formal treaty of peace will suffer the same fate and that wars will one day end at the armistice table."[5] The armistice achieves cessation of hostilities even as "an armistice does *not* terminate the state of war existing between the belligerents, either *de jure* or *de facto*, and . . . the state of war continues to exist."[6] A cessation that does not end war can endure as an exemplary mode of governance in the details its provides, in its protocols, in its ability to outlast violations (as has been the case in Korea), in its bringing together of consenting parties to oppose each other.[7] Peace will result from the elaboration not from a formal treaty.

Four years earlier, Levie had been assigned to the United Nations Armistice Commission, the only lawyer on the negotiating team in Korea. Levie's task was to create a document that rendered negotiations among representatives of the Korean People's Army (KPA), the Chinese People's Volunteer Army (CPVA), and the United Nations Command (UNC) into legal language. He would draft an armistice, drawing on the June 12, 1935 Peace Protocol ending the combat phase of the Chaco War (the armistice agreement that established a line of separation between the Bolivian and Paraguayan armies) and other modern truce agreements (particularly those that referenced a DMZ).[8] Talks broke off in October 1952, but when they resumed in 1953, Levie's draft appears formative; indeed, "what both sides signed on 27 July 1953 essentially was what Levie had written."[9] While the extent of Levie's authorship may be overstated, what remains important is the claim. The Korean Armistice distills the recent history of truce arrangements while ushering in a new era. The armistice is thus a compilation that itself became a template.

Like Schelling (future Nobel laureate, who fused game theory to nuclear weapons policy and security studies more broadly), Levie would rise to the top of his field, his work on prisoners of war, Status of Forces Agreements (SOFA), and global terrorism helping to define the post-1945 subfield of the law of war. Taken together, Schelling and Levie were translators of discord and nonretreat, offering mediation through words themselves—through bargaining, through contracts. The movement of words into praxis (via consensus, legally binding documents) tells a story of conflict resolution. This is also the story of a kind of architecture, where mediation transforms words into a thing, into a durability. Here is where the limit is made real. And here is where risk management meets the post-1945 management of decolonization.

The July 1953 armistice was not proper to Korea but was from its beginning global in scope and intent, drawing on what was available and making it readily applicable to other sites and arrangements. The armistice organizes the exercises, deployments of three standing armies on the peninsula (DPRK, US, ROK) and extends to an array of international alliances and security guarantees. As a mode of governance, the armistice undergirds US force posture in the transpacific, providing the legal apparatus for its westernmost border (the United States maintains administrative control of the southern portion of the DMZ via the UNC).

The armistice arranges and maintains the formal division of Korea into two states. The point of nonretreat becomes a form of advance in other directions, in competing, mirroring mobilizations (both civilian and military). Address to the armistice can also take the form of nonreturn, evident in Pak Yŏngjun's wartime literary trajectory, which comes to a close in the final installment of *Chŏnsŏn munhak* (see chapter 9). Pak's repatriated POW protagonist ultimately rejects entrance into the postarmistice order forming in the ROK. He jumps. We are left to image his body in the sea, off the coast. Yi Hoch'ŏl will reflect on this history from the vantage point of the mid-1960s (see chapter 12). For Yi, wartime Busan is where the front meets the rear, where survival requires incorporation into the US transpacific. Busan promises a transactional, postarmistice future propelled by the flourishing of the petty bourgeoisie (emblematic of the ROK social, economic, and cultural order). If Pak Yŏngjun writes of nonreturn, Yi Hoch'ŏl calls for a new beginning, the mid-1960s serving as the point from which to reflect on the past and depart.

In its reach, in its making real, the armistice achieves form. Armies, weaponry, alliances, negotiations—all are mobilized upon the premise of deterrence, continuous prevention of what might happen. As a mode, an agreement to set arms aside, the armistice tells a story of the sovereignty of an interim based on potential death (most obvious in the militarizations brought to bear on the peninsula). The armistitial order, what we might call an armistitium, resides in the possibility that a highly disproportionate, incommensurable level of death and destruction will be meted out on the Korean people. Here, the potential is of something short of nuclear war (although that is possible): Another limited war, with massive Korean casualties. Erin Twyford points out that "Thanatopower takes on both the active 'make live' element of biopower and the active 'make die' component of sovereign power, offering a 'make live and make die' dual imperative."[10] The armistitium, though, does not proceed via the power to make two things happen at once. The formulation shifts via the introduction of possibility, a temporal order. The armistitium represents a meta-sovereignty in which the imperative to "make live" in the present rests on the premise of a virtuality, the possibility of mass death.

If the armistice is a legal rendering of limited-war thinking, the interim blends life in the present (a survivable present) with past and future, turning both to wartime images of death (what happened in Korea) and images of death in a potential future (what might happen in Korea). The armistice subjects those residing on the Korean peninsula to the spectral portent of repetition. From its inception, the limit line dividing the peninsula spoke to a particular form of hiatus, to the necessity of deterring the irruption of a wartime past in the future. To appeal to deterrence, to incline to the future in this way, is to demand that decolonization of the peninsula take place under armistitial mediation. And to reside under armistice is to live in some relation, north or south, to the multilayered horizons that present themselves by way of the limit line, sign of an end that is not an end.

As this book has shown, appeals to the hortatory, celebratory, condemning, sorrowful, loving, racist, sentimental, angry, masculinist, feminist (and more) occur within a distribution of approaches to the highly incommensurate loss of life, violence, destruction, and suffering that took place during the civil and international war in Korea. The thanatographic imagination, though, does not dwell only upon the past or the inert. Wartime and postarmistice thanatographies seek multiple forms of truth from the dead and in doing so write and image an entanglement of pasts, presents, and futures that unsettle the convenience, staying power, and aspirations of a catch-all designation (thinglike in its own way), the "cold war."

ACKNOWLEDGMENTS

Numerous conversations, more than I can possibly list here, contributed greatly to the making of this book. Over the years, many people have shared personal and family histories related to the Korean War with me, and I found those stories coming to mind throughout the writing process. I am particularly grateful to students in my English classes in Masan and Changwon many years ago, who taught me much more than I could teach them.

Two conferences in the summer of 2018 proved formative for this book. I would like to thank Sabine Hake for inviting me to participate in "The Proletarian Moment: Interdisciplinary Approaches, Comparative Perspectives" at ZiF, Bielefeld University's Institute for Advanced Study. The chance to meet scholars working all over the world was invaluable. Conversations during walks and over dinner with John Lear, Natalia Murray, and Magnus Nilsson led me in new directions. I also benefited immensely from the time I was able to spend at Yanbian University that summer and would like to express my gratitude to Baek Moonim, Hwang Hoduk, and Choe Il for helping me take a fresh look at my project.

A 2018–2019 Heyman Center Fellowship at Columbia University allowed for sustained interaction among colleagues working across a variety of disciplines; these discussions were key to the path this book eventually took. I thank Eileen Gillooly and Mark Mazower for their leadership of this program. I would also like to thank all of the Heyman Fellows, particularly Matt Jones, Katharina Volk, and Naor Ben-Yehoyada. Special thanks to Alma Igra for comments after my presentation at the Heyman Center; her advice sparked a change in the framing of the book. Alan Slatas generously opened his house in Massachusetts for a week-long gathering that just happened to take place right after the Heyman year. Conversations there with Stephen DiRado and Anne Geller, often within the quasi-performances that constitute Stephen's "Across the Table" photographic series, set the stage for the expansion of my ideas about the visual materials that now populate this book. The book began to move into its present form at that place and time.

I cannot hope to name everyone to whom I owe a profound debt. Among those who provided advice and support related to this project in different ways are Jinsoo An, Heekyoung Cho, Kyeong-Hee Choi, Steve Chung, Han Mansu, Kelly Jeong, Kim Jaeyong, Jina Kim, Suzy Kim, Lee Sang-kyung, So-Rim Lee, John Lie, Hwasuk Nam, Paik Won-dam, Kyunghee Pyun, Jooyeon Rhee, and We Jung Yi. Jungwon Kim, Seong Uk Kim, Sohl Lee, Sunyoung Park, and Theodore Jun Yoo also offered much-needed words of encouragement. Over the years, I have greatly benefited from seminar discussions with scholars who were once graduate students at universities in the tristate area, including Ksenia Chizhova, Monica Cho, Jae Won Chung, I Jonathan Kief, Se-Mi Oh, Jenny Wang Medina, Mi-Ryong Shim, Jeong Eun Annabel We, and Christina Yi. I often thought of the advice about academic life and work given by my senior colleagues, Nancy Abelmann at the University of Illinois Urbana-Champaign and Ja Hyun Kim Haboush at Columbia. Nancy and Ja have passed; the generosity and kindness of their words remained as I wrote this book, from start to finish.

As this book project began to enter its final stages, I had the good fortune to spend time as Shinhan Visiting Professor at Yonsei University. I thank Helen Lee for her support. This was a crucial moment for the book, and long conversations with Henry Em, Lisa Min, and Seunghei Clara Hong were the source of much inspiration. I thank Hwang Jongyon and Heonik Kwon for their kind words in support of the book as presented at a talk during the Shinhan Visiting Professorship. I am also grateful to Kwon Boduerae for encouraging words at a subsequent Korea University workshop. I thank Sarah Cole (Dean of Humanities at Columbia) for a grant under the War and Peace Initiative at Columbia that allowed for a late research trip to Seoul. Youngju Ryu offered much-needed advice when I was not sure how to move the project through to its close.

I am deeply grateful to Christine Dunbar, the editor at Columbia University Press, for her interest in this project, for her patience with my many delays, and for her guidance and advice from beginning to end. It was truly a pleasure to work with the Columbia University Press team of Leslie Kriesel, Chang Jae Lee, and Miriah Ralston. I thank Lis Pearson for copyediting and Magdalena Zapędowska for her work on the index. I could not have written this book without the support of Hee-sook Shin, Korean studies librarian at Columbia. I thank her for all of her help locating hard-to-find primary sources. Karen Green, curator for comics and cartoons at Columbia, also stepped in at a crucial moment to help me with original materials. I thank two anonymous readers of the manuscript for their comments and suggestions, all of which were tremendously helpful. Any errors in the book are my own.

Lt. John Hughes: Fair winds and following seas.

NOTES

INTRODUCTION

1. Such moments approach but do not coincide with the uniformity of what Achille Mbembe calls a "death world." Achille Mbembe, *Necropolitics* (Duke University Press, 2019), 92.
2. Eleanor Lattimore, "Pacific Ocean or American Lake?," *Far Eastern Survey* 14, no. 22 (November 1945): 313–16.
3. Eleanor Lattimore, "Pacific Ocean or American Lake?," 315.
4. Robert Jervis, "The Impact of the Korean War on the Cold War," *The Journal of Conflict Resolution* 24, no. 4 (December 1980): 581.
5. Robert Jervis, "The Impact of the Korean War," 584.
6. Robert Jervis, "The Impact of the Korean War," 588.
7. Robert E. Osgood, *Limited War Revisited* (Westview Press, 1979), 6.
8. Robert E. Osgood, *Limited War Revisited*, 3.
9. Robert E. Osgood, *Limited War Revisited*, 4.
10. Joseph Darda, *Empire of Defense: Race and the Cultural Politics of Permanent War* (University of Chicago Press, 2019), 31.
11. Joseph Darda, *Empire of Defense*, 32.
12. Heonik Kwon, *The Other Cold War* (Columbia University Press, 2010), 6–7.
13. Heonik Kwon, *The Other Cold War*, 6–7.
14. Paik Nak-chung, "South Korean Democracy and Korea's Division System," *Inter-Asia Cultural Studies* 14, no. 1 (2013): 162.
15. Paik Nak-chung, "South Korean Democracy," 160 (emphasis in original).
16. Paik Nak-chung, *The Division System in Crisis: Essays on Contemporary Korea* (University of California Press, 2011), 71.
17. Paik Nak-chung, *The Division System in Crisis*, 71.
18. For elaboration on the limits observed by combatants, see Morton H. Halperin, "The Limiting Process in the Korean War," in *Korea and the Theory of Limited War*, ed. Allen Guttmann (D.C. Heath and Co., 1967), 93.
19. "Korean War Armistice Agreement," https://catalog.archives.gov/id/5730903.
20. The notion of "hot spot" accompanies the framing of war as cold. See, for example, Army Heritage Center Foundation, "The Hot Spot in the Cold War: Korea 1950–1953," https://www.armyheritage.org/soldier-stories-information/the-hot-spot-in-the-cold-war-korea-1950-1953/.

21. For the history of trusteeship, see Mark Caprio, "The Politics of Trusteeship and the Perils of Korean Reunification," *Seoul Journal of Korean Studies* 32, no. 2 (2019): 263–91.
22. Su-kyoung Hwang, *Korea's Grievous War* (University of Pennsylvania Press, 2015), 51.
23. The most common term used for the Korean War in the ROK, 6/25 denoting the day and month of the war's outbreak in 1950.

1. JEJU ISLANDS

1. *Foreign Relations of the United States, 1951, Korea and China*, Vol. VII, Part 1, 795.00/1–1351: Telegram (Washington, January 13, 1951), https://history.state.gov/historicaldocuments/frus1951v07p1/d61.
2. *Foreign Relations of the United States, 1951, Korea and China*, Vol. VII, Part 1, 795.00/1–1351: Telegram (Washington, January 13, 1951), https://history.state.gov/historicaldocuments/frus1951v07p1/d61.
3. *Foreign Relations of the United States, 1951, Korea and China*, Vol. VII, Part 1, 795.00/1–1351: Telegram (Washington, January 13, 1951), https://history.state.gov/historicaldocuments/frus1951v07p1/d61.
4. *Foreign Relations of the United States, 1951, Korea and China*, Vol. VII, Part 1, 795.00/1–1251: Telegram (Washington, January 12, 1951), https://history.state.gov/historicaldocuments/frus1951v07p1/d52.
5. *Foreign Relations of the United States, 1951, Korea and China*, Vol. VII, Part 1, 795.00/1–1251: Telegram (Washington, January 12, 1951), https://history.state.gov/historicaldocuments/frus1951v07p1/d52.
6. *Foreign Relations of the United States, 1951, Korea and China*, Vol. VII, Part 1, 795.00/1–1251: Telegram (Washington, January 12, 1951), https://history.state.gov/historicaldocuments/frus1951v07p1/d55.
7. Truman indicates he found the CIA's report, "International Implications of Maintaining a Beachhead in Korea," helpful on this point. *Foreign Relations of the United States, 1951, Korea and China*, Vol. VII, Part 1, 795.00/1–1251: Telegram (Washington, January 12, 1951), https://history.state.gov/historicaldocuments/frus1951v07p1/d55.
8. James F. Schnabel and Robert J. Watson, *The Joint Chiefs of Staff and National Policy Volume III 1950–1951, The Korean War Part One* (Office of Joint History, Office of the Chairman of the Joint Chiefs of Staff, Washington, D.C., 1998), 195.
9. See John Merrill, "Reflections on the Jeju 4.3 Incident: Korea's 'Dark History' and Its Implications for Current Policy," in *The Jeju 4.3 Mass Killing: Atrocity, Justice, and Reconciliation*, ed. Jeju 4.3 Peace Foundation (Yonsei University Press, 2018).
10. Hal M. Friedman, *Creating an American Lake: United States Imperialism and Strategic Security in the Pacific Basin, 1945–1947* (Praeger, 2000), 1–4. See also Moon-ho Jung, *Menace to Empire: Anticolonial Solidarities and the Transpacific Origins of the US Security State* (University of California Press, 2022).
11. For an account of the early stages of the Jeju 4.3 Uprising, see Heonik Kwon, *After the Korean War: An Intimate History* (Cambridge University Press, 2020), 141–42.
12. For USAMGIK's role in the Jeju 4.3 Uprising, see Jeong-Sim Yang, "The Jeju 4.3 Uprising and the United States: Remembering Responsibility for the Massacre," *S/N Korean Humanities* 4, no. 2 (2018): 39–65. See also Bryan R. Gibby, *The Will to Win: American Military Advisors in Korea, 1946–1953* (University of Alabama Press, 2012).
13. Su-kyoung Hwang, *Korea's Grievous War* (University of Pennsylvania Press, 2016), 50.

1. JEJU ISLANDS   261

14. For elaboration on the beginning of the Korean War on Jeju Island, see Allan Millet's *The War for Korea, 1945–1950: A House Burning* (University of Kansas Press, 2015).
15. For an account of this meeting, see National Committee for Investigation of the Truth About the Jeju 4.3 Incident, ed., *The Jeju 4.3 Incident Investigation Report* (Jeju 4.3 Peace Foundation, 2014), 257–60.
16. *Rodong sinmun*, May 9, 1948, 4; *Minju Chosŏn*, May 9, 1948, 2.
17. *Rodong sinmun*, April 3, 1949, 4. For the designation of the 4.3 Uprising as the beginning of resistance in the south, see *Rodong sinmun*, April 3, 1950, 2; and *Rodong sinmun*, April 3, 1951, 2. Commemorative articles also appear in April 1952 and 1953.
18. *Munhak yesul*, May 1949, 4. First published in 1947, *Chosŏn munhak*, changed its name to *Munhak yesul* in 1948. The title reverted to *Chosŏn munhak* in October 1953 and has remained the same to the present.
19. *Munhak yesul*, May 1949, 4.
20. *Munhak yesul*, May 1949, 4.
21. Born in 1915, Ham was known for his lyricism and romantic leanings, as well as an affinity for island settings. An established and prominent playwright during the Japanese colonial period, he penned a number of plays aligned with Japanese imperial interests. Following the Japanese surrender in 1945, Ham moved to the left, departing for the DPRK in the late 1940s. Ham subsequently accompanied DPRK forces during the taking of Seoul on June 28, 1950 only to die in an accident the next day.
22. The 2016 *T'ongil munhak chakp'um sŏnjip* version gives 1948 as the date of publication for the entirety of Ham's play. The original publication of the play took place in four installments, one in December 1949, the remaining three in January, February, and March of 1950. For groundbreaking research on Ham's *Mountain People*, see Kim Tongyun, "Ham Sedŏk hŭigok *San saramdŭl* yŏn'gu: t'eksŭt'ŭ munje wa Jeju 4.3 chungsim ŭro" [Study of Ham Sedŏk's play *Mountain People*, with a focus on textual provenance and Jeju 4.3], *Han'guk munhak nonch'ong* 55 (August 2010): 93–125. According to Kim Tongyun, *Mountain People* was likely first performed in August 1948 at Haeju; the play was also almost certainly performed in Pyongyang in February 1949 and May 1950. See Kim Tongyun, "Ham Sedŏk hŭigok *San saramdŭl* yŏn'gu," 107. As a *wŏlbuk chakka*, or "writer gone to the north," all of Ham's work was censored in the ROK until the lifting of the ban on *wŏlbuk chakka* in 1988, year of the Seoul Olympics.
23. *Munhak yesul*, December 1949, 120.
24. *Munhak yesul*, December 1949, 121.
25. *Munhak yesul*, December 1949, 122.
26. *Munhak yesul*, December 1949, 124.
27. *Munhak yesul*, December 1949, 127.
28. *Munhak yesul*, December 1949, 145.
29. *Munhak yesul*, December 1949, 150.
30. *Munhak yesul*, December 1949, 152.
31. While Cho, Song, An, and Dean appear under their names in the 1950 version of *Mountain People*, Lt. Col. Kim's name is altered to Ch'oe Chinyŏl. Song and An, who would both later leave the ROK for the DPRK, are referred to only by their titles in the 2016 reprint of the play. Ch'oe Chinyŏl is likely a composite of Kim Ingnyŏl and the hardliner Pak Chin'gyŏng. Pak, who was not present at the meeting, was assassinated shortly after replacing Kim. For details, see Kim Tongyun, "Ham Sedŏk hŭigok *San saramdŭl* yŏn'gu."
32. *Munhak yesul*, February 1950, 120.
33. *Munhak yesul*, February 1950, 120.
34. *Munhak yesul*, February 1950, 131.
35. *Munhak yesul*, February 1950, 132.

36. *Munhak yesul*, February 1950, 133.
37. *Munhak yesul*, February 1950, 135.
38. *Munhak yesul*, February 1950, 138.
39. *Munhak yesul*, February 1950, 138.
40. *Munhak yesul*, February 1950, 138.
41. *Munhak yesul*, February 1950, 141.
42. *Munhak yesul*, February 1950, 141.
43. *Munhak yesul*, March 1950, 119.
44. *Munhak yesul*, March 1950, 120.
45. *Munhak yesul*, March 1950, 123.
46. *Munhak yesul*, March 1950, 144.
47. *Munhak yesul*, March 1950, 144.
48. *Munhak yesul*, March 1950, 145–46.
49. *Munhak yesul*, March 1950, 145–46.
50. *Munhak yesul*, March 1950, 147.
51. *Munhak yesul*, March 1950, 150.
52. *Munhak yesul*, March 1950, 152.
53. William F. Dean (as told to William L. Worden), *General Dean's Story* (Viking Press, 1954), 147. Worden was a contract reporter for *The Saturday Evening Post* during the Korean War.
54. William F. Dean, *General Dean's Story*, 147.
55. William F. Dean, *General Dean's Story*, 148.
56. William F. Dean, *General Dean's Story*, 148.
57. William F. Dean, *General Dean's Story*, 148–49.
58. For Dean's extensive involvement in the military operations taking place in Jeju, see *The Jeju 4.3 Incident Investigation Report*, 256–62.
59. William F. Dean, *General Dean's Story*, 149.
60. Monica Kim, *The Interrogation Rooms of the Korean War: The Untold History* (Princeton University Press, 2019), 217.
61. Monica Kim, *The Interrogation Rooms*, 217.
62. William F. Dean, *General Dean's Story*, 294.
63. Hye Seung Chung, "Hollywood Goes to Korea: Biopic Politics and Douglas Sirk's *Battle Hymn* (1957)," *Historical Journal of Film, Radio and Television* 25, no. 1 (2005): 56.
64. For the interrelations among collateral damage, fear/trauma, and US fighter-bomber pilots, see Su-kyoung Hwang, *Korea's Grievous War*, 136–38.
65. See Daniel Y. Kim, *The Intimacies of Conflict: Cultural Memory and the Korean War* (New York University Press, 2020), 134.
66. Gwisook Gwon argues that the Jeju 4.3 Uprising, in fact, opened a paradigm shift for the acceptance of Christianity by the local Jeju population. See Gwisook Gwon, "Reframing Christianity on Cheju During the Korean War," *Journal of Korean Religions* 6, no. 2 (October 2015): 93–120.
67. Daniel Y. Kim, *The Intimacies of Conflict*, 137.
68. Dean E. Hess, *Battle Hymn* (McGraw-Hill, 1956), 180.
69. Dean E. Hess, *Battle Hymn*, 236.
70. In a 1968 oral history, Partridge speaks of Nichols (without naming him): "I had an intelligence unit headed by an American major—a crazy man. He had about sixty or eighty Koreans. He was funded by the Far East Air Forces headquarters, and he was a one-man intelligence section, I'll tell you." Richard H. Kohn and Joseph P. Harahan, eds., *Air Interdiction in World War II, Korea, and Vietnam: An Interview with General Earle E. Partridge, General Jacob E. Smart, and General John W. Vogt Jr.* (USAF Warrior Studies, 1986), 50. In a diary entry, General George E. Stratemeyer, Far East Air Forces commander, writes of Nichols in a similar vein: "This fellow is a one-man army in Korea. He has been there some 4 1/2 years and on several occasions with a GI or two

1. JEJU ISLANDS   263

and a group of Koreans he has performed the impossible." William T. Y'Blood, ed., *The Three Wars of Lt. Gen. George E. Stratemeyer: His Korean War Diary* (Air Force History and Museums Program, 1999), 197.
71. Hye Seung Chung notes the fictitious dimensions of Partridge's introduction. Hess was called back to military service in 1948, not 1950; he did not return to the pulpit after World War II (he was studying history in a PhD program at Ohio State University when recalled to active duty); a town named West Hampton does not exist in Ohio. Hye Seung Chung, "Hollywood Goes to Korea," 55–56.
72. Dean E. Hess, *Battle Hymn*, 181.
73. Christine Hong, *A Violent Peace: Race, U.S. Militarism, and Cultures of Democratization in Cold War Asia and the Pacific* (Stanford University Press, 2020), 19.
74. The terms *haegol pudae* and *paekkol pudae* are used synonymously in Hŏ's work. The White Skull is a well-known ROK infantry unit. In the early 1950s it was made up of large numbers of Northwest Youth; the white skull insignia was considered symbolic of the willingness to fight to the death to recover the lost northern homeland.
75. *Munye*, February 1950, 12.
76. *Munye*, February 1950, 13.
77. *Munye*, February 1950, 13.
78. *Munye*, February 1950, 13. Camellias are closely associated with Jeju Island.
79. *Munye*, February 1950, 13.
80. Pak P'ilhyŏn points out that mention of the SKWP and the KPA advance pales in relation to the intensity of the blood-based and spiritual belonging to the island the clan leaders enact in the ritual. Pak P'ilhyŏn, "P'ongnyŏk ŭi kyŏnghŏm kwa kŭndaejŏk minjok kukka: ch'ogi 4.3 sosŏl ŭl chungsim ŭro [The experience of violence and the formation of a modern nation-state, with a focus on early 4.3 fiction], *Hyŏndae munhak iron yŏn'gu* 63 (2015): 233–34.
81. *Munye*, February 1950, 17.
82. *Munye*, February 1950, 18.
83. *Munye*, February 1950, 19.
84. *Munye*, February 1950, 19.
85. *Munye*, February 1950, 20–21, 25.
86. *Munye*, February 1950, 20.
87. *Munye*, February 1950, 21.
88. *Munye*, February 1950, 22.
89. *Munye*, February 1950, 23.
90. *Munye*, February 1950, 25.
91. I follow Pak P'ilhyŏn's analysis of the role of violence in mediating the formation on Jeju of the ROK as nation-state. See Pak P'ilhyŏn, "P'ongnyŏk ŭi kyŏnghŏm," 244–45.
92. *Munye*, February 1950, 28.
93. A mainlander, O Yŏng-su is well known for his lyrical descriptions of rural and seashore settings.
94. *Hyŏndae munhak*, June 1960, 125.
95. *Hyŏndae munhak*, June 1960, 126.
96. *Hyŏndae munhak*, June 1960, 128.
97. *Hyŏndae munhak*, June 1960, 128.
98. *Hyŏndae munhak*, June 1960, 129.
99. *Hyŏndae munhak*, June 1960, 129.
100. *Hyŏndae munhak*, June 1960, 129.
101. *Hyŏndae munhak*, June 1960, 130.
102. *Hyŏndae munhak*, June 1960, 130
103. *Hyŏndae munhak*, June 1960, 131.
104. *Hyŏndae munhak*, June 1960, 131.
105. See Heonik Kwon, *After the Korean War: An Intimate History* (Cambridge University Press, 2020).

106. *Hyŏndae munhak*, June 1960, 137.
107. See Dong-Choon Kim, *The Unending Korean War: A Social History* (Tamal Vista, 2009).

2. SEOUL REQUIEM

1. *Rodong sinmun*, August 1, 1953, 2.
2. Cheehyung Harrison Kim, "Pyongyang Modern: Architecture of Multiplicity in Postwar North Korea," *Journal of Korean Studies* 26, no. 2 (2021): 281.
3. Katerina Clark, *Moscow, the Fourth Rome: Stalinism, Cosmopolitanism, and the Evolution of Soviet Culture, 1931–1941* (Harvard University Press, 2011), 103.
4. Tatiana Gabroussenko, *Soldiers on the Cultural Front: Developments in the Early History of North Korean Literature and Literary Policy* (University of Hawai'i Press, 2010), 29.
5. *Munhak sinmun*, September 26, 1957, 2.
6. *Munhak sinmun*, September 26, 1957, 2.
7. *Munhak sinmun*, October 10, 1957, 1.
8. Yun Sep'yŏng, "P'yŏngyang kwa munhak" [Pyŏngyang and literature], *Munhak sinmun*, October 10, 1957, 2.
9. *Rodong sinmun*, June 29, 1950, 1.
10. *Minju Chosŏn*, July 5, 1950, 3.
11. *Minju Chosŏn*, September 29, 1950, 3.
12. *Minju Chosŏn*, September 30, 1950, 2.
13. *Minju Chosŏn*, October 6, 1950, 2. *Rodong sinmun* also carried an article on the last stand at Wŏlmi Island in its October 7, 1950 edition.
14. Sheila Miyoshi Jager, *Brothers at War: The Unending Conflict in Korea* (W. W. Norton, 2013), 185.
15. For an incisive discussion of late 1940s DPRK literary history, see Benoit Berthelier, "High Among the People: Social Distinction, Aesthetic Hierarchies, and Workers' Poetry in North Korea," *Azalea: Journal of Korean Literature & Culture* 13 (2020): 289–323.
16. O T'aeho, "Haebanggi (1945–1950) Pukhan munhak ŭi 'kosanghan riŏllijŭm' nonŭi ŭi chŏn'gae kwajŏng koch'al: *Munhwa chŏnsŏn, Chosŏn munhak, Munhak yesul*, tŭng ŭl chungsim ŭro" [A consideration of developments in North Korea's literary debates on "lofty realism" in the liberation period (1945–1950): focusing on *Munhwa chŏnsŏn, Chosŏn munhak, Munhak yesul*], *Uri munhak yŏn'gu* 46 (2013): 339. For a genealogy of the *kosanghan* that highlights Han's use of the term to legitimize a form of revolutionary romanticism, see p. 349.
17. Han Hyo, "Kosanghan riallijŭm ŭi ch'edŭk: munhak ch'angjo e taehan Kim Ilsŏng changgun ŭi kyohun" [Incorporating lofty realism: General Kim Il Sung's teachings on creative writing], *Chosŏn munhak*, September 1947, 280.
18. Han Hyo, "Kosanghan riallijŭm," 282.
19. Han Hyo, "Kosanghan riallijŭm," 284. Evgeny Dobrenko writes that at the First Congress of Soviet Writers, Andrei Zhadnov called for "a combination of the most stern and sober practical work with the loftiest heroism and grandiose perspectives." Dobrenko notes that such a move could be reworked for different position-takings: Boris Bialik's later "apparently innocent appeal to writers to 'lift up reality,' make it 'poetic' and 'lofty,' thus 'fusing realism and romanticism,' amounted in effect to a questioning and upsetting of the balance asserted by Zhdanov." Han Hyo's own move follows that of Bialik. See Evgeny Dobrenko, "Literary Criticism and the Institution of Literature in the Era of War and Late Stalinism, 1941–1953," in *A History of Russian Literary Theory and Criticism: The Soviet Age and Beyond*, ed. Evgeny Dobrenko and Galin Tihanov (University of Pittsburgh Press, 2011), 179.

20. Han Hyo, "Kosanghan riallijŭm," 286.
21. Han Hyo, "Chosŏn munhak e issŏsŏ sahoejuŭi reallijŭm ŭi palsaeng chogŏn kwa kŭ palsaeng chogŏn e issŏsŏ ŭi che t'ŭkching" [Characteristics of the emergence of socialist realism in Chosŏn literature], *Chosŏn munhak*, June 1952, 69.
22. Han Hyo, "Chosŏn munhak e issŏsŏ sahoejuŭi reallijŭm," 69.
23. Han Hyo, "Chosŏn munhak e issŏsŏ sahoejuŭi reallijŭm," 70.
24. Han Hyo, "Chosŏn munhak e issŏsŏ sahoejuŭi reallijŭm," 72–74.
25. *Munhak yesul*, August 1951, 4 (ellipses in original).
26. *Munhak yesul*, August 1951, 4.
27. *Munhak yesul*, August 1951, 5.
28. *Munhak yesul*, August 1951, 5.
29. *Munhak yesul*, August 1951, 4.
30. *Munhak yesul*, August 1951, 6.
31. *Munhak yesul*, August 1951, 7.
32. *Munhak yesul*, August 1951, 12.
33. See Han Hyo's four-part "Chayŏnjuŭi rŭl pandaehanŭn t'ujaeng e issŏsŏ ŭi Chosŏn munhak" [Chosŏn literature in the struggle against naturalism], *Munhak yesul*, January–April 1953.
34. *Munhak yesul*, August 1951, 21.
35. *Munhak yesul*, August 1951, 22.
36. *Munhak yesul*, August 1951, 23.
37. *Munhak yesul*, August 1951, 24.
38. Ŏm Hosŏk, "Choguk haebang chŏnjaeng kwa munhak ŭi angyang" [Literary exaltation and the fatherland liberation war], *Munhak yesul*, May 1952), 89.
39. Ŏm Hosŏk, "Choguk haebang," *Munhak yesul*, May 1952, 85.
40. Ŏm Hosŏk, "Choguk haebang," *Munhak yesul*, May 1952, 87.
41. *Munhak yesul*, September 1949, 71.
42. *Munhak yesul*, August 1951, 40.
43. *Munhak yesul*, August 1951, 41.
44. *Munhak yesul*, August 1951, 41.
45. Argyrios K. Pisiotis, "Images of Hate in the Art of War," in *Culture and Entertainment in Wartime Russia*, ed. Richard Stiles (University of Indiana Press, 1995), 143.
46. *Munhak yesul*, August 1951, 35.
47. *Munhak yesul*, August 1951, 35.
48. *Munhak yesul*, August 1951, 45.
49. *Munhak yesul*, September 1951, 27.
50. *Munhak yesul*, September 1951, 28.
51. *Munhak yesul*, September 1951, 28.
52. *Munhak yesul*, September 1951, 29.
53. *Munhak yesul*, September 1951, 30–31.
54. For the importance of music to revolution in North Korea, see Keith Howard, *Songs for "Great Leaders": Ideology and Creativity in North Korean Music and Dance* (Oxford University Press, 2020).
55. *Munhak yesul*, September 1951, 31.
56. *Munhak yesul*, September 1951, 31
57. *Munhak yesul*, September 1951, 46.
58. *Munhak yesul*, September 1951, 46.
59. *Munhak yesul*, October 1951, 34.
60. *Munhak yesul*, October 1951, 34.
61. *Munhak yesul*, October 1951, 38.
62. *Munhak yesul*, October 1951, 39.

63. *Munhak yesul*, October 1951, 43.
64. *Munhak yesul*, October 1951, 46 (ellipses in original).

3. HORIZONS OF HAPPINESS

1. The *Rodong sinmun* featured these columns with some frequency, particularly in 1953.
2. *Happiness* first appeared in the February 1953 issue of *Munhak yesul* as a single installment, a note on its final page indicating that Hwang's work was written in July 1952. For a detailed account of shifts in the DPRK literary criticism on *Happiness* and "Island Ablaze," see Nam Wŏnjin, "Aejŏng kwa yŏng'ung: Hwang Kŏn ŭi *Haengbok* ŭi ch'angjak kwa p'yŏngga ŭi puch'im e taehan yŏn'gu" [Affect and the heroic: a study of Hwang Kŏn's *Happiness* and its changing critical appraisal], *Han'guk kŭndae munhak yŏn'gu* 29 (April 2014), 311–16.
3. *Rodong sinmun*, January 21, 1952.
4. *Rodong sinmun*, January 21, 1952.
5. *Munhak yesul*, February 1953, 11.
6. *Munhak yesul*, February 1953, 15.
7. *Munhak yesul*, February 1953, 9.
8. *Munhak yesul*, February 1953, 16.
9. *Munhak yesul*, February 1953, 16.
10. *Munhak yesul*, February 1953, 16.
11. *Munhak yesul*, February 1953, 22.
12. *Munhak yesul*, February 1953, 22. For the transnational circulation of the notion of red love, see Ruth Barraclough, Heather Bowen-Struyk, and Paula Rabinowitz, eds., *Red Love Across the Pacific: Political and Sexual Revolutions of the Twentieth Century* (Palgrave Macmillan, 2015).
13. *Munhak yesul*, February 1953, 42.
14. *Munhak yesul*, February 1953, 43.
15. *Munhak yesul*, February 1953, 45.
16. *Munhak yesul*, February 1953, 45–46.
17. *Munhak yesul*, Februrary 1953, 46–47.
18. *Minju Chosŏn*, November 7, 1950, 2. Regular mention is made of the Soviet Union's Great Patriotic War as model and precedent for Korean War. See also *Minju Chosŏn*, May 8, 1951, 2.
19. Mun Sangmin, "3.1 undong kwa Chosŏn munhak" [The March 1st movement and Chosŏn literature], *Munhak sinmun*, February 28, 1957, 1.
20. *Munhak sinmun*, August 15, 1957, 2.
21. *Munhak sinmun*, August 15, 1957, 2.
22. *Munhak sinmun*, August 15, 1957, 2. For a rehearsal of this history, see the commemoration of the October Revolution in *Munhak sinmun*, November 7, 1957. For an overview of the North Korean navigation of Soviet literature and literary criticism in the late 1940s and early 1950s, see Tatiana Gabroussenko, *Soldiers on the Cultural Front: Developments in the Early History of North Korean Literature and Literary Policy* (University of Hawai'i Press, 2010), 14–46.
23. *Munhak sinmun*, August 15, 1957, 2.
24. "SSobet'ŭ munhak ŭn uri munhak ŭi mobŏmida" [Soviet literature is the model for our literature], *Munhak sinmun*, March 21, 1957, 1.
25. *Munhak sinmun*, March 21, 1957, 1.
26. *Munhak sinmun*, March 21, 1957, 1.
27. *Munhak sinmun*, March 21, 1957, 28.
28. For the immense popularity and subsequent critique of Fadeev's novel as lacking proper emphasis on the leadership of the party, see Juliane Furst, *Stalin's Last Generation: Soviet Post-War Youth*

and the Emergence of Mature Socialism (Oxford University Press, 2010), 149–59. For a discussion of Gerasimov's film as offering a vision of transcendental sacrifice rather than martyrdom in the name of Stalin's personality cult, see Maksim Kazyuchits, "Sergei Gerasimov's *The Young Guard*: Artistic Method and the Conflict of Discourses of History and Power," *Studies in Russian and Soviet Cinema* 13, no. 2 (2019): 169.

29. *Munhak yesul*, February 1953, 28.
30. *Munhak yesul*, February 1953, 28.
31. *Munhak yesul*, February 1953, 29.
32. As their titles imply, the journals *Cho-Sso munhwa* (Chosŏn-Soviet Culture) and *Cho-Sso Ch'insŏn* (Chosŏn-Soviet Friendship) aimed to create a shared socialist cultural sphere with the Soviet Union. Content would shift from the assumption of the Soviet Union as model to a more DPRK-centered emphasis in the late 1950s.
33. Yun Tuhŏn, "*Kyohyŏngsu ŭi sugi* rŭl ilkko" [On reading *Notes from the Gallows*], *Munhak yesul*, August 1949, 133.
34. Ko Ilhwan, "Ssobaet'ŭ munhak chakp'um esŏ padŭn yŏnghyang kwa uri munhak ŭi sŏnggwa" [Influences of Soviet literary works and our literary achievements], *Munhak yesul*, October 1949, 52.
35. Ko Ilhwan, "Ssobaet'ŭ munhak chakp'um," 52.
36. Han Hyo, "Chayŏnjuŭi rŭl pandaehanŭn t'ujaeng e issŏsŏ ŭi Chosŏn munhak" [Chosŏn literature in the struggle against naturalism], *Munhak yesul*, January–April 1953, in *Han Hyo p'yŏngnon sŏnjip* [Collected literary criticism of Han Hyo], ed. O T'ae-ho (Chimanji, 2015), 129.
37. Han Hyo, "Chayŏnjuŭi," 128.
38. *Munhak yesul*, February 1953, 52.
39. *Munhak yesul*, February 1953, 52.
40. *Munhak yesul*, February 1953, 53.
41. *Munhak yesul*, February 1953, 53.
42. *Munhak yesul*, February 1953, 53.
43. *Munhak yesul*, February 1953, 54.
44. *Munhak yesul*, February 1953, 57.
45. *Munhak yesul*, February 1953, 57.
46. *Munhak yesul*, February 1953, 57.
47. *Munhak yesul*, February 1953, 69 (all ellipses in original).
48. Nam Wŏnjin notes that the September 1953 version of *Happiness* (its first publication in book form) alters the ending to hint at Ryeju's survival, thus offering a "heightened sense of revolutionary optimism." Nam Wŏnjin, "Aejŏng kwa yŏng'ung," 305.
49. Andrei Lankov, *Crisis in North Korea: The Failure of De-Stalinization, 1956* (University of Hawai'i Press, 2005), 41.
50. *Chosŏn nyŏsŏng*, August 1960, 1.

4. MOTION IN STILLNESS

1. *Chosŏn nyŏsŏng*, August 1960, 3.
2. *Chosŏn nyŏsŏng*, August 1960, 3.
3. Han Hyo, "Chayŏnjuŭi rŭl pandaehanŭn t'ujaeng e issŏsŏ ŭi Chosŏn munhak" [Chosŏn literature in the struggle against naturalism], *Munhak yesul*, January–April 1953, in *Han Hyo p'yŏngnon sŏnjip* [Collected literary criticism of Han Hyo], ed. O T'ae-ho (Chimanji, 2015), 259.
4. Han Hyo, "Chayŏnjuŭi," 268–69.
5. Han Hyo, "Chayŏnjuŭi," 290–91.
6. Han Hyo, "Chayŏnjuŭi," 291.

7. Im Sundŭk, "Friendship," included in Yi Sanggyŏng, *Im Sundŭk, taeanjŏk yŏsŏng chuch'e rŭl hyanghayŏ* [Im Sundŭk, toward an alternative women's subjectivity] (Somyŏng ch'ulpansa, 2012), 304. Yi Sanggyŏng's book is the locus classicus for scholarship on Im Sundŭk.
8. Im Sundŭk, "Friendship," 300.
9. Im Sundŭk, "Friendship," 309.
10. Im Sundŭk, "Friendship," 310.
11. Im Sundŭk, "Friendship," 312.
12. Im Sundŭk, "Friendship," 312.
13. Im Sundŭk, "Friendship," 312–13.
14. Im Sundŭk, "Friendship," 332.
15. Im Sundŭk, "Friendship," 325.
16. Kil Chinsŏp, "Choguk haebang chŏnjaeng misul chŏllamhoe p'yŏng" [Evaluation of the fatherland liberation war art exhibition], *Munhak yesul*, September 1952, 119–20.
17. As Yun-Jong Lee points out, the 1954 film *Partisan Maiden* (Ppalchisan ch'ŏnyŏ) starring Mun Yebong was based on the life of Cho Okhŭi. See Yun-Jong Lee, "Mun Yebong, a Partisan Maiden in a 'Partisan State,'" *Korea Journal* 60, no. 3 (2020): 358.
18. Kil Chinsŏp, "Choguk haebang chŏnjaeng misul chŏllamhoe p'yŏng," 20.
19. For Kil Chinsŏp's later, more positive assessment of the same painting, see Hong Chisŏk, "Tu kae ŭi kŭndae: Mun Haksu (1916–1988) ŭi haebang chŏnhu" [Two modernities: Mun Haksu before and after liberation], *Inmul misul sahak* 8 (2012): 23.
20. For groundbreaking work on the transnational women's alliance in opposition to the Korean War, see Suzy Kim, *Among Women Across Worlds: North Korea in the Global Cold War* (Cornell University Press, 2023).
21. Ŏm Hosŏk, "Chosŏn munhak e nat'anan Kim Ilsung Changgun ŭi hyŏngsang" [The portrayal of General Kim in Chosŏn literature], *Munhak yesul*, May 1950, 20.
22. Ŏm Hosŏk, "Chosŏn munhak," 20.
23. Ŏm Hosŏk, "Chosŏn munhak," 27.
24. *Munhak yesul*, June 1951, 20.
25. *Munhak yesul*, June 1951, 20.
26. *Munhak yesul*, June 1951, 18.
27. *Munhak yesul*, June 1951, 18.
28. *Munhak yesul*, June 1951, 18.
29. *Munhak yesul*, June 1951, 19.
30. *Munhak yesul*, June 1951, 22.
31. *Munhak yesul*, June 1951, 22.
32. *Munhak yesul*, June 1951, 23.
33. *Munhak yesul*, June 1951, 24.
34. *Munhak yesul*, June 1951, 24. For the status of women in early North Korea and the 1946 Gender Equality Law, see Suzy Kim, *Everyday Life in the North Korean Revolution, 1945–1950* (Cornell University Press, 2013), 174–203.
35. *Munhak yesul*, June 1951, 26.
36. *Munhak yesul*, June 1951, 24.
37. *Munhak yesul*, June 1951, 26. "Civilized" (*munmyŏnghan*) and "travel in the mysterious orient" (*sinbiroun tongyang ŭi ryŏhaeng*) in quotes in the original.
38. *Munhak yesul*, June 1951, 27.
39. *Munhak yesul*, June 1951, 30.
40. *Munhak yesul*, June 1951, 31.
41. *Munhak yesul*, June 1951, 32.
42. *Munhak yesul*, June 1951, 32.
43. *Munhak yesul*, June 1951, 33.

44. *Munhak yesul*, June 1951, 35.
45. *Munhak yesul*, June 1951, 35.
46. *Munhak yesul*, June 1951, 35.
47. Ŏm Hosŏk, "Rodong kyegŭp ŭi hyŏngsang kwa mihaksang ŭi myŏt kaji munje" [Portrayal of the working class and several problems of aesthetics], *Munhak yesul*, January 1953, in *Munhak yesul ŭi hyŏngmyŏngjŏk chŏnhwan: PukHan ŭi pip'yŏng*, ed. Kim Chonghwoe (Kukhak charyowŏn, 2012), 114.
48. Cited in Evgeny Dobrenko, "Literary Criticism and the Institution of Literature in the Era of War and Late Stalinism," in *A History of Russian Literary Theory and Criticism: The Soviet Age and Beyond*, ed. Evgeny Dobrenko and Galin Tihanov (University of Pittsburgh Press, 2011), 179.
49. Ŏm Hosŏk, "Rodong kyegŭp," 113.
50. See Andrei Lankov, *Crisis in North Korea: The Failure of De-Stalinization, 1956* (University of Hawai'i Press, 2005); and Cheehyung Harrison Kim, *Heroes and Toilers: Work as Life in Postwar North Korea, 1953–1961* (Columbia University Press, 2018), 83–92.
51. *Chosŏn munhak*, June 1957, 41.
52. *Chosŏn munhak*, June 1957, 34. Yi Sanggyŏng points out that "Bereaved" turns upon a story "within the surface story," namely Chŏngdŏk's sympathy for her younger counterpart as indication of her own wish to leave. See Yi Sanggyŏng, *Im Sundŭk*, 216–18.
53. *Chosŏn munhak*, June 1957, 32.
54. *Chosŏn munhak*, June 1957, 36.
55. *Chosŏn munhak*, June 1957, 36.
56. *Chosŏn munhak*, June 1957, 37.
57. *Chosŏn munhak*, June 1957, 37.
58. *Chosŏn munhak*, June 1957, 42.
59. *Chosŏn munhak*, June 1957, 42.
60. *Chosŏn munhak*, June 1957, 42.
61. *Munhak sinmun*, September 19, 1957, 3.
62. *Munhak sinmun*, September 19, 1957, 3.
63. *Munhak sinmun*, September 19, 1957, 3.
64. *Munhak sinmun*, December 5, 1957, 2.
65. Jein Do and Mincheol Park argue against the assumption that gendered hierarchies in the 1950s DPRK derive from a broad-based patriarchy, emphasizing instead how "the political crisis of legitimacy in the mid-1950s situated tradition at the core of the regime's ideological education and cultural management of revolutionary *Joseon nyeoseong* [North Korean women]." Jein Do and Mincheol Park, "Dressing Socialism: *Joseonot* and Revolutionary Womanhood in North Korea, 1955–1960," *Korea Journal* 61, no. 2 (Summer 2021): 247.

5. OCEAN'S EDGE

1. Joseph Heller, *Catch-22* (Simon & Schuster, 2011 [1961]), 46.
2. *Playboy*, June 1975, 61. Heller makes the point in another interview: "Virtually none of the attitudes in the book... coincided with my experiences as a bombardier in World War II. The antiwar and antigovernment feelings in the book belong to the period following World War II: the Korean War, the cold war of the Fifties." See Lynda Rosen Obst, ed., *The Sixties: The Decade Remembered Now by the People who Lived it Then* (Rolling Stone Press, 1977), 50.
3. *Playboy*, June 1975, 68 (emphasis in original).
4. Eugene Rabinowitch, "The Narrowing Way," *Bulletin of the Atomic Scientists* 9, no. 8 (October 1953): 294.
5. Eugene Rabinowitch, "The Narrowing Way," 295.

6. Eugene Rabinowitch, "The Narrowing Way," 295.
7. Eugene Rabinowitch, "The Narrowing Way," 295.
8. Eugene Rabinowitch, "The Narrowing Way," 295.
9. Bosthley Crowther, " 'One Minute to Zero,' a Korean War Picture with Robert Mitchum, at Criterion," *New York Times*, September 20, 1952.
10. Hye Seung Chung, *Hollywood Diplomacy: Film Regulation, Foreign Relations, and East Asian Representations* (Rutgers University Press), 96. Chung questions the power of DoD in Hollywood, noting DoD's failure "to persuade the profit-driven commercial industry to implement desired changes" (ibid., 128).
11. Richard Hallion, "The Air War in Korea: Coalition Air Power in the Context of Limited War," in *In from the Cold: Reflections on Australia's Korean War*, ed. John Blaxland et al. (ANU Press, 2020), 140.
12. Richard Hallion, "The Air War in Korea," 140.
13. UNC moved to Seoul in 1957, leaving behind a small and frequently overlooked entity called United Nations Command-Rear. UNC-R (currently a four-person unit) provides the legal framework for the US stationing and movement of military forces in Japan. Taken together, UNC and UNC-R, play a major role in the legal codification of US military power in the transpacific. US four-star generals continue to wear the "triple hat," serving concurrent terms as United Nations, Combined Forces Command (CFC), and United States Forces Korea (USFK) commanders in Korea. Seven US bases in Japan are UNC-designated.
14. The duet is followed by Steve's whistling "When I Fall in Love," a song later made famous by Doris Day and Nat King Cole.
15. Daniel Kim, *The Intimacies of Conflict: Cultural Memory and the Korean War* (New York University Press, 2020), 132.
16. Howard Hughes would refuse the DoD request to edit the scene out of the picture, leading DoD to deny approval of the film even after providing extensive support (no acknowledgment of DoD assistance appears in the film credits). See Steve Fore, "Howard Hughes' 'Authoritarian Fictions': RKO, *One Minute to Zero*, and the Cold War," *The Velvet Light Trap* (Spring 1993): 23–24.
17. Steve Fore maintains that the sequence derives from Osborne's *TIME* article, which lets the "incident stand without explicit resolution as an evocative moral quandary." Steve Fore, "Howard Hughes," 20. For a nuanced analysis of Osborne's *LIFE* article, see Daniel Kim, *The Intimacies of Conflict*, 119–27.
18. Reinhold Niebuhr, "The Children of Light and the Children of Darkness: A Vindication of Democracy and a Critique of its Traditional Defence," in *Reinhold Niebuhr: Major Works on Religion and Politics*, ed. Elisabeth Sifton (Library of America, 2015), 368.
19. Reinhold Niebuhr, "The Children of Light," 368.
20. William Haines Wister, *One Minute to Zero (1952): Shooting Script* (Alexander Street Press, 2007), 100.
21. *The Hollywood Reporter*, September 4, 1953, 3.
22. Daniel Immerwahr, *How to Hide an Empire: A History of the Greater United States* (Farrar, Straus and Giroux, 2019), 360–62.

6. JET SUBLIME

1. The German Messerschmitt ME 262 was the only jet fighter to engage in combat in World War II, action limited to the war's closing months. For a comprehensive history of jets in combat, see Bill Gunston with Peter Gilchrist, *Jet Bombers: From the Messerschmitt Me 262 to the Stealth B-2* (Osprey Aerospace, 1993).

2. Although, as Steffen Hantke points out, *Top Gun* fetishizes airplanes to a degree difficult to find in jet films of the 1950s. See Steffen Hantke, "We Own the Sky: Jet Airplanes and Cold-War Propaganda in American Cinema after the Korean War," *Journal of Popular Film and Television* 45, no. 4 (2017): 208.
3. For an overview of Salter's work, see Jeffrey Meyers, "James Salter's Strange Career," *Salmagundi* no. 220–221 (Fall 2023/Winter 2024): 117–31. James Salter is the pen name used by James Arnold Horowitz. For the influential role of the Iowa Writer's Workshop in "the chastening of American literature after 1945" as containment to the self, see Eric Bennet, *Workshops of Empire: Stegner, Engle, and American Creative Writing During the Cold War* (University of Iowa Press, 2015), 164.
4. Although the majority of Glenn's combat missions in Korea were actually in a close air support (CAS) role, he shot down three MIG-15s in the weeks prior to the July 27, 1953 armistice.
5. Heonik Kwon, *The Other Cold War* (Columbia University Press, 2010), 6 (emphasis in original).
6. Heonik Kwon, *The Other Cold War*, 9.
7. James Salter, *The Hunters* (Harper, 1956), 20.
8. James Salter, *The Hunters*, 21.
9. James Salter, *The Hunters*, 34.
10. James Salter, *The Hunters*, 191.
11. James Salter, "Preface to the 1997 Edition," in *The Hunters* (Counterpoint, 1997), xv.
12. James Salter, *The Hunters*, 150.
13. James Salter, *The Hunters*, 202.
14. James Salter, *The Hunters*, 133.
15. James Salter, *The Hunters*, 133.
16. James Salter, *The Hunters*, 134.
17. James Salter, *The Hunters*, 239.
18. James Salter, *The Hunters*, 243.
19. Arthur M. Schlesinger Jr., *The Vital Center: The Politics of Freedom* (Houghton and Mifflin, 1962 [1948]), 218.
20. *LIFE*, July 6, 1953, 66.
21. *LIFE*, July 6, 1953, 70.
22. *LIFE*, July 6, 1953, 59.
23. *LIFE*, July 6, 1953, 72.
24. *LIFE*, July 6, 1953, 86.
25. *LIFE*, July 6, 1953, 59.
26. *LIFE*, July 6, 1953, 69.
27. *LIFE*, July 6, 1953, 79.
28. *LIFE*, July 6, 1953, 79.
29. *LIFE*, July 6, 1953, 69.
30. *LIFE*, July 6, 1953, 74.
31. *LIFE*, July 6, 1953, 75.
32. *LIFE*, July 6, 1953, 83.
33. *LIFE*, July 6, 1953, 83.
34. *LIFE*, July 6, 1953, 86.
35. Stephen Prince, *Classical Film Violence: Designing and Regulating Brutality in Hollywood Cinema, 1930–1968* (Rutgers University Press, 2003), 247.
36. Stephen Prince, *Classical Film Violence*, 247.
37. *LIFE*, July 6, 1953), 87.
38. *LIFE*, July 6, 1953, 69.
39. *LIFE*, July 6, 1953, 69.

7. DEATH IN *LIFE*

1. Erika Doss, "*Life*'s Impact: Circulation, Copycats and Reader Response," in *Life Magazine and the Power of Photography*, ed. Katherine A. Bussard and Kristen Gresh (Princeton Art Museum, 2020), 117. See also James L. Baughman, "Who Read *Life*? The Circulation of America's Favorite Magazine," in *Looking at Life Magazine*, ed. Erika Doss (Smithsonian Institution Press, 2001), 41–51.
2. Qiana Whitted, *EC Comics: Race, Shock, and Social Protest* (Rutgers University Press, 2019), 9.
3. Amy Kiste Nyberg, *Seal of Approval: The History of the Comics Code* (University Press of Mississippi, 1998), 59.
4. For the innovative and meticulous artistic process Kurtzman brought to *Two-Fisted Tales* and *Frontline Combat*, see Denis Kitchen and Paul Buhle, *The Art of Harvey Kurtzman: The Mad Genius of Comics* (Abrams ComicArts, 2009), 66–67.
5. Michael Dean, ed., *The Comics Journal Library Volume 10: The EC Artists Part 2* (Fantagraphics Books, 2016), 47.
6. M. Thomas Inge, "Harvey Kurtzman and Modern American Satire," in *Seeing Mad: Essays on Mad Magazine's Humor and Legacy*, ed. John Bird and Judith Yaross Lee (University of Missouri Press, 2020), 74.
7. *LIFE*, January 8, 1951, 18.
8. *LIFE*, January 8, 1951, 14 (capitals in original).
9. C. P. FitzGerald, "The Chinese Revolution and the West," *Pacific Affairs* 24, no. 1 (March 1951): 7.
10. C. P. FitzGerald, "The Chinese Revolution," 10.
11. C. P. FitzGerald, "The Chinese Revolution," 8.
12. C. P. FitzGerald, "The Chinese Revolution," 8.
13. W. Macmahon Ball, "The Communist Problem in East Asia-A Western View," *Pacific Affairs* 24, no. 3 (September 1951): 248.
14. W. Macmahon Ball, "The Communist Problem," 255.
15. *Two-Fisted Tales* #26, March–April 1952 (bold in original).
16. *LIFE*, December 25, 1950, 9–13.
17. *LIFE*, December 25, 1950, 20.
18. "The Trap!," *Two-Fisted Tales* #26, March–April, 1952. Art by John Severin.
19. Harvey Kurtzman had offered a sustained, horror-inspired reflection on mourning the adversary's dead body the previous month in "Corpse on the Imjin!," *Two-Fisted Tales* #25, January–February, 1952.
20. Qiana Whitted, *EC Comics*, 16–17.
21. "Link-Up!," *Two-Fisted Tales* #26, March–April 1952. Art by John Severin.
22. Christine Hong, *A Violent Peace: Race, U.S. Militarism, and Cultures of Democratization in Cold War Asia and the Pacific* (Stanford University Press, 2020), 12.
23. "Hungnam!," *Two-Fisted Tales* #26, March–April 1952. Art by Wally Wood.
24. "Hungnam!," *Two-Fisted Tales* #26, March–April 1952. Art by Wally Wood.
25. "Hungnam!," *Two-Fisted Tales* #26, March–April 1952. Art by Wally Wood.
26. "Hungnam!," *Two-Fisted Tales* #26, March–April 1952. Art by Wally Wood.
27. James J. Kimble, "Spectral Soldiers: Domestic Propaganda, Visual Culture, and Images of Death on the World War II Home Front," *Rhetoric and Public Affairs* 19, no. 4 (2016): 547.
28. James J. Kimble, "Spectral Soldiers," 547.
29. James J. Kimble, "Spectral Soldiers," 556.
30. *LIFE*, July 17, 1950, 27.
31. *LIFE*, July 24, 1950, 21.
32. Cited in Harvey Kurtzman et al., *Atom Bomb and Other Stories* (Fantagraphics Books, 2020), vii.

33. Harvey Kurtzman et al., *Atom Bomb and Other Stories*, vii.
34. The July–August 1951 issue of *Two-Fisted Tales* would be the last to include "He-Man Adventure" on its cover, its place taken for the duration by "War and Fighting Men."
35. *Two-Fisted Tales* #20, March–April 1951.
36. Harvey Kurtzman, *Corpse on the Imjin! And Other Stories* (Fantagraphics Books, 2012), 211. Also cited in Bill Schelly, *Harvey Kurtzman: The Man Who Created Mad and Revolutionized Humor in America* (Fantagraphics Books, 2015), 198.
37. Bill Schelly, *Harvey Kurtzman*, 197.
38. Junghyun Hwang, "Seen Through the Camera Obscura: *Life* Photographs of the Korean War and Cold War Anxiety of the American Self," *Cultural Critique*, no. 121 (2023): 149.
39. *LIFE*, October 9, 1950, 32.
40. "Big 'If!,'" *Frontline Combat* #5, March 1952.
41. "Big 'If!,'" *Frontline Combat* #5, March 1952.
42. In an interview, Kurtzman indicates that much of the material for his Korean War comics came from military personnel themselves. Pressed by his interlocutor (who notes that Kurtzman has been vague on this point previously), he responds that "I usually contacted them through the various services. The Army would send me to veterans who were still there, in the Army." Harvey Kurtzman, *Corpse on the Imjin!*, 211.
43. "B-26 Invader!," *Frontline Combat* #12, May–June 1953. Art by Jack Davis.
44. "B-26 Invader!," *Frontline Combat* #12, May–June 1953. Art by Jack Davis (bold and ellipses in original).
45. "B-26 Invader!," *Frontline Combat* #12, May–June 1953. Art by Jack Davis (ellipses in original).
46. "B-26 Invader!," *Frontline Combat* #12, May–June 1953. Art by Jack Davis (ellipses in original.
47. "B-26 Invader!," *Frontline Combat* #12, May–June 1953. Art by Jack Davis.
48. "B-26 Invader!," *Frontline Combat* #12, May–June 1953. Art by Jack Davis.
49. *MAD* #11, May 1954.
50. *LIFE*, May 11, 1953, 142.
51. Hillary L. Chute. *Disaster Drawn: Visual Witness, Comics, and Documentary Form* (Belknap Press, 2016), 96.
52. Dan Byrne-Smith, "Harvey Kurtzman and the Influence of Mad Magazine," in *The Cambridge History of the Graphic Novel*, ed. Jan Baetens et al. (Cambridge University Press, 2018), 93.

8. THE BREAKING POINT

1. "NSC 68: United States Objectives and Programs for National Security" (S/S–NSC Files: Lot 63D351: NSC 68 Series), 8. https://history.state.gov/historicaldocuments/frus1950v01/d85.
2. "NSC 68: United States Objectives and Programs for National Security" (S/S–NSC Files: Lot 63D351: NSC 68 Series), 8. https://history.state.gov/historicaldocuments/frus1950v01/d85.
3. "NSC 68: United States Objectives and Programs for National Security" (S/S–NSC Files: Lot 63D351: NSC 68 Series), 8. https://history.state.gov/historicaldocuments/frus1950v01/d85.
4. George Kennan, "Communism and Conformity," *Bulletin of the Atomic Scientists* 9, no. 8 (October 1953): 297.
5. George Kennan, "Communism," 304.
6. George Kennan, "Communism," 304.
7. Marsha Gordon, *Film is Like a Battleground: Sam Fuller's War Movies* (Oxford University Press, 2017), 66.

8. For a detailed account of the contemporary controversy surrounding *The Steel Helmet*, see Marsha Gordon, *Film is like a Battleground*, 80–94.
9. Daniel Kim, *The Intimacies of Conflict: Cultural Memory and the Korean War* (New York University Press, 2020), 33.
10. Short Round's correction is likely the result of MPAA head Joseph Breen's letter to producer Robert Lippert asking for a number of changes to the shooting script, one of them being that "the expression 'gook' both here [p. 5] and throughout the script be eliminated." Breen to Lippert, October 16, 1950, Margaret Herrick Library, Hollywood, Censorship, and the Motion Picture Production Code, 1927–1968 Collection, https://www.gale.com/primary-sources.
11. *Men in War* (1957; dir., Anthony Mann) would also offer an extended treatment of war trauma in Korea via its portrayal of a colonel completely incapacitated and unable to speak.
12. Albert J. Glass, "Current Problems in Military Psychiatry," *Journal of the American Medical Association* 150, no. 1(1952): 6.
13. Albert J. Glass, "Current Problems," 6.
14. Albert J. Glass, "Current Problems," 6.
15. Albert J. Glass, "Current Problems," 7.
16. Albert J. Glass, "Current Problems," 315.
17. Albert J. Glass, "Current Problems," 318.
18. Raymond Sobel "The 'Old Sergeant' Syndrome." *Psychiatry* 10, no. 3 (1947): 321.
19. Harry Brown, "A Walk in the Sun," *Liberty*, September 16, 1944, 41.
20. Cited in Nicholas J. Cull, "Samuel Fuller on Lewis Milestone's *A Walk in the Sun* (1946): *The Legacy of All Quiet on the Western Front* (1930)," *Historical Journal of Film, Radio and Television* 20 no. 1, (2000): 84. Cull includes Fuller's letter in its entirety.
21. Nicholas J. Cull, "Samuel Fuller," 83.
22. Lisa Dombrowski notes that Fuller's war diary contains the sketch for a war film set in Germany that would serve as the basis for *The Steel Helmet*. See Lisa Dombrowski, *The Films of Samuel Fuller: If You Die, I'll Kill You* (Wesleyan University Press, 2008), 41–42. For the relation between Fuller's combat experience and his war films, see Samuel Fuller, *A Third Face: My Tale of Writing, Fighting, and Filmmaking* (Alfred A. Knopf, 2003).
23. For more on Hunter, brainwashing discourse, and classified research related to hypnosis, drugs, and mind control (Project Bluebird, Project Artichoke, MK-Ultra), see Birkbeck, University of London's online "Hidden Persuaders Project," http://www7.bbk.ac.uk/hiddenpersuaders/.
24. Edward Hunter, *Brainwashing: The Story of Men Who Defied It* (Farrar, Straus and Cudahy, 1956), 200, 236.
25. Edward Hunter, *Brainwashing*, 253.
26. Edward Hunter, *Brainwashing*, 22, 24, 259.
27. Edward Hunter, *Brainwashing*, 253.
28. Edward Hunter, *Brainwashing*, 248.
29. Edward Hunter, *Brainwashing*, 91.
30. Edward Hunter, *Brainwashing*, 114.
31. Edward Hunter, *Brainwashing*, 115.
32. Edward Hunter, *Brainwashing*, 309.
33. "Defense Advisory Committee Report," included in *The U.S. Fighting Man's Code*, (Office of Armed Forces Information and Education) (November 1955), 1.
34. "Defense Advisory Committee Report," 13.
35. "Defense Advisory Committee Report," 15.
36. "Defense Advisory Committee Report," 15–16.
37. "Defense Advisory Committee Report," 31.

9. HABITATIONS

38. For US Steel and the contemporary cultural scene, see Cynthia B. Meyers, "Advertising, the Red Scare, and the Blacklist: BBDO, US Steel, and 'Theatre Guild on the Air,' 1945–1952," *Cinema Journal* 55, no. 4 (Fall 2016): 55–83.
39. Robert Lindner, *Must You Conform?* (Rinehart, 1956), 174. This volume is comprised of material Lindner previously published or presented in lectures in 1953–1954; Joost Meerloo, *The Rape of the Mind: The Psychology of Thought Control—Menticide and Brainwashing* (World Publishing, 1956), 19.
40. Eric Bennett, *Workshops of Empire: Stegner, Engle, and American Creative Writing During the Cold War* (University of Iowa Press, 2015), 34–35.
41. Joost Meerloo, *The Rape of the Mind*, 19.
42. Joost Meerloo, *The Rape of the Mind*, 27, 35.
43. Reinhold Niebuhr, *The Irony of American History*, in *Major Works on Religion and Politics*, ed. Reinhold Niebuhr (Library of America, 2015 [1952]), 589.
44. Reinhold Niebuhr, *The Children of Light and the Children of Darkness*, in *Major Works on Religion and Politics*, ed. Reinhold Niebuhr (Library of America, 2015 [1944]), 378.
45. Reinhold Niebuhr, *The Irony of American History*, 586.
46. Reinhold Niebuhr, *The Irony of American History*, 586.
47. Hans J. Morgenthau, *Politics Among Nations: The Struggle for Power and Peace* (Knopf, 1948 [Third Edition, 1960]), 4.
48. Arthur M. Schlesinger Jr., *The Vital Center: The Politics of Freedom* (Houghton Mifflin, 1962 [1948]), 250.
49. Hans J. Morgenthau, *Politics Among Nations*, 3.
50. Rod Serling exhibited a profound suspicion of the utilitarian call for sacrifice in the name of the greater good in his first, and often forgotten, treatment of the Korean War, "The Strike" (aired on CBS on June 7, 1954).
51. Rod Serling, *Patterns: Four Television Plays with the Author's Personal Commentaries* (Simon & Schuster, 1957), 141.
52. Robert Lindner, *Must You Conform?*, 84–92, 157.
53. Robert Lindner, *Must You Conform?*, 176.
54. Robert Lindner, *Must You Conform?*, 141.
55. Robert Lindner, *Must You Conform?*, 175–76.
56. Robert Lindner, *Must You Conform?*, 205.
57. Robert Lindner, *Must You Conform?*, 210 (emphasis in original).
58. For classified experiments on human behavior under extreme pressure (including isolation) in the 1950s, see David Price, *Cold War Anthropology: The CIA, the Pentagon, and the Growth of Dual Use Anthropology* (Duke University Press, 2015).
59. Erik Mortenson, "A Journey into the Shadows: *The Twilight Zone*'s Visual Critique of the Cold War," *Science Fiction Film and Television* 7, no. 1 (2014): 59–60.

9. HABITATIONS

1. Kang Yongjun, "Ch'ŏljomang" [Barbed wire], *Sasanggye*, July 1960, 299–300. Kang Yongjun (1931–?) was born in Hwanghae Province, in what is now the DPRK. In 1950, while attending school in Pyongyang, Kang was conscripted into the KPA and captured by UN forces shortly after. He spent three years as a POW in various UN prison camps, including Kŏje Island. Designated an "anticommunist prisoner" (*pan'gong p'oro*), Kang was allowed to escape along with 27,000 others by order of Syngman Rhee to his commanders on June 18, 1953, a date that would be commemorated in the

ROK for years to come. Kang was commissioned as a second lieutenant in the ROKA in 1954 and was serving in the Army Corps of Engineers when he wrote "Barbed Wire."
2. Kang Yongjun, "Barbed Wire," 307.
3. Kang Yongjun, "Barbed Wire," 307.
4. Kang Yongjun, "Barbed Wire," 286.
5. See Chŏn Chini, "1950nyŏndae ch'oban chonghapchi *Hŭimang* ŭi pan'gong ch'ŏngnyŏn p'yosang yŏn'gu" [A study of representations of anticommunist youth in the journal *Hope* in the early 1950s], *Ŏmun nonch'ong* 68 (2016): 369–400.
6. As a label, *pan'gong* has been applied to any number of entities. Among these was the Anticommunist Literary Prize (*pan'gong munhaksang*), first awarded on June 25, 1976, the twenty-sixth anniversary of the outbreak of the Korean War. The highest level of the prize, the Presidential Award, was, in fact, given to Kang Yongjun in recognition of his anticommunist literary achievements.
7. For the US POW camp as the "explicit site of the workings of US liberal power," see Monica Kim, *The Interrogation Rooms of the Korean War: The Untold History* (Princeton University Press, 2019), 8–9. For the relation between "voluntary repatriation" and the articulation of cold war positionality in ROK fictional accounts and memoirs of the POW camps, see Chang Sejin, "Ŭnyu rosŏ ŭi p'oro: suyongso ŭi salm kwa 'chŏk/tongji' ŭi kubyŏl chŏngch'i" [POW as metaphor: life in POW camps and the politics of distinguishing between 'enemies and allies'], *Sanghŏ hakpo* 46 (2016): 9–61.
8. Pak Yŏngjun would win the inaugural Freedom Literature Prize in 1953 for a short story collection that included "Dark Night" and "Partisan." Sponsored by the Asia Foundation, the Freedom Literature Prize played a significant role in the early organization of the ROK literary field (the program was discontinued after 1959). For the Freedom Literature Prize, see Yi Pongbŏm, "Naengjŏn kwa wŏnjo, wŏnjo sidae naengjŏn munhwa kuch'uk ŭi yŏktongsŏng: 1950~60nyŏndae Miguk min'gan chaedan ŭi wŏnjo wa Han'guk munhwa" [Cold war and aid: the dynamism of cold war cultural construction in the aid era, with a focus on Korean culture and aid provided by US private foundations in the 1950s and 1960s], *Han'gukhak yŏn'gu* 39 (2015): 252–61. For a sustained analysis of the Asia Foundation as a CIA front working to shape academic discourse in both Asia and the United States, see David H. Price, *Cold War Deceptions: The Asia Foundation and the CIA* (University of Washington Press, 2024).
9. The term "Korean War" (*Han'guk chŏnjaeng*) has been used with increased frequency over the years.
10. For an analysis of how a "specific historical sense" of kinship "became the primary target of politics in the Korean War, and how it continued to be a vital site of the state's disciplinary actions throughout the long Cold War," see Heonik Kwon, *After the Korean War: An Intimate History* (Cambridge University Press, 2020), 10.
11. Yi Muyŏng, "Chŏnjaeng kwa munhak" [War and literature], *Chŏnsŏn munhak*, May 1953, 4.
12. *Chŏnsŏn munhak*, May 1953, 5.
13. Pak Kijun, "Han'guk chakka ŭi pansŏng" [Self-reflections of Korean writers], *Chŏnsŏn munhak*, April 1952, 14.
14. Pak Kijun, "Han'guk chakka ŭi pansŏng," 15.
15. Pak Yŏngjun (1911–1976) was born in Pyongyang, the son of a pastor and independence fighter. He debuted on the colonial literary scene in the mid-1930s and gained a reputation as a writer of fiction addressing impoverished conditions in the countryside (he would spend five months behind bars in 1935). Post-1945, Pak would hold various professorships and administrative posts both within the university and in the literary world.
16. *Chŏnsŏn munhak*, April 1952, 24. This is *Chŏnsŏn munhak*'s inaugural issue.
17. I Jonathan Kief underscores the ways in which the wartime mobilization of writers aimed not only to combat communism but also had a "second target," those who remained in Seoul under DPRK occupation or were suspected of going north, even if temporarily. Pak Yŏngjun falls in the latter

category. See I Jonathan Kief, "Anthropological Fictions: 'Humanism' and Its Doubles in 1930s–1960s Korea," (PhD diss., Columbia University, 2016), 67.
18. *Chŏnsŏn munhak*, April 1952, 26.
19. *Chŏnsŏn munhak*, April 1952, 26–27.
20. *Chŏnsŏn munhak*, April 1952, 27.
21. Heonik Kwon, *After the Korean War*, 125.
22. *Chŏnsŏn munhak*, April 1952, 27.
23. *Chŏnsŏn munhak*, April 1952, 29.
24. Kim Oksŏn underscores the importance of this figure of the "ideal soldier" (strong, responsible, benevolent, a soldier who knows how to show affection for subordinates) in "Dark Night," as well as in the pages of *Chŏnsŏn munhak* more generally. See Kim Oksŏn, "Chŏnsŏn muhak e nat'anan kamjŏng chŏngch'i" [The politics of emotion in *Frontline Literature*], *Inmunhak nonch'ong*, February 2011, 114; See also Seungsook Moon, *Militarized Modernity and Gendered Citizenship in South Korea* (Duke University Press, 2005).
25. *Sinch'ŏnji* 7, May 1952.
26. *Sinch'ŏnji* 7, May 1952, 131.
27. *Sinch'ŏnji* 7, May 1952, 132.
28. *Sinch'ŏnji* 7, May 1952, 135.
29. *Sinch'ŏnji* 7, May 1952, 135.
30. *Sinch'ŏnji* 7, May 1952, 136.
31. *Sinch'ŏnji* 7, May 1952, 138–39.
32. *Sinch'ŏnji* 7, May 1952, 140.
33. *Chŏnsŏn munhak*, December 1952, 17.
34. For an analysis of this "third way," see I Jonathan Kief, "Anthropological Fictions," 61–108.
35. "Chŏnjaeng munhak ŭi panghyang" [Directions for war literature], *Chŏnsŏn munhak*, February 1953, 61.
36. "Chŏnjaeng munhak ŭi panghyang," 62.
37. "Chŏngsin ŭi pin'gon" [The poverty of spirit], *Chŏnsŏn munhak*, April 1953, 4–5.
38. "Chŏngsin ŭi pin'gon," 5.
39. "Munhwa chŏnsŏn ŭn hyŏngsŏng twoeŏttnŭnga" [Has a cultural front taken form?], *Chŏnsŏn munhak*, December 1952, 5.
40. "Munhwa chŏnsŏn ŭn hyŏngsŏng twoeŏttnŭnga," 5.
41. "Munhwa chŏnsŏn ŭn hyŏngsŏng twoeŏttnŭnga," 7.
42. *Chŏnsŏn munhak*, December 1953, 60.
43. *Chŏnsŏn munhak*, December 1953, 62.
44. *Chŏnsŏn munhak*, December 1953, 62.
45. *Chŏnsŏn munhak*, December 1953, 63.
46. *Chŏnsŏn munhak*, December 1953, 65.
47. For a repatriated ROK soldier's reminiscence of life, death, and interrogations on Yongch'o Island, see Pak Chinhong, *Toraon p'aeja: 6/25 kukkun p'oro ch'ehŏmgi* [Return of the defeated: the true story of an ROK POW] (Yŏksa pip'yŏngsa, 2009), 202–21.
48. *Chŏnsŏn munhak*, December 1953, 73.
49. *Chŏnsŏn munhak*, December 1953, 74.
50. *Chŏnsŏn munhak*, December 1953, 74.
51. *Chŏnsŏn munhak*, December 1953, 71.
52. *Chŏnsŏn munhak*, December 1953, 72.
53. Kwŏn Podŭrae contrasts both An Tongmin's *Hell Island* (1957) and Kang Yongjun's "Barbed Wire" (1960) with Ch'oe Inhun's *The Square*. If the former texts (lesser known) depict the Kŏje Island camp as site of kidnapping, torture, murder, a place where "humans have become animals,"

the latter is as a "war novel without war, a POW novel without a POW." See Kwŏn Podŭrae, *"Kwangjang* ŭi chŏnjaeng kwa p'oro: Han'guk chŏnjaeng ŭi p'oro sŏsa wa 'chungnip' ŭi chwap'yo" [War and the POW in *The Square*: narratives of the Korean war POW and the question of "neutrality"], *Han'guk hyŏndae munhak yŏn'gu* 53 (2017): 155, 159. For an incisive comparison of Ch'oe's *The Square* and the prominent writer Pak Wansŏ's sustained address of wartime and post-armistice history, see We Jung Yi, *Worm-Time: Memories of Division in South Korean Aesthetics* (Cornell University Press, 2024), 17–72.

54. *Chŏnsŏn munhak*, December 1953, 75.
55. *Chŏnsŏn munhak*, December 1953, 77.
56. *Chŏnsŏn munhak*, December 1953, 77.

10. CROSSINGS

1. See Nan Kim, *Memory, Reconciliation, and Reunions in South Korea: Crossing the Divide* (Lexington Books, 2015), 2.
2. Nam Haeyŏng, "Na ŭi wŏllam ilgi" [My recollection of crossing south], *Saegajŏng*, June 1957, 23.
3. Nam Haeyŏng, "Na ŭi wŏllam ilgi," 23.
4. Henry Em, "Christianity, the Cold War, and the Construction of the Republic of Korea," *Korea Journal* 60, no. 4 (2020): 10–11 (emphasis in original).
5. Recipient of the Tongin Literary Prize for his short story "Flowers of Fire" (pulkkot, 1957), Sŏnu Hwi (1922–1986) is widely considered one of the representative authors of the post–Korean War generation. Hailing from P'yŏng'an Province in what is now the DPRK, Sŏnu served as an ROKA officer in the Korean War and was discharged at the rank of colonel in 1959. Like Pak Yŏngjun and Kang Yongjun, Sŏnu Hwi was born in what is now the DPRK. He would occupy influential positions in the ROK literary and cultural scenes throughout his life, working at the *Chosŏn Daily* for twenty-five years and eventually rising to the position of editor in chief.
6. Sŏnu Hwi, *Kwihwan* [*Return*] (Ch'ŏnggu ch'ulp'ansa, 1954), 1.
7. Sŏnu Hwi, *Kwihwan*, 7.
8. Sŏnu Hwi, *Kwihwan*, 7.
9. Chŏn Kapsaeng, "Suyongso e kat'in kwihwan yongsa: 'chiokto' Yongch'odo ŭi kwihwan'gun chipkyŏlso wa sasang simnijŏn" [Repatriated warriors in a prison camp: ideology and psychological warfare at hell island, the Yongch'o Island returnee collection point], *Yŏksa pip'yŏng* 2 (Spring 2017): 382.
10. Sŏnu Hwi, *Kwihwan*, 184.
11. Sŏnu Hwi, *Kwihwan*, 185.
12. Sŏnu Hwi, *Kwihwan*, 186.
13. Sŏnu Hwi, *Kwihwan*, 187.
14. Sŏnu Hwi, *Kwihwan*, 190.
15. Sŏnu Hwi, *Kwihwan*, 195.
16. Sŏnu Hwi, *Kwihwan*, 196.
17. Sŏnu Hwi, *Kwihwan*, 197.
18. Sŏnu Hwi, *Kwihwan*, 198.
19. Sŏnu Hwi, *Kwihwan*, 199.
20. Sŏnu Hwi, *Kwihwan*, 200.
21. Sŏnu Hwi, *Kwihwan*, 200–201.
22. For psychoanalytic critiques of authoritarian rule, see Matt Ffytche and Daniel Pick, eds., *Psychoanalysis in the Age of Totalitarianism* (Routledge, 2016).

23. *Wŏllam chŏnhu* was serialized in *Munhak yesul* in six installments from July 1956 through December 1956.
24. *Munhak yesul*, December 1956, 108.
25. Born in Kilchu, North Hamgyŏng Province, Im Ogin (1915–1995) established herself on the colonial period literary scene with the publication of her short stories "Balsam Flower" (Pongsŏnhwa, 1939) and "Record of a Second Wife" (Huch'ŏgi, 1940). She came south in the aftermath of the 1945 liberation from Japanese colonial rule and became a prominent figure on the ROK literary scene in the late 1940s and 1950s. Im obtained a series of professorships at major universities and served in a number of administrative positions during her long career, including president of the Christian Writers Association, president of the Women Writers Association, and president of the Seoul YWCA.
26. Cho Tong-jae et al., *A Partner for Change: Six Decades of the Asia Foundation in Korea* (The Asia Foundation, 2017), 40.
27. Chang Sejin, "Wŏnhan, nosŭt'aeljiŏ, kwahak—wŏllam chisigindŭl kwa 1960nyŏndae PukHan hakchi ŭi sŏngnip sajŏng" [Ressentiment, nostalgia, science: intellectuals who crossed south and conditions surrounding the establishment of North Korean studies in the 1960s], *SAI* 17 (2014): 143. For the formation of North Korean studies within the framework of Sovietology in the United States, see Ryu Kihyŏn, "Han'guk chŏnjaenggi Mi kungmubu chŏngbo chosaguk ŭi PukHan hyŏnji chosa wa Pukhan yŏn'gu ŭi t'aedong: PukHan-Soryŏn wisŏng kukka sarye yŏn'gu rŭl chungsim ŭro" [Wartime investigations of the United States department of state research mission to Korea and the birth of North Korean studies: focusing on *North Korea: A Case Study of a Soviet Satellite*], *Yŏksa munje yŏn'gu* 24, no. 2 (2020): 335–72.
28. *Munhak yesul*, August 1956, 83.
29. *Munhak yesul*, September 1956, 75.
30. *Munhak yesul*, September 1956, 76.
31. *Munhak yesul*, July 1956, 32.
32. For groundbreaking work that highlights the importance of Japan as a post-1945 site for "cross-border circulation" among DPRK, ROK, and diasporic writers, see I Jonathan Kief's "Closed Borders and Open Letters in the Cold War Koreas," in *The Routledge Companion to Korean Literature*, ed. Heekyoung Cho (Routledge, 2022), 427–40.
33. *Munhak yesul*, October 1956, 96–97.
34. *Munhak yesul*, October 1956, 86.
35. Janet Poole, *When the Future Disappears: The Modernist Imagination in Late Colonial Korea* (Columbia University Press, 2014), 86.
36. Cho Yŏnhyŏn, "Han'guk chŏnjaeng kwa Han'guk munhak" [The Korean war and Korean literature], *Chŏnsŏn munhak* 5 (May 1953): 18.
37. Cho Yŏnhyŏn, "Hanguk chŏnjaeng," 18.
38. Cho Yŏnhyŏn, "Hanguk chŏnjaeng," 19.
39. Cho Yŏnhyŏn, "Hanguk chŏnjaeng," 20.
40. *Munhak yesul*, October 1956, 86.
41. For an early account of Yi T'aejun's departure for the north, see Hyŏn Su (pseudonym for Pak Namsu), *Chŏkch'i yungnyŏn ŭi PukHan mundan* [The North Korean literary scene: six years under the reds] (1952), reprinted in *Han'guk chŏnjaenggi charyojip* [Korean wartime sourcebook] XIV (K'ep'oi puksŭ, 2013). Hyŏn underscores the extent to which Yi's choice was a complete surprise. Unlike others, "Yi T'aejun was in his bones (*saengnijŏgŭro*) utterly disinclined toward Marxist beliefs," 481; original pagination, 153. For Yi T'aejun's purge, see Sonia Ryang, *Language and Truth in North Korea* (University of Hawai'i Press, 2021), 30–37.
42. *Munhak yesul*, October 1956, 97.
43. *Munhak yesul*, October 1956, 97.

44. *Munhak yesul*, October 1956, 99.
45. For the discourse surrounding Hŏ Chŏngsuk's feminist and socialist trajectory under Japanese colonialism and in the DPRK, see Ruth Barraclough, "Red Love and Betrayal in the Making of North Korea: Comrade Hŏ Jŏng-suk," *History Workshop Journal* 77 (Spring 2014): 86–102.
46. *Munhak yesul*, September 1956, 84.
47. *Munhak yesul*, September 1956, 94.
48. *Munhak yesul*, October 1956, 81.
49. *Munhak yesul*, October 1956, 79.
50. *Munhak yesul*, October 1956, 89.
51. *Munhak yesul*, October 1956, 89.
52. *Munhak yesul*, December 1956, 94.
53. *Munhak yesul*, December 1956, 94.
54. *Munhak yesul*, December 1956, 94–5.
55. *Munhak yesul*, December 1956, 95.
56. Jae Won Edward Chung offers a nuanced analysis of the "aesthetics of vitalism" and *kaesŏng* in his "Vitalism and Existentialism in Early South Korean Literature," in *The Routledge Companion to Korean Literature*, ed. Heekyoung Cho (Routledge, 2022), 320–22.
57. *Munhak yesul*, October 1956, 79.
58. *Munhak yesul*, December 1956, 107 (ellipsis in original).
59. Hyaeweol Choi, *New Women in Colonial Korea: A Sourcebook* (Routledge, 2012), 11.

11. YET TO DIE, YET TO LIVE

1. For a detailed analysis of the reorganization of the film industry in the early 1960s, see Ham Ch'ungbŏm, "1960nyŏndae chŏnban'gi Pak Chŏnghŭi chŏnggwŏn ŭi yŏnghwa chŏngch'aek e taehan yŏnghwagye ŭi pan'ŭng mit hwaldong yangsang yŏn'gu: yŏnghwabŏp ŭl tullŏssan 'yŏnghyŏp' kwa 'chehyŏp' ŭi ipchang kwa t'aedo rŭl chungsim ŭro" [A study of the response of the film world to the Pak Chŏnghŭi regime's film policy of the early 1960s: focusing on the stance and attitude taken by the motion picture association and the film producers association to the film laws], *Hyŏndae yŏnghwa yŏn'gu* 21, no. 1 (July 2015): 149–88.
2. See Hye Seung Chung, *Cinema Under National Reconstruction: State Censorship and South Korea's Cold War Film Culture* (Rutgers University Press, 2025).
3. Hieyoon Kim, *Celluloid Democracy: Cinema and Politics in Cold War South Korea* (University of California Press, 2023), 58.
4. For the ap'ŭre kŏl's fall into a promiscuity at once unavoidable and devoid of sexual pleasure (a trajectory signaling the "popularization of existentialist freedom"), see Kwŏn Podŭrae, "Silchon, *Chayu puin*, p'ŭraegŭmŏt'ijŭm: 1950syŏndae ŭi tu kaji 'chayu' kaenyŏm kwa munhwa" [Existentialism, *Madame Freedom*, pragmatisim: 1950s cultural practices and the two notions of "freedom"], *Han'guk munhak yŏn'gu* 35 (2008): 121–22.
5. For patricide in *Hero Without a Service Number*, see Pak Yuhŭi, "Salbu ŭi yulli wa p'ipchinsŏng ŭi kiyul: Kunbŏn ŏmnŭn yongsa (1966) rŭl t'onghae pon Yi Manhŭi ŭi yŏnghwa segye" [The ethics of patricide and the disciplining of verisimilitude: Yi Manhŭi's filmic world as seen through *Hero Without a Service Number* (1966)], *Yŏngsang munhwa* 19 (December 2015): 9–25.
6. For Yi Manhŭi's approach to censorship, with emphasis on his banned film *A Day Off*, see Hieyoon Kim, *Celluloid Democracy*, 52–70.
7. The censor's report was summarized in *Kyŏnghyang sinmun*, February 5, 1965. For this and other original censorship documents related to *Seven Women*, see the Korean Film Archive's digital collection: https://www.kmdb.or.kr/history/leaflet.

8. *Kyŏnghyang sinmun*, February 5, 1965.
9. For Michelangelo Antonioni's postwar modernism, see Matilde Nardelli, *Antonioni and the Aesthetics of Impurity: Remaking the Image in the 1960s* (Edinburgh University Press, 2020). See also Slawomir Maslon, *Secret Violences: The Political Cinema of Michelangelo Antonioni, 1960–1975* (Bloomsbury, 2023).
10. Hong Chinhyŏk, "*Kwiro* ŭi modŏnijŭm sŭt'ail, simni ŭi kongganhwa" [Modernist style in *Homeward*: the spatialization of psychology], *Hyŏndae yŏnghwa yŏn'gu* 27 (2017): 336.
11. See Eunjung Kim, *Curative Violence: Rehabilitating Disability, Gender, and Sexuality in Modern Korea* (Duke University Press, 2017).
12. For a sustained analysis of melodramatic desire and modernist form in this sequence and the earlier combat flashback sequence, see Chŏng Yŏnggwŏn, "1960nyŏndae Han'guk chŏnjaeng mellodŭrama ŭi yongmang kwa chwajŏl: *I saengmyŏng tahadorok* kwa *Kwiro* rŭl chungsim ŭro [Desire and frustration in the war melodrama of 1960s Korea: focusing on *To the Last Day* and *Homeward*] *Yŏnghwa yŏn'gu* 33 (September 2007): 119–26.
13. Active as a writer in three wars, Ch'oe Chŏnghŭi lectured and wrote on behalf of the Japanese mobilization effort during the Asia Pacific War, served as an embedded writer (*chonggun chakka*) with the ROK Air Force in the Korean War, and was the leader of the ROK cultural support group sent to Vietnam in 1967. As was the case with many others who remained in Seoul during its occupation by DPRK forces in the late summer of 1950, Ch'oe Chŏnghŭi (1906–1990) was compelled to write a testimonial outlining her activities under DPRK occupation and stating her unequivocal support for the ROK government and anticommunist cause (the departure of her husband, the poet Kim Tonghwan, for the north likely added precarity to her position). Ch'oe would assume a position of considerable power in the 1950s and 1960s literary scene. She published numerous works in the 1950s while serving in high-profile positions such as editor in chief for a major women's magazine (*Chubu saenghwal*); she was also a regular on literary award committees. She would go on to become the president of the Korean Women Writers Association in 1969 and was made a member of the Republic of Korea National Academy of Arts in 1970. Much of the scholarship on Ch'oe Chŏnghŭi's work turns to her controversial personal history. Yi Pyŏngsun, for example, divides her post-1945 work into two strands. The first occurs in an autobiographical mode that seeks exculpation from her past as "collaborator-leftist-traitor: she is a victim, a 'weak woman' forced to make choices in circumstances beyond her control." The second takes place after she becomes a wartime embedded writer: She now "increasingly moves away . . . from portrayals of a suffering object to an increasingly fervent anticommunism that calls for active participation in the war as subject." See Yi Pyŏngsun, Ch'oe Chŏnghŭi sosŏl e nat'anan chŏnjaeng ŭi ŭimi [The meaning of war in Ch'oe Chŏnghŭi's novels], *Han'guk sasang kwa munhwa* 50 (2009): 57.
14. Kang Soyŏn, "1950nyŏndae yŏsŏng chapchi e p'yosangtoen Miguk munhwa wa yŏsŏng tamnon" [The discourse on women and representations of US culture in 1950s women's magazines] *Sanghŏ hakpo* 18 (2006): 107–36.
15. *Chosŏn ilbo*, September 8, 1955, 4.
16. Steven Chung, "Regimes Within Regimes: Film and Fashion Cultures in the Korean 1950s," in *The Korean Popular Culture Reader*, ed. Kyung Hyun Kim and Youngmin Choe (Duke University Press, 2013), 105.
17. *Chosŏn ilbo*, September 8, 1955, 4.
18. *Chosŏn ilbo*, September 8, 1955, 4. Edith Head would win the Academy Award for Costume Design for her work on *A Place in the Sun*, as well as for *Samson and Delilah*, one of the films advertised in the *Chosŏn ilbo* during the serialization of "Maelstrom."
19. *Chosŏn ilbo*, September 9, 1955, 4.
20. *Chosŏn ilbo*, September 9, 1955, 4
21. For colonial period debates on "new women," appearance, and westernization, see Theodore Jun Yoo, *The Politics of Gender in Colonial Korea: Education, Labor, and Health, 1910–1945*

(University of California Press, 2008), 74–81. For the modern girl/new woman distinction, see Hyaeweol Choi, *New Women in Colonial Korea: A Sourcebook* (Routledge, 2013), 10–12.
22. *Chosŏn ilbo*, August 30, 1955, 4.
23. *Chosŏn ilbo*, August 31, 1955, 4.
24. *Chosŏn Ilbo*, August 31, 1955, 4.
25. *Chosŏn ilbo*, September 7, 1955, 4.
26. *Chosŏn ilbo*, September 13, 1955, 4.
27. *Chosŏn ilbo*, September 6, 1955, 4. I draw here on my location of Yunsu's Mother's precarity and Ch'oe's "Maelstrom" in a more expansive post-1945 history of enemy property in the ROK. See Theodore Hughes, "Under Occupation, After Armistice: Stories of Enemy and Traitorous Property," in *Korea Journal* 65 (2025): 68–93.
28. *Chosŏn ilbo*, September 13, 1955, 4.
29. *Chosŏn ilbo*, September 13, 1955, 4.

12. DIVISION AS METHOD

1. For Kim Il Sung's prewar vision of peaceful reunification and rescue of the impoverished southern people from Syngman Rhee's oppression and US imperialism, see his "Choguk ŭi p'yŏnghwajŏk t'ongil pangch'aek e taehan sŏnŏnsŏ wa kwallyŏnhayŏ" [On the declaration concerning the plan for peaceful reunification of the fatherland] (August 2, 1949), in Kim Il Sung, *Choguk t'ongil e kwanhan widaehan suryŏng Kim Ilsŏng tongji ŭi munhŏn* [Documents on the reunification of the fatherland by the great leader comrade Kim Il Sung], (Samhaksa, 1981), 53–56.
2. Kim Il Sung, "Modŭn kŏsŭl chŏnhu inmin kyŏngje pokku paljŏnŭl wihayŏ" [All things for the sake of the recovery and development of the postwar people's economy] (August 5, 1953), in Kim Il Sung, *Choguk t'ongil*, 62. Subtitled "Chŏngjŏn wa choguk ŭi t'ongil munje e kwanhayŏ" [On armistice and the issue of reunification of the fatherland], this document was a report Kim Il Sung gave to the central committee of the Chosŏn Worker's Party on August 5, 1953. Kim Il Sung was a signatory to the armistice in his capacity of supreme commander of the Korean People's Army.
3. Kim Il Sung, "Modŭn kŏt ŭl," 62.
4. Kim Il Sung, "Modŭn kŏt ŭl," 62–63.
5. Kim Il Sung, "Chosŏn nodongdang che3 ch'a taehoe esŏ han chung'ang wiwŏnhoe saŏp ch'onghwa pogo" [General report of the central committee at the third meeting of the Chosŏn worker's party] (April 23, 1956), in Kim Il Sung, *Choguk t'ongil*, 66. The term *pukpŏl* clearly refers to Rhee's advocacy of *pukchin t'ongil* but has a longer history, stretching back to the Chosŏn dynasty.
6. For the history and implications of Rhee's "Unification by Northward Advance" policy, see Joong-Seok Seo, *Korean Nationalism Betrayed* (Brill, 2007), 129–91.
7. Syngman Rhee to Dwight D. Eisenhower, April 9, 1953, in *I sŭngman (1): T'ŭruman, Aijenhawŏ taet'ongnyŏng ŭi sŏsin* [Syngman Rhee: epistolary exchanges with presidents Truman and Eisenhower], ed. Yang Sŭngham et al. (Yŏnse taehakkyo kukka kwalli yŏn'guwŏn, 2010), 142.
8. Syngman Rhee to Dwight D. Eisenhower, May 30, 1953, in Yang Sŭngham et al., *I sŭngman (1)*, 148.
9. Dwight D. Eisenhower to Syngman Rhee, June 6, 1953, in Yang Sŭngham et al., *I sŭngman (1)*, 150.
10. Christine Hong, *A Violent Peace: Race, U.S. Militarism, and Cultures of Democratization in Cold War Asia and the Pacific* (Stanford University Press, 2020), 17.
11. Dwight D. Eisenhower to Syngman Rhee, June 6, 1953, in Yang Sŭngham et al., *I sŭngman (1)*, 151.
12. Syngman Rhee to Dwight D. Eisenhower, June 17, 1953, in Yang Sŭngham et al., *I sŭngman (1)*, 156.
13. Robert E. Osgood, "The Uses of Military Power in the Cold War," in *America Armed: Essays on United States Military Policy*, ed. Robert A. Goldwin (Rand McNally, 1963).

14. No author given, "Let's Create a Greater, More High-Spirited Epic and Poetic Canvas of the Fatherland Liberation War!" (Choguk haebang chŏnjaeng e taehan taesŏsasijŏk hwap'oktŭl tŏ hullyunghage tŏ wangsŏnghage ch'angjakhaja!) *Chosŏn munhak*, June 1965, 6.
15. "Let's Create a Greater, More High-Spirited Epic," 4.
16. "Let's Create a Greater, More High-Spirited Epic," 5.
17. "Let's Create a Greater, More High-Spirited Epic," 5 (emphasis in original).
18. Ri Yunyŏng, "Chŏkhu ŭi saebyŏk" [Dawn behind enemy lines], *Chosŏn munhak*, June 1965, 7.
19. *Chosŏn munhak*, June 1965, 9.
20. *Chosŏn munhak*, June 1965, 9.
21. *Chosŏn munhak*, June 1965, 9.
22. *Chosŏn munhak*, June 1965, 11.
23. *Chosŏn munhak*, June 1965, 11.
24. *Chosŏn munhak*, June 1965, 12.
25. *Chosŏn munhak*, June 1965, 12.
26. *Chosŏn munhak*, June 1965, 12.
27. *Chosŏn munhak*, June 1965, 13.
28. *Chosŏn munhak*, June 1965, 13.
29. *Chosŏn munhak*, June 1965, 13–14.
30. *Chosŏn munhak*, June 1965, 14.
31. *Chosŏn munhak*, June 1965, 14.
32. *Chosŏn munhak*, June 1965, 14.
33. Pang Hyŏnsŭng, "Choguk haebang chŏnjaeng ŭl panyŏnghan chakp'um ch'angjak ŭl wihayŏ [To create literary works reflecting the fatherland liberation war], *Chosŏn munhak*, February 1965, 36.
34. Pang Hyŏnsŭng, "Choguk haebang," 41.
35. Pang Hyŏnsŭng, "Choguk haebang," 41.
36. Marc J. Selverstone, "It's a Date: Kennedy and the Timetable for a Vietnam Troop Withdrawal," *Diplomatic History* 34, no. 1 (June 2010): 489.
37. Marc J. Selverstone, *The Kennedy Withdrawal: Camelot and the American Commitment to Vietnam* (Harvard University Press, 2022), 6. Selverstone argues that Kennedy had no intention of ending US aid to South Vietnam at the time of his assassination.
38. Selverstone, *The Kennedy Withdrawal*, 6.
39. Robert E. Osgood, *Limited War: The Challenge to American Strategy* (University of Chicago Press, 1957), 283–84.
40. Robert E. Osgood, *Limited War*, 279.
41. Robert E. Osgood, *Limited War*, 279.
42. Robert E. Osgood, *Limited War*, 281–82.
43. Robert Osgood, *Ideals and Self-Interest in America's Foreign Relations* (University of Chicago Press, 1953), 5.
44. David Rees, *Korea: The Limited War* (St. Martin's Press, 1964), xi.
45. David Rees, *Korea: The Limited War*, xvi.
46. David Rees, *Korea: The Limited War*, xvi.
47. T. R. Fehrenbach, *This Kind of War: A Study in Unpreparedness* (Macmillan, 1963), 4.
48. T. R. Fehrenbach, *This Kind of War*, 658.
49. T. R. Fehrenbach, *This Kind of War*, 658.
50. T. R. Fehrenbach, *This Kind of War*, 659.
51. T. R. Fehrenbach, *This Kind of War*, 660.
52. Bruce Cumings, *The Korean War: A History* (Modern Library, 2010), 243.
53. Su-kyoung Hwang, *Korea's Grievous War* (University of Pennsylvania Press, 2016), 150.
54. T. R. Fehrenbach, *This Kind of War*, 660.

55. See Julie Reshe, *Negative Psychoanalysis for the Living Dead: Philosophical Pessimism and the Death Drive* (Springer International Publishing, 2023).
56. *Sasanggye*, January 1959, 130–31,
57. *Sasanggye*, January 1959, 135.
58. See Paik Nak-chung [Paek Nakch'ŏng], "Simin munhak non" [On citizen's literature] [1969], in *Minjok munhak kwa segye munhak* I [National literature and world literature I] (Ch'angjak kwa pip'yŏngsa, 1978), 58.
59. Paik Nak-chung, "Simin munhak non," 11.
60. Born in Wŏnsan, South Hamgyŏng Province, in the northern half of the Korean peninsula, Yi Hoch'ŏl (1932–2016) served briefly in the PLA during the Korean War. He was captured, escaped, and made his way to the south in December 1950. He later worked as a guard at a US military installation in the 1950s while writing short stories, eventually emerging as a major literary figure.
61. *Sedae*, August 1964, 367.
62. For wartime Busan, see Janice Kim, "Pusan at War: Refuge, Relief, and Resettlement in the Temporary Capital, 1950–1953," *Journal of American-East Asian Relations* 24, no. 2/3 (2017): 103–27.
63. *Sedae*, September 1964, 353. The lengthy debates between the narrator and Chŏng have been considerably altered in the 1991 version of the text appearing in volume six of Yi's collected works (published by Ch'ŏnggye yŏn'guso). Many of the exchanges have been deleted. The narrator's former ambivalence toward Chŏng disappears, replaced solely by sympathy.
64. *Sedae*, February 1965, 363. The 1991 softening of the conflict between Chŏng and the narrator is likely the reason the passage has been deleted.
65. *Sedae*, February 1965, 363.
66. *Sedae*, August 1965, 409.
67. *Sedae*, August 1965, 409.
68. *Sedae*, August 1965, 406.
69. *Sedae*, August 1965, 408.
70. *Sedae*, August 1965, 409.
71. *Sedae*, August 1965, 409.

EPILOGUE

1. Thomas C. Schelling, "Bargaining, Communication, and Limited War," *Conflict Resolution* 1, no. 1 (1957): 34.
2. Thomas C. Schelling, "Bargaining," 30.
3. Thomas C. Schelling, "Bargaining," 33.
4. Howard S. Levie, "The Nature and Scope of the Armistice Agreement," *The American Journal of International Law* 50, no. 4 (1956): 880.
5. Howard S. Levie, "The Nature and Scope," 906.
6. Howard S. Levie, "The Nature and Scope," 884 (italics in original).
7. For UNC violations of the armistice, see Steven Lee, "The Korean Armistice and the End of Peace: The US-UN Coalition and the Dynamics of War-Making in Korea, 1953–76," *The Journal of Korean Studies* 18, no. 2 (2013): 183–224.
8. Fred L. Borch, "The Cease-Fire on the Korean Peninsula: The Story of the Judge Advocate Who Drafted the Armistice Agreement that Ended the Korean War," *The Army Lawyer*, August 2013, 2.
9. Fred L. Borch, "The Cease-Fire on the Korean Peninsula," 2.
10. Erin Twyford, "A Thanatopolitical Visualisation of Accounting History: Giorgio Agamben and Nazi Germany," *Accounting History* 26, no. 3 (2021): 355.

SELECTED BIBLIOGRAPHY

Ball, W. Macmahon. "The Communist Problem in East Asia—A Western View." *Pacific Affairs* 24, no. 3 (September 1951): 241–55.
Barraclough, Ruth. "Red Love and Betrayal in the Making of North Korea: Comrade Hŏ Jŏng-suk." *History Workshop Journal* 77 (Spring 2014): 86–102.
Barraclough, Ruth, Heather Bowen-Struyk, and Paula Rabinowitz, eds. *Red Love Across the Pacific: Political and Sexual Revolutions of the Twentieth Century.* Palgrave Macmillan, 2015.
Baughman, James L. "Who Read *Life*? The Circulation of America's Favorite Magazine." In *Looking at Life Magazine*, edited by Erika Doss, 41–51. Smithsonian Institution Press, 2001.
Bennett, Eric. *Workshops of Empire: Stegner, Engle, and American Creative Writing During the Cold War.* University of Iowa Press, 2015.
Berthelier, Benoit. "High Among the People: Social Distinction, Aesthetic Hierarchies, and Workers' Poetry in North Korea." *Azalea: Journal of Korean Literature & Culture* 13 (2020): 289–323.
Borch, Fred L. "The Cease-Fire on the Korean Peninsula: The Story of the Judge Advocate Who Drafted the Armistice Agreement that Ended the Korean War." *The Army Lawyer* (August 2013): 1–3.
Breen, Joseph. Joseph Breen to Robert Lippert, October 16, 1950. *Hollywood, Censorship, and the Motion Picture Production Code, 1927–1968*, selected from the holdings of the Margaret Herrick Library of the Academy of Motion Picture Arts and Sciences in Beverly Hills, CA.
Brown, Harry. *"A Walk in the Sun." Liberty*, September 16, 1944.
Byrne-Smith, Dan. "Harvey Kurtzman and the Influence of *Mad* Magazine." In *The Cambridge History of the Graphic Novel*, edited by Jan Baetens, Hugo Frey, and Stephen E. Tabachnick, 92–106. Cambridge University Press, 2018.
Caprio, Mark. "The Politics of Trusteeship and the Perils of Korean Reunification." *Seoul Journal of Korean Studies* 32, no. 2 (2019): 263–91.
Chang Sejin. "Ŭnyu rosŏ ŭi p'oro: suyongso ŭi salm kwa 'chŏk/tongji' ŭi kubyŏl chŏngchi" [POW as metaphor: Life in POW camps and the politics of distinguishing between 'enemies' and allies]. *Sanghŏ hakpo* 46 (2016): 9–61.
Chang Sejin. "Wŏnhan, nosŭt'aeljiŏ, kwahak—wŏllam chisigindŭl kwa 1960nyŏndae Pukhan hakchi ŭi sŏngnip sajŏng" [Ressentiment, nostalgia, science: intellectuals who crossed south and conditions surrounding the establishment of North Korean studies in the 1960s]. *SAI* 17 (2014): 141–80.
Cho Tong-jae, Park Tae-jin, and Edward Reed. *A Partner for Change: Six Decades of the Asia Foundation in Korea.* Asia Foundation, 2017.

Cho Yŏnhyŏn, "Han'guk chŏnjaeng kwa Han'guk munhak" [The Korean war and Korean literature]. *Chŏnsŏn munhak*, May 1953, 18–21.

Ch'oe Chŏnghŭi. "Soyongdori" [Maelstrom]. *Chosŏn ilbo*, August 30, 1955–September 13, 1955.

Choi, Hyaeweol. *New Women in Colonial Korea: A Sourcebook*. Routledge, 2012.

Chŏn Chini. "1950nyŏndae ch'oban chonghapchi *Hŭimang* ŭi pan'gong ch'ŏngnyŏn p'yosang yŏn'gu" [A study of representations of anticommunist youth in the journal *Hope* in the early 1950s]. *Ŏmun nonch'ong* 68 (2016): 369–400.

Chŏn Kapsaeng. "Suyongso e kat'in kwihwan yongsa: 'chiokto' Yongch'odo ŭi kwihwan'gun chipkyŏlso wa sasang simnijŏn" [Repatriated warriors in a prison camp: ideology and psychological warfare at hell island, the Yongch'o island returnee collection point]. *Yŏksa pip'yŏng* 2 (Spring 2017): 381–406.

Chŏng Yŏnggwŏn. "1960nyŏndae Han'guk chŏnjaeng mellodŭrama ŭi yongmang kwa chwajŏl: *I saengmyŏng tahadorok* kwa *Kwiro* rŭl chungsim ŭro" [Desire and frustration in the war melodrama of 1960s Korea: focusing on *To the Last Day* and *Homeward*]. *Yŏnghwa yŏn'gu* 33 (September 2007): 119–26.

Chung, Hye Seung. *Cinema Under National Reconstruction: State Censorship and South Korea's Cold War Film Culture*. Rutgers University Press, 2025.

Chung, Hye Seung. *Hollywood Diplomacy: Film Regulation, Foreign Relations, and East Asian Representations*. Rutgers University Press, 2020.

Chung, Hye Seung. "Hollywood Goes to Korea: Biopic Politics and Douglas Sirk's *Battle Hymn* (1957)." *Historical Journal of Film, Radio and Television* 25, no. 1 (2005): 51–80.

Chung, Jae Won Edward. "Vitalism and Existentialism in Early South Korean Literature." In *The Routledge Companion to Korean Literature*, edited by Heekyoung Cho, 316–29. Routledge, 2022.

Chung, Steven. "Regimes Within Regimes: Film and Fashion Cultures in the Korean 1950s." In *The Korean Popular Culture Reader*, edited by Kyung Hyun Kim and Youngmin Choe, 103–25. Duke University Press, 2013.

Chute, Hillary L. *Disaster Drawn: Visual Witness, Comics, and Documentary Form*. Belknap Press of Harvard University Press, 2016.

Clark, Katerina. *Moscow, the Fourth Rome: Stalinism, Cosmopolitanism, and the Evolution of Soviet Culture, 1931–1941*. Harvard University Press, 2011.

Crowther, Bosthley. "'One Minute to Zero,' a Korean War Picture with Robert Mitchum, at Criterion." *New York Times*, September 20, 1952.

Cull, Nicholas J. "Samuel Fuller on Lewis Milestone's *A Walk in the Sun* (1946): The Legacy of *All Quiet on the Western Front* (1930)." *Historical Journal of Film, Radio and Television* 20, no. 1 (2000): 79–87.

Cumings, Bruce. *The Korean War: A History*. Modern Library, 2010.

Darda, Joseph. *Empire of Defense: Race and the Cultural Politics of Permanent War*. University of Chicago Press, 2019.

Dean, Michael, ed. *The Comics Journal Library*. Vol. 10, *The EC Artists*, pt. 2. Fantagraphics Books, 2016.

Dean, William F. (as told to William L. Worden). *General Dean's Story*. Viking Press, 1954.

Do, Jein, and Mincheol Park. "Dressing Socialism: *Joseonot* and Revolutionary Womanhood in North Korea, 1955–1960." *Korea Journal* 61, no. 2 (Summer 2021): 241–65.

Dobrenko, Evgeny. "Literary Criticism and the Institution of Literature in the Era of War and Late Stalinism, 1941–1953." In *A History of Russian Literary Theory and Criticism: The Soviet Age and Beyond*, edited by Evgeny Dobrenko and Galin Tihanov, 163–83. University of Pittsburgh Press, 2011.

Dombrowski, Lisa. *The Films of Samuel Fuller: If You Die, I'll Kill You*. Wesleyan University Press, 2008.

Doss, Erika. "*Life*'s Impact: Circulation, Copycats and Reader Response." In *Life Magazine and the Power of Photography*, edited by Katherine A. Bussard and Kristen Gresh, 110–23. Princeton Art Museum, 2020.

Em, Henry. "Christianity, the Cold War, and the Construction of the Republic of Korea." *Korea Journal* 60, no. 4 (2020): 5–29.

Fehrenbach, T. R. *This Kind of War: A Study in Unpreparedness*. Macmillan, 1963.
FitzGerald, C. P. "The Chinese Revolution and the West." *Pacific Affairs* 24, no. 1 (March 1951): 3–17.
Ffytche, Matt, and Daniel Pick, eds. *Psychoanalysis in the Age of Totalitarianism*. Routledge, 2016.
Fore, Steve. "Howard Hughes' 'Authoritarian Fictions': RKO, *One Minute to Zero*, and the Cold War." *The Velvet Light Trap* (Spring 1993): 15–26.
Friedman, Hal M. *Creating an American Lake: United States Imperialism and Strategic Security in the Pacific Basin, 1945–1947*. Praeger, 2000.
Fuller, Samuel, with Christa Lang Fuller and Jerome Henry Rudes. *A Third Face: My Tale of Writing, Fighting, and Filmmaking*. Alfred A. Knopf, 2003.
Furst, Juliane. *Stalin's Last Generation: Soviet Post-War Youth and the Emergence of Mature Socialism*. Oxford University Press, 2010.
Gabroussenko, Tatiana. *Soldiers on the Cultural Front: Developments in the Early History of North Korean Literature and Literary Policy*. University of Hawai'i Press, 2010.
Gibby, Bryan R. *The Will to Win: American Military Advisors in Korea, 1946–1953*. University of Alabama Press, 2012.
Glass, Albert J. "Current Problems in Military Psychiatry." *Journal of the American Medical Association* 150, no. 1 (1952): 6–10.
Glennon, John P., Harriet D. Schwar, and Paul Claussen, eds. *Korea and China*. Vol. 7, pt. 1 of *Foreign Relations of the United States, 1951*. Edited by Frederick Aandahl. United States Government Printing Office, 1983. https://history.state.gov/historicaldocuments/frus1951v07p1.
Gordon, Marsha. *Film is like a Battleground: Sam Fuller's War Movies*. Oxford University Press, 2017.
Gunston, Bill, with Peter Gilchrist. *Jet Bombers: From the Messerschmitt Me 262 to the Stealth B-2*. Osprey Aerospace, 1993.
Gwon, Gwisook. "Reframing Christianity on Cheju During the Korean War." *Journal of Korean Religions* 6, no. 2 (October 2015): 93–120.
Hallion, Richard. "The Air War in Korea: Coalition Air Power in the Context of Limited War." In *In from the Cold: Reflections on Australia's Korean War*, edited by John Blaxland, Michael Kelly, and Liam Brewin Higgins, 121–42. ANU Press, 2020.
Halperin, Morton H. "The Limiting Process in the Korean War." In *Korea and the Theory of Limited War*, edited by Allen Guttmann, 92–106. D. C. Heath, 1967.
Ham Ch'ungbŏm. "1960nyŏndae chŏnban'gi Pak Chŏnghŭi chŏnggwŏn ŭi yŏnghwa chŏngch'aek e taehan yŏnghwagye ŭi pan'ŭng mit hwaldong yangsang yŏn'gu: yŏnghwa pŏp ŭl tullŏssan 'yŏnghyŏp' kwa 'chehyŏp' ŭi ipchang kwa t'aedo rŭl chungsim ŭro" [A study of the response of the film world to the Pak Chŏnghŭi regime's film policy of the early 1960s: focusing on the stance and attitude taken by the motion picture association and the film producers association under the film laws]. *Hyŏndae yŏnghwa yŏn'gu* 21, no. 1 (July 2015): 149–88.
Ham Sedŏk. *San saramdŭl* [Mountain people]. *Munhak yesul*, December 1949–March 1950.
Han Hyo. "Chayŏnjuŭi rŭl pandaehanŭn t'ujaeng e issŏsŏ ŭi Chosŏn munhak" [Chosŏn literature in the struggle against naturalism]. Pts. 1, 2, 3, and 4. *Munhak yesul*, January–April 1953. In *Han Hyo p'yŏngnon sŏnjip* [Collected literary criticism of Han Hyo], edited by O T'ae-ho, 111–350. Chimanji, 2015.
Han Hyo. "Chosŏn munhak e issŏsŏ sahoejuŭi realrijŭm ŭi palsaeng chogŏn kwa kŭ palsaeng chogŏn e issŏsŏ ŭi che t'ŭkching" [Characteristics of the emergence of socialist realism in Chosŏn literature]. *Munhak yesul*, June 1952, 83–102.
Han Hyo. "Kosanghan riallijŭm ŭi ch'edŭk: munhak ch'angjo e taehan Kim Ilsŏng changgun ŭi kyohun" [Incorporating lofty realism: General Kim Il Sung's teachings on creative writing]. *Chosŏn munhak*, September 1947, 279–86.
Han Hyo. *Sŏul saramdŭl* [Seoul people]. *Munhak yesul*, August 1951–October 1951.
Hantke, Steffen. "We Own the Sky: Jet Airplanes and Cold-War Propaganda in American Cinema After the Korean War." *Journal of Popular Film and Television* 45, no. 4 (2017): 202–10.

Heller, Joseph. *Catch-22*. Simon & Schuster, 2011 [1961].
Hess, Dean E. *Battle Hymn*. McGraw-Hill, 1956.
Hŏ Yunsŏk. "Haenyŏ" [Women Divers]. *Munye*, February 1950, 12–28.
Hong Chinhyŏk. "*Kwiro* ŭi modŏnijŭm sŭt'ail, simni ŭi kongganhwa" [Modernist style in *Homeward*: The spatialization of psychology]. *Hyŏndae yŏnghwa yŏn'gu* 27 (2017): 321–49.
Hong Chisŏk. "Tu kae ŭi kŭndae: Mun Haksu (1916–1988) ŭi haebang chŏnhu" [Two modernities: Mun Haksu before and after liberation]. *Inmul misul sahak* 8 (2012): 9–34.
Hong, Christine. *A Violent Peace: Race, U.S. Militarism, and Cultures of Democratization in Cold War Asia and the Pacific*. Stanford University Press, 2020.
Howard, Keith. *Songs for "Great Leaders": Ideology and Creativity in North Korean Music and Dance*. Oxford University Press, 2020.
Hughes, Theodore. "Under Occupation, After Armistice: Stories of Enemy and Traitorous Property," in *Korea Journal* 65 (2025): 68–93.
Hunter, Edward. *Brainwashing: The Story of Men Who Defied It*. Farrar, Straus and Cudahy, 1956.
Hwang, Junghyun. "Seen Through the Camera Obscura: *Life* Photographs of the Korean War and Cold War Anxiety of the American Self." *Cultural Critique*, no. 121 (2023): 138–61.
Hwang Kŏn. *Haengbok* [Happiness]. *Munhak yesul*, February 1953.
Hwang Kŏn. "Pul t'anŭn sŏm" [Island ablaze]. *Rodong sinmun*, January 21, 1952.
Hwang, Su-kyoung. *Korea's Grievous War*. University of Pennsylvania Press, 2016.
Hyŏn Su (pseudonym for Pak Namsu). *Chŏkch'i yungnyŏn ŭi Pukhan mundan* [The North Korean literary scene: six years under the reds] (1952). In *Hanguk chŏnjaenggi charyojip* [Korean wartime sourcebook] XIV. K'ep'oi puksŭ, 2013.
Im Ogin. *Wŏllam chŏnhu* [Crossing south: before and after]. *Munhak yesul*, July 1956– December 1956.
Im Sundŭk. "Cho Okhŭi" [Cho Okhŭi]. *Munhak yesul*, June 1951, 16–36
Im Sundŭk. "Friendship." In *Im Sundŭk, taeanjŏk yŏsŏng chuch'e rŭl hyanghayŏ* [Im Sundŭk, toward an alternative women's subjectivity], by Yi Sanggyŏng, 296–332. Somyŏng ch'ulpansa, 2012.
Im Sundŭk. "Ŏnŭ han yugajok ŭi iyagi" [Tale of a bereaved family]. *Chosŏn munhak*, June 1957, 31–42.
Immerwahr, Daniel. *How to Hide an Empire: A History of the Greater United States*. Farrar, Straus and Giroux, 2019.
Inge, M. Thomas. "Harvey Kurtzman and Modern American Satire." In *Seeing Mad: Essays on Mad Magazine's Humor and Legacy*, edited by John Bird and Judith Yaross Lee, 67–83. University of Missouri Press, 2020.
Jager, Sheila Miyoshi. *Brothers at War: The Unending Conflict in Korea*. W. W. Norton, 2013.
Jervis, Robert. "The Impact of the Korean War on the Cold War." *The Journal of Conflict Resolution* 24, no. 4 (December 1980): 563–92.
Jung, Moon-ho. *Menace to Empire: Anticolonial Solidarities and the Transpacific Origins of the US Security State*. University of California Press, 2022.
Kang Soyŏn. "1950nyŏndae yŏsŏng chapchi e p'yosangtoen Miguk munhwa wa yŏsŏng tamnon" [The discourse on women and representations of US culture in 1950s women's magazines]. *Sanghŏ hakpo* 18 (2006): 107–36.
Kang Yongjun. "Ch'ŏljomang" [Barbed wire]. *Sasanggye*, July 1960, 276–307.
Kazyuchits, Maksim. "Sergei Gerasimov's *The Young Guard*: Artistic Method and the Conflict of Discourses of History and Power." *Studies in Russian and Soviet Cinema* 13, no. 2 (2019): 162–71.
Kennan, George. "Communism and Conformity." *Bulletin of the Atomic Scientists* 9, no. 8 (October 1953): 296–98.
Kief, I Jonathan. "Anthropological Fictions: 'Humanism' and its Doubles in 1930s–1960s Korea." PhD diss., Columbia University, 2016.
Kief, I Jonathan. "Closed Borders and Open Letters in the Cold War Koreas." In *The Routledge Companion to Korean Literature*, edited by Heekyoung Cho, 427–40. Routledge, 2022.

Kil Chinsŏp. "Choguk haebang chŏnjaeng misul chŏllamhoe p'yŏng" [Evaluation of the fatherland liberation war art exhibition]. *Munhak yesul*, September 1952, 106–36.

Kim Il Sung. *Choguk t'ongil e kwanhan widaehan suryŏng Kim Ilsŏng tongji ŭi munhŏn* [Documents on the reunification of the fatherland by the great leader comrade Kim Il Sung]. Samhaksa, 1981.

Kim Oksŏn. "Chŏnsŏn munhak e nat'anan kamjŏng chŏngch'i" [The politics of emotion in *Frontline Literature*]. *Inmunhak nonch'ong* 25 (February 2011): 103–29.

Kim Tongyun. "Ham Sedŏk hŭigok *San saramdŭl* yŏn'gu: t'eksŭt'ŭ munje wa Jeju 4.3 chungsim ŭro" [Study of Ham Sedŏk's play *Mountain People*, with a focus on textual provenance and Jeju 4.3]. *Han'guk munhak nonch'ong* 55 (August 2010): 93–125.

Kim, Cheehyung Harrison. *Heroes and Toilers: Work as Life in Postwar North Korea, 1953–1961*. Columbia University Press, 2018.

Kim, Cheehyung Harrison. "Pyongyang Modern: Architecture of Multiplicity in Postwar North Korea." *Journal of Korean Studies* 26, no. 2 (2021): 271–96.

Kim, Daniel Y. *The Intimacies of Conflict: Cultural Memory and the Korean War*. New York University Press, 2020.

Kim, Dong-Choon. *The Unending Korean War: A Social History*. Tamal Vista, 2009.

Kim, Eunjung. *Curative Violence: Rehabilitating Disability, Gender, and Sexuality in Modern Korea*. Duke University Press, 2017.

Kim, Hieyoon. *Celluloid Democracy: Cinema and Politics in Cold War South Korea*. University of California Press, 2023.

Kim, Janice. "Pusan at War: Refuge, Relief, and Resettlement in the Temporary Capital, 1950–1953." *Journal of American–East Asian Relations* 24, no. 2/3 (2017): 103–27.

Kim, Monica. *The Interrogation Rooms of the Korean War: The Untold History*. Princeton University Press, 2019.

Kim, Nan. *Memory, Reconciliation, and Reunions in South Korea: Crossing the Divide*. Lexington Books, 2015.

Kim, Suzy. *Among Women Across Worlds: North Korea in the Global Cold War*. Cornell University Press, 2023.

Kim, Suzy. *Everyday Life in the North Korean Revolution, 1945–1950*. Cornell University Press, 2013.

Kimble, James J. "Spectral Soldiers: Domestic Propaganda, Visual Culture, and Images of Death on the World War II Home Front." *Rhetoric and Public Affairs* 19, no. 4 (2016): 535–70.

Kitchen, Denis, and Paul Buhle, *The Art of Harvey Kurtzman: The Mad Genius of Comics*. Abrams ComicArts, 2009.

Ko Ilhwan. "Ssobaet'ŭ munhak chakp'um esŏ padŭn yŏnghyang kwa uri munhak ŭi sŏnggwa" [Influences of Soviet literary works and our literary achievements]. *Munhak yesul*, October 1949, 52–55.

Kohn, Richard H., and Joseph P. Harahan, eds. *Air Interdiction in World War II, Korea, and Vietnam: An Interview with General Earle E. Partridge, General Jacob E. Smart, and General John W. Vogt Jr*. USAF Warrior Studies, 1986.

Korean Film Archive's Digital Collection. Accessed February 14, 2025. https://www.kmdb.or.kr/history/leaflet.

Korean Film Archive's Film and Magazine Collection. Accessed February 14, 2025. https://www.koreafilm.or.kr/collection/CI_00000009.

"Korean War Armistice Agreement." July 27, 1953. Treaties and Other International Acts. General Records of the United States Government, Record Group 11. National Archives at Washington, D.C. https://catalog.archives.gov/id/5730903.

Kurtzman, Harvey, *Corpse on the Imjin! And Other Stories*. Fantagraphics Books, 2012.

Kurtzman, Harvey (w/a). "Big 'If!'" In *Frontline Combat* #5. Entertaining Comics Group, March 1952.

Kurtzman, Harvey (w), and Jack Davis (a). "B-26 Invader!" In *Frontline Combat* #12. Entertaining Comics Group, May–June 1953.

Kurtzman, Harvey, Jerry De Fuccio, Carl Wessler, Wallace Wood, and Archie Goodwin. *Atom Bomb and Other Stories*. Fantagraphics Books, 2020.

Kurtzman, Harvey (w), and John Severin (a). "Hungnam!" In *Two-Fisted Tales* #26. Entertaining Comics Group, March–April 1952.

Kurtzman, Harvey (w), and John Severin (a). "Link-Up!" In *Two-Fisted Tales* #26. Entertaining Comics Group, March–April 1952.

Kurtzman, Harvey (w), and John Severin (a). "The Trap!" In *Two-Fisted Tales* #26. Entertaining Comics Group, March–April 1952.

Kwŏn Podŭrae. "*Kwangjang* ŭi chŏnjaeng kwa p'oro: Han'guk chŏnjaeng ŭi p'oro sŏsa wa 'chungnip' ŭi chwap'yo" [War and the POW in *The Square*: Narratives of the Korean war POW and the question of "neutrality"]. *Han'guk hyŏndae munhak yŏn'gu* 53 (2017): 151–93.

Kwŏn Podŭrae. "Silchon, *Chayu puin*, p'ŭraegŭmŏt'ijŭm: 1950nyŏndae ŭi tu kaji 'chayu' kaenyŏm kwa munhwa" [Existentialism, *Madame Freedom*, pragmatism: 1950s cultural practices and the two notions of "freedom"]. *Han'guk munhak yŏn'gu* 35 (2008): 101–47.

Kwon, Heonik. *After the Korean War: An Intimate History*. Cambridge University Press, 2020.

Kwon, Heonik. *The Other Cold War*. Columbia University Press, 2010.

Lankov, Andrei. *Crisis in North Korea: The Failure of De-Stalinization, 1956*. University of Hawai'i Press, 2005.

Lattimore, Eleanor. "Pacific Ocean or American Lake？" *Far Eastern Survey* 14, no. 22 (November 1945): 313–16.

Lee, Steven. "The Korean Armistice and the End of Peace: The US-UN Coalition and the Dynamics of War-Making in Korea, 1953–76." *The Journal of Korean Studies* 18, no. 2 (2013): 183–224.

Lee, Yun-Jong. "Mun Yebong, a Partisan Maiden in a 'Partisan State.'" *Korea Journal* 60, no. 3 (2020): 349–70.

Levie, Howard S. "The Nature and Scope of the Armistice Agreement." *The American Journal of International Law* 50, no. 4 (1956): 880–906.

LIFE 29 no. 3, July 17, 1950. Time, Inc.

LIFE 29 no. 4, July 24, 1950. Time, Inc.

LIFE 29 no. 15, October 9, 1950. Time, Inc.

LIFE 29 no. 26, December 25, 1950. Time, Inc.

LIFE 30 no. 2, January 8, 1951. Time, Inc.

LIFE 34 no. 19, May 11, 1953. Time, Inc.

Lindner, Robert. *Must You Conform?* Rinehart, 1956.

MAD #11, May 1954. Entertaining Comics Group.

Maslon, Slawomir. *Secret Violences: The Political Cinema of Michelangelo Antonioni, 1960–1975*. Bloomsbury, 2023.

Mbembe, Achille. *Necropolitics*. Duke University Press, 2019.

Meerloo, Joost. *The Rape of the Mind: The Psychology of Thought Control—Menticide and Brainwashing*. World Publishing, 1956.

Merrill, John. "Reflections on the Jeju 4.3 Incident: Korea's 'Dark History' and its Implications for Current Policy." In *The Jeju 4.3 Mass Killing: Atrocity, Justice, and Reconciliation*, edited by Jeju 4.3 Peace Foundation, 321–49. Yonsei University Press, 2018.

Meyers, Cynthia B. "Advertising, the Red Scare, and the Blacklist: BBDO, US Steel, and 'Theatre Guild on the Air,' 1945–1952." *Cinema Journal* 55, no. 4 (Fall 2016): 55–83.

Meyers, Jeffrey. "James Salter's Strange Career." *Salmagundi* no. 220–221 (Fall 2023/Winter 2024): 117–31.

Michener, James. *The Bridges at Toko-Ri*. *LIFE*, July 6, 1953.

Millet, Allan. *The War for Korea, 1945–1950: A House Burning*. University of Kansas Press, 2015.

Moon, Seungsook. *Militarized Modernity and Gendered Citizenship in South Korea*. Duke University Press, 2005.

Morgenthau, Hans J. *Politics Among Nations: The Struggle for Power and Peace*. 3rd ed. Knopf, 1960 [1948].
Mortenson, Erik. "A Journey into the Shadows: *The Twilight Zone*'s Visual Critique of the Cold War," *Science Fiction Film and Television* 7, no. 1 (2014): 55–76.
Mun Sangmin. "3.1 undong kwa Chosŏn munhak" [The March 1st movement and Chosŏn literature]. *Munhak sinmun*, February 28, 1957.
Nam, Haeyŏng. "Na ŭi wŏllam ilgi" [My recollection of crossing south]. *Saegajŏng*, June 1957, 22–23.
Nam Wŏnjin. "Aejŏng kwa yŏng'ung: Hwang Kŏn ŭi *Haengbok* ŭi ch'angjak kwa p'yŏngga ŭi puch'im e taehan yŏn'gu" [Affect and the heroic: A study of Hwang Kŏn's *Happiness* and its changing critical appraisal]. *Han'guk kŭndae munhak yŏn'gu* 29 (April 2014): 311–16.
Nardelli, Matilde. *Antonioni and the Aesthetics of Impurity: Remaking the Image in the 1960s*. Edinburgh University Press, 2020.
National Committee for Investigation of the Truth About the Jeju 4.3 Incident, ed. *The Jeju 4.3 Incident Investigation Report*. Jeju 4.3 Peace Foundation, 2014.
Niebuhr, Reinhold. *Major Works on Religion and Politics*. Edited by Elisabeth Sifton. Library of America, 2015.
"NSC 68: United States Objectives and Programs for National Security," S/S-NSC Files: Lot 63D351: NSC 68 Series. In *National Security Affairs; Foreign Economic Policy*. Edited by Neal H. Petersen, John P. Glennon, David W. Mabbon, Ralph R. Goodwin, and William Z. Slany. Vol. 1 of *Foreign Relations of the United States, 1950*. Edited by S. Everett Gleason, Frederick Aandahl. United States Government Printing Office, 1977. https://history.state.gov/historicaldocuments/frus1950v01/d85.
Nyberg, Amy Kiste. *Seal of Approval: The History of the Comics Code*. University Press of Mississippi, 1998.
O T'aeho. "Haebanggi (1945–1950) Pukhan munhak ŭi 'kosanghan riŏllijŭm' non ŭi chŏn'gae kwajŏng koch'al: *Munhwa chŏnsŏn, Chosŏn munhak, Munhak yesul*, tŭng ŭl chungsim ŭro" [A consideration of developments in North Korea's literary debates on "lofty realism" in the liberation period (1945–1950): Focusing on *Munhwa chŏnsŏn, Chosŏn munhak, Munhak yesul*]. *Uri munhak yŏn'gu* 46 (2013): 319–57.
O Yŏngsu. "Huildam" [Afterword]. *Hyŏndae munhak*, June 1960, 125–37.
Obst, Lynda Rosen, ed. *The Sixties: The Decade Remembered Now by the People Who Lived It Then*. Rolling Stone Press, 1977.
Ŏm Hosŏk. "Choguk haebang chŏnjaeng kwa munhak ŭi angyang" [Literary exaltation and the fatherland liberation war]. *Munhak yesul*, May 1952, 84–111.
Ŏm Hosŏk. "Chosŏn munhak e nat'anan Kim Ilsung Changgun ŭi hyŏngsang" [The portrayal of General Kim in Chosŏn Literature]. *Munhak yesul*, May 1950, 20–32.
Ŏm Hosŏk. "Rodong kyegŭp ŭi hyŏngsang kwa mihaksang ŭi myŏt kaji munje" [Portrayal of the working class and several problems of aesthetics]. *Munhak yesul*, January 1953. In *Munhak yesul ŭi hyŏngmyŏngjŏk chŏnhwan: PukHan ŭi pip'yŏng*, edited by Kim Chonghwoe, 105–38. Kukhak charyowŏn, 2012.
Osgood, Robert. *Ideals and Self-Interest in America's Foreign Relations*. University of Chicago Press, 1953.
Osgood, Robert E. *Limited War Revisited*. Westview Press, 1979.
Osgood, Robert E. *Limited War: The Challenge to American Strategy*. University of Chicago Press, 1957.
Osgood, Robert E. "The Uses of Military Power in the Cold War." In *America Armed: Essays on United States Military Policy*, edited by Robert A. Goldwin, 1–21. Rand McNally, 1963.
Paik Nak-chung. *The Division System in Crisis: Essays on Contemporary Korea*. University of California Press, 2011.
Paik Nak-chung [Paek Nakch'ŏng]. "Simin munhak non" [On citizen's literature] (1969). In *Minjok munhak kwa segye munhak* I [National literature and world literature I], 9–76. Ch'angjak kwa pip'yŏngsa, 1978.
Paik Nak-chung. "South Korean Democracy and Korea's Division System." *Inter-Asia Cultural Studies* 14, no. 1 (2013): 156–69.
Pak Chinhong. *Toraon p'aeja: 6/25 kukkun p'oro ch'ehŏmgi* [Return of the defeated: The true story of an ROK prisoner of war]. Yŏksa pip'yŏngsa, 2009.

Pak Kijun. "Han'guk chakka ŭi pansŏng" [Self-reflections of Korean writers]. *Chŏnsŏn munhak*, April 1952, 13–15.

Pak P'ilhyŏn. "P'ongnyŏk ŭi kyŏnghŏm kwa kŭndaejŏk minjok kukka: ch'ogi 4.3 sosŏl ŭl chungsim ŭro" [The experience of violence and the formation of a modern nation-state, with a focus on early 4.3 fiction]. *Hyŏndae munhak iron yŏn'gu* 63 (2015): 225–50.

Pak Yŏngjun. "Amya" [Dark Night]. *Chŏnsŏn munhak*, April 1952, 24–29.

Pak Yŏngjun. "Ppalch'isan" [Partisan]. *Sinch'ŏnji*, May 1952, 129–40.

Pak Yŏngjun. "Yongch'odo kŭnhae" [In the sea off Yongch'o Island]. *Chŏnsŏn munhak*, December 1953, 60–77.

Pak Yuhŭi. "Salbu ŭi yulli wa p'ipchinsŏng ŭi kiyul: Kunbŏn ŏmnŭn yongsa (1966) rŭl t'onghae pon Yi Manhŭi ŭi yŏnghwa segye" [The ethics of patricide and the disciplining of verisimilitude: Yi Manhŭi's filmic world as seen through *Hero without a Service Number* (1966)]. *Yŏngsang munhwa* 19 (December 2015): 9–25.

Pang Hyŏnsŭng. "Choguk haebang chŏnjaeng ŭl panyŏnghan chakp'um ch'angjak ŭl wihayŏ" [To create literary works reflecting the fatherland liberation war]. *Chosŏn munhak*, February 1965, 36–43.

Pisiotis, Argyrios K. "Images of Hate in the Art of War." In *Culture and Entertainment in Wartime Russia*, edited by Richard Stiles, 141–56. University of Indiana Press, 1995.

Poole, Janet. *When the Future Disappears: The Modernist Imagination in Late Colonial Korea*. Columbia University Press, 2014.

Price, David H. *Cold War Anthropology: The CIA, the Pentagon, and the Growth of Dual Use Anthropology*. Duke University Press, 2015.

Price, David H. *Cold War Deceptions: The Asia Foundation and the CIA*. University of Washington Press, 2024.

Prince, Stephen. *Classical Film Violence: Designing and Regulating Brutality in Hollywood Cinema, 1930–1968*. Rutgers University Press, 2003.

Rabinowitch, Eugene. "The Narrowing Way." *Bulletin of the Atomic Scientists* 9, no. 8 (October 1953): 294–95.

Rees, David. *Korea: The Limited War*. St. Martin's Press, 1964.

Rhee, Syngman. *I sŭngman (1): T'ŭruman, Aijenhawŏ taet'ongnyŏng ŭi sŏsin* [Syngman Rhee: Epistolary exchanges with presidents Truman and Eisenhower]. Edited by Yang Sŭngham, Pak Myŏngnim, and Yun Sangjin. Yŏnse taehakkyo kukka kwalli yŏn'guwŏn, 2010.

Ri Yunyŏng, "Chŏkhu ŭi saebyŏk" [Dawn behind enemy lines]. *Chosŏn munhak*, June 1965.

Ryang, Sonia. *Language and Truth in North Korea*. University of Hawai'i Press, 2021.

Ryu Kihyŏn. "Han'guk chŏnjaenggi Mi kungmubu chŏngbo chosaguk ŭi Pukhan hyŏnji chosa wa Pukhan yŏn'gu ŭi t'aedong: Pukhan-Soryŏn wisŏng kukka sarye yŏn'gu rŭl chungsim ŭro" [Wartime investigations of the department of state research mission to Korea and the birth of North Korean studies: focusing on *North Korea: A Case Study of a Soviet Satellite*]. *Yŏksa munje yŏn'gu* 24, no. 2 (2020): 335–72.

Salter, James. *The Hunters*. Harper, 1956.

Salter, James. Preface to the 1997 edition of *The Hunters*. Counterpoint, 1997.

Schelly, Bill. *Harvey Kurtzman: The Man Who Created Mad and Revolutionized Humor in America*. Fantagraphics Books, 2015.

Schlesinger, Arthur M., Jr. *The Vital Center: The Politics of Freedom*. Houghton Mifflin, 1962 [1948].

Schnabel, James F., and Robert J. Watson, eds. *The Joint Chiefs of Staff and National Policy*. Vol. 3, pt. 1, *1950–1951: The Korean War*. Historical Division, Joint Chiefs of Staff, 1998.

Selverstone, Marc J. "It's a Date: Kennedy and the Timetable for a Vietnam Troop Withdrawal." *Diplomatic History* 34, no. 1 (June 2010): 485–95.

Selverstone, Marc J. *The Kennedy Withdrawal: Camelot and the American Commitment to Vietnam*. Harvard University Press, 2022.

Seo, Joong-Seok. *Korean Nationalism Betrayed*. Brill, 2007.

Serling, Rod. *Patterns: Four Television Plays with the Author's Personal Commentaries.* Simon & Schuster, 1957.
Sobel, Raymond. "The 'Old Sergeant' Syndrome." *Psychiatry* 10, no. 3 (1947): 315–21.
Sŏnu Hwi. *Kwihwan* [Return]. Ch'ŏnggu Ch'ulp'ansa, 1954.
Twyford, Erin. "A Thanatopolitical Visualisation of Accounting History: Giorgio Agamben and Nazi Germany." *Accounting History* 26, no. 3 (2021): 352–74.
United States Office of Armed Forces Information and Education. *The U.S. Fighting Man's Code.* Office of Armed Forces Information and Education, Department of Defense, 1955.
Whitted, Qiana. *EC Comics: Race, Shock, and Social Protest.* Rutgers University Press, 2019.
Wister, William Haines. *One Minute to Zero (1952): Shooting Script.* Alexander Street Press, 2007.
Yang, Jeong-Sim. "The Jeju 4.3 Uprising and the United States: Remembering Responsibility for the Massacre." *S/N Korean Humanities* 4, no. 2 (2018): 39–65.
Y'Blood, William T., ed. *The Three Wars of Lt. Gen. George E. Stratemeyer: His Korean War Diary.* Air Force History and Museums Program, 1999.
Yi Hoch'ŏl. *Sosimin* [Petty bourgeoisie]. *Sedae,* July 1964–August 1965.
Yi Muyŏng. "Chŏnjaeng kwa munhak" [War and literature]. *Chŏnsŏn munhak,* May 1953, 4–8.
Yi Pongbŏm. "Naengjŏn kwa wŏnjo, wŏnjo sidae naengjŏn munhwa kuch'uk ŭi yŏktongsŏng: 1950~60nyŏndae Miguk min'gan chaedan ŭi wŏnjo wa Han'guk munhwa" [Cold war and aid: the dynamism of cold war cultural construction in the aid era, with a focus on Korean culture and aid provided by US private foundations in the 1950s and 1960s]. *Hangukhak yŏn'gu* 39 (2015): 252–61.
Yi Pyŏngsun. "Ch'oe Chŏnghŭi sosŏl e nat'anan chŏnjaeng ŭi ŭimi" [The meaning of war in Ch'oe Chŏnghŭi's novels]. *Han'guk sasang kwa munhwa* 50 (2009): 137–61.
Yi, We Jung. *Worm-Time: Memories of Division in South Korean Aesthetics.* Cornell University Press, 2024.
Yoo, Theodore Jun. *The Politics of Gender in Colonial Korea: Education, Labor, and Health, 1910–1945.* University of California Press, 2008.
Yun Sep'yŏng. "P'yŏngyang kwa munhak" [Pyŏngyang and literature]. *Munhak sinmun,* October 10, 1957.
Yun Tuhŏn. "*Kyohyŏngsu ŭi sugi* rŭl ilkko" [On reading *Notes from the Gallows*]. *Munhak yesul,* August 1949, 126–32.

FILM AND TELEVISION

David Davidson, dir. "P.O.W." (US Steel Hour, 1953).
Samuel Fuller, dir. *The Steel Helmet* (1951).
Tay Garnet, dir. *One Minute to Zero* (1952).
Sergei Gerasimov, dir. *The Young Guard* (1948).
Louis King, dir. *Sabre Jet* (1953).
Karl Malden, dir. *Time Limit* (1957).
Lewis Milestone, dir. *A Walk in the Sun* (1946).
Mark Robson, dir. *The Bridges at Toko-Ri* (1954).
Rod Serling, dir. "The Rack" (US Steel Hour, 1955).
Rod Serling, dir. "Where is Everybody?" (*The Twilight Zone,* 1959).
Douglas Sirk, dir. *Battle Hymn* (1957).
Yi Manhŭi, dir. *Kunbŏn ŏmnŭn yongsa* [Hero without a service number], 1966.
Yi Manhŭi, dir. *Kwiro* [Homeward], 1967.
Yi Manhŭi, , dir. *Ssarikkol ŭi sinhwa* [The legend of Ssarikkol], 1967.

INDEX

Page numbers in *italics* indicate figures. When the figure is on the same page as the related text, only the text is indexed.

4/3 Jeju Uprising (1948), 6; in "Afterword," 37–40; as environmental warfare, 34; events, 18; in *General Dean's Story*, 27–28; and ghostliness, 36, 38–40; massacre, 18, 24–25, 38–39, 40; in *Mountain People*, 21–26; torture, 38–39; as trauma and possibility, 7, 18–19. *See also* Jeju Island

6/25 War (1950, term for Korean War in ROK), 9, 10; aftermath, in film 216–21; anticommunist representation of, 211–15; combat experience, 37, 217; as defense of human dignity, 191; and disability, 216–18; and family, 214–15, 230; in film, 210, 211–15; as intra-ethnonational war, 184, 186, 212; and Jeju Uprising, 38, 40; as literary topic, 205–6; and living dead, 177; patricide in, 213–15; in *Return*, 199–200; and sacrifice, 184, 190–91; temporalities of, 199; as war upon *koeroe*, 187, 230. *See also* Fatherland Liberation War; Korean War; POW

Acheson, Dean, 16

adoption trope, 30, 35–36

afterdeath and afterdead, 10, 11, 59; in "Barbed Wire," 183; and military sublime, 125–27; in Kurtzman's comics, 144

"Afterword" (Huildam, O Yŏngsu), 6, 32, 37–40

"American Lake," 2, 17–18, 100

An Chaehong, 23

anticommunism, 10, 203, 276n6; and armistice, 237; in "Barbed Wire," 182, 183; and belonging, 183; and censorship, 211–12, 215; central to ROK cultural production, 179; and familial paradigm, 229–30; film as vehicle of, 10, 212–15, 216, 229–30; and fratricide, 185, 187; hateful, 169. *See also* communism; containment; *koeroe*

"anticommunist prisoner" (*pan'gong p'oro*), 182

après girl (*ap'ŭre kŏl*), 212–13, 221–26; as corpse, 227, 228–29; 230; influenced by Hollywood, 221, 223–25, 226; as virtual widow, 230

armistice, 3–6; as governance, 2, 10–11, 233, 245, 251–53; Kim Il Sung's views on, 234–35, 237; as prevention of death, 253; as respite and stop, 231; Rhee's views on, 236–37; and *sosimin* depravity, 247–48; as unwar, 179; and US global management, 236

Armistice Agreement (1953), 3, 251–52; and DMZ, 246, 251

armistitium, 252

artists, directives for, 20–21, 48

auto-thanatography, 28, 150

awakescape, 193–94

Baek Young-soo, 221, 223–24, *225*, *227*, *228*, 229

Ball, W. Macmahon, 137–38

"Barbed Wire" (Ch'ŏljomang, Kang Yongjun): and non-return, 195; as thanatography, 9, 181–83
Battle Hymn (book by Hess), 31–32
Battle Hymn (film by Sirk), 6, 28–32; in *Twilight Zone*, 175–76
Battle in Defense of Seoul (Chang Myŏngnyong), 62–64
becoming communist, and *koeroe*, 185–88, 204
becoming-corpse, 130, 131, 148; and horror, 153
belonging: autochthonous, 22; ethnonational, 202, 208, 215; in free world, 199; global, 41, 73; national, 183; revolutionary, 59
Bennett, Eric, 167–68
border consciousness, 9, 181–82
border-making: crossing south as, 9, 198; global, 7; and thanatography, 250; transpacific, 90, 100; in *War Hunt*, 245
brainwashing, 8, 154, 163–68, 170; and Black experience, 163–64; and breaking point, 165; under communism, 163; and fragility, 156–57; vs. *koeroe*, 179; management of, 170–71; on television, 165–66
breaking point, 155–68, 170–77; and brainwashing, 165; and fragility, 8, 98, 154; military psychiatry on, 156, 160–62, 163, 176; and mobilization, 168; prevention of, 162; and self-empowerment, 156, 165, 172; and white masculinity, 160, 166–67
Bridges at Toko-Ri (film by Robson), 113, 120–28
Bridges at Toko-Ri (novella by Michener), 8, 113–14, 120–28
Brown, Harry, 162
Busan, 10; and postarmistice future, 252; and *sosimin*, 247–48; as US transpacific edge, 249; and war profiteering, 194
Byrne-Smith, Dan, 154

Catch-22 (Heller), 97–98, 269n2
censorship: of comics, 130; and depicting combat death, 144; under Park regime, 211–12, 280n7
Chang Myŏngnyong, 62
Chang Sejin, 203
Chernyshevsky, Nikolai, 92
children: and adoption, 30, 35–36; care of, 92–93; massacred, 53–54, 67, 89; orphaned, 29–31, 238–39
China: as communist enemy, 135–36, 137; DPRK's affiliation with, 7; in Truman's plans, 15

Ch'oe Chŏnghŭi, 213, 221–29, 282n13
Chŏnsŏn munhak (Frontline Literature), 184–85, 189–90, 192, 195
"Cho Okhŭi" (Cho Okhŭi, story by Im Sundŭk), 80, 86–91
"Cho Okhŭi, Hero" (painting by Mun Haksu), 84–86, 88
Cho Pyŏngok, *20*, 23
Chosŏn munhak (Korean Literature), 48, 80, 237–38
Chosŏn nyŏsŏng (Chosŏn Women), 76, 78, *79*
Cho Yŏnhyŏn, 205–6
Chung, Hye Seung, 28–29, 263n71
Chung, Steven, 223
Chute, Hillary, 154
cold war, 1, 120; and *Catch-22*, 97–98; as cosmopolitanism, 114, 117; and hot spot, 98, 115–16; and Korean War, 3–4, 8; and limited-war thinking, 5; unsettled by thanatography, 253
Collins, Joseph, 16
combat killing, and murder, 243, 245
combat zone, 95
communism: accounts of life under, 203–6; and anticolonialism, 137–38; and brainwashing, 156, 163–64; and capitalism, 190–91, 194, 246; containment of, 134–38; critiqued, 167, 168–69, 190–91, 194, 246; global struggle against, 15–17, 31; holy war against, 184–85; as *koeroe*, 179, 183, 187–88; recantation of, and crossing south, 188, 194; rejection of, 182; as slavery, 29, 141, 155; as ultimate evil, 243. *See also* anticommunism; *koeroe*
communist in the mirror, 186, 188
containment, 134, 137, 153; and armistice, 237; limited war as, 242–43
corpses: and après girl, 226–29; in "Barbed Wire," 181; bound, 105, 146, 158; brainwashed minds as, 163; communists as, 138; and horror, 147–48, 149–50; in "Island Ablaze," 66; in *LIFE* magazine, 105, 139–41, 144–46; and military sublime, 125–27; and the north within, 238–40; POW as, 203; prophetic, 246; visual representation, 8–9, 130–31, 136, 138, *227*
cosmopolitanism, cold war as, 114, 117
crossing south (*wŏllam*), 179; vs. crossing north, 208–9; as flight from communism, 197–99; as repatriation, 200; and suicide, 195, 201–2, 252

INDEX   ✤   297

Crossing South (*Wŏllam chŏnhu*, Im Ogin), 9, 196; and border-making, 198; 203–10; and colonial remains, 205–6
Crowther, Bosley, 100–101, 103
cultural front, 191
Cumings, Bruce, 243

Darda, Joseph, 3–4
"Dark Night" (Amya, Pak Yŏngjun), 184, 186–88; as thanatography, 9
Davidson, David, 8, 157, 166
"Dawn Behind Enemy Lines" (Chŏkhu ŭi saebyŏk, Ri Yunyŏng), 233, 238–40
Dean, William F., 6, 18, *20*; *General Dean's Story*, 26–28; as Ttin in *Mountain People*, 23–24
death: armistice as management of, 4–5, 8, 252–53; joyful, 41, 71–72, 74–75; living, 13, 39, 156, 177, 189; multiple valences, 1, 7–11; POW camp as site of, 193–94, 202; proximal, 111; and rebirth, 13, 26; sacrificial, 90–91; virtual, 13, 27–28, 100. *See also* corpses; massacre; mourning; thanatography
deathscapes, 129, 131, 148
decolonization: and feelings, 68; in Im Sundŭk's fiction, 80, 83, 91; Kim Il Sung's views on, 236, 237; and limited-war thinking, 4–5; management of, 252–53
demilitarized zone. *See* DMZ
Department of Defense (DoD), 101, 107, 270n16; and film, 120, 157; Kurtzman's relationship with, 147, 150, 273n42
dividing point, 234, 249
division of Korea, 6–7, 9, 59–60; and armistice, 252–53; in *Crossing South*, 206; and *koeroe*, 207; and liberation, 197; and limit line, 7; and lived reality, 4; as method, 233–34; 250; vs. regional affiliations, 210; as unsettled state, 231
DMZ (demilitarized zone), 231, 233; in film, 245–46
Dobrenko, Evgeny, 264n19
domesticity, 8, 29–30, 108–11; après girl as threat to, 212–13, 221, 225–26
Doomsday Clock, 99
Doss, Erika, 129
doubt, 50–51, 112; and suspicion, 183, 186–87, 195
DPRK (Democratic People's Republic of Korea): accounts of life in, 203–4; as agent of reunification, 43–45, 234–36; directives for writers, 20–21, 48–49, 70, 72; disillusionment with, 194–95; emancipation and loss of Seoul, 45–47; established, 6; and internationalist socialism, 65; postarmistice reconstruction, 43, 77, 80, 92; and revolutionary mourning, 41, 47; as Soviet puppet, 203
Duncan, David Douglas, *132–36*, *139–40*, 148–49

Eisenhower, Dwight D., 236–37
election in southern Korea (1948): and USAMGIK, 6, 18; and unrest on Jeju, 18, 24, 25; critiques in DPRK press, 19; Dean on, 27–28
Em, Henry, 199
emancipation, women's, 76, 78, 80; and communist feminism, 207
embedded writers, 9, 65, 66, 184, 186, 195, 281n13
Ermilov, Vladimir, 91–92
escalation, 24, 105–6; and temporality, 103–4
ethnonation. *See* nation
exceptionalism, American, 118

Fadeev, Alexander, 70–73, 75
family, 30–31; après girl as threat to, 212–13, 221, 225–26; bereaved, 92–95; central to anticommunist film, 215, 229–30; and corpse, 227–28; and Japan-US amity, 123; *koeroe*'s disruption of, 185–88, 212–15; nation as, 36
Far East Command, 17, 100
Fatherland Liberation War (*Choguk haebang chŏnjaeng*, term for Korean War in DPRK), 7, 20, 46–47, 61; commemorated in literature, 237–38, 240; in "Happiness," 67–68, 74–76; in "Island Ablaze," 65–68; and joyful death, 71–72, 74–75; in painting, 62–64; and portrayals of Soviet Great Patriotic War, 64, 86; in *Seoul People*, 47, 49–52, 53–59
Fatherland Liberation War Exhibition (1952), 84
FBI (Federal Bureau of Investigation), 146–47
feelings: in "Cho Okhŭi," 87–88; circulation in socialist world, 61, 64–65; in combat, 149; in *Happiness*, 67–68, 71–72; lofty, 49–50; the north as, 239–40; revolutionary, 47, 50–52, 59, 62; in *Seoul People*, 49–52; transferred by way of Soviet texts, 70–71, 240; transformed by war, 108–10; and typicality, 84; as women's realm, 103, 111. *See also* pathos
Fehrenbach, T. R., 242–43
feminism, 77, 198, 207
FitzGerald, C. P., 137, 138

frailty, 8, 155–56; and white masculinity, 160, 165. *See also* breaking point
fratricide, 9, 186–87; 215
Friedman, Hal, 17
"Friendship" (Ujŏng, Im Sundŭk), 80, 81–83
Frontline Combat (Kurtzman), 9; as thanato-comic, 130, 150; and thanatographics, 129–31
Frontline Literature (*Chŏnsŏn munhak*), 184–85, 189–90, 192, 195
Fučik, Julius, 72
Fuller, Samuel, 156, 157, 162–63
future: armistice as, 233–34; cold war as, 119–20; crossing into, by crossing south, 200; Hungnam evacuation as advance into, 137; Jeju and, 17–18, 22, 40; Korean War as template for, 3–4, 241–43; loss of Seoul and, 47–48; revolutionary, 83, 87; and sacrificial death, 91–92; women creating, 78–79
Fyodorov, Alexei, 52

Gabroussenko, Tatiana, 44
Gaines, William, 130
Garnet, Tay, 100
Gender Equality Law (1946), in DPRK, 76
gender roles, 62, 77, 86; in combat, 88–89, 91, 104; disrupted by *koeroe*, 229; and duty, 100, 105–6, 108–11, 215; postarmistice, 95, 269n65. *See also* masculinity; pilots; women
General Dean's Story (Dean), 27–28
ghostliness, 28, 215; and Jeju Uprising, 36, 38–40
Glass, Albert J., 160–62

"Haenyŏ" (Hŏ Yunsŏk), 6, 32–37
haenyŏ (sea woman), 21–22, 25, 32–37
Hallion, Richard, 101
Ham Sedŏk, 261n21; *Mountain People*, 6, 18, 21–26
Han Hyo, 7, 264n19; on "lofty realism," 48–49, 52–53; against naturalism, 80–81; *Seoul People*, 46–50, 86; on typicality, 73;
Han Pyŏngik, 66
Han Sŏrya, 49
Happiness (*Haengbok*, Hwang Kŏn), 7, 65–76, 266n2; and Fadeev's *Young Guard*, 70–72, 75
hate: for enemy, 51, 55; 67–68, 75, 123; for oneself, 201
Heller, Joseph, 97–98, 269n2
Hero Without a Service Number (*Kunbŏn ŏmnŭn yongsa*, Yi Manhŭi), 214
Hess, Dean, 18, 28–32, 263n71
Hodge, John R., 18

Hollywood films: and Korean War, 8, 107, 113, 119, 120; in "Maelstrom," 221, 223–25, 226
home as traitorous property, 226–28, 229
home front, 144–45, 146; and horror, 149
Homeward (*Kwiro*, Yi Manhŭi), 10, 212, 216–21; combat flashback in, 217–18; and survivability, 230
homosociality: and competition, 113, 118, 127–28; and fratricide, 186; in "Friendship," 80, 83
Hong Chinhyŏk, 216
Hong, Christine, 142
horror: and brain death, 153; and comics, 130; and mourning, 272n19; and play of the seen and unseen, 128, 147–48, 149–50, 151–52; in *Sabre Jet*, 110–11; as visual regime, 8–9
Hŏ Yunsŏk, 6, 18
Hughes, Howard, 270n16
Hungnam evacuation: in *LIFE* magazine, 131–38; and retreat as advance, 131, 137, 138; in *Two-Fisted Tales*, 138–39, 141–44
Hunter, Edward, 163–64, 167, 175
Hunters (Salter), 8, 113–14, 115–18; as thanatography, 118
Huston, John, 29
Hwang, Junghyun, 149
Hwang Kŏn, 7, 60–61; *Happiness*, 65, 67–76, 266n2; "Island Ablaze," 46, 65–67
Hwang, Su-kyoung, 18, 243

icon-making, 80, 86, 89, 91
Im Hwa, 51, 80
Immerwahr, Daniel, 108
Im Ogin, 9, 196, 279n25; *Crossing South*, 203–10; and Yi T'aejun, 198, 204–6
Im Sundŭk, 7–8, 77, 251; "Cho Okhŭi," 80, 86–91; "Friendship," 80, 81–83; perversity of, 82; "Tale of a Bereaved Family," 80, 92–95
indigeneity, 7, 22, 33, 35, 36
Inge, M. Thomas, 131
internationalism, 56, 72–74, 87; proletarian, 81, 91
interoperability, 101, 104, 107
"In the Sea off Yongch'o Island" (Yongch'odo kŭnhae, Pak Yŏngjun), 184, 192–95; and *Return*, 202; as thanatography, 9
intra-ethnonational war (*tongjok sangjan*). *See* 6/25 War
"Island Ablaze" (Pul t'anŭn sŏm, Hwang Kŏn, 1952), 46, 65–67
Itazuke Air Base, 100, 103, 107–8

Jager, Sheila Miyoshi, 46
Japan: defeated army as specters, 204; friendship with US, 123–25; as host for US power, 100, 103, 107–8, 270n13; as imperial power, 87, 184; Jeju islanders' connection with, 17; as safe haven, 8; in Truman's plans, 15
Jeju Island, 6–7, 13, 40; in "Afterword," 37–40; and anti-imperialist resistance, 21–26; as base for anticommunist resistance, 15–18, 24, 31; and Christianity, 262n66; devastation of, 33; and *haenyŏ*, 21–22, 23; and Japan, 17; and repressed history, 37; as site of redemption, 29–30, 32. *See also* 4/3 Jeju Uprising
Jeju Uprising. *See* 4/3 Jeju Uprising.
Jervis, Robert, 2–3

Kang Soyŏn, 223
Kang Yongjun, 9, 181–83, 195, 275n1, 276n6
Kennan, George, 155
Kennedy, John F., 241
Kil Chinsŏp, 84, 88
Kimble, James, 144–45
Kim Chaeha, 94–95
Kim Chung Yul, 31
Kim, Daniel, 30, 104, 158
Kim Il Sung, 43, 45, 79; in DPRK literature, 86–87; as model for women, 78–79, 88; pivot away from Soviet Union, 64, 76–77, 80; and POW indoctrination, 201; views on armistice and reunification, 234–36, 237, 282n1; views on literature, 48–49
Kim Ingnyŏl, 19, 20, 23
Kim, Monica, 28
Kim Namch'ŏn, 51, 80
Kim, Nan, 197
Kim P'albong, 190–91
Kim Sŏngsik, 246
Kim Tongyun, 261n22
King, Louis, 100, 107
koeroe (puppet), 179, 183–88, 196; and battle within, 188; and becoming communist, 204; disrupts family and gender relations, 229; in film, 210, 211–12; and forgiveness, 214–15; and national division, 207–8; and parricide/patricide, 213–14; as self-other, 212
Ko Ilhwan, 72
Korea Artista Proleta Federatio/Korean Artists Proletarian Federation, 48, 70

Korean People's Army (KPA): and emancipation of Seoul, 45–46; ghostliness of, 215; in "Haenyŏ," 34; as puppet army (*koeroegun*), 186, 188, 192; as revolutionaries, 50, 56
Korean War: biblical mapping of, 139–41; and cold war, 1–4; combat deaths in, 18; disparate experiences of, 5, 119; implications for future wars, 241–43, 250; inconclusive, 106; and limits, 176–77; and masculinities, 114, 128; and potential death, 8; as war that was not a war, 98, 119, 146, 177; without strict end, 250. *See also* 6/25 War; Fatherland Liberation War
Kurtzman, Harvey, 8–9; depiction of Hungnam withdrawal, 138–44; and *LIFE* photo-essays, 130–31, 138–44, 148–59, 153
Kwak Haksong, 45
kwisun (defection): in "Haenyŏ," 33–37, 39; in *Hero Without a Service Number*, 214–15
Kwon, Heonik, 4, 39, 115, 186

Lankov, Andrei, 76
Last Report (Han Pyŏngik), 66–67
Lattimore, Eleanor H., 2
Legend of Ssarikkol (*Ssarikkol ŭi sinhwa*, Yi Manhŭi), 213–14
Lenin, Vladimir, 81, 86–87, 248
Levie, Howard S., 251–52
liberation, from Japanese colonial rule, 6, 81, 204; in "Cho Okhŭi," 90; commemorated, 76–77, 226, 229; and crossing south, 197–98; in "Happiness," 68–69
LIFE magazine, 9, 105; biblical mapping of war, 139–41; and Hungnam evacuation, 131–38, 141–44; photo-essays reworked by Kurtzman, 130–31, 138–44, 148–59, 153; publication of *Bridges at Toko-Ri*, 119, 120–28; thanatographics of, 129–30
limit, 1–2, 6; of human power, 168–69, 170
limited war, 3–4, 8; and escalation, 103–4; global and timeless, 127; as global governance, 127, 251; and Hungnam evacuation, 137; and limitlessness, 5–6; and limits of heroism, 168; and mourning, 95, 103; postarmistice theorizations, 241–43; and sublime, 112, 118; temporality of, 100, 103–4; as thanatographic, 2; vs. total war, 138; and white masculinity, 113. *See also* "limited war thinking"
"limited war thinking" (Osgood), 3, 4–5, 253. *See also* limited war

limitlessness: and armistice, 10–11; and cold war, 3, and limit, 1; and limited war, 5–6, 98
Lindner, Robert, 172–73
literary front, 184
literature, program for, 20–21, 48–49, 70, 72–73, 205–6. *See also* writers
lofty, the, 41, 47, 73; and everyday life; 92; and feelings, 49; Han on, 48–49; vs. massacre, 53–54; in *Seoul People*, 49–51
"lofty realism," 48–49, 52
Luce, Henry, 9, 129, 137

MacArthur, Douglas, 15–16, 60
MAD magazine, 9, 130, 153–54
"Maelstrom" (Soyongdori, Ch'oe Chŏnghŭi), 213, 221–25
Malden, Karl, 8, 157
Marines Who Never Returned (*Toraoji annŭn haebyŏng*, Yi Manhŭi), 10, 212
marriage, 81–83, 108, 111, 217–20, 225, 226–28
masculinity, 128, 212: and breaking point, 160, 166–67; and disability, 217–18; and feelings in combat, 149; and *koeroe*, 187; jet pilots as models of, 8, 113, 116, 118; and limited-war sublime, 112–15, 124; and military sublime, 125–27; and positive rebellion, 173; and reluctance, 114, 119–20, 122, 123, 127; soporific, 152–53; violent, 36
massacre: of children, 53–54, 67, 89; in "Cho Okhŭi," 89–90; and escalatory temporality, 104, 105; on Jeju, 18, 24–25, 38–39, 40; vs. the lofty, 53–54
McConnell, John, 114
Meerloo, Joost, 168, 245
memorializing, 83
menticide, 1, 154, 168. *See also* brainwashing
Michener, James, 8, 9, 113–14, 118–28
Milestone, Lewis, 162
militarization, 8, 17, 24, 112; and armistice, 4–5, 98, 253
military-civilian nexus, 165, 170, 177
Military Demarcation Line (MDL), 234, 246
military realism, 111
mobilization, 8; and armistice, 3, 5, 98, 252; economic, 43; and everyday life, 218; filmic, 230; literary, 184–85, 240; and self-empowerment, 156; in "Tale of a Bereaved Family," 94
Morgenthau, Hans, 169

Mortenson, Erik, 176
Moscow, as model for Pyongyang, 44–45
Mountain People (*San saramdŭl*, Ham Sedŏk), 6, 21–26, 32, 261n22, 261n31; and postcolonial future, 22
mourning: and desire, 220; gendered, 98; in *LIFE* magazine, 146; and limited war, 103; in Pak Yŏngjun's fiction, 184; of potential death, 8; as praxis of the present, 92–95; proleptic, 100, 111; revolutionary, 7–8, 40–41, 47, 48; vitalist, 94; of the war dead, 80, 92–95. *See also* self-mourning; virtual widows; widows
Munhak sinmun (*Literary Weekly*), 94–95
Mun Haksu, 84–86, *85*, 88
Munhak yesul (*Literary Arts*), 20–21, 46, 261n18

Nam Haeyŏng, 198–99
Nam Wŏnjin, 267n48
nation (*minjok*): and belonging, 202, 208, 215; and crossing south, 200; defined by anticommunism, 184–85, 211–12, 215, 237; in "Haenyŏ," 35–36; and *inmin*, 20–21; *koeroe* and, 186–87, 207; return to, 192–93; Seoul as symbol of, 46
naturalism, condemned, 51, 80–81, 190
Nichols, Donald, 31, 262n70
Niebuhr, Reinhold, 106, 168–69
North Korea. *See* DPRK
Northwest Youth, 19, 22, 35, 53, 55, 262n74
Nyberg, Amy, 130

October Revolution, 69, 71, 86–87
Ŏm Hosŏk, 52, 86–87, 91–92
One Minute to Zero (Garnet), 8, 100–106; interoperability in, 101, 103–4; Korean language in, 104, 106
orientalism, 89, 150
orphans, 29–31, 238–39. *See also* children
Osgood, Robert, 3, 237, 241–42
O T'aeho, 48
O Yŏngsu, 6, 19, 37–40, 263n93

Paik Nak-chung, 4, 246–47, 249
Pak Kijun, 184–85
Pak Yŏngjun, 9, 184, 252, 276n8, 276n15; "Dark Night," 186–88; "In the Sea off Yongch'o Island," 192–95; "Partisan," 188–89
Pang Hyŏnsŭng, 240

INDEX

Park Chung Hee, 211
"Partisan" (Ppalch'isan, Pak Yŏngjun), 184, 188–89; as thanatography, 9
Partridge, Earle E., 31, 262n70, 263n71
pathos (*ppap'osŭ*), 70, 94
patriarchal order, 80, 213; and *koeroe*, 208, 213–14, 215, 229
patrilineage, 80, 94, 187
people (*inmin*), 73, 84; betrayal of, 202; definition, in "Cho Okhŭi," 86, 88; and gender roles, 88–89, 91; in lofty realism, 48–50; loyalty to Kim Il Sung, 238; in *Mountain People*, 22–25; and Pyongyang, 43; as revolutionary subjects, 8, 19, 20–21, 47, 49
petty bourgeoisie (*sosimin*), 246–47, 249, 252
Petty Bourgeoisie (*Sosimin*, Yi Hoch'ŏl), 233, 247–49, 252, 284n63
pilots: and imagining cold war, 115; and masculinity, 8, 111–18, 152–53; and military sublime, 124–27; and religion, 30
Pisiotis, Argyrios, 54
Poole, Janet, 205
"positive rebellion" (Lindner), 172–73
POW (prisoners of war): and brainwashing, 8, 156, 164–65; death and limit-consciousness, 181–82; as *koeroe*, 185–88; murdered, 157–58; and redemption, 199–203; in Serling's television drama, 169–72; and suicide, 195; as warriors, 168–69
"P.O.W." (Davidson), 8, 157, 166–67
Pyongyang, reconstruction of, 43–45

Rabinowitch, Eugene, 99
racialization, 105, 112, 114
"Rack" (Serling), 8, 157, 169–71
readiness, 5, 8, 99, 100; women's worry as 111. *See also* mobilization
recantation (*chŏnhyang*), 194, 201; *koeroe* and, 183, 214; and *kwisun*, 33; and return from living dead, 188–89
redemption, 9–10, 18, 144–45, 176; crossing south as, 199–203; and postcolonial history, 198; sacrifice as, 29–30, 32
Rees, David, 242
religion, Christian, 30, 106, 199; and crossing south, 202; as ethical frame, 214–15
reluctance, 106, 112; and American exceptionalism, 118–19; as duty, 127–28; and voluntary men, 114, 119–20, 122

return (*kwihwan*), 183, 184; impossible, 192–95; as rebirth, 202–3; and suicide, 194–95
Return (*Kwihwan*, Sŏnu Hwi), 9, 195–96, 198–203, 209; and "In the Sea off Yongch'o Island," 202
reunification, 3, 9, 62; cartoon representation of, 60; foreclosed, 7, 46, 59; peaceful, 43, 45, 47, 234–36, 237
"reunification literature" (DPRK), 21
revolution: in "Cho Okhŭi," 86–91; and combat, 74–76; global, 21, 47, 69; in "Happiness," 67–68, 74–76; in "Island Ablaze," 65–68; and joyful death, 71–72, 74–75; manifest vs potential, 45, 47, 60; redefined, 80; in *Seoul People*, 49–59. *See also* Fatherland Liberation War
revolutionary intertextuality, 69–72
revolutionary mourning, 7, 47–48, 55, 57, 77
Rhee, Syngman, 31, 34, 37, 40, 49; as enemy, 56, 60; views on armistice, 236–37
Ri Yunyŏng, 233, 238–40
Robson, Mark, 120–21, 125
Rodong sinmun (*Workers' Daily*), 19–20, 43, 64–65
ROK (Republic of Korea): as agent of emancipatory history, 191; anticommunism vs. *koeroe*, 179, 183, 186; anticommunist film, 212–15; and cultural front, 191; directives for writers, 184–85; established, 6, 18; as geopolitical island, 32; modernization and westernization, 212–13, 221–26; Park regime and Motion Picture Laws, 211–12; portrayals of postarmistice Seoul, 216–20; Rhee's insistence on northward advance, 236–37
ROKA (Republic of Korea Army): in film, 213–15; as national army (*kukkun*), vs. puppet army 188–89
Rusk, Dean, 16

Sabre Jet (King), 100, 107–11
Salter, James, 8, 113–14, 115–18
Sanders, Denis, 233
Schelling, Thomas, 250–51, 252
Schelly, Bill, 148
Schlesinger, Jr., Arthur M., 118, 169
security imperialism, 2, 3, 5
self-mourning, 5, 212
Selverstone, Marc J., 241

Seoul: battles for, 46, 62; communist occupation of, 226; DPRK vs. ROK representations of, 45, 46; loss of, 15, 41; as modernist cityscape, 216–18. *See also* Seoul People

Seoul People (*Sŏul saramdŭl*, Han Hyo), 7; 46–50, 86; as epic poem, 49–50; massacre in, 53–54; and revolutionary feelings, 51–52, 56–57; and revolutionary mourning, 47–48, 55, 57

Serling, Rod, 8, 157, 169–71, 175–76, 275n50

Seven Women POWs (*7in ŭi yŏp'oro*, Yi Manhŭi), 215

sexism, 80, 88, 91

sexuality, 9, 33, 193; and virtual widows, 216–21

Sickles, Noel, 120–24, 127, 128

Sirk, Douglas, 18, 28

Sobel, Raymond, 162

socialist realism: in Hwang's fiction, 66–67, 71; Im Sundŭk's departure from, 80–81; and proletarian true story, 91; Soviet, 72; and thanatography, 74; and typicality, 73, 84

Sŏ Manil, 70

Song Hosŏng, *20*, 23

Sŏnu Hwi, 9, 213, 195–96, 198–203, 209, 278n5

South Korea. *See* ROK

Soviet cultural production, 61, 64, 86; glorified, 64–65; as model for DPRK literature, 70–73; influence on "Cho Okhŭi, Hero," 85–86; and socialist realism, 49; and transfer of feelings, 7, 70–71, 240

Soviet people, praise of, 52–53

Soviet Union, 6, 7; as communist enemy, 135, 137; DPRK's friendship with, 76–77; Kim Il Sung's pivot away from, 64, 76–77, 80, 267n32; as model, 19–20, 61, 65, 266n18; occupation of northern Korea, 198, 204; in Truman's plans, 15

Stalin, 49, 81, 90, 201

Steel Helmet (Fuller), 156–60, 163, 175, 176, 274n10

subjectivity (*chuch'e*), 76, 185

sublime: proletarian, 56–57; and future, 120; limited-war, 112, 118; military, 125–27

suicide, 9, 10, 184, 194; and crossing south, 194–95, 201–2, 252; and virtual widows, 216

survivability, 230, 247

suspicion, and *koeroe*, 183, 185–87, 228, 229

"Tale of a Bereaved Family" (*Ŏnŭ han yugajok ŭi iyagi*, Im Sundŭk), 80, 92–95

temporality: and *koeroe*, 229; of limited war, 100, 103–4, 127

testimonials of crossing south, 198–203

thanatographic imagination, 1–2, 8, 10–11, 77, 253

thanatographics, 129–30; and containment, 138; critical, 150; in *MAD* magazine, 154; of survival, 158

thanatography, 1, 9; of absence, 152; "Barbed Wire" as, 181–83; and border-making, 250; and cold war, 252; and hagiography, 89, 90; *Hunters* as, 118; and socialist realism, 74. *See also* auto-thanatography

Time Limit (Malden), 8, 157, 171–72

torture, 51, 71, 165; in "Afterword," 38–39; in "Barbed Wire," 181; and breaking point, 166–67; in "Cho Okhŭi," 84, 90; in *Crossing South*, 206

transpacific military network, 100, 103, 270n13. *See also* "American Lake"

trauma, 29, 40; and brainwashing, 157; and breakdown, 160, 175; in combat, 218, 274n11

Truman, Harry, 2, 15–16, 146, 155, 260n7

Truman Doctrine, 2

Twilight Zone (Serling), 157, 173–76

twisteroo, 142–44, 147, 150

Two-Fisted Tales (Kurtzman), 9, 153; and horror, 146–48, 151; Hungnam evacuation in, 138–39, 141–44; as thanato-comics, 130, 150; and thanatographics 129–31

Twyford, Erin, 253

typicality: and commemorating war, 238; and feelings, 84; and internationalism, 72–74; intervisual, 86; and the lofty, 52; and portraying Cho Okhŭi, 84, 86, 88, 91

UN. *See* United Nations

unification. *See* reunification

United Nations (UN): and election in southern Korea, 6, 18; idealism vs. US military power, 101, 105; and interracial coalition, 142–43; and militarization of the transpacific, 270n13

United States Air Force, 101, 107; and horror, 151–52; and interoperability, 101, 104, 107; jets in, 113

United States Military Government in Korea. *See* USAMGIK

United States of America: bombing of Hiroshima and Nagasaki, 17; and division of Korea, 6–7; as enemy, 88; and foreign policy, 2–4, 15;

geostrategy, 7, 15, 32; and global management, 236, 241; and limited war, 241–42; militarization in, 8; in *Mountain People*, 23; occupation of Japan, 123; sacrifice in Korean War, 236. *See also* USAMGIK

United States Steel Hour, 165–66, 169

universal breaking point. *See* breaking point.

USAMGIK (United States Military Government in Korea), 17, 26; critiqued in DPRK press, 19–21; and Jeju Uprising, 6, 18, 19; in *Mountain People*, 23; supports Northwest Youth, 28

Vandenberg, Hoyt, 16

Van Fleet, James A., 153

virtual widows, 8, 10; as après girls, 221, 226, 228–29, 230; and desire, 220–21; as flaneurs, 216–17; and precarity, 228–29, 282n27; and sacrifice, 217, 219; and self-mourning, 212; and sexuality, 216–17; and suicide, 216

visual regimes of war, 129–30, 150–51; and authenticity, 153–54; and communism as *koeroe*, 179

voluntary men, 114, 119, 125, 127

War Hunt (Sanders), 233, 243–46

weapon fetishism, 118, 127, 151

Wertham, Fredric, 130

White Skulls (*haegol pudae*), 32–33, 34, 35, 36, 263n74

Whitted, Qiana, 130, 142

widows, 77, 80, 101; and desire, 93; and proper mourning, 95. *See also* virtual widows

witnessing, 32, 53–54, 68, 105; and crossing south, 198, 200

wives, of pilots, 100, 103, 107–8

women: in combat, 41, 62, 89–90; feelings of, 51–52, 67–68, 74–76; as figures of happiness, 234, *235*; and heroic death, 65–67; and Kim Il Sung, 78–79; as *koeroe*, 208; as leaders of collective, 92–93; as martyrs, 41, 61, 77, 88; and motherhood, 87–88; and proletarian sublime, 56, 58–59; as revolutionaries, 51–52, 55–56; and revolutionary history, 83; and revolutionary mourning, 7–8; in socialist realism, 80; tortured, 38–39; transformed by war, 103–5; and US cultural forms, 223. *See also* après girl; *haenyŏ*; virtual widows; widows; wives, of pilots

World War II, 29, 97; and depicting the dead, 144, 146

writers: Kim Il Sung's directives for, 48–49; and lofty realism, 49, 52; proper stance for, 184–85; and representing war, 206, 237–38, 240; and revolutionary history, 20–21; and typicality, 52, 73

Yi Hoch'ŏl, 233, 247–49, 252, 284n60

Yi Hŏn'gu, 191

Yi Manhŭi, 10, 212–21; *Homeward*, 216–21, 230

Yi Muyŏng, 184

Yi T'aejun, 198, 204–5, 206, 208, 209; purge of, 81

Yŏm Sangsŏp, 45

Young Guard (book by Fadeev), in *Happiness*, 70–72, 75

Young Guard (film by Gerasimov), *85*, 86

Yun Tuhŏn, 72

GPSR Authorized Representative: Easy Access System Europe, Mustamäe tee
50, 10621 Tallinn, Estonia, gpsr.requests@easproject.com

www.ingramcontent.com/pod-product-compliance
Lightning Source LLC
Chambersburg PA
CBHW022037290426
44109CB00014B/891